LINUX
DEVICE DRIVERS

LINUX
DEVICE DRIVERS

ALESSANDRO RUBINI

O'REILLY®

Beijing · Cambridge · Farnham · Köln · Paris · Sebastopol · Taipei · Tokyo

Linux Device Drivers
by Alessandro Rubini

Copyright © 1998 O'Reilly & Associates, Inc. All rights reserved.
Printed in the United States of America.

Published by O'Reilly & Associates, Inc., 101 Morris Street, Sebastopol, CA 95472.

Editors: Andy Oram and Ellen Siever

Production Editor: David Futato

Printing History:

February 1998:   First Edition.

ISBN: 1-56592-292-1
[M]

[2/00]

TABLE OF CONTENTS

CHAPTER THREE
CHAR DRIVERS _____ 41

CHAPTER FOUR
DEBUGGING TECHNIQUES _____ 69

CHAPTER FIVE
ENHANCED CHAR DRIVER OPERATIONS _____ 94

CHAPTER SIX
FLOW OF TIME _____ 131

CHAPTER FIFTEEN
OVERVIEW OF PERIPHERAL BUSES _____341

CHAPTER SIXTEEN
PHYSICAL LAYOUT OF THE KERNEL SOURCE _____362

PREFACE

As an electronic engineer and a do-it-yourself kind of person, I have always enjoyed using the computer to control external hardware. Ever since the days of my father's Apple-2e, I have been looking for another platform where I could connect my custom circuitry and write my own driver software. Unfortunately, the PC of the eighties wasn't powerful enough, at either the software or the hardware level—the internal design of the PC was much worse than that of the Apple-2e, and the available documentation for a long time was unsatisfying. But then Linux appeared, and I decided to give it a try by buying an expensive 386 motherboard and no commercial software at all.

At the time, I was using Unix systems at the university, and was greatly excited by the smart operating system, particularly when supplemented by the even smarter utilities that the GNU project donates to the user base. Running Linux on my own PC motherboard has always been an interesting experience, and I could even write my own device drivers and play with the soldering iron once again. I continue to tell people "when I grow up, I wanna be a hacker," and Linux is the perfect platform for such dreams. That said, I don't know if I will ever grow up.

As Linux matures, more and more people get interested in writing drivers for custom circuitry and for commercial devices. As Linus Torvalds noted, "We're back to the times when men were men and wrote their own device drivers."

Not being able to write innovative code, I began writing technical articles for *Linux Journal* as a contribution to the Linux community; later, Andy Oram at O'Reilly expressed an interest in having me write a whole book about device drivers, and I accepted this task. Although real hackers can find all the necessary information in the official kernel sources, a written text can be helpful in developing programming skills. The text you are approaching is the result of hours of patient grepping through the kernel sources, and I hope the final result is worth the effort it took. I hope this book will be useful as a starting point for people who want to become kernel hackers but don't know where to start.

Audience of This Book

On the technical side, this text should offer a hands-on approach to understanding the kernel internals and some of the design choices made by the Linux developers. Although the main and official target of the book is teaching how to write device drivers, the enclosed material should give an intriguing overview of kernel implementation as well.

This book should be an interesting source of information both for people who want to play with their computer and for technical programmers who need to deal with the inner levels of a Linux box. Note that "a Linux box" is a wider concept than "a PC running Linux" as many platforms are supported by our operating system, and kernel programming is by no means bound to a specific platform.

The Linux enthusiast should find in this book enough food for her mind to start playing with the code base, and then be able to join the group of developers who are continuously working on new capabilities and performance enhancements. Linux is still a work-in-progress, and there's always a place for new programmers to jump into the game.

If, on the other hand, you are just trying to write a device driver for your own device and don't want to muck with the kernel internals, the text should be modularized enough to fit your needs as well. If you don't want to go deep into the details, you can just skip the most technical sections and stick to the standard API used by device drivers to seamlessly integrate with the rest of the kernel.

The main target of this book is writing kernel modules for version 2.0 of the Linux kernel. A *module* is object code that can be loaded at run time to add new functionality to a running kernel. The discussion also covers version 1.2 of the kernel, and the last chapter describes the changes that the driver interface underwent from version 2.0 to version 2.1.43 (the latest-and-greatest at the time the book went to technical review).

Organization of the Material

The book introduces its topics in ascending order of complexity and can be divided into two parts. The first part (Chapters 1 through 10) begins with the proper setup of kernel modules, and goes on to describe the various aspects of programming that you'll need in order to write a full-featured driver for a char-oriented device. Every chapter covers a distinct problem and includes a "symbol table" at the end, which can be used as a reference during actual development. As I wrote my own drivers, I found myself referring back to my own chapters, and I hope you too will exploit the symbol tables.

Throughout the first part of the book, the organization of the material moves roughly from the software-oriented concepts to the hardware-related ones. This is meant to allow you to test the software on your own computer as far as possible without the need to plug external hardware into the machine. Every chapter includes source code and points to sample drivers that you can run on any Linux computer. In Chapters 8 and 9, however, I'll ask you to connect an inch of wire to the parallel port in order to test out hardware handling, but this requirement should be manageable by everyone.

The second half of the book describes block drivers and network interfaces and goes deeper into more advanced topics. Most likely you won't need this information to write actual drivers, but I hope you appreciate the first part enough to be induced to go on reading.

As a matter of fact, most of the material I present can be interesting independent of the actual need to write device drivers. Several students were referred to me for Linux information for their theses while I was writing this book; all of them enjoyed reading the appropriate chapter to support their work, even if their task didn't involve writing a driver.

Background Information

In order to be able to face this book, you need to be confident with C programming. A little Unix expertise is needed as well, as I often refer to Unix commands and pipelines.

At the hardware level, no previous expertise is required, as long as the general concepts are clear in advance. The text isn't based on specific PC hardware, and I provide all the needed information when I do refer to specific hardware.

Being able to connect to the Internet would be beneficial for the reader because many interesting documents and upgrades can be retrieved from the network. Being wired is, however, not strictly necessary, and I myself have quite poor connectivity (mainly due to the high rates of the Italian telecommunication company).

As far as the software is concerned, you'll need to have Linux installed on your computer to run the sample drivers, but any distribution will do (and almost any hardware platform as well). A complete list of the needed software packages is found in Chapter 1, as many readers just wouldn't receive the information if it was in the Preface. (I expect many will skip Chapter 1 as well; most of the readers are hackers, aren't you?)

Sources for Further Information

Most of the information I provide in this book is extracted directly from the kernel sources. As long as you have them installed in your system, you'll rarely need other documents to supplement the information. There are a few interesting books out there that can help in writing device drivers, although the main sources of information are the kernel sources and the technical documentation about your devices. Needless to say, you'll appreciate the manuals that describe your own computer platform.

As far as kernel hacking is concerned, the best information (after the source files) is available on the Internet. *Linux Journal* also hosts some interesting technical articles. Check the "Kernel Korner" column, but skip my own articles, as I tend to repeat myself; non–Kernel Korner articles are interesting as well, but rarely as technical as the average reader of this book will appreciate.

On the Internet, I'd suggest looking in the following places:

http://www.redhat.com:8080/
> The "HyperNews" server at Red Hat carries the *Kernel Hacker's Guide*, an interesting document about the kernel internals. Some of its chapters are quite old, but some have been introduced or updated recently. The material is quite interesting, in my opinion.

http://www.kernel.org/
ftp://ftp.kernel.org/
> This site is the home of Linux kernel development. You'll find the latest kernel release and related information. Note that the FTP site is mirrored throughout the world, so you'll most likely find a mirror near you.

ftp://sunsite.unc.edu/pub/Linux/docs/
ftp://tsx-11.mit.edu/pub/linux/docs/
> The "Linux Documentation Project" carries a lot of interesting documents called "HOWTOs"; some of them are pretty technical and cover kernel-related topics. Sunsite and tsx-11 also carry most of the programs available for Linux; they are interesting in general, not only for their *docs/* directory. Well, I'm sure you know about these archives already, but I think it's worth mentioning them.

http://www.ssc.com/
> SSC, Specialized System Consultants, are the publishers of *Linux Journal*, and their site carries the HTML version of most of the articles they've published. Any interesting article they print is converted to HTML shortly after publication and is made available on the Web.

http://www.conecta.it/linux/

> This Italian site is one of the places where a Linux enthusiast keeps updated information about all the ongoing projects involving Linux. Maybe you already know an interesting site with HTTP links about Linux development; if not, this one is a good starting point.

Relevant Books

In addition to source code and Internet resources, a number of good books cover some of the topics discussed in this book. The following list represents my *personal* anthology in the field. The books I list here either document software features of Unix systems or describe interesting hardware topics. I won't name any books about the PC architecture, as there are too many of them. Unfortunately, I also can't suggest any book about the Sparc architecture, as I found none. If you need information, I'm pretty sure a quick search through the Web will fill the gap.

[0] Bach, Maurice. *The Design of the Unix Operating System*. Prentice Hall. 1986.

> This book, though quite old, covers all the issues related to Unix implementations. It has been the main source of inpiration for Linus to write the first Linux versions.

[1] Beck, Michael. *Linux Kernel Internals*. Addison-Wesley. 1997.

> This book concentrates on the internal data structures and algorithms of Linux; you'll like it if you appreciate detailed descriptions. The first edition treated version 1.2; I don't know how far through later versions the new edition has moved. Version 2.0 and later are quite different from 1.2 in their internal details.

[2] Stevens, Richard. *Advanced Programming in The Unix Environment*. Addison-Wesley. 1992.

> Every detail of Unix system calls is described herein. The book is a good companion when implementing advanced features in the device methods. Any conceivable doubt about Unix semantics can be solved by referring to this book.

[3] Stevens, Richard. *Unix Network Programming*. Prentice Hall. 1990.

> As you might imagine, this book is a high-quality reference about networking issues. It matches "Advanced Programming" in both quality and coverage of the subject matter. The books is full of source code to test every bit of user-space networking.

[4] Comer, Douglas, and Stevens, David. *Internetworking with TCP/IP Vols I, II and III*. Prentice Hall. 1991.

> This heavy collection of networking information is a complete tutorial about everything in the Internet field. The books describe the suite of Internet Protocols and their implementation.

[5] Shanley, Tom, and Anderson, Don. *PCI Sytem Architecture*. Addison-Wesley. 1995.

> This book thoroughly describes the PCI bus and its interface standard. You'll find similar "System Architecture" titles for most of the hardware topics, all by the same authors. All these books are very interesting, although somehow PC-biased. This volume about PCI is the one I liked best. I disliked at least one of the books, but a careful analysis revealed that the book is good and just describes a bad architecture.

[6] Digital Semiconductor. *Alpha AXP Architecture Handbook*. Digital Semiconductor. 1994.

> This book and the "Alpha AXP Reference Manual" are available for free from Digital Semiconductor. They describes the machine language of the Alpha processors and the underlying design issues that have been dealt with. The order number for this book is EC-QD2KA-TE.

Conventions Used in This Book

The following is a list of the typographical conventions used in this book.

Italic

> is used for file and directory names, program and command names, command-line options, email addresses and path names, URLs, and for emphasizing new terms.

Boldface

> is used to symbolize keystrokes (i.e., **Ctrl-N**).

`Constant Width`

> is used in examples to show the contents of code files or the output from commands, and to indicate environment variables and keywords that appear in code.

`Constant Italic`

> is used to indicate variable options, keywords, or text that the user is to replace with an actual value.

`Constant Bold`

> is used in examples to show commands or other text that should be typed literally by the user.

We'd Like to Hear from You

We have tested and verified all of the information in this book to the best of our ability, but you may find that features have changed (or even that we have made mistakes!). Please let us know about any errors you find, as well as your suggestions for future editions, by writing:

O'Reilly & Associates, Inc.
101 Morris Street
Sebastopol, CA 95472
1-800-998-9938 (in the US or Canada)
1-707-829-0515 (international/local)
1-707-829-0104 (FAX)

You can also send us messages electronically. To be put on the mailing list or request a catalog, send email to:

info@oreilly.com   (via the Internet)

To ask technical questions or comment on the book, send email to:

bookquestions@oreilly.com (via the Internet)

Finally, we can be found on the World Wide Web at *http://www.oreilly.com/*.

Acknowledgments

This book isn't completely mine: I've had external help both in hardware material and human support. I want to thank Mr. Dreyer of Quant-X for loaning me an Alpha computer so I could test portability of the sample code included in this book. Sun-Italia has been kind as well, by loaning me a Sparc machine; this allowed me to upgrade the box from their OS to mine. ImageNation helped by donating a PCI frame grabber, which I used to dissect PCI and DMA features.

Surely this book would never have been finished without the help of Andy Oram and Michael Johnson, and the psychological support of Federica, my girlfriend—ehm, wife. Andy has been my mighty editor, and Michael is the one who asked me to write for the *Linux Journal* and then sent me to Andy—if someone is guilty for this work, that's Michael. I'd like to thank Georg van Zezschwitz, who introduced me to the fascinating world of kernel modules and helped in writing for the *Linux Journal.* I want to thank Silvana Ranzoli, my teacher of English at high school, for her relentless (though sometimes perceived as cruel) commitment to the benefit of her classroom. I am grateful to Ellen Siever, who fixed all the linguistic misfeatures I learned after high school; she patiently dealt with my tendency towards hackerisms and subtleties—I'm never satisfied with rewritings.

My text has been technically reviewed by Alan Cox, Greg Hankins, Hans Lermen, Heiko Eissfeldt, and Miguel de Icaza (in alphabetic order by first name). Their comments and suggestions have been very useful in pinpointing oversights and deficiencies of mine. I wish to thank them for spending their qualified time over my writing, which looks so irrelevant to their guru's activity.

I also want to acknowledge people who allowed me to take time from "real jobs" to concentrate on the Linux kernel. This includes Virginio Cantoni, Alberto Biancardi, and other people in the Vision Lab at the University, as well as Davide Yachaya and the staff at *systemy.it,* where I help as network administrator.

Thanks also to the O'Reilly staff: David Futato, the copyeditor and production editor; Chris Reilley, the technical illustrator; Jane Ellin and Nicole Gipson Arigo for quality assurance; Seth Maislin, who produced the index; Len Muellner and Chris Maden for tools support; Edie Freedman for the cover design; Nancy Priest, who did the interior design; and Sheryl Avruch, the production manager.

Last but not least, I thank the Linux developers for their relentless work. This includes both the kernel programmers and the user-space people, who often get forgotten. In this book I chose never to call them by name in order to avoid being unfair to someone I might forget. I sometimes made an exception to this rule and called Linus by name—hope he doesn't mind.

## CHAPTER ONE

AN INTRODUCTION TO THE LINUX KERNEL

People all around the world are delving into the Linux kernel, mostly to write device drivers. While each driver is different, and you have to know your specific device, many principles and basic techniques are the same from one driver to another. In this book, you'll learn to write your own device drivers and to hack around in related parts of the kernel. This book covers device-independent programming techniques, without binding the examples to any specific device.

This chapter doesn't actually get into writing code. However, I'm going to introduce some background concepts about the Linux kernel that you'll be glad you know later, when we do launch into writing code.

As you learn to write drivers, you will find out a lot about the Linux kernel in general; this may help you understand how your machine works and why things aren't always as fast as you expect or don't do quite what you want. We'll introduce new ideas smoothly, starting off with very simple drivers and building upon them; every new concept will be accompanied by sample code that doesn't need special hardware to be tested.

The Role of the Driver Writer

As a programmer, you will be able to make your own choices about your driver, choosing an acceptable tradeoff between the programming time required and the flexibility of the result. Though it may appear strange to say that a driver is "flexible," I like this word because it emphasizes that the role of a device driver is providing *mechanisms*, not *policies*.

The distinction between mechanism and policy is one of the best ideas behind the Unix design. Most programming problems can indeed be split into two parts: "what needs to be done" (the mechanism) and "how can the program be used" (the policy). If the two issues are addressed by different parts of the program, or even by different programs altogether, the software package is much easier to develop and to adapt to particular needs.

For example, Unix management of the graphic display is split between the X server, which knows the hardware and offers a unified interface to user programs, and the window manager, which implements a particular policy without knowing anything about the hardware. People can use the same window manager on different hardware, and different users can run different configurations on the same workstation. Another example is the layered structure of TCP/IP networking: the operating system offers the socket abstraction, which is policy-free, while different servers are in charge of the services. Moreover, a server like `ftpd` provides the file transfer mechanism, while users can use whatever client they prefer; both command-line and graphic clients exist, and anyone can write a new user interface to transfer files.

Where drivers are concerned, the same role-splitting applies. The floppy driver is policy-free—its role is only to show the diskette as a continuous byte array. How to use the device is the role of the application: *tar* writes it sequentially, while *mkfs* prepares the device to be mounted, and *mcopy* relies on the existence of a specific data structure on the device.

When *writing* drivers, a programmer should pay particular attention to this fundamental problem: we need to write kernel code to access the hardware, but we shouldn't force particular policies on the user, since different users have different needs. The driver should only deal with hardware handling, leaving all the issues about *how* to use the hardware to the applications. A driver, then, is "flexible" if it offers access to the hardware capabilities without adding constraints. Sometimes, however, some policy decisions must be made.

You can also look at your driver from a different perspective: it is a software layer that lies between the applications and the actual device. This privileged role of the driver allows the driver programmer to choose exactly how the device should appear: different drivers can offer different capabilities, even for the same device. The actual driver design should be a balance between many different considerations. For instance, a single device may be used concurrently by different programs, and the driver programmer has complete freedom to determine how to handle concurrency. You could implement memory mapping on the device independently of its hardware capabilities, or you could provide a user library to help application programmers implement new policies on top of the available primitives, and so forth. One major consideration is the tradeoff between the desire to present the user with as many options as possible, balanced against the time you have to do the writing and the need to keep things simple so that errors don't creep in.

If a driver is designed for both synchronous and asynchronous operations, if it allows itself to be opened multiple times, and if it is able to exploit all the hardware capabilities without adding a software layer "to simplify things"—like converting binary data to text or other policy-related operations—then it will turn out to be easier to write and to maintain. Being "policy-free" is actually a common target for software designers.

Most device drivers, indeed, are released together with user programs to help with configuration and access to the target device. Those programs can range from simple configuring utilities to complete graphical applications. Usually a client library is provided as well.

The scope of this book is the kernel, so we'll try not to deal with policy issues, nor with application programs or support libraries. Sometimes I'll talk about different policies and how to support them, but I won't go into much detail about programs using the device or the policies they enforce. You should understand, however, that user programs are an integral part of a software package and that even policy-free packages are distributed with configuration files that apply a default behavior to the underlying mechanisms.

Splitting the Kernel

In a Unix system, several concurrent *processes* attend to different tasks. Each process asks for system resources, be it computing power, memory, network connectivity, or some other resource. The kernel is the big chunk of executable code in charge of handling all such requests. Though the distinction between the different kernel tasks isn't always clearly marked, the kernel's role can be split, as shown in Figure 1-1, into the following parts:

Process management
> The kernel is in charge of creating and destroying processes, and handling their connection to the outside world (input and output). Communication among different processes (through signals, pipes, or interprocess communication primitives) is basic to the overall system functionality, and is also handled by the kernel. In addition, the scheduler, probably the most critical routine in the whole operating system, is part of process management. More generally, the kernel's process management activity implements the abstraction of several processes on top of a single CPU.

Memory management
> The computer's memory is a major resource, and the policy used to deal with it is a critical one for system performance. The kernel builds up a virtual addressing space for any and all processes on top of the limited available resources. The different parts of the kernel interact with the memory-management subsystem through a set of function calls, ranging from simple *malloc/free* equivalents to much more exotic functionalities.

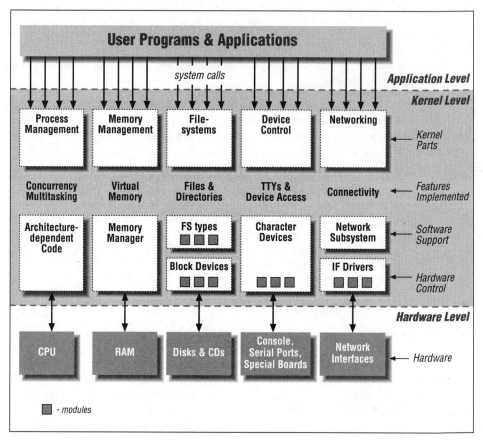

Figure 1-1: A split view of the kernel

Filesystems

Unix is heavily based on the filesystem concept; almost everything in Unix can be treated as a file. The kernel builds a structured filesystem on top of unstructured hardware, and the resulting file abstraction is heavily used throughout the whole system. In addition, Linux supports multiple filesystem types, i.e., different ways of organizing data on the physical medium.

Device control

Almost every system operation eventually maps to a physical device. With the exception of the processor, memory, and a very few other entities, any and all device control operations are performed by code that is specific to the device being addressed. That code is called a *device driver*. The kernel must have embedded in it a device driver for every peripheral present on your system, from the hard drive to the keyboard and the tape streamer. This aspect of the kernel's functions is our primary interest in this book.

Networking

Networking must be managed by the operating system because most network operations are not specific to a process: incoming packets are asynchronous events. The packets must be collected, identified, and dispatched before a process takes care of them. The system is in charge of delivering data packets across program and network interfaces, and it must correctly put to sleep and wake programs waiting for data from the network. Additionally, all the routing and address resolution issues are implemented within the kernel.

Towards the end of this book, in Chapter 16, *Physical Layout of the Kernel Source*, you'll find a roadmap to the Linux kernel, but these few words should suffice for now.

One of the good features of Linux is the ability to expand the kernel code at run time. This means that you can add functionality to the kernel while the system is up and running.

Each piece of code that can be added to the kernel is called a *module*. The Linux kernel offers support for quite a few different types (or "classes") of modules, including, but not limited to, device drivers. Each *module* is made up of object code (not linked to be a complete executable) that can be dynamically linked to the running kernel by the *insmod* program and can be unlinked by the *rmmod* program.

In Figure 1-1, you can identify different classes of modules in charge of specific tasks—a module is said to belong to a specific class according to the functionality it offers.

Classes of Devices and Modules

The Unix way of looking at devices distinguishes between three device types, each devoted to a different task. Linux can load each device type in the form of a module, thus allowing users to experiment with new hardware while still being able to run up-to-date kernel versions and to follow development.

As far as modules are concerned, each module usually implements only one driver, and thus is classifiable, for example, as a *char module*, or a *block module*. This division of modules into different types, or classes, is not a rigid one; the programmer can choose to build huge modules implementing different drivers in a single chunk of code. Good programmers, nonetheless, usually create a different module for each new functionality they implement.

Going back to devices, the three flavors are the following:

Character devices

A character (char) device is one that can be accessed like a file, and a char driver is in charge of implementing this behavior. Such a driver usually implements the *open, close, read,* and *write* system calls. The console and the parallel ports are examples of char devices, as they are well represented by the stream abstraction. Char devices are accessed by means of filesystem nodes, such as */dev/tty1* and */dev/lp1*. The only relevant difference between a char device and a regular file is that you can always step back and forth in the regular file, while most char devices are just a data channel, which you can only access sequentially. There exist, nonetheless, char devices that look like a data area, and you can step back and forth in them.

Block devices

A block device is something that can host a filesystem, such as a disk. In most Unix systems, a block device can only be accessed as multiples of a block, where a block is usually one kilobyte of data. Linux allows you to read and write a block device like a char device—it permits the transfer of any number of bytes at a time. As a result, block and char devices differ only in the way data is managed internally by the kernel, and thus in the kernel/driver software interface. Like a char device, each block device is accessed through a filesystem node and the difference between them is transparent to the user. A block driver interfaces with the kernel through the same interface as a char driver, as well as through an additional block-oriented interface that is invisible to the user or application.

Network interfaces

Any network transaction is made through an interface, i.e., a device that is able to exchange data with other hosts. Usually, an interface is a hardware device, but it might also be a software tool, like the loopback interface. A network interface is in charge of sending and receiving data packets, driven by the network subsystem of the kernel, without knowing how individual transactions map to the actual packets being transmitted. Though both "telnet" and "ftp" connections are stream-oriented, they transmit using the same device; the device doesn't see the individual streams, but only the data packets.

Not being a stream-oriented device, a network interface isn't easily mapped to a node in the filesystem, as */dev/tty1* is. The Unix way to call interfaces is by assigning a unique name to them (such as `eth0`). Such a name doesn't have a corresponding entry in the filesystem. Communication between the kernel and a network device driver is completely different from that used with char and block drivers. Instead of *read* and *write*, the kernel calls functions related to packet transmission.

As a matter of fact, there is another class of "driver modules" in Linux: the SCSI* drivers. Although every peripheral connected to the SCSI bus appears in */dev* as either a char device or a block device, the internal organization of the software is different.

---

* SCSI is an acronym for Small Computer Systems Interface; it is an established standard in the workstation market and is becoming common also for PCs.

Just as network interfaces provide the network subsystem with hardware-related functionality, a SCSI controller provides the SCSI subsystem with access to the actual interface cable. SCSI is a communication protocol between the computer and peripheral devices, and every SCSI device responds to the same protocol, independently of what controller board is plugged into the computer. The Linux kernel therefore embeds a SCSI "implementation" (i.e., the mapping of file operations to the SCSI communication protocol). The driver writer has to implement the mapping between the SCSI abstraction and the physical cable. This mapping depends on the SCSI controller and is independent of the devices attached to the SCSI cable.

In addition to device drivers, there are other drivers, both hardware and software, that are modularized in the kernel. The most important class of modules not specifically implementing a device driver is that of filesystems. A filesystem type is concerned with the way information is organized on a block device in order to represent a tree of directories and files. Such an entity is not a "device driver," in that there's no explicit device associated with the way the information is laid down; the filesystem type is instead a software driver, because it structures raw data into higher level information.

If you think of how strongly a Unix system depends on the underlying filesystem, you'll realize that such a software concept is vital to system operation. The ability to decode filesystem information stays at the lowest level of the kernel hierarchy and is of utmost importance; even if you write a block driver for your new CD-ROM, it is useless if you are not able to run *ls* or *cp* on the data it hosts. Linux supports filesystem modules, whose software interface declares the different operations that can be performed on a filesystem inode, directory, file, and superblock. Such an interface is completely independent of the actual data transfer to and from the disk, which is accomplished by a block device driver. It's quite unusual for a programmer to actually need to write a filesystem module, because the official kernel already includes code for the most important filesystem types.

Security Issues

Talking about security issues is fashionable these days, and most programmers are concerned about their systems' security, so I'll address the problem at the beginning to avoid later misunderstandings.

Security has two faces. One problem is what a user can achieve through the misuse of existing programs, or by exploiting bugs; a different issue is what kind of (mis)functionality a programmer can implement. The programmer has, obviously, much more power than a plain user. In other words, it's more dangerous to run as root a program you got from a friend than to give him or her a root shell once in a while. Although having access to a compiler is not a security hole *per se*, the hole can appear when compiled code is actually executed; be careful with modules, because a kernel module can do anything. A module is much more powerful than a superuser shell, in that its privileged status is acknowledged by the CPU.

Any security check in the system is enforced by kernel code. If the kernel has security holes, then the system has holes. In the official kernel distribution, only root can load modules; the system call *create_module* checks the user ID of the invoking process. Thus with the official kernel, only the superuser, or an intruder who has succeeded in becoming root, can exploit the power of privileged code.

Fortunately, when writing a device driver or other module, there's little need to be concerned about security because processes accessing the device are already constrained by more general blocking techniques. With block devices, for example, security is handled by the permissions on the filesystem node and the *mount* command, so usually nothing has to be checked in the actual block driver.

Be careful, however, when receiving software from third parties, especially when the kernel is concerned: since everybody has access to the source code, everybody can break and recompile things. While you can trust precompiled kernels found in your distribution, you should avoid running kernels compiled by an untrusted friend—if you wouldn't run a precompiled binary as root, then you'd better not run a precompiled kernel. For example, a maliciously modified kernel could allow anyone to load a module, thus opening an unexpected back door via *create_module*.

If you are really concerned about system security in relation to modules, I'd urge you to look at how the **securelevel** kernel variable is used. As I write this, there is ongoing discussion in the Linux community about the prevention of module loading and unloading under the control of **securelevel**. It's interesting to note that with recent kernels, support for modules can be removed at kernel compile time, thus closing any related security hole.

Version Numbering

As the last point before digging in to programming, I'd like to comment on the unusual version numbering scheme used in Linux and what version this book refers to.

First of all, note that *every* software package used in a Linux system has its own release number, and there are often interdependencies across them: you need a particular version of one package to run a particular version of another package. The creators of Linux distributions usually handle the messy problem of matching packages, and the user who installs from a prepackaged distribution doesn't need to deal with version numbers. Those who replace and upgrade system software, on the other hand, are on their own. Fortunately, some modern distributions allow the upgrade of single packages by checking interpackage dependencies, and this greatly simplifies things for the user who needs to keep system software up to date.

In this book, I'll assume you have version 2.6.3 or newer of the *gcc* compiler, version 1.3.57 or newer of the module utilities, and a recent-enough version of the GNU tools (the most important being *gmake*) for program development. Those requirements aren't particularly strict, as nearly every Linux installation is equipped with GNU tools, and these versions are relatively old (besides, kernel versions 2.0 and later refuse to compile with a *gcc* older than 2.6). Note that recent kernels include a file called *Documentation/Changes*, which lists the software needed to proficiently compile and run that kernel version. This file is missing from the 1.2 sources.

As far as the kernel is concerned, I'll concentrate on the 2.0.*x* and 1.2.13 versions, trying to write code that can work with both of them.

The even-numbered kernel versions (i.e., 1.2.*x* and 2.0.*x*) are the stable ones and are intended for general distribution. The odd versions, on the contrary, are development snapshots and are quite ephemeral; the latest of them represents the current status of development, but becomes obsolete in a few days.

There should be no general reason to ever run a 1.3 or 2.1 kernel, unless it is the latest one. Sometimes, however, you will choose to run a development kernel, either because it has some features you need that are missing in the stable distributions, or simply because you have made your personal changes to that version, and you lack the time to upgrade your patch. Note, however, that there's no guarantee on experimental kernels, and nobody will help you if you lose your data because of a bug in a non-current odd-numbered kernel. Nonetheless, this book supports development versions of the kernel up to 2.1.43, as the last chapter describes how to write drivers that are aware of interface differences between 2.0 and 2.1.*x*.

As far as 1.2.13 is concerned, I feel it is an important kernel version, though quite old. While 2.0.*x* is faster than 1.2.13 on most new hardware, 1.2.13 is considerably smaller, and might be a good choice for someone who runs old hardware. Inexpensive systems based on a 386 processor with a small RAM supply are good candidates for embedded systems or automated controllers, and they might be faster with 1.2.13 than with 2.0.*x*. Since 1.2.13 is a bugfix release over previous 1.2.*x* versions, I won't consider earlier 1.2 kernels.

Whenever there is some incompatibility between 1.2.13 and 2.0, or in the latest 2.1 kernels, I'll report it.

My *main* target version is nonetheless Linux 2.0, and some features introduced in this book are not available in older kernels. Most sample modules will compile and run on a wide range of kernel versions; in particular, they have all been tested with version 2.0.30, and most of them with 1.2.13. Sometimes I won't support version 1.2 in the sample modules, but this only happens in the second part of the book, which is more advanced by design and can thus live without reference to older kernels.

Another feature of Linux is that it is a platform-independent operating system, as it isn't only "a Unix clone for PC clones" anymore: it is successfully being used with Axp-Alpha, the Sparc processors, Mips Rx000, and a few other platforms, in addition to the x86. This book is platform-independent as far as possible, and all the code samples have been tested on PCs, an Alpha platform, and a Sparc machine. Since the code has been tested on both 32-bit and 64-bit (the Alpha) processors, it should compile and run on all the other platforms. As you might expect, the code samples that rely on particular hardware don't work on all the supported platforms, but this is always stated in the source code.

License Terms

Linux is licensed with the GNU "General Public License" (GPL), a document devised for the GNU project by the Free Software Foundation. The GPL allows anybody to redistribute, and also sell, a GPL'd product, as long as the recipient is allowed to rebuild an exact copy of the binary files from source. Additionally, any software product derived from a GPL'd product must be released under the GPL.

The main goal of such a licence is to allow the growth of knowledge by permitting everybody to modify programs at will; at the same time, people selling software to the public can still do their job. Despite this simple objective, there's an ongoing discussion about the GPL and its use. If you want to read the license, you can find it in several places in your system, including the directory */usr/src/linux*, as a file called *COPYING*.

As far as third-party and custom modules are concerned, they're not part of the Linux kernel, and thus you're not forced to license them under the GPL. A module *uses* the kernel through a well-defined interface, but is not part of it, similar to the way user programs use the kernel through system calls.

In brief, if your code goes in the kernel, you must use the GPL as soon as you release the code. Although personal use of your changes doesn't force the GPL on, if you distribute your code you must include the source code in the distribution— people acquiring your package must be allowed to rebuild the binary at will. If you write a module, on the other hand, you are allowed to distribute it in binary form. However, this is not always practical, as modules should in general be recompiled for each kernel version that they will be linked with (as explained in Chapter 2, *Building and Running Modules*, in the section "Version Dependency," and Chapter 11, *Kerneld and Advanced Modularization*, in the section "Version Control in Modules"). The common objection to binary distribution of modules is that a module embeds code defined or declared in the kernel headers; this objection doesn't apply, however, because header files are part of the public interface of the kernel, and thus are not subject to licensing.

As far as this book is concerned, most of the code is freely redistributable, either in source or binary form, and neither O'Reilly & Associates nor I retain any license on any derived works. All the programs are available through FTP from *ftp://ftp.ora.com/pub/examples/linux/drivers/*, and the exact licence terms are stated in the file *LICENSE* in the same directory.

When sample programs include parts of the kernel code, the GPL applies: the text accompanying source code is very clear about that. This only happens for a pair of source files that are very minor to the topic of this book.

Overview of the Book

From here on, we enter the world of kernel programming. Chapter 2 introduces modularization, explaining the secrets of the art and showing the code for running modules. Chapter 3, *Char Drivers*, talks about char drivers and shows the complete code for a memory-based device driver that can be read and written for fun. Using memory as the hardware base for the device allows anyone to run the sample code without the need to acquire special hardware.

Debugging techniques are vital tools for the programmer and are introduced in Chapter 4, *Debugging Techniques*. Then, with our new debugging skills, we'll move to advanced features of char drivers, such as blocking operations, the use of *select* and the ever-popular *ioctl* call; these topics are the subject of Chapter 5, *Enhanced Char Driver Operations*.

Before dealing with hardware management, we'll dissect a few more of the kernel's software interfaces: Chapter 6, *Flow of Time*, shows how time is managed in the kernel, and Chapter 7, *Getting Hold of Memory*, explains memory allocation.

Next we focus on hardware: Chapter 8, *Hardware Management*, describes the management of I/O ports and memory buffers that live on the device; after that comes interrupt handling, in Chapter 9, *Interrupt Handling*. Unfortunately, not everyone will be able to run the sample code for these chapters, because some hardware support *is* actually needed to test the software interface to interrupts. I've tried my best to keep required hardware support to a minimum, but you still need to put your hands on the soldering iron to build your hardware "device." The device is a single jumper wire that plugs into the parallel port, so I hope this is not a problem.

Chapter 10, *Judicious Use of Data Types*, offers some additional suggestions about writing kernel software and about portability issues.

In the second part of this book, we get more ambitious; thus Chapter 11 starts over with modularization issues, going deeper into the topic.

Chapter 12, *Loading Block Drivers*, then describes how block drivers are implemented, outlining the aspects that differentiate them from char drivers. Following that, Chapter 13, *Mmap and DMA*, explains what we left out from the previous treatment of memory management: *mmap* and DMA. At this point, everything about char and block drivers has been introduced.

The third main class of drivers is introduced next: Chapter 14, *Network Drivers*, talks in some detail about network interfaces and dissects the code of the sample network driver.

A few features of device drivers depend directly on the interface bus where the peripheral fits, so Chapter 15, *Overview of Peripheral Buses*, provides an overview of the main features of the bus implementations most frequently found nowadays, with a special focus on PCI support offered in the kernel.

Finally, Chapter 16 is a sort of tour of the kernel source: it is meant to be a starting point for people who want to understand the overall design, but who may be scared by the huge amount of source code that makes up Linux.

Soon after Linux 2.0 was released, the 2.1 development tree began introducing incompatibilities; the most important ones were introduced in the first months. Chapter 17, *Recent Developments*, which can be considered almost an appendix, gathers all the known incompatibilities introduced before 2.1.43 and offers software fixes for them. By the end of the chapter, you'll be able to write device drivers that compile and run on 1.2.13 and all kernels between 2.0 and 2.1.43. Hopefully, 2.2 will turn out to be quite similar to 2.1.43, and your software will be ready for the event.

CHAPTER TWO

BUILDING AND RUNNING MODULES

I t's high time now to begin programming. This chapter is going to introduce all the essential concepts about modules and kernel programming. In these few pages, we'll build and run a complete module. Building such expertise is an essential foundation for any kind of modularized driver. To avoid throwing in too many concepts, this chapter only talks about modules, without referring to any device class.

All the kernel items (functions, variables, header files, and macros) that are introduced here are described in a reference section at the end of the chapter.

For the impatient reader, the following code is a complete "Hello, World" module (which does nothing in particular). This code will compile and run under Linux 2.0 and later versions, but not under 1.2, as explained later in this chapter.*

```
#define MODULE
#include <linux/module.h>

int init_module(void)      { printk("<1>Hello, world\n"); return 0; }
void cleanup_module(void)  { printk("<1>Goodbye cruel world\n"); }
```

The *printk* function is defined in the Linux kernel and behaves similarly to *printf*; the module can call *printk*, because after *insmod* has loaded it, the module is linked to the kernel and can access its symbols. The string <1> is the priority of the message. I've specified a high priority in this module because a message with the default priority might not show on the console if you use version 2.0.*x* of the kernel and an old *klogd* daemon (you can ignore this issue for now; we'll explain it in the section "Printk," in Chapter 4, *Debugging Techniques*).

---

* This example, and all the others presented in this book, are available on the O'Reilly FTP site, as explained in Chapter 1, *An Introduction to the Linux Kernel*.

You can test the module by calling *insmod* and *rmmod*, as shown in the screen dump below. Note that only the superuser can load and unload a module.

```
root# gcc -c hello.c
root# insmod hello.o
Hello, world
root# rmmod hello
Goodbye cruel world
root#
```

As you see, writing a module *is* easy. We'll go deeper into the topic throughout this chapter.

Modules Versus Applications

Before we go further, it's worth underlining the various differences between a kernel module and an application.

While an application performs a single task from beginning to end, a module registers itself in order to serve future requests, and its "main" function terminates immediately. In other words, the task of *init_module()* (the module's entry point) is to prepare for later invocation of the module's functions; it's as though the module is saying, "Here I am, and this is what I can do." The second entry point of a module, *cleanup_module*, gets invoked just before the module is unloaded. It should tell the kernel, "I'm not there any more, don't ask me to do anything else." The ability to unload a module is one of the features of modularization that you'll most appreciate, because it helps cut down development time; you can test successive versions of your new driver without going through the lengthy shutdown/reboot cycle each time.

As a programmer, you know that an application can call functions it doesn't define: the linking stage resolves external references using the appropriate library of functions. *printf* is one of those callable functions and is defined in *libc*. A module, on the other hand, is linked only to the kernel, and the only functions it can call are the ones exported by the kernel. The *printk* function used in *hello.c* above, for example, is the version of *printf* defined within the kernel and exported to modules; it behaves exactly like the original function, except that it has no floating-point support.

Figure 2-1 shows how function calls and function pointers are used in a module to add new functionality to a running kernel.

Since no library is linked to modules, source files should *never* include the usual header files. Anything related to the kernel is declared in headers found in */usr/include/linux* and */usr/include/asm*. The header files that reside in these directories are also used indirectly when compiling applications; kernel code is thus protected by #ifdef __KERNEL__. The two directories of kernel headers are usually symbolic links to the place where the kernel sources reside. If you

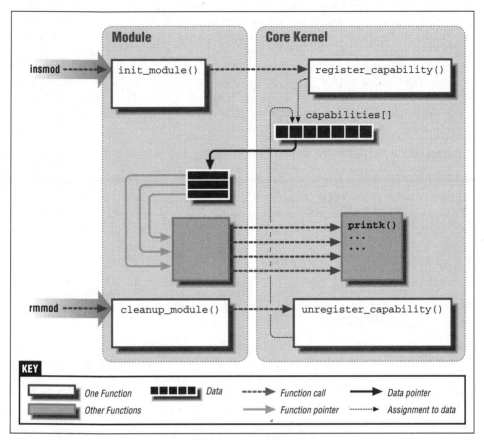

Figure 2-1: Linking a module to the kernel

don't want the complete Linux source tree on your system, you still need at least these two directories of header files. In recent kernels, you also find the *net* and *scsi* header directories in the kernel sources, but it's very unusual for modules to need them.

The role of the kernel headers will be introduced later, as each of them is needed.

Kernel modules also differ from applications in requiring that you watch out for "namespace pollution." When writing small programs, programmers frequently don't care about the program's namespace, but this causes problems when the small programs are going to become part of a huge application. Namespace pollution is what happens when there are many functions and global variables, and their names aren't meaningful enough to be easily distinguished. The programmer who is forced to deal with such an application expends much mental energy just to remember the "reserved" names and to find unique names for new symbols.

We can't afford to fall into such an error when writing kernel code, because even the smallest module is going to be linked to the whole kernel. The best approach to prevent namespace pollution is to declare all your symbols as `static` and to use a well-defined prefix for the symbols you leave global. Alternatively, you can avoid declaring `static` symbols by declaring a symbol table, as described in "Registering Symbol Tables," later in this chapter. Using the chosen prefix even for private symbols within the module can sometimes simplify debugging. Prefixes used in the kernel are, by convention, all lowercase, and we'll stick to the same convention.

The last difference between kernel programming and application programming is in how faults are handled: while a segmentation fault is harmless during application development and a debugger can always be used to trace the error to the problem in the source code, a kernel fault is fatal at least for the current process, if not for the whole system. We'll see how to trace kernel errors in Chapter 4, in the section "Debugging System Faults."

User Space and Kernel Space

We can summarize our discussion by saying that a module runs in the so-called "kernel space," while applications run in "user space." This concept is at the basis of operating systems theory.

The role of the operating system, in practice, is to provide programs with a consistent view of the computer's hardware. In addition, the operating system must account for independent operation of programs and protection against unauthorized access to resources. This non-trivial task is only possible if the CPU enforces protection of system software from the applications.

Every modern processor is able to enforce this behavior. The chosen approach is to implement different operating modalities (or levels) in the CPU itself. The levels have different roles, and some operations are disallowed at the lowest levels; program code can switch from one level to another only through a limited number of "gates." Unix systems are designed to take advantage of this hardware feature, but they only use two such levels (while, for example, Intel processors have four levels). Under Unix, the kernel executes in the highest level (also called "supervisor mode"), where everything is allowed, while applications execute in the lowest level (the so-called "user mode"), where the processor inhibits direct access to hardware and unauthorized access to memory.

As mentioned before, when dealing with software, we usually refer to the execution modes as "kernel space" and "user space," with reference to the different memory mappings, and thus the different "address spaces" used by program code.

Unix transfers execution from user space to kernel space through system calls and hardware interrupts. Kernel code executing a system call is working in the context of a process—it operates on behalf of the calling process and is able to access data in the process's address space. Code that handles interrupts, on the other hand, is asynchronous with respect to processes and is not related to any particular process.

The role of a module is to extend kernel functionality; modularized code runs in kernel space. Usually a driver performs both the tasks outlined above: some functions in the module are executed as part of system calls, and some are in charge of interrupt handling.

Concurrency in the Kernel

One of the first questions new kernel programmers ask is how multitasking is managed. Actually, there's nothing special about multitasking except in the scheduler proper, and the scheduler is beyond the scope of the average programmer's activity. You can face this task, but module writers don't need to know anything about it, except to learn the following principles.

Unlike application programs, which run sequentially, the kernel works asynchronously, executing system calls on behalf of the applications. The kernel is in charge of input/output and resource management for every process in the system.

Kernel (and module) functions are completely executed in a single thread, usually in the context of a single process, unless they "go to sleep"—a driver should be able to support concurrency by allowing the interwoven execution of different tasks. For example, a device can be read by two processes at the same time. The driver responds sequentially to several *read* calls, each belonging to either process. Since the code needs to keep each flow of data distinct, the kernel (and driver) code must maintain internal data structures to be able to tell the different operations apart. That's not unlike the way a student keeps track of the interweaving of lessons: a different notebook is devoted to each course. An alternative way of dealing with the problem of multiple access would be to avoid it by prohibiting concurrent access to a device, but this lazy technique isn't even worth discussing here.

Context switches can't happen unexpectedly while kernel code is executing, so driver functions don't need to be reentrant, unless they call *schedule* by themselves. Functions that must wait for data call *sleep_on*, which in turn calls *schedule*. However, you must be careful, as there are other functions that can unexpectedly sleep, notably any access to user space. Making use of "natural non-preemption" is generally a bad practice. I won't deal with reentrant functions until "Writing Reentrant Code," in Chapter 5, *Enhanced Char Driver Operations*.

As far as multiple access to the driver is concerned, there are various approaches to keeping things separate, all relying on task-specific data. This data can be either global kernel variables or process-specific arguments to driver functions.

The most important global variable that can be used for tracking processes is `current`: a pointer to `struct task_struct`, which is declared in `<linux/sched.h>`. The `current` pointer refers to the user process currently executing. During the execution of a system call, such as *open* or *read*, the current process is the one that invoked the call.* Kernel code can use process-specific information by using `current`, if it needs to do so. An example of this technique is presented in "Access Control on a Device File," in Chapter 5.

The compiler handles `current` just like the external reference *printk*. A module can refer to `current` wherever it wants and all the references are resolved by *insmod* at load time. For example, the following statement prints the process ID and the command name of the current process, by accessing certain fields in `struct task_struct`:

```
printk("The process is \"%s\" (pid %i)\n",
       current->comm, current->pid);
```

The command name stored in `current->comm` is the basename of the executable file that was last executed by the current process.

Compiling and Loading

The rest of this chapter is devoted to writing a complete, though typeless, module. That is, the module will not belong to any of the classes listed in "Classes of Devices and Modules," in Chapter 1. The sample driver shown in this chapter is called *skull*, short for "Simple Kernel Utility for Loading Localities." You can reuse the *skull* source to load your own local code to the kernel, after removing the sample functionality it offers.†

Before we deal with the roles of *init_module* and *cleanup_module*, however, we'll write a *Makefile* that builds object code that the kernel can load.

First, we need to define the `__KERNEL__` symbol in the preprocessor before we include any headers. This symbol is used to select which parts of the headers are actually used. Applications end up including kernel headers because *libc* includes them,‡ but the applications don't need all the kernel prototypes. Therefore, `__KERNEL__` is used to mask the extra ones out via `#ifdef`. Exporting kernel symbols and macros to user-space programs would greatly contribute to program namespace pollution. If you are compiling for an SMP (Symmetric Multi-Processor)

---

* In version 2.0, `current` is a macro that expands to `current_set[this_cpu]`, to be SMP-compliant. 2.1.37 optimized access to `current` by storing the value in the stack, thus removing any global symbol.

† I use the word "local" here to denote personal changes to the system, in the good old Unix tradition of */usr/local*.

‡ This is true for version 5 and previous versions of the library. With version 6 (*glibc*) this may change, but discussion is not over as I write this.

machine, you also need to define `__SMP__` before including the kernel headers. This requirement may seem unfriendly, but is going to disappear as soon as the developers find the right way to be SMP-transparent.

Another important symbol is `MODULE`, which must be defined before including `<linux/module.h>`. This symbol is always defined, except when compiling drivers that are directly linked to the kernel image. Since none of the drivers covered in this book are directly linked to the kernel, they all define the symbol.

A module writer must also specify the *−O* flag to the compiler, because many functions are declared as `inline` in the header files. *gcc* doesn't expand inlines unless optimization is enabled, but it can accept both the *−g* and *−O* options, allowing you to debug code that uses inline functions.*

Finally, in order to prevent unpleasant errors, I suggest that you use the *−Wall* (all warnings) compiler flag, and also that you fix all errors in the code to eliminate all compiler warnings, even if this requires changing your usual programming style.

All the definitions and flags I've introduced so far are best located within the `CFLAGS` variable used by *make*.

In addition to a suitable `CFLAGS`, the *Makefile* being built needs a rule for joining different object files. The rule is needed only if the module is split into different source files, but that is not uncommon with modules. The modules are joined through the `ld -r` command, which is not really a linking operation, even though it uses the linker. This is because the output is another object file, which incorporates all the code from the input files. The *−r* option means "relocatable"; the output file is relocatable because it doesn't yet embed absolute addresses.

The following *Makefile* implements all the features described above, and it builds a module made up of two source files. If your module is made up of a single source file, just skip the entry containing `ld -r`.

```
# Change it here or specify it on the "make" commandline
INCLUDEDIR = /usr/include

CFLAGS = -D__KERNEL__ -DMODULE -O -Wall -I$(INCLUDEDIR)

# Extract version number from headers.
VER = $(shell awk -F\" '/REL/ {print $$2}' \
        $(INCLUDEDIR)/linux/version.h)

OBJS = skull.o

all: $(OBJS)
```

---

* Note, however, that using any optimization more than *−O2* is risky, as the compiler might inline functions that are not declared as `inline` in the source. This may be a problem with kernel code, as some functions expect to find a standard stack layout when they are called.

```
skull.o: skull_init.o skull_clean.o
        $(LD) -r $^ -o $@

install:
        install -d /lib/modules/$(VER)/misc /lib/modules/misc
        install -c skull.o /lib/modules/$(VER)/misc
        install -c skull.o /lib/modules/misc

clean:
        rm -f *.o *~ core
```

The tricky `install` rule in the file above is meant to install the module in a version-dependent directory, as explained below. The VER variable in *Makefile* is set to the correct version number, extracted from `<linux/version.h>`.

Next, after the module is built, it must be loaded into the kernel. As I've already suggested, *insmod* does the job for you. The program is like *ld*, as it links any unresolved symbol in the module to the symbol table of the running kernel. Unlike the linker, however, it doesn't modify the disk file, but rather the in-memory image. *insmod* accepts a number of command-line options (for details, see the man page), and it can change the value of integer and string variables in your module before linking the module to the current kernel. Thus, if a module is correctly designed, it can be configured at load time; load-time configuration gives the user more flexibility than compile-time configuration, which unfortunately is still used sometimes. Load-time configuration is explained in "Automatic and Manual Configuration," later in this chapter.

Interested readers may want to look at how the kernel supports *insmod*: it relies on a few system calls defined in *kernel/module.c*. *sys_create_module* allocates *kernel* memory to hold a module (this memory is allocated with *vmalloc*; see "vmalloc and Friends" in Chapter 7, *Getting Hold of Memory*), the system call *get_kernel_syms* returns the kernel symbol table in order to link the module, and *sys_init_module* copies the relocated object code to kernel space and calls the module's initialization function.

If you actually look in the kernel source, you'll find that the name of the system calls is prefixed with `sys_`. This is true for all system calls and no other functions; it's useful to keep this in mind when grepping for the system calls in the sources.

Version Dependency

Bear in mind that your module's code has to be recompiled for each version of the kernel that it will be linked to. Each module defines a symbol called `kernel_version`, which *insmod* matches against the version number of the current kernel. Recent kernels define the symbol for you in `<linux/module.h>` (that's why *hello.c* above didn't declare it). That also means that if your module is made up of multiple source files, you only have to include `<linux/module.h>` from one of your sources. When compiling against Linux 1.2, on the other hand, `kernel_version` must be defined in your sources.

In case of version mismatch, you can still try to load a module against a different kernel version, by specifying the *–f* ("force") switch to *insmod*, but this operation isn't safe and can fail. It's also difficult to tell in advance what will happen. Loading can fail because of mismatching symbols, in which case you'll get an error message, or it can fail because of an internal change in the kernel. If that happens, you'll get serious errors at run time and possibly a system panic—a good reason to be wary of version mismatches. Actually, version mismatches can be handled more gracefully by using "versioning" in the kernel (a topic that is more advanced and is introduced later in "Version Control in Modules" in Chapter 11, *Kerneld and Advanced Modularization*).

If you want to compile your module for a particular kernel version, you have to include the specific header files for that kernel (for example, by declaring a different `INCLUDEPATH`) in the *Makefile* above.

In order to deal with version dependency at load time, *insmod* follows a particular search path; if it doesn't find the module in the current directory, it looks for it in a version-dependent directory, and then in */lib/modules/misc* if that fails. The `install` rule in the *Makefile* above follows this convention.

The tricky task is writing code that can be compiled and run on any kernel version from 1.2.13 to 2.0.*x* and on. The interface to modularization has changed to make setup easier. You can see in *hello.c* above that there's no need to declare anything, as long as you deal only with recent kernels. A portable interface, on the other hand, looks like the following:

```
#define __NO_VERSION__  /* don't define kernel_version in module.h */
#include <linux/module.h>
#include <linux/version.h>

char kernel_version [] = UTS_RELEASE;
```

In 2.0 and newer kernels, the file *version.h* is included by *module.h*, which also defines `kernel_version` unless `__NO_VERSION__` is defined.

The `__NO_VERSION__` symbol can also be used if you need to include `<linux/module.h>` in several source files that will be linked together to form a single module—if you need preprocessor macros declared in *module.h*, for example. Declaring `__NO_VERSION__` before including *module.h* prevents automatic declaration of the string `kernel_version` in source files where you don't want it (*ld -r* would complain about the multiple definition of the symbol). Sample modules in this book use `__NO_VERSION__` to this aim.

Other dependencies based on the kernel version can be solved with preprocessor conditionals—*version.h* defines the integer macro `LINUX_VERSION_CODE`. The macro expands to the binary representation of the kernel version, one byte for each part of the version release number. For example, the code for 1.3.5 is 66309 (i.e., 0x10305).* With this information, you can easily determine what version of the kernel you are dealing with.

Writing the number in decimal isn't too practical when you have to check against a particular version. In order to support multiple kernel versions from the same source file, I'll use the following macro to build a version code from the three component parts of the version number:

```
#define VERSION_CODE(vers,rel,seq) (((vers)<<16) | ((rel)<<8) | (seq))
```

The Kernel Symbol Table

We've seen how *insmod* resolves undefined symbols against the table of public kernel symbols. The table contains global kernel items—functions and variables—that are needed to implement modularized drivers. The public symbol table can be read in text form from the file */proc/ksyms*.

When your module is loaded, any global symbol you declare becomes part of the kernel symbol table, and you can see it appear in */proc/ksyms* or in the output of the *ksyms* command.

New modules can use symbols exported by your module, and you can stack new modules on top of other modules. Module stacking is implemented in the mainstream kernel sources as well: the *msdos* filesystem relies on symbols exported by the *fat* module, and the *ppp* driver stacks on the header compression module.

Module stacking is useful in complex projects. If a new abstraction is implemented in the form of a device driver, it might offer a plug for hardware-specific implementations. For example, a frame buffer video driver can export symbols to be used by a lower-level VGA driver. Each user loads the frame buffer module and the specific VGA module for his or her installed hardware.

Layered modularization can help reduce development time by simplifying each layer. This is similar to the separation between mechanism and policy that we discussed in Chapter 1.

Registering Symbol Tables

An alternative to exporting all the global symbols of your module is to use the function *register_symtab*, which is the official kernel interface to symbol-table management. The programming interface described here applies to the 1.2.13 and

---

* This allows up to 256 development versions between stable versions.

2.0 kernels. See the section "Modularization" in Chapter 17, *Recent Developments*, for details about changes introduced in the 2.1 development kernels.

The function *register_symtab*, as its name suggests, is used to register a whole symbol table in the kernel's main table. This technique is somewhat cleaner than relying on static and global symbols, in that the programmer centralizes the information about what is made available to other modules and what isn't. This is a better approach than scattering `static` declarations all over the source file.

If a module calls *register_symtab* from its initialization function, global symbols are no longer exported; only symbols that are listed in the explicit symbol table are exported to the kernel.

The advantage of declaring a centralized symbol table is most relevant when writing modules that span multiple source files. Many functions and variables can be left global so the source files can share the relevant information; the symbol table later selects what really needs to be exported for use by other modules.

Filling a symbol table structure is a tricky task, but kernel developers have written header files to simplify the task. The following lines of code show how a symbol table is declared and exported:

```
static struct symbol_table skull_syms = {

#include <linux/symtab_begin.h>
        X(skull_fn1),
        X(skull_fn2),
        X(skull_variable),
#include <linux/symtab_end.h>
        };

register_symtab(&skull_syms);
```

Interested readers can examine `<linux/symtab_begin.h>`, but it's one of the most difficult headers in the kernel. It's not actually necessary to understand the X macro to benefit from its use.

register_symtab is able to override the static or global declaration of symbols because it is called *after* the module has been loaded into the running kernel. *register_symtab* replaces the public symbols exported by default for the current module with the explicit symbol table.

The override is possible because *insmod* hands the table of global symbols to the system call *sys_init_module*, which in turn registers the table *before* calling *init_module*. Any explicit call to *register_symtab* thus replaces the symbol table associated with the module.

If your module doesn't need to export any symbols, and you don't want to declare everything as **static**, just hide global symbols by adding the following line to *init_module*. This call to *register_symtab* simply overwrites the module's default symbol table with an empty one:

```
register_symtab(NULL);
```

If the source file does not offer hooks for additional modules to be stacked on it, it's always a good idea to hide all the symbols by using the one-liner above.

When the module is unloaded from the kernel, any public symbol it declared is automatically discarded from the main symbol table. This applies to both global symbols and explicit symbol tables.

Initialization and Shutdown

As already suggested, *init_module* registers any facility offered by the module. By "facility," I mean a new functionality, be it a whole driver or a new software abstraction, that can be accessed by an application.

Registration of a new facility is performed by calling a kernel function. The arguments passed are usually a pointer to a data structure describing the new facility and the name of the facility being registered. The data structure usually embeds pointers to module functions, which is how functions in the module body get called.

In addition to the "main" facilities that are used to identify the class of each module (such as char and block drivers), a module can register the following items:

Miscellaneous devices
> These were once called mice because this kind of facility was only used by bus-mice. They are spare devices, generally simpler than full-featured ones.

Serial ports
> A serial driver can be added to the system at run time; this is how PCMCIA modems are supported.

Line disciplines
> The line discipline is a software layer that handles the tty data streams. A module can register a new line discipline to handle tty transactions in a nonstandard way. The *kmouse* module, for example, uses a discipline to steal incoming data from serial mice.

tty drivers
> A tty driver is the set of functions that implement low-level data handling over a tty. Both the console and the serial driver register their drivers in order to create terminal devices. Multiport serial ports have their own driver as well.

/proc files

/proc contains files that are used to access information in the kernel. Because they can be used in debugging, /proc files are covered in "Using the /proc Filesystem," in Chapter 4.

Binary formats

For every file marked as executable, the kernel scans a list of "binary formats" to actually execute it. Modules can implement new formats, as the *Java* module does.

Exec domains

In order to offer binary compatibility with other flavors of Unix, a few of the kernel internal tables must be modified. An "execution domain" is a set of mappings from the conventions of another operating system to Linux. For example, the iBCS2 module defines the execution domain to execute SCO binary files.

Symbol tables

These have already been covered in "Registering Symbol Tables," earlier in this chapter.

The items above are device types not considered in the previous chapter and support facilities that usually integrate the driver's functionality, such as /proc files and line disciplines. The reason why mice and other miscellaneous drivers are not managed like "complete" char drivers is mainly for convenience. The reason will be apparent in a while, when you read the section "Major and Minor Numbers," in Chapter 3, *Char Drivers.*

There are indeed other facilities that can be registered as add-ons for certain drivers, but their use is so specific that it's not worth talking about them; they use the stacking technique, as described above in "Registering Symbol Tables." If you want to probe further, you can grep for *register_symtab* in the kernel sources and find the entry points offered by different drivers. Most registration functions are prefixed with `register_`, so another possible way to find them is to grep for "`register_`" in /proc/ksyms.

Error Handling in init_module

If any errors occur when you register utilities, you must undo any registration performed before the failure. An error can happen, for example, if there isn't enough memory in the system to allocate a new data structure. Though unlikely, it might happen, and good program code must be prepared to handle this event.

Linux doesn't keep a per-module registry of facilities that have been registered to the module, so the module must back out everything if *init_module* fails at some point. If you ever fail to unregister what you got, the kernel is left in an unstable state: you can't register your facilities again by reloading the module because they will appear to be "busy," and you can't unregister them because you'd need the same pointer you used to register and you're not likely to be able to figure out the address. Recovery from such situations is tricky, and rebooting the system is often the best solution.

I suggest that you deal with error recovery by using the `goto` statement. I hate to use `goto`, but in my opinion this is one situation (well, the *only* situation) where it is useful. In the kernel, `goto` is often used as shown here to deal with errors.

The following sample code behaves correctly both in the case of success and in the case of failure:

```
int init_module(void)
{
int err;

    /* registration takes a pointer and a name */
    err = register_this(ptr1, "skull");
    if (err) goto fail_this;
    err = register_that(ptr2, "skull");
    if (err) goto fail_that;
    err = register_those(ptr3, "skull");
    if (err) goto fail_those;

    return 0; /* success */

    fail_those: unregister_that(ptr2, "skull");
    fail_that:  unregister_this(ptr1, "skull");
    fail_this:  return err; /* propagate the error */
}
```

The return value (`err`) is an error code. In the Linux kernel, error codes are negative numbers, belonging to the set defined in `<linux/errno.h>`. If you want to generate your own error codes instead of returning what you get from other functions, you should include `<linux/errno.h>` in order to use symbolic values like `-ENODEV`, `-ENOMEM`, and so on. It is always good practice to return appropriate error codes, because user programs can turn them to meaningful strings using *perror* or similar means.

Obviously, *cleanup_module* must undo any registration performed by *init_module*:

```
void cleanup_module(void)
{
    unregister_those(ptr3, "skull");
    unregister_that(ptr2, "skull");
    unregister_this(ptr1, "skull");
    return;
}
```

The Usage Count

The system keeps a usage count for every module, in order to determine whether the module can be safely removed. The system needs this information because a module can't be unloaded if it is busy: you can't remove a filesystem type while the filesystem is mounted, and you can't drop a char device while a process is using it.

The usage count is maintained by three macros:

MOD_INC_USE_COUNT
> Increments the count for the current module.

MOD_DEC_USE_COUNT .XET N .XE1 "MOD_DEC_USE_COUNT module"
./XET
> Decrements the count.

MOD_IN_USE
> Evaluates to true if the count is not zero.

The macros are defined in <linux/module.h>, and they act on internal data structures that shouldn't be accessed directly by the programmer. As a matter of fact, the internals of module management changed a lot during 2.1 development and have been completely rewritten in 2.1.18 (see "Modularization" in Chapter 17 to probe further).

Note that there's no need to check for MOD_IN_USE from within *cleanup_module*, because the check is performed by the system call *sys_delete_module* (defined in *kernel/module.c*) before calling the cleanup function.

You won't be able to unload a module if you lose track of the usage count. This situation may very well to happen during development, so you should keep it in mind. For example, if a process gets destroyed because your driver dereferenced a NULL pointer, the driver won't be able to close the device, and the usage count won't fall back to 0. One possible solution is to completely disable the usage count during the debugging cycle by redefining both MOD_INC_USE_COUNT and MOD_DEC_USE_COUNT to no-ops. Another solution is to use some other method to force the counter to zero (you'll see this done in the section "Using the ioctl Argument," in Chapter 5). Sanity checks should never be circumvented in a production module. For debugging, however, sometimes a brute-force attitude helps save time and is therefore acceptable.

The current value of the usage count is found in the third field of each entry in */proc/modules*. This file shows the modules currently loaded in the system, with one entry for each module. The fields are the name of the module, the number of pages of memory it uses, and the current usage count. This is a typical */proc/modules*:

```
plip            3           0
isofs           5           1 (autoclean)
nfs            12           4
kmouse          3           4 (autoclean)
```

The (autoclean) marker identifies modules managed by *kerneld* (see Chapter 11). New parenthesized flags have been introduced in recent kernels, but the basic structure of */proc/modules* is the same except for one thing: in kernel 2.1.18 and newer the length is expressed in bytes instead of pages.

Unloading

To unload a module, use the *rmmod* command. Its task is much simpler than loading, as no linking has to be performed. The command invokes the *delete_module* system call, which calls *cleanup_module* in the module itself if the usage count is zero.

The *cleanup_module* implementation is in charge of unregistering every item that was registered by the module. Only the symbol table is removed automatically.

Using Resources

A module can't accomplish its task without using system resources, such as memory, I/O ports, and interrupt lines, as well as DMA channels if you use the mainboard's DMA controller.

As a programmer, you are already accustomed to managing memory allocation, and writing kernel code is no different in this regard. Your program obtains a memory area using *kmalloc* and releases it using *kfree*. These functions behave like *malloc* and *free*, except that *kmalloc* takes an additional argument, the priority. Most of the time, a priority of GFP_KERNEL will do. The GFP acronym stands for "Get Free Page."

Requesting I/O ports and interrupt lines, on the other hand, looks strange at first, because normally a programmer accesses them with explicit instructions in the code, without telling the operating system about it. "Allocating" ports and interrupts is different from memory allocation in that memory is allocated from a pool, and every address behaves the same; I/O ports have individual roles, and a driver needs to work with specific ports, not just *some* ports.

Ports

The job of a typical driver is, for the most part, writing and reading ports. This is true both at initialization time and during normal work. A device driver must be guaranteed exclusive access to its ports in order to prevent interference from other drivers—if a module probing for its hardware should happen to write to ports owned by another device, weird things would undoubtedly happen.

The developers of Linux chose to implement a request/free mechanism for ports, mainly as a way to prevent collisions between different devices. However, unauthorized port access doesn't produce any error condition equivalent to "segmentation fault"—the hardware can't enforce port registration.

Information about registered ports is available in text form in the file */proc/ioports*, which looks like the following:

```
0040-005f : timer
0060-006f : kbd
0070-007f : rtc
00f0-00ff : npu
0170-0177 : ide1
01f0-01f7 : ide0
02f8-02ff : serial(auto)
0300-031f : NE2000
0376-0376 : ide1
03c0-03df : vga+
03f6-03f6 : ide0
```

Each entry in the file specifies (in hex) a range of ports locked by a driver. No other driver should try to access those ports before they are released by the driver holding them.

Collision is avoided in two ways. First, a user adding a new device to the system can check */proc/ioports* in order to configure the new device to use free ports—this assumes the device is configured by moving jumpers around. Later, when the software driver initializes itself, it can autodetect the new device without risking harm to other devices: the driver won't probe I/O ports already in use by other drivers.

In practice, collision avoidance based on the I/O registry works best for modularized drivers, while it may fail for drivers directly linked into the kernel. Although we're not concerned with such drivers, it's worth noting that a driver initializing itself at boot time might misconfigure other devices by using ports that will be registered at a later time. Nonetheless, there's no way for a compliant driver to interact with hardware that has already been configured in the system, unless the previously loaded driver didn't register its ports. As a matter of fact, ISA probing is a risky task, and several drivers distributed with the official Linux kernel refuse to perform probing when loaded as modules, to avoid corrupting system operation by interacting with hardware whose module has yet to be loaded.

The problem with device probing is that the only way to identify the hardware is by trying to write and read the candidate ports—the processor (and thus any program) can only look at electric signals on its data lines. Driver writers know that *if* a device is connected to a particular port, it will reply to queries with particular codes. But if another device is connected to the port, it will nonetheless be written to, and nobody can foresee how it will react to the unexpected probing. Sometimes port probing can be avoided by reading the peripheral's BIOS looking for a known string; this technique is exploited by several SCSI drivers, but not every device carries its own BIOS.

A compliant driver should call *check_region* to find out if a range of ports is already locked by other drivers, *request_region* to lock ports for later use, and *release_region* when it's done. The prototypes for these functions reside in <linux/ioport.h>.

The typical sequence for registering ports is the following (the function *skull_probe_hw* embeds device-specific code and is not shown here):

```
#include <linux/ioport.h>
#include <linux/errno.h>
static int skull_detect(unsigned int port, unsigned int range)
{
    int err;

    if ((err=check_region(port,range)) < 0) return err; /* busy */
    if (skull_probe_hw(port,range) != 0) return -ENODEV; /* not found */

    request_region(port,range,"skull"); /* always succeeds */
    return 0;
}
```

Ports are released by *cleanup_module*:

```
static void skull_release(unsigned int port, unsigned int range)
{
    release_region(port,range);
}
```

A similar request/free policy is used for interrupt lines, but managing interrupts is trickier than handling ports, and a detailed explanation of the whole story is deferred to Chapter 9, *Interrupt Handling*.

The request/free approach to resources is similar to the register/unregister task described earlier for facilities and fits well into the goto-based implementation scheme already outlined.

The problems related to probing are not encountered by programmers writing drivers for PCI devices. I'll introduce PCI in Chapter 15, *Overview of Peripheral Buses*.

ISA Memory

This section is quite technical, and can easily be skipped if you are not (yet) confident dealing with hardware issues.

On Intel platforms, target devices fitting into an ISA slot may offer on-board memory in the range 640KB-1MB (0xA0000 to 0xFFFFF); this is another kind of system resource used by a device driver.

This memory layout dates back to the old days of the 8086 processor, which could address only one megabyte of memory. The designers of the PC decided that the low 640KB would host the RAM, while the other 384KB would be reserved for ROM and memory-mapped devices. Nowadays even the most powerful personal computers still have this memory hole in the first meg. The PC version of Linux marks the region as reserved and simply doesn't consider it. The code presented in this section of the book can be used to access the memory in this range, though its use is limited to the x86 platforms and to Linux kernels up to and including version 2.0.*x*, for any "x." Version 2.1 changed the way physical memory is accessed, such that I/O memory in the 640KB-1MB range can't be accessed in this way any more. The correct way to access I/O memory is the topic of the section "ISA Memory Below 1M," in Chapter 8, *Hardware Management*, and is outside the scope of this chapter.

Although the kernel supports a request/free mechanism for ports and interrupts, it doesn't currently support anything similar for I/O memory ranges, so you're on your own. This won't ever change, if I understand Linus' attitude towards the PC architecture.

Sometimes it happens that a driver needs to detect ISA memory during initialization; for example, I needed to locate a free memory area to tell a frame grabber where to map the grabbed image. The problem is that, without probing, you can't tell how address areas in that range are used. The probe needs to be able to identify three different cases: RAM is mapped to the address, ROM is there (the VGA BIOS, for example), or the area is free.

The *skull* sample source shows a way to deal with such memory, but since *skull* is not related to any physical device, it just prints information about the 640KB–1MB memory region and then exits. However, the code used to analyze memory is worth describing, because it must deal with race conditions. A *race condition* is a situation where two tasks might contend for the same resource, and where unsynchronized access can cause system damage.

While driver writers don't need to handle multitasking, we must always remember that interrupts can happen in the middle of our code, and an interrupt handler can modify global items without telling us about it. Although the kernel offers several utilities to deal with race conditions, the following simple rules state the general way to deal with the problem; a complete treatment of the issue appears in the section "Race Conditions," in Chapter 9.

- If the shared item is read and not written, declare it as `volatile`, asking the compiler to skip optimization. Thus, the compiled code actually reads the item every time the source code reads it.

- If the code needs to check and change the value, interrupts must be disabled during the operation to prevent other processes from changing the item after we have checked it, but before our change takes effect.

The suggested sequence for temporarily disabling interrupts is the following:

```
unsigned long flags;
save_flags(flags);
cli();

/* critical code */

restore_flags(flags);
```

where *cli* means "clear interrupt flag." The functions shown above are defined in `<asm/system.h>`.

The classic sequence *cli* and *sti* should be avoided, as there are times when you can't tell if interrupts are enabled before you disable them. Calling *sti* in such situations can lead to sporadic errors that are very difficult to track down.

The code to check for RAM segments makes use of both `volatile` declarations and *cli*, because these regions can be identified only by physically writing and rereading data, and real RAM might be changed by other drivers in the middle of our tests during an interrupt. The following code is not completely foolproof, because it might mistake RAM memory on acquisition boards for empty regions if a device is actively writing to its own memory while this code is scanning the area. However, this situation is quite unlikely to happen.

In the source code below, each *printk* is prefixed with the `KERN_INFO` symbol. This symbol is a priority string that gets concatenated to the format string and is defined in `<linux/kernel.h>`. Its expansion is similar to the `<1>` strings used in *hello.c* at the beginning of this chapter.

```
volatile unsigned char *ptr;  /* pointed data is volatile  */
unsigned char oldval, newval; /* values read from memory    */
unsigned long flags;          /* used to hold system flags */
unsigned long add, i;

/* probe all the memory hole in 2KB steps */
for (add = 0xA0000; add < 0x100000; add += 2048) {
    ptr = (unsigned char *)add;

    save_flags(flags);
    cli();
    oldval = *ptr;      /* read a byte */
    *ptr= oldval^0xff; /* change it    */
```

```
    newval=*ptr;        /* re-read     */
    *ptr=oldval;        /* restore     */
    restore_flags(flags);

    /* FIXME--user getmem_fromio or such */
    if ((oldval^newval) == 0xff) { /* we re-read our change: it's ram */
        printk(KERN_INFO "%lx: RAM\n", (long)ptr);
        continue;
    }
    if ((oldval^newval) != 0) {     /* random bits changed: it's empty */
        printk(KERN_INFO "%lx: empty\n",(long)ptr);
        continue;
    }

    /*
     * Expansion rom (executed at boot time by the bios)
     * has a signature of 0x55, 0xaa, and the third byte tells
     * the size of such rom
     */
    if ( (*ptr == 0x55) && (*(ptr+1) == 0xaa)) {
        int size = 512 * *(ptr+2);
        printk(KERN_INFO "%lx: Expansion ROM, %i bytes\n",
                (long)ptr, size);
        add += (size & ~2048) - 2048; /* skip it */
        continue;
    }

    /*
     * If the tests above failed, we still don't know if it is ROM or
     * empty. Since empty memory can appear as 0x00, 0xff, or the low
     * address byte, we must probe multiple bytes: if at least one of
     * them is different from these three values, then this is rom
     * (though not boot rom).
     */
    printk(KERN_INFO "%lx: ", (long)ptr);
    for (i=0; i<5; i++) {
        ptr+=57; /* a "random" value */
        if (*ptr && *ptr!=0xFF && *ptr!=((long)ptr&0xFF))
            break;
    }
    printk("%s\n", i==5 ? "empty" : "ROM");
}
```

Detecting memory doesn't cause collisions with other devices, as long as you take care to restore any byte you modified while you were probing.*

---

* Note that in some cases writing to memory can have side effects, as some devices can map I/O registers to memory addresses. This and other considerations lead to the conclusion that the code just shown should definitely be avoided in production drivers. It is nonetheless a simple introductory module and is shown here as such.

An attentive reader might ask now about ISA memory in the 15MB–16M address range. Unfortunately, that's a more difficult issue, which we'll discuss in the section "ISA Memory Above 1M," in Chapter 8.

Automatic and Manual Configuration

Several parameters that a driver needs to know can change from system to system. For instance, the driver must know the hardware's actual I/O addresses, or memory range.

Note that most of the problems discussed in this section don't apply to PCI devices (described in Chapter 15.

Depending on the device, there may be other parameters in addition to the I/O address that affect the driver's behavior, such as device brand and release number. It's essential for the driver to know the value of these parameters in order to work correctly. Setting up the driver with the correct values (i.e., configuring it) is one of the tricky tasks that need to be performed during driver initialization.

Basically, there are two ways to obtain the correct values: either the user specifies them explicitly or the driver autodetects them. While autodetection is undoubtedly the best approach to driver configuration, user configuration is much easier to implement; a suitable tradeoff for a driver writer is to implement automatic configuration whenever possible, while allowing user configuration as an option to override autodetection. An additional advantage of this approach to configuration is that the initial development can be done without autodetection, by specifying the parameters at load time, and autodetection can be implemented later.

Parameter values can be assigned at load time by *insmod*, which accepts specification of integer and string values on the command line. The command can modify all the global variables defined in the module. For example, if your source contains the variables:

```
int skull_ival=0;
char *skull_sval;
```

then the following command can be used to load the module:

```
insmod skull skull_ival=666 skull_sval="the beast"
```

A sample run using *printk* will show that the assignments are already in effect when *init_module* gets invoked. Note that *insmod* can assign a value to any integer or char-pointer variable in the module. It does this for both static and global variables, whether they are part of the public symbol table or not. Strings declared as arrays, on the other hand, can't be assigned at load time because the pointer is resolved at compile time and can't be changed after that.

Automatic configuration, then, can be designed to work this way: "If the configuration variables have the default value, perform autodetection; otherwise, keep the current value." In order for this technique to work, the "default" value should be one that the user would never actually want to specify at load time.

The following code shows how *skull* autodetects the port address of a device. In this example, autodetection is used to look for multiple devices, while manual configuration is restricted to a single device. Note that the function *skull_detect* was shown above, while *skull_init_board* is in charge of device-specific initialization, and thus is not shown.

```
/*
 * port ranges: the device can reside between
 * 0x280 and 0x300, in step of 0x10. It uses 0x10 ports.
 */
#define SKULL_PORT_FLOOR 0x280
#define SKULL_PORT_CEIL  0x300
#define SKULL_PORT_RANGE 0x010

/*
 * the following function performs autodetection, unless a specific
 * value was assigned by insmod to "skull_port_base"
 */

static int skull_port_base=0; /* 0 forces autodetection */

static int skull_find_hw(void) /* returns the # of devices */
{
    /* base is either the load-time value or the first trial */
    int base = skull_port_base ? skull_port_base
                        : SKULL_PORT_FLOOR;
    int result = 0;

    /* loop one time if value assigned, try them all if autodetecting */
    do {
        if (skull_detect(base, SKULL_PORT_RANGE) == 0) {
            skull_init_board(base);
            result++;
        }
        base += SKULL_PORT_RANGE; /* prepare for next trial */
    }
    while (skull_port_base == 0 && base < SKULL_PORT_CEIL);

    return result;
}
```

A real driver can avoid using the prefix (in this case, `skull_`) for the configuration variables in order to make things easier for the user who specifies them on the *insmod* command line, provided that those symbols are not going to be published in the main symbol table. If they are, a good choice can be to declare two symbols: one without the prefix, which is assigned at load time and one with the prefix, which is published by *register_symtab*.

Doing It in User Space

At this point, a Unix programmer who's addressing kernel issues for the first time might well be nervous about writing a module. Writing a user program that reads and writes directly to the device ports is much easier.

Indeed, there are some arguments in favor of user-space programming, and sometimes writing a so-called "user-space device driver" is a wise alternative to kernel hacking.

The advantages of user-space drivers can be summarized as follows:

- The full C library can be linked in. The driver can perform many exotic tasks without resorting to external programs (the utility programs implementing usage policies that are usually distributed along with the driver itself).

- A conventional debugger can be run on the driver code, without having to go through contortions to debug a running kernel.

- If a user-space driver hangs, you can simply kill it. Problems with the driver are unlikely to hang the entire system, unless the hardware being controlled is *really* misbehaving.

- User memory is swappable, unlike kernel memory. An infrequently used device with a huge driver won't occupy RAM that other programs could be using, except when it is actually in use.

- A well-designed driver program can still allow concurrent access to a device.

An example of a user-space driver is the X server: it knows exactly what the hardware can do and what it can't, and it offers the graphic resources to all X clients. The library *libsvga* is another similar beastie.

Usually, the writer of a user-space driver implements a "server" process, taking over from the kernel the task of being "the single agent in charge of hardware control." Client applications can then connect to the server to perform actual communication with the device; a smart driver process can thus allow concurrent access to the device. This is exactly how the X server works.

Another example of a user-space driver is the *gpm* mouse server: it performs arbitration of the mouse device between clients, so that several mouse-sensitive applications can run on different virtual consoles.

Sometimes, though, the user-space driver grants device access to a single program. This is how *libsvga* works. It gets linked to the application, thus supplementing the application's capabilities without resorting to a central authority (e.g., a server). This approach usually gives you better performance because it skips the communication overhead, but it requires the application to run as a privileged user.

But the user-space approach to device driving has a number of drawbacks. The most important are:

- Interrupts are not available in user space. There is no way around this, unless you learn to use the new *vm86* system call and can deal with a little performance penalty.

- Direct access to memory is possible only by mmapping */dev/mem*, and only a privileged user can do that.

- Access to I/O ports is available only after calling *ioperm* or *iopl*, and only a privileged user can do that.

- Response time is slower, because a context switch is required to transfer information or actions between the client and the hardware.

- Worse yet, if the driver has been swapped to disk, response time is unacceptably long. Using the *mlock* system call might help, but usually you'll need to lock several memory pages, as a user-space program depends on a lot of library code.

- The most important devices can't be handled in user space, including, but not limited to, network interfaces and block devices.

As you see, user-space drivers can't do that much, after all. Interesting applications nonetheless exist: for example, support for SCSI scanner devices. Scanner applications exploit the "SCSI generic" kernel driver, which exports low-level SCSI functionality to user-space programs so they can drive their own hardware.

In order to write a user-space driver, some hardware knowledge is sufficient, and there's no need to understand the subtleties of kernel software. I won't discuss user-level drivers any further in this book, but will concentrate on kernel code instead.

When dealing with unusual hardware, on the other hand, you might want to start by writing software in user space. This way you can learn to manage your hardware without the risk of hanging the whole system. Once you've done that, encapsulating the software in a kernel module should be a painless operation.

Quick Reference

This section summarizes the kernel functions, variables, macros, and */proc* files that we've touched on in this chapter. It is meant to act as a reference. Each item is listed after the relevant header file, if any. A similar section appears at the end of every chapter from here on, summarizing the new symbols introduced in the chapter.

`__KERNEL__`
`MODULE`
　Preprocessor symbols, which must both be defined to compile modularized kernel code.

`int init_module(void);`
`void cleanup_module(void);`
　Module entry points, which must be defined in the module object file.

`#include <linux/module.h>`
　Required header. It must be included by a module source.

`MOD_INC_USE_COUNT;`
`MOD_DEC_USE_COUNT;`
`MOD_IN_USE`
　Macros that act on the usage count.

/proc/modules
　The list of currently loaded modules. Entries contain the module name, the amount of memory they occupy, and the usage count. Extra strings are appended to each line to specify flags that are currently active for the module.

`int register_symtab(struct symbol_table *);`
　Function used to specify the set of public symbols in the module. This function doesn't exist any more in Linux 2.1.18 and newer kernels. See "Modularization" in Chapter 17 for details.

`int register_symtab_from(struct symbol_table *, long *);`
　Version 2.0 exports this function instead of *register_symtab*, which is a preprocessor macro instead. You'll see *register_symtab_from* in */proc/ksyms*, but the source code doesn't need to cope with it.

`#include <linux/symtab_begin.h>`
`X(symbol),`
`#include <linux/symtab_end.h>`
　Headers and preprocessor macro used to declare a symbol table with 1.2 and 2.0 kernels. The interface to symbol tables changed in 2.1.1.

#include <linux/version.h>
>   Required header. It is included by <linux/module.h>, unless
>   __NO_VERSION__ is defined (see below).

LINUX_VERSION_CODE
>   Integer macro, useful to #ifdef version dependencies.

char kernel_version[] = UTS_RELEASE;
>   Required variable in every module. <linux/module.h> defines it, unless
>   __NO_VERSION__ is defined (see below).

__NO_VERSION__
>   Preprocessor symbol. Prevents declaration of kernel_version in
>   <linux/module.h>.

#include <linux/sched.h>
>   One of the most important header files. It's unlikely you could do without it.

struct task_struct *current;
>   The current process.

struct task_struct *current_set[];
>   Linux 2.0 supports symmetric multiprocessor boards and defines current as
>   a macro that expands to current_set[*this_cpu*]. You'll see cur-
>   rent_set in */proc/ksyms*, but code in the module still uses current. 2.1
>   development kernels introduced faster ways to access current without
>   exporting a kernel symbol. See "Other Changes" in Chapter 17.

current->pid
current->comm
>   The process ID and command name for the current process.

#include <linux/kernel.h>
int printk(const char * fmt, ...);
>   The analogue of *printf* for kernel code.

#include <linux/malloc.h>
void *kmalloc(unsigned int size, int priority);
void kfree(void *obj);
>   Analogue of *malloc* and *free* for kernel code. Use the value of GFP_KERNEL
>   as the priority.

#include <linux/ioport.h>
int check_region(unsigned int from, unsigned int extent);
void request_region(unsigned int from, unsigned int extent,
                        const char *name);

`void release_region(unsigned int from, unsigned int extent);`
> Functions used to register and release I/O ports. Version 2.1.30 changed the `unsigned int` arguments to `unsigned long`, but this change doesn't affect driver code.

`#include <asm/system.h>`
> This header defines macros like *save_flags* and *restore_flags* that access specific machine registers.

`save_flags(long flags);`
`restore_flags(long flags);`
> Preprocessor macros meant to allow temporary modification of one processor flag.

`cli();`
`sti();`
> Disable and enable interrupts. *sti* shouldn't be used; use *save_flags* and *restore_flags* instead.

/proc/ksyms
> The public kernel symbol table.

/proc/ioports
> The list of ports used by installed devices.

CHAR DRIVERS

The goal of this chapter is to write a complete char device driver. We'll develop a character driver because this class is suitable for most simple hardware devices. Char drivers are also easier to understand than, for example, block drivers. Our ultimate aim is to write a *modularized* char driver, but I won't talk about modularization issues in this chapter.

Throughout the chapter, I'll present code fragments extracted from a real device driver: *scull*, short for "Simple Character Utility for Loading Localities." *scull* is a char driver that acts on a memory area as though it were a device. A side effect of this behavior is that as far as *scull* is concerned, the word "device" can be used interchangeably with "the memory area used by *scull*."

The advantage of *scull* is that it isn't hardware dependent, since every computer has memory. *scull* just acts on some memory, which is allocated using *kmalloc*. Anyone can compile and run *scull*, and *scull* is portable across the computer architectures on which Linux runs. On the other hand, the device doesn't do anything "useful" other than demonstrating the interface between the kernel and char drivers and allowing the user to run some tests.

The Design of scull

The first step of driver writing is defining the capabilities (the "mechanism") the driver will offer to user programs. Since our "device" is part of the computer's memory, we're free to do what we want with it. It can be a sequential or random-access device, one device or many, and so on.

In order for *scull* to be useful as a template for writing real drivers for real devices, I'll show you how to implement several device abstractions on top of the computer memory, each with a different personality.

The *scull* source implements the following devices. Each kind of device implemented by the module is referred to as a "type":

scull0-3

Four devices consisting of four memory areas that are both global and persistent. "Global" means that if the device is opened multiple times, the data is shared by all the file descriptors that opened it. "Persistent" means that if the device is closed and reopened, data isn't lost. This device can be fun to work with, because it can be accessed and tested using conventional commands, like *cp*, *cat*, and the shell I/O redirection; we'll examine its internals in this chapter.

scullpipe0-3

Four "fifo" devices, which act like pipes. One process reads what another process is writing. If more processes read the same device, they contend for data. The internals of scullpipe will show how blocking and nonblocking read and write can be implemented; this happens without having to resort to interrupts. Although real drivers synchronize with their devices using hardware interrupts, the topic of blocking and nonblocking operations is an important one and is conceptually detached from interrupt handling (covered in Chapter 9, *Interrupt Handling*).

scullsingle
scullpriv
sculluid
scullwuid

These devices are similar to scull0, but with some limitations on when an *open* is permitted. The first (scullsingle) allows only one process at a time to use the driver, while scullpriv is private to each virtual console (the device is private to the console). sculluid and scullwuid can be opened multiple times, but only by one user at a time; the former returns -EBUSY if another user is locking the device, while the latter implements blocking *open*. These devices will be used to show how different access policies can be implemented.

Each of the *scull* devices demonstrates different features of a driver, and presents different difficulties. This chapter covers the internals of scull0-3; the more advanced devices will be covered in Chapter 5, *Enhanced Char Driver Operations*: scullpipe is described in "A Sample Implementation: scullpipe" and the others in "Access Control on a Device File."

Major and Minor Numbers

Char devices are accessed through names (or "nodes") in the filesystem, usually located in the */dev* directory. Device files are special files and are identified by a "c" in the first column of the output of *ls –l*, indicating that they are char nodes. Block devices appear in */dev* as well, but they are identified by a "b"; even if some of the following information applies also to block devices, I am now focusing on char drivers.

If you issue the *ls* command, you'll see two numbers (separated by a comma) on the device file entries before the date of last modification, where the file length normally appears. These numbers are the "major" and "minor" numbers for the particular device. The following listing shows a few devices as they appear on my system. Their major numbers are 10, 1, and 4, while the minors are 0, 3, 5, 64–65, and 128–129.

```
crw-rw-rw-   1 root     root      10,    3 Nov 30   1993 bmouseatixl
crw-rw-rw-   1 root     sys        1,    3 Nov 30   1993 null
crw-rw-rw-   1 root     root       4,  128 Apr 30 13:02 ptyp0
crw-rw-rw-   1 root     root       4,  129 Apr 30 13:02 ptyp1
crw-rw-rw-   1 rubini   staff      4,    0 Jan 30   1995 tty0
crw-rw-rw-   1 root     tty        4,   64 Jan 25   1995 ttyS0
crw-rw-rw-   1 root     root       4,   65 May  1 00:04 ttyS1
crw-rw-rw-   1 root     sys        1,    5 Nov 30   1993 zero
```

The major number identifies the driver associated with the device. For example, */dev/null* and */dev/zero* are both managed by driver 1, while all the tty's and pty's are managed by driver 4. The kernel uses the major number to associate the appropriate driver with its device.

The minor number is only used by the device driver; other parts of the kernel don't use it, and merely pass it it along to the driver. It isn't unusual for a driver to control several devices (as in the example above)—the minor number provides a way to differentiate among them.

Adding a new driver to the system means assigning a major number to it. The assignment should be made at driver (module) initialization by calling the following function, defined in `<linux/fs.h>`:

```
int register_chrdev(unsigned int major, const char *name,
                struct file_operations *fops);
```

The return value is the error code. A negative return code indicates an error; a zero or positive return code means successful completion. The `major` argument is the major number being requested, `name` is the name of your device, which will appear in */proc/devices*, and `fops` is the pointer to a jump table used to invoke the driver functions, as explained in "File Operations," later in this chapter.

The major number is a small integer that serves as the index into a static array of char drivers. In 1.2.13 and early 2.x kernels, the array holds 64 elements, while 2.0.26 and 2.1.11 raised the number to 128. Minor numbers aren't passed to *register_chrdev*, because only the driver cares about them.

Once the driver has been registered in the kernel table, whenever an operation is performed on a character file whose major number matches your driver's major number, the kernel invokes the correct function in the driver's code by indexing into the `fops` jump table.

The next question is how to give programs a name by which they can request your driver. A name must be inserted into the */dev* directory and associated with your driver's major and minor numbers.

The command to create a device node on a filesystem is *mknod*, and you must be the superuser to create devices. The command takes three arguments in addition to the name of the node being created. For example, the command:

```
mknod /dev/scull0 c 127 0
```

creates a char device (c) whose major number is 127 and whose minor number is 0. Minor numbers should be in the range 0–255, because, for historical reasons, they are sometimes stored in a single byte. There are sound reasons to extend the range of available minor numbers, but for the time being, the 8-bit limit is still in force.

Dynamic Allocation of Major Numbers

Some major device numbers are statically assigned to the most common devices. A list of those devices can be found in *Documentation/devices.txt* within the kernel source tree. Because many numbers are already assigned, choosing a unique number for a new driver can be difficult—there are more custom drivers than available major numbers.

Fortunately (or rather, thanks to someone's ingenuity), you can request dynamic assignment of a major number. If the argument `major` is set to zero when you call *register_chrdev*, the function selects a free number and returns it. The major number is always positive and thus can't be mistaken for an error code.

I strongly suggest that you use dynamic allocation to obtain your major device number, rather than choosing a number randomly from the ones that are currently free.

The disadvantage of dynamic assignment is that you can't create the device nodes in advance, because the major number assigned to your module can't be guaranteed to always be the same. This is hardly a problem, however, because once the number has been assigned, you can read it from */proc/devices*. To load a driver, the invocation of *insmod* can be replaced by a simple script that reads */proc/devices* to get the newly assigned major number in order to create the node(s).

A typical */proc/devices* looks like the following:

```
Character devices:
 1 mem
 2 pty
 4 ttyp
 7 vcs
10 misc
63 scull
```

```
Block devices:
 3 ide0
22 ide1
```

The script to load a module that has been assigned a dynamic number can thus be written using a tool such as *awk* to retrieve information from */proc/devices* in order to create the files in */dev*.

The following script, *scull_load*, is part of the *scull* distribution. The user of a driver that is distributed in the form of a module can invoke such a script from */etc/rc.d/rc.local* or call it manually whenever the module is needed. There is also a third option: using *kerneld*. This and other advanced features of modularization are covered in Chapter 11, *Kerneld and Advanced Modularization*.

```
#!/bin/sh
module="scull"
device="scull"
group="wheel"
mode="664"

# invoke insmod with all arguments we got
/sbin/insmod -f $module $* || exit 1

# remove stale nodes
rm -f /dev/${device}[0-3]

major=`cat /proc/devices | awk "\\$2==\"$module\" {print \\$1}"`

mknod /dev/${device}0 c $major 0
mknod /dev/${device}1 c $major 1
mknod /dev/${device}2 c $major 2
mknod /dev/${device}3 c $major 3

# give appropriate group/permissions
chgrp $group /dev/${device}?
chmod $mode  /dev/${device}?
```

The script can be adapted for another driver by redefining the variables and adjusting the *mknod* lines. The script shown above creates four devices because four is the default in the *scull* sources.

The last two lines of the script may seem obscure: why change the group and mode of a device? The reason is that the node is created by root and is thus owned by root. The permission bits default so that only root has write access, while anyone can get read access. Normally, a device node requires a different policy, and some change is needed. Access to a device is usually granted to a group of users, but the details depend on the device and on the system administrator. Security is a huge problem, beyond the scope of this book. The chmod and chgrp lines in *scull_load* are there only as a hint about handling permissions.

Later, in the section "Access Control on a Device File" in Chapter 5, the code for sculluid will demonstrate how the driver can enforce its own kind of authorization for device access.

If repeatedly creating and destroying */dev* nodes sounds like overkill, there is a useful workaround. If you look at the kernel source, in *fs/devices.c,* you can see that dynamic numbers are assigned starting from 127 (or 63) and moving down, so you can create long-living nodes with 127 as the major number and avoid calling the script every time the associated device is loaded. This trick won't work if you use several dynamic drivers, or if a new kernel release changes the behavior of dynamic allocation. (Code that you've written based on having peeked at the internals of the kernel isn't guaranteed to keep working if the kernel changes.) Nonetheless, you might find this technique useful during development, when the module is constantly being loaded and unloaded.

The best way to assign major numbers, in my opinion, is by defaulting to dynamic allocation while leaving yourself the option of specifying the major number at load time, or even at compile time. The code I suggest using is similar to the code introduced for autodetection of port numbers. The *scull* implementation uses a global variable, scull_major, to hold the chosen number. The variable is initialized to SCULL_MAJOR, defined in *scull.h.* The default value of SCULL_MAJOR in the distributed source is zero, which means "select dynamic assignment." The user can accept the default or choose a particular major number, either by modifying the macro before compiling, or by specifying a value for scull_major on the *insmod* command line. Finally, by using the *scull_load* script, the user can pass arguments to *insmod* on *scull_load*'s command line.

Here's the code I use in *scull.c* to get a major number:

```
result = register_chrdev(scull_major, "scull", &scull_fops);
if (result < 0) {
    printk(KERN_WARNING "scull: can't get major %d\n",scull_major);
    return result;
}
if (scull_major == 0) scull_major = result; /* dynamic */
```

Removing a Driver from the System

When a module is unloaded from the system, the major number should be released. This is accomplished with the following function, which is called from *cleanup_module*:

```
int unregister_chrdev(unsigned int major, const char *name);
```

The arguments are the major number being released and the name of the associated device. The kernel compares the name to the registered name for that number: if they differ, −EINVAL is returned. The kernel also returns −EINVAL if the major number is out of the allowed range for majors or is not assigned to a driver.

Failing to unregister the resource from *cleanup_module* has unpleasant effects. */proc/devices* will generate a fault the next time you try to read it, because one of the **name** strings still points to the module's memory, which is no longer mapped. This kind of fault is called an *Oops* because that's the message the kernel prints when it tries to access invalid addresses.*

When you unload the driver without unregistering the major number, the situation is unrecoverable, even from a "rescue" module written for that purpose, because the *strcmp* call in *unregister_chrdev* will use the unmapped **name** string and will oops when trying to release the number. Needless to say, any attempt to *open* a device node associated with the phantom major number will oops as well.

In addition to unloading the module, you'll often need to remove the device nodes for the driver being unloaded. If the device nodes were created at load time, a simple script can be written to remove them at unload time. The script *scull_unload* does the job for our sample device. If dynamic nodes are not removed from */dev*, there's a possibility of unexpected errors: a spare */dev/framegrabber* on a developer's computer might refer to a fire-alarm device one month later if both used dynamic assignment to get a major number. "No such file or directory" is a friendlier response to opening */dev/framegrabber* than the new device would produce.

dev_t and kdev_t

So far we've talked about the major number. Now it's time to discuss the minor number and how the driver uses the minor number to differentiate among devices.

Every time the kernel calls a device driver, it tells the driver what device is being acted upon. The major and minor numbers are paired in a single data type that is then used to identify a particular device. The combined device number (the major and minor numbers concatenated together) resides in the field **i_rdev** of the "inode" structure, which is introduced later. Every driver function receives a pointer to **struct inode** as the first argument. The pointer is usually called **inode** as well, and the function can extract the device number by looking at **inode->i_rdev**.

Historically, Unix declared **dev_t** (device-type) to hold the device numbers. It used to be a 16-bit integer value defined in **<sys/types.h>**. Nowadays, more than 256 minor numbers are needed at times, but changing **dev_t** is difficult, because there are applications (and the C library itself) that know the internals of **dev_t** and would break if the structure were to change. The **dev_t** type, therefore, hasn't been changed; it is still a 16-bit integer, and the minor numbers are restricted to the range 0–255.

---

* The word "Oops" is used as both a noun and a verb by Linux freaks.

Within the Linux kernel, however, a new type, `kdev_t`, is used. This new type is designed to be a black box for every kernel function. The idea is that user programs won't even know about `kdev_t`. If `kdev_t` remains hidden, it can change from one kernel version to the next as needed, without requiring changes to everyone's device drivers.

The information about `kdev_t` is confined in `<linux/kdev_t.h>`, which is mostly comments. The header makes instructive reading if you're interested in the philosophy behind the code. There's no need to include the header explicitly in the drivers, however, because `<linux/fs.h>` does it for you.

The `kdev_t` type, unfortunately, is a "modern" idea and was missing from kernel version 1.2. In recent kernels, all the kernel variables and structure fields referring to devices are `kdev_t` items, but in 1.2.13 the same variables are in `dev_t`. This is not a problem if your driver uses only structure fields it receives, without declaring its own variables. If you need to declare your own device-type variable, you should add the following lines to your headers in order to ensure portability:

```
#if LINUX_VERSION_CODE < VERSION_CODE(1,3,28)
#   define kdev_t dev_t
    /* two conversion functions are defined in newer kernels */
#   define kdev_t_to_nr(dev) (dev)
#   define to_kdev_t(dev)    (dev)
#endif
```

This code is part of the *sysdep.h* header in the sample source files. I won't refer to `dev_t` any more in the code, but will assume the previous conditional statement has been executed.

The following macros and functions are the operations you can perform on `kdev_t`:

`MAJOR(kdev_t dev);`
> Extract the major number from a `kdev_t` structure.

`MINOR(kdev_t dev);`
> Extract the minor number.

`MKDEV(int ma, int mi);`
> Return a `kdev_t` built from major and minor numbers.

`kdev_t_to_nr(kdev_t dev);`
> Convert a `kdev_t` type to a number (a `dev_t`).

`to_kdev_t(int dev);`
> Convert a number to `kdev_t`. Note that `dev_t` is not defined in kernel mode and therefore `int` is used.

The headers associated to Linux 1.2 defined the same functions to act on `dev_t` quantities, with the exception of the two conversion functions. That's why the conditional code shown earlier defines them simply to return their argument.

File Operations

In the next few sections, we'll look at the various operations a driver can perform on the devices it manages. The device is identified internally by a `file` structure, and the kernel uses the `file_operations` structure to access the driver's functions. This design is the first evidence we've seen of the object-oriented design of the Linux kernel. We'll see more evidence of object-oriented design later. The structure `file_operations` is a table of function pointers, defined in `<linux/fs.h>`. The structure `struct file` is going to be described next.

The `fops` pointer, which we've already seen as an argument to the *register_chrdev* call, points to a table of operations (*open, read,* and so on). Each entry in the table points to the function defined by the driver to handle the requested operation. The table can contain NULL pointers for the operations you don't support. The exact behavior of the kernel when a NULL pointer is specified is different for each function, as the list in the next section shows.

The `file_operations` structure has been slowly getting bigger as new functionality is added to the kernel (although no new fields were added between 1.2.0 and 2.0.*x*). There should be no side effects from this increase, because the C compiler takes care of any size mismatch by zero-filling uninitialized fields in global or static `struct` variables. New items are added at the end of the structure,* so a NULL value inserted at compile time will select the default behavior (remember that the module needs to be recompiled in any case for each new kernel version it will be loaded into).

A few of the function prototypes associated to `fops` fields, actually changed slightly during 2.1 development. These differences are covered in "File Operations," in Chapter 17, *Recent Developments.*

Overview of the Different Operations

The following list introduces all the operations that an application can invoke on a device. These operations are often called "methods," using object-oriented programming terminology to denote actions declared by an object to act on itself.

I've tried to keep the list brief so it can be used as a reference, merely summarizing each operation and the default kernel behavior when a NULL pointer is used. You can skip over this list on your first reading and return to it later.

The rest of the chapter, after describing another important data structure (the `file`), explains the role of the most important operations and offers hints, caveats, and real code examples. We'll defer discussion of the more complex operations to a later chapter, because we aren't yet ready to dig into memory management and asynchronous notification.

---

* For example, version 2.1.31 added a new field called *lock.*

The operations appear in `struct file_operations` in this order, and their return value is 0 for success or a negative error code to signal an error, unless otherwise noted:

`int (*lseek) (struct inode *, struct file *, off_t, int);`
> The *lseek* method is used to change the current read/write position in a file, and the new position is returned as a (positive) return value. Errors are signalled by a negative return value. If the function is not specified for the driver, a seek relative to end-of-file fails, while other seeks succeed by modifying the position counter in the `file` structure (described in "The file Structure"). The prototype of this function changed in 2.1.0, as explained in "Prototype Differences" in Chapter 17.

`int (*read) (struct inode *, struct file *, char *, int);`
> Used to retrieve data from the device. A null pointer in this position causes the *read* system call to fail with `-EINVAL` ("Invalid argument"). A non-negative return value represents the number of bytes successfully read.

`int (*write) (struct inode *, struct file *, const char *,`
`              int);`
> Sends data to the device. If missing, `-EINVAL` is returned to the program calling the *write* system call. Note that the `const` specifier was missing in 1.2 headers. If you include `const` in your own *write* method, a warning is generated when compiling against older Linux headers. If you don't include `const`, a warning is generated for newer versions; you can safely ignore the warning in either case. The return value, if non-negative, represents the number of bytes successfully written.

`int (*readdir) (struct inode *, struct file *, void *,`
`                filldir_t);`
> This field should be `NULL` for device nodes; it is used only for directories.

`int (*select) (struct inode *, struct file *, int,`
`               select_table *);`
> *select* is used by programs to ask if the device is readable or writable, or if an "exception" condition has happened. If the pointer is `NULL`, the device is assumed to be both readable and writable, with no exceptions pending. The meaning of "exception" is device-dependent. The implementation of *select* is completely different in the current 2.1 development kernels. (See "The poll Method," in Chapter 17.) The return value tells whether condition is met (1) or not (0).

`int (*ioctl) (struct inode *, struct file *, unsigned int,`
`              unsigned long);`
> The *ioctl* system call offers a way to issue device-specific commands (like formatting a track of a floppy disk, which is neither reading nor writing).

Additionally, a few *ioctl* commands are recognized by the kernel without referring to the `fops` table. If the device doesn't offer an *ioctl* entry point, the system call returns `-EINVAL` for any request that isn't predefined. A non-negative return value is passed back to the calling program to indicate a successful completion.

`int (*mmap) (struct inode *, struct file *,`
`          struct vm_area_struct *);`
> *mmap* is used to request a mapping of device memory to a process's memory. If the device doesn't provide this method, the *mmap* system call returns `-ENODEV`.

`int (*open) (struct inode *, struct file *);`
> Though this is always the first operation performed on the device node, the driver is not required to declare a corresponding method. If this entry is `NULL`, opening the device always succeeds, but your driver isn't notified.

`void (*release) (struct inode *, struct file *);`
> This operation is invoked when the node is closed. Like *open*, *release* can be missing. In 2.0 and earlier kernel versions, the *close* system call never fails; this changed in 2.1.31 (see Chapter 17).

`int (*fsync) (struct inode *, struct file *);`
> Flush the device. If not supported, the *fsync* system call returns `-EINVAL`.

`int (*fasync) (struct inode *, struct file *, int);`
> This operation is used to notify the device of a change in its `FASYNC` flag. Asynchronous notification is an advanced topic and will be described in "Asynchronous Notification" in Chapter 5. The field can be `NULL` if the driver won't support asynchronous notification.

`int (*check_media_change) (kdev_t dev);`
> *check_media_change* is only used with block devices, especially removable media like floppies. The method is called by the kernel to determine if the physical medium (e.g., the floppy disk) in the device has changed since the last operation (return value is 1) or not (0). This function doesn't need to be declared for char devices.

`int (*revalidate) (kdev_t dev);`
> This is the last entry, which is meaningful only for block drivers. *revalidate* is related to buffer cache management, as is the previous method. We'll discuss *revalidate* in "Removable Devices" in Chapter 12, *Loading Block Drivers*.

The `file_operations` structure used in the *scull* driver is the following:

```
struct file_operations scull_fops = {
    scull_lseek,
    scull_read,
    scull_write,
    NULL,          /* scull_readdir */
```

```
        NULL,           /* scull_select */
        scull_ioctl,
        NULL,           /* scull_mmap */
        scull_open,
        scull_release,
                        /* nothing more, fill with NULLs */
};
```

A few of the prototypes above have changed slightly in the latest kernel development. The list was extracted from a 2.0.*x* header, and the prototypes as shown are correct for a wide range of kernels. The differences introduced in the 2.1 kernel (and the fix needed to make our modules portable) are detailed in the section pertaining to each specific operation and in "File Operations" in Chapter 17.

The file Structure

`struct file`, defined in `<linux/fs.h>`, is the second most important data structure used in device drivers. Note that a `file` has nothing to do with the FILEs of user-space programs. A FILE is defined in the C library and never appears in kernel code. A `struct file`, on the other hand, is a kernel structure that never appears in user programs.

The `file` structure represents an "open file." It is created by the kernel on *open* and is passed to any function that operates on the file, until *close*. After the file is closed, the kernel releases the data structure. An "open file" is different from a "disk file," which is represented by `struct inode`.

In the kernel sources, a pointer to `struct file` is usually called either `file` or `filp` ("file pointer"). I'll consistently call the pointer `filp` to prevent ambiguities with the structure itself—`filp` is a pointer (as such, it is one of the arguments to device methods), while `file` is the structure itself.

The most important fields of `struct file` are shown below. As in the previous section, the list can be skipped on a first reading. In the next section though, when we face some real C code, I'll discuss some of the fields, so they are here for you to refer back to.

`mode_t f_mode;`
> The file mode is identified by the bits **FMODE_READ** and **FMODE_WRITE**. You might want to check this field for read/write permission in your *ioctl* function, but you don't need to check permissions for *read* and *write* because the kernel checks before invoking your driver. An attempt to write without permission, for example, is rejected without the driver even knowing about it.

`loff_t f_pos;`
> The current reading or writing position. `loff_t` is a 64-bit value (`long long` in *gcc* terminology). The driver can read this value if it needs to know the current position. The *lseek* method, if defined, should update the value of `f_pos`. The read and write methods should update it when transferring data.

`unsigned short f_flags;`
> These are the file flags, such as `O_RDONLY`, `O_NONBLOCK`, and `O_SYNC`. A driver needs to check the flag for nonblocking operation, while the other flags are seldom used. In particular, read/write permission should be checked using `f_mode` instead of `f_flags`. All the flags are defined in the header `<linux/fcntl.h>`.

`struct inode *f_inode;`
> The inode associated with the open file. The `inode` pointer is the first argument passed by the kernel to all file operations, so you don't usually need to access the field in `file`. In those cases when you have access only to a `struct file`, you can find the corresponding inode here.

`struct file_operations *f_op;`
> The operations associated with the file. The kernel assigns the pointer at *open* time and then reads it when it needs to dispatch any operations. The value in `filp->f_op` is never saved for later reference; this means that you can change the file operations associated with your file whenever you want, and the new methods will be effective the next time a method is invoked for that open file. For example, the code for *open* associated with major number 1 (*/dev/null*, */dev/zero*, and so on) substitutes the operations in `filp->f_op` depending on which minor number is being opened. This practice makes it possible to distinguish between devices with the same major number without introducing overhead at each system call. The ability to replace the file operations is called "method overriding" in object-oriented programming.

`void *private_data;`
> The *open* system call sets this pointer to NULL before calling the *open* method for the driver. The driver is free to make its own use of the field or to ignore it. The driver can use the field to point to allocated data, but then must clear it again in the *release* method before the `file` structure is destroyed by the kernel. `private_data` is a great resource for preserving state information across system calls and is used by most of our sample modules.

The real structure has a few more fields, but they aren't useful to device drivers. We can safely ignore those fields because drivers never fill `file` structures; they only access structures created elsewhere.

Open and Close

Now that we've taken a quick look at the fields, we'll start using them in real *scull* functions.

The open Method

The *open* method is provided for a driver to do any initialization in preparation for later operations. In addition, *open* usually increments the usage count for the device, so the module won't be unloaded before the file is closed.

In most drivers, *open* does the following:

- Checks for device-specific errors (like device-not-ready or similar hardware problems).

- Initializes the device, if it is being opened for the first time.

- Identifies the minor number and updates the `f_op` pointer, if necessary.

- Allocates and fills any data structure to be put in `filp->private_data`.

- Increments the usage count.

In *scull*, most of the preceding tasks depend on the minor number of the device being opened. Therefore, the first thing to do is identify which device is involved. We can do that by looking at `inode->i_rdev`.

We've already talked about how the kernel doesn't use the minor number of the device, so the driver is free to use it at will. In practice, different minor numbers are used to access different devices, or to open the same device in a different way. For example, */dev/ttyS0* and */dev/ttyS1* refer to different serial ports, whereas */dev/cua0* is the same physical device as */dev/ttyS0*, but it acts differently. *cua*s are "callout" devices; they aren't ttys, and they don't get all the software support that is needed for terminals (i.e., they don't have a line discipline* attached). All the serial devices feature different device numbers, so the driver can tell them apart: a *ttyS* is different from a *cua*.

A driver never actually knows the name of the device being opened, just the device number—and users can play on this indifference to names by aliasing new names to a single device for their own convenience. If you look in your */dev* directory, you'll find different names associated with the same major/minor pair; the devices are one and the same, and there's no way to differentiate between them. For example, on many systems, both */dev/psaux* and */dev/bmouseps2* exist, and they have the same device number; they can be used interchangeably. The latter is an historical relic, and may be missing from your own system.

---

* The "line discipline" is a software module dealing with tty I/O policies.

The *scull* driver uses the minor number like this: the most significant nibble (4 bits) identifies the type (personality) of the device, and the least significant nibble lets you distinguish between devices if the type supports more than one instance (`scull0-3` and `scullpipe0-3`). Thus, `scull0` is different from `scullpipe0` in the top nibble, while `scull0` and `scull1` differ in the bottom nibble.* Two macros (TYPE and NUM) are defined in the source to extract the bits from a device number, as we'll see shortly.

For each device type, *scull* defines a specific `file_operations` structure, which is substituted in `filp->f_op` at open time. The following code shows how bit-splitting and multiple `fops` are implemented:

```
#define TYPE(dev)    (MINOR(dev) >> 4)   /* high nibble */
#define NUM(dev)     (MINOR(dev) & 0xf)   /* low nibble */

struct file_operations *scull_fop_array[]={
    &scull_fops,       /* type 0 */
    &scull_priv_fops, /* type 1 */
    &scull_pipe_fops, /* type 2 */
    &scull_sngl_fops, /* type 3 */
    &scull_user_fops, /* type 4 */
    &scull_wusr_fops  /* type 5 */
};
#define SCULL_MAX_TYPE 5
```

The kernel invokes *open* according to the major number; *scull* uses the minor number in the macros shown above. **TYPE** is used to index into `scull_fop_array`, in order to extract the right set of methods for the device type being opened.

What I did in *scull* is assign the correct `filp->f_op` according to the type of the minor number. The *open* method declared in the new `fops` is then invoked. Usually, a driver doesn't invoke its own `fops`, which are used by the kernel to dispatch the right driver method. But when your *open* method has to deal with different device types, you might want to call `fops->open` after modifying the `fops` pointer according to the minor number being opened.

The actual code for *scull_open* follows. It uses the **TYPE** and **NUM** macros defined in the previous code snapshot to split the minor number:

```
int scull_open (struct inode *inode, struct file *filp)
{
    int type = TYPE(inode->i_rdev);
    int num = NUM(inode->i_rdev);
    Scull_Dev *dev; /* device information */

    /* manage peculiar types first */
```

---

* Bit-splitting is a typical way to use minor numbers. The IDE driver, for example, uses the top two bits for the disk number, and the bottom six bits for the partition number.

```
        if (type) {
            if (type > SCULL_MAX_TYPE) return -ENODEV;
            filp->f_op = scull_fop_array[type];
            /* dispatch to specific open */
            return filp->f_op->open(inode, filp);
        }

        /* type 0, check the device number */
        if (num >= scull_nr_devs) return -ENODEV;
        dev = &scull_devices[num];

        /* now trim to 0 the length of the device if open was write-only */
        if ( (filp->f_flags & O_ACCMODE) == O_WRONLY)
            scull_trim(dev); /* ignore errors */

        /* and use filp->private_data to point to the device data */
        filp->private_data = dev;

        MOD_INC_USE_COUNT;
        return 0;                /* success */
    }
```

A few explanations are due here. The data structure used to hold the region of memory is `Scull_Dev`, which will be introduced shortly. The internals of `Scull_Dev` and `scull_trim` (discussed in "Scull's Memory Usage") aren't used here. The global variables `scull_nr_devs` and `scull_devices[]` (all lower-case) are the number of available devices and the actual array of pointers to `Scull_Dev`.

The code looks pretty sparse because it doesn't do any particular device handling when *open* is called. It doesn't need to, because the `scull0-3` device is global and persistent by design. Specifically, there's no action like "initializing the device on first open," because we don't keep an open count for *sculls*, just the module-usage count.

The only real operation performed on the device is truncating it to a length of zero when the device is opened for writing. This truncation is part of the *scull* design: overwriting the device with a shorter file results in a shorter device data area, similar to the way opening a regular file for writing truncates it to zero.

This "truncation on open", however, has a serious drawback: if for some reason the device memory is being used, releasing it results in a system fault. Though unlikely, this kind of situation can happen: if either the *read* or *write* method sleeps during data transfer, another process may be able to open the device for writing, thus asking for trouble. Facing a race condition is quite an advanced topic, and I'll deal with it in "Race Conditions," in Chapter 9. The *scull* device solves the problem simply by not releasing memory when it is in use, as shown later in "Scull's Memory Usage."

We'll see later how a real initialization works when we look at the code for the other *scull* personalities.

The release Method

The role of the *release* method is the reverse of *open*. The device method is sometimes called *close*. It should:

- Decrement the usage count.

- Deallocate anything that *open* allocated in `filp->private_data`.

- Shut down the device on last close.

The basic form of *scull* does not need to do a shutdown, so the code required is minimal:*

```
void scull_release (struct inode *inode, struct file *filp)
{
    MOD_DEC_USE_COUNT;
}
```

Decrementing the usage count is important, because the kernel will never be able to unload the module if the counter doesn't drop to zero.

How can the counter remain consistent if sometimes a file is closed without having been opened? We all know that *dup* and *fork* make two open files from one without calling *open*, but each of the files is then closed at program termination. For example, most programs don't open their `stdin` file (or device), but all of them end up closing it.

The answer is simple. If *open* was not called, then *release* isn't called either. The kernel keeps a counter of how many times a `file` structure is being used. Neither *fork* nor *dup* create a new data structure; they just increment the counter in the existing structure.

A new `struct file` is created only by *open*. The *close* system call executes the *close* method only when the counter for the structure drops to zero, which happens when the structure is destroyed. This relationship between the *close* method and the *close* system call guarantees that the usage count for modules is always consistent.

---

* The other flavors of the device are closed by different functions, because *scull_open* substituted `filp->f_op` for them, and we'll see those later.

Scull's Memory Usage

Before introducing the *read* and *write* operations, we'd better look at how and why *scull* performs memory allocation. "How" is needed to thoroughly understand the code, and "why" demonstrates the kind of choices a driver writer needs to make, although *scull* is definitely not typical as a device.

This section deals only with the memory allocation policy in *scull* and doesn't show the hardware management skills you'll need to write real drivers. Those skills are introduced in Chapter 8, *Hardware Management*, and in Chapter 9. Therefore, you can skip this section if you're not interested in understanding the inner workings of the memory-oriented *scull* driver.

The region of memory used by *scull*, which is also called a "device" here, is variable in length. The more you write, the more it grows; trimming is performed by overwriting the device with a shorter file.

The implementation chosen for *scull* is not a smart one. The source code for a smart implementation would be more difficult to read, and the aim of this section is to show *read* and *write*, not memory management. That's why the code only uses *kmalloc* and *kfree*, without resorting to allocation of whole pages, although that would be more efficient.

On the flip side, I didn't want to limit the size of the "device" area, for both a philosophical reason and a practical one. Philosophically, it's always a bad idea to put arbitrary limits on data items being managed. Practically, *scull* can be used to temporarily eat up your system's memory in order to run tests under low-memory conditions. Running such tests might help you understand the system's internals. You can use the command *cp /dev/zero /dev/scull0* to eat all the real RAM with *scull*, and you can use the *dd* utility to choose how much data is copied to the *scull* device.

In *scull*, each device is a linked list of pointers, each of which points to Scull_Dev. Each such structure can refer to at most four million bytes, through an array of intermediate pointers. The released source uses an array of 1000 pointers to areas of 4000 bytes. I call each memory area a "quantum" and the array (or its length) a "quantum set." A *scull* device and its memory areas are shown in Figure 3-1.

The chosen numbers are such that writing a single byte in *scull* consumes eight thousand bytes of memory: four for the quantum and four for the quantum set (a pointer is four bytes on most platforms; the set uses eight thousand bytes when compiled for the Alpha, which has eight-byte pointers). On the other hand, if you write a huge amount of data, the overhead of stepping through the linked list is not too bad, because there is only one list element for every four megabytes of data, and the maximum size of the device is limited to a few megs, as it cannot be bigger than the computer's memory.

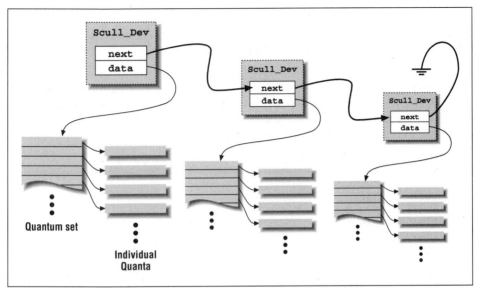

Figure 3-1: The layout of a scull device

Choosing the appropriate values for the quantum and the quantum set is a question of policy, rather than mechanism, and the optimal sizes depend on how the device is used. The source addresses this issue by allowing the user to change the values:

- At compile time, the macros SCULL_QUANTUM and SCULL_QSET can be changed in *scull.h*.

- At load time, the integer values scull_quantum and scull_qset can be changed by *insmod*.

- At run time, the *ioctl* method allows you to change the default and current values. *ioctl* is explained in the section "ioctl" in Chapter 5.

Using a macro and an integer value to allow both compile-time and load-time configuration is reminiscent of how the major number is selected. I use this technique for whatever value in the driver is arbitrary, or related to policy.

The only question left is how the default numbers have been chosen. Driver writers don't face exactly the same issue when writing their modules, though a similar pre-tuning of configurable parameters is sometimes needed. In this particular case, the problem is finding the best balance between the waste of memory deriving from half-filled quanta and quantum sets and the overhead of allocation, deallocation, and pointer-chaining that occurs if quanta and sets are small.

Additionally, the internal design of *kmalloc* must be taken into account. I won't go into the details now and the rule that "slightly less than a power of two is the best allocation size" will suffice. The innards of *kmalloc* are explored in "The Real Story of kmalloc" in Chapter 7, *Getting Hold of Memory*.

The choice of default numbers derives from the assumption that most program-mers aren't limited to four megs of physical RAM, and that massive amounts of data are likely to be written to *scull*. Several tens of megabytes will be written to the device by owners of big computers for testing. The default values are thus optimized for a medium-sized system and massive usage.

The data structure used to hold device information is as follows:

```
typedef struct Scull_Dev {
    void **data;
    struct Scull_Dev *next;    /* next listitem */
    int quantum;               /* the current quantum size */
    int qset;                  /* the current array size */
    unsigned long size;
    unsigned int access_key;   /* used by sculluid and scullpriv */
    unsigned int usage;        /* lock the device while using it */
} Scull_Dev;
```

The next code shows in practice how `Scull_Dev` is used to hold data. The func-tion shown is in charge of freeing the whole data area and is invoked by *scull_open* when the file is opened for writing. If device memory is currently being used, the function does not release it (as suggested above in "The open Method"); otherwise, it simply walks through the list and frees any quantum and quantum set it finds.

```
int scull_trim(Scull_Dev *dev)
{
    Scull_Dev *next, *dptr;
    int qset = dev->qset;    /* "dev" is not-null */
    int i;

    if (dev->usage)
        return -EBUSY; /* scull_open ignores this error and goes on */

    for (dptr = dev; dptr; dptr = next) { /* all the list items */
        if (dptr->data) {
            for (i = 0; i < qset; i++)
                if (dptr->data[i])
                    kfree(dptr->data[i]);
            kfree(dptr->data);
            dptr->data=NULL;
        }
        next=dptr->next;
        if (dptr != dev) kfree(dptr); /* all of them but the first */
    }
    dev->size = 0;
```

```
        dev->quantum = scull_quantum;
        dev->qset = scull_qset;
        dev->next = NULL;
        return 0;
}
```

Read and Write

Reading and writing a *scull* device means transferring data between the kernel address space and the user address space. The operation cannot be carried out through pointers in the usual way, or through *memcpy*, because pointers operate in the current address space, and the driver's code is executing in kernel space, while the data buffers are in user space.

If the target device is an expansion board instead of RAM, the same problem arises, because the driver must nonetheless copy data between user buffers and kernel space. In fact, the role of a device driver is mainly managing data transfers between devices (kernel space) and applications (user space).

Cross-space copy is performed in Linux by special functions, which are defined in `<asm/segment.h>`. The functions devoted to performing such a copy are optimized for different data sizes (`char`, `short`, `int`, `long`); most of them will be introduced in "Using the ioctl Argument" in Chapter 5.

Driver code for *read* and *write* in *scull* needs to copy a whole segment of data to or from the user address space. This capability is offered by the following functions, which copy an arbitrary array of bytes:

```
void memcpy_fromfs(void *to, const void *from, unsigned long count);
void memcpy_tofs(void *to, const void *from, unsigned long count);
```

The names of the functions date back to the first Linux versions, when the only supported architecture was the i386 and there was a lot of assembler code peeking through the C. On Intel platforms, Linux addresses user space through the FS segment register, and the two functions have kept the old name through Linux 2.0. Things *did* change with Linux 2.1, but 2.0 is the main target of this book. See "Accessing User Space" in Chapter 17 for details.

Although the functions introduced above look like normal *memcpy* functions, a little extra care must be used when accessing user space from kernel code; the user pages being addressed might not be currently present in memory, and the page-fault handler can put the process to sleep while the page is being transferred into place. This happens, for example, when the page must be retrieved from swap space. The net result for the driver writer is that any function that accesses user space must be reentrant and must be able to execute concurrently with other driver functions. That's why the *scull* implementation refuses to release device memory when `dev->usage` is not 0: the *read* and *write* methods increment the `usage` counter before using either *memcpy* function.

As far as the actual device methods are concerned, the task of the read method is to copy data from the device to user space (using *memcpy_tofs*), while the write method must copy data from user space to the device (using *memcpy_fromfs*). Each *read* or *write* system call requests transfer of a specific number of bytes, but the driver is free to transfer less data—the exact rules are slightly different for reading and writing.

Both *read* and *write* return a negative value if an error occurs. A number greater than or equal to zero tells the calling program how many bytes have been successfully transferred. If some data is transferred correctly and then an error happens, the return value must be the count of bytes successfully transferred, while the error does not get reported until the next time the function is called.

The role of the different arguments to *read* is depicted in Figure 3-2.

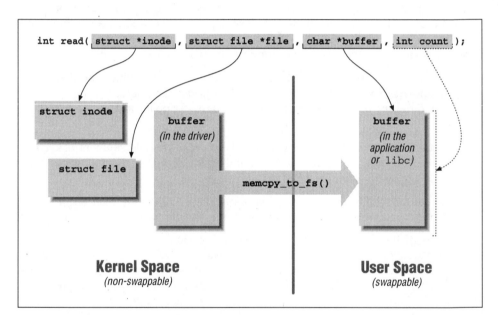

Figure 3-2: The arguments to read

While kernel functions return a negative number to signal an error, and the value of the number indicates the kind of error that occurred (as introduced in Chapter 2, *Building and Running Modules*, in "Error Handling in init_module"), programs that run in user space always see –1 as the error return value. These application programs need to access the `errno` variable to find out what happened. The difference in behavior is dictated by the library conventions on one hand and the advantage of not dealing with `errno` in the kernel on the other hand.

As far as portability is concerned, it's interesting to note that the `count` argument to both the *read* and *write* methods has always been `int`, but changed to `unsigned long` with release 2.1.0 of the kernel. Also, the return value for the methods has been changed from `int` to `long`, because it represents either a `count` or a negative error code.

This type change is beneficial: `unsigned long` is a better choice than `int` for a `count` item because of its wider range. The choice is so good that the Alpha team changed the typing before 2.1 was released (mainly because the GNU C library uses `unsigned long` in its definition of system calls).

Although beneficial, this change introduces some platform dependency in driver code. To circumvent the problem, all the sample modules available on the O'Reilly FTP site use the following definitions (from *sysdep.h*):

```
#if defined(__alpha__) || (LINUX_VERSION_CODE >= VERSION_CODE(2,1,0))
# define count_t unsigned long
# define read_write_t long
#else
# define count_t int
# define read_write_t int
#endif
```

After the macros have been evaluated, the `count` argument to *read* and *write* is always declared as `count_t`, and the return value as `read_write_t`. I chose to use a preprocessor definition instead of `typedef` because the `typedef` introduces more compiler warnings than it removes (see "Interface-Specific Types" in Chapter 10, *Judicious Use of Data Types*). On the other hand, an uppercase type name in function prototypes is really bad-looking, so I named the new "type" using the standard `typedef` convention.

Portability to version 2.1 is more thoroughly described in Chapter 17.

The read Method

The return value for *read* is interpreted by the calling program as follows:

- If the value equals the `count` argument passed to the *read* system call, the requested number of bytes has been transferred. This is the optimal case.

- If the value is positive, but smaller than `count`, only part of the data has been transferred. This may happen for a number of reasons, depending on the device. Most often, the program will retry the read. For instance, if you read using the *fread* function, the library function reissues the system call till completion of the requested data transfer.

- If the value is zero, it is interpreted to mean that end-of-file was reached.

- A negative value means there was an error. The value specifies what the error was, according to `<linux/errno.h>`.

What is missing from the preceding table is the case of "there is no data, but it may arrive later." In this case, the *read* system call should block. We won't deal with blocking input until "Blocking I/O" in Chapter 5.

The *scull* code takes advantage of these rules. In particular, it takes advantage of the partial-read rule. Each invocation of *scull_read* deals only with a single data quantum, without implementing a loop to gather all the data; this makes the code shorter and easier to read. If the reading program really wants more data, it reiterates the call. If the standard library is used to read the device, the application won't even notice the quantization of the data transfer.

If the current read position is greater than the device size, the *read* method of *scull* returns 0 to signal that there's no data available (in other words, we're at end-of-file). This situation can happen if process A is reading the device while process B opens it for writing, thus truncating the device to a length of 0. Process A suddenly finds itself past end-of-file, and the next *read* call returns 0.

Here is the code for *read*:

```
read_write_t scull_read (struct inode *inode, struct file *filp,
                         char *buf, count_t count)
{
    Scull_Dev *dev = filp->private_data; /* the first listitem */
    int quantum = dev->quantum;
    int qset = dev->qset;
    int itemsize = quantum * qset; /* how many bytes in the listitem */
    unsigned long f_pos = (unsigned long)(filp->f_pos);
    int item, s_pos, q_pos, rest;

    if (f_pos > dev->size)
        return 0;
    if (f_pos + count > dev->size)
        count = dev->size - f_pos;
    /* find listitem, qset index, and offset in the quantum */
    item = f_pos / itemsize;
    rest = f_pos % itemsize;
    s_pos = rest / quantum; q_pos = rest % quantum;

    /* follow the list up to the right position (defined elsewhere) */
    dev = scull_follow(dev, item);

    if (!dev->data)
        return 0; /* don't fill holes */
    if (!dev->data[s_pos])
        return 0;
    if (count > quantum - q_pos)
```

```
        count = quantum - q_pos; /* read only up to */
                                 /* the end of this quantum */

    dev->usage++; /* the following call may sleep */
    memcpy_tofs(buf, dev->data[s_pos]+q_pos, count);
    dev->usage--;

    filp->f_pos += count;
    return count;
}
```

The write Method

write, like *read*, can transfer less data than was requested, according to the following rules for the return value:

* If the value equals `count`, the requested number of bytes has been transferred.

* If the value is positive, but smaller than `count`, only part of the data has been transferred. Again, the program will most likely retry writing the rest of the data.

* If the value is zero, nothing was written. This result is not an error, and there is no reason to return an error code. Once again, the standard library retries the call to *write*. We'll examine the significance of this case in a later chapter, when blocking *write* is introduced.

* A negative value means an error occurred; the semantics are the same as for *read*.

Unfortunately, there are a few misbehaving programs that issue an error message and abort when a partial transfer is performed. Most notably, a not-so-old version of the GNU file utilities has such a bug. If your installation dates back to 1995 (for example, Slackware 2.3), your *cp* will fail to handle *scull*. You'll know you have this version if you see the message `/dev/scull0: no such file or directory` when *cp* writes a data chunk bigger than the *scull* quantum. The GNU *dd* implementation refuses to read or write partial blocks by design, and *cat* refuses to write partial blocks. Therefore, *cat* shouldn't be used with the *scull* module and *dd* should be passed a block size equal to *scull*'s quantum. Note that this limitation in the *scull* implementation could be fixed, but I didn't want to complicate the code more than necessary.

The *scull* code for *write* deals with a single quantum at a time, as the *read* method does:

```
    read_write_t scull_write (struct inode *inode, struct file *filp,
                              const char *buf, count_t count)
    {
        Scull_Dev *dev = filp->private_data;
```

```
    Scull_Dev *dptr;
    int quantum = dev->quantum;
    int qset = dev->qset;
    int itemsize = quantum * qset;
    unsigned long f_pos = (unsigned long)(filp->f_pos);
    int item, s_pos, q_pos, rest;

    /* find listitem, qset index and offset in the quantum */
    item = f_pos / itemsize;
    rest = f_pos % itemsize;
    s_pos = rest / quantum; q_pos = rest % quantum;

    /* follow the list up to the right position */
    dptr = scull_follow(dev, item);
    if (!dptr->data) {
        dptr->data = kmalloc(qset * sizeof(char *), GFP_KERNEL);
        if (!dptr->data)
            return -ENOMEM;
        memset(dptr->data, 0, qset * sizeof(char *));
    }
    if (!dptr->data[s_pos]) {
        dptr->data[s_pos] = kmalloc(quantum, GFP_KERNEL);
        if (!dptr->data[s_pos])
            return -ENOMEM;
    }
    if (count > quantum - q_pos)
        count = quantum - q_pos; /* write only up to */
                                 /*the end of this quantum */

    dev->usage++; /* the following call may sleep */
    memcpy_fromfs(dptr->data[s_pos]+q_pos, buf, count);
    dev->usage--;

    /* update the size */
    if (dev->size < f_pos + count)
        dev-> size = f_pos + count;
    filp->f_pos += count;
    return count;
}
```

Playing with the New Devices

Once you are equipped with the four methods just described, the driver can be compiled and tested; it retains any data you write to it until you overwrite it with new data. The device acts like a data buffer whose length is limited only by the amount of real RAM available. You can try using *cp*, *dd*, and input/output redirection to test out the driver.

The *free* command can be used to see how the amount of free memory shrinks and expands according to how much data is written into *scull*.

To get more confident with reading and writing one quantum at a time, you can add a *printk* at an appropriate point in the driver and watch what happens while an application reads or writes large chunks of data. Alternatively, use the *strace* utility to monitor the system calls issued by a program, together with their return values. Tracing a *cp* or an *ls –l* > */dev/scull0* will show quantized reads and writes. Monitoring (and debugging) techniques are presented to some detail in the next chapter.

Quick Reference

This chapter introduced the following symbols and header files. The list of the fields in `struct file_operations` and `struct file` is not repeated here.

`#include <linux/fs.h>`
The "File System" header is the header required for writing device drivers. All the important functions are declared in here.

`int register_chrdev(unsigned int major, const char *name,`
                                `struct file_operations *fops);`
Registers a character device driver. If the major number is not zero, it is used unchanged; if the number is zero, then a dynamic number is assigned for this device.

`int unregister_chrdev(unsigned int major, const char *name);`
Deregisters the driver at unload time. Both `major` and the `name` string must contain the same values that were used to register the driver.

`kdev_t inode->i_rdev;`
The device "number" for the current device is accessible from the `inode` argument passed to every device method.

`int MAJOR(kdev_t dev);`
`int MINOR(kdev_t dev);`
These macros extract the major and minor numbers from a device item.

`kdev_t MKDEV(int major, int minor);`
This macro builds a `kdev_t` data item from the major and minor numbers.

`#include <asm/segment.h>`
This header defines functions related to cross-space copying in all kernels up to and including 2.0. The functions are the ones used to copy data from the user segment to the kernel segment and vice versa. Version 2.1 changed the header's name as well as the functions (see "Accessing User Space" in Chapter 17 for more information).

```
void memcpy_fromfs(void *to, const void *from,
                    unsigned long count);
void memcpy_tofs(void *to, const void *from,
                  unsigned long count);
```

These functions are used to copy an array of bytes from user space to kernel space and vice versa. "FS" is the i386 segment register used to address user space from kernel code. These functions changed in 2.1.

CHAPTER FOUR

DEBUGGING TECHNIQUES

One of the most compelling problems for anyone writing kernel code is how to approach debugging. Kernel code cannot be easily executed under a debugger, nor can it be traced, because it is a set of functionalities not related to a specific process.

This chapter introduces techniques you can use to monitor kernel code and trace errors.

Debugging by Printing

The most common debugging technique is monitoring, which in applications programming is done by calling *printf* at suitable points. When you are debugging kernel code, you can accomplish the same goal with *printk*.

Printk

We used the *printk* function in earlier chapters with the simplifying assumption that it works like *printf*. Now it's time to introduce some of the differences.

One of the differences is that *printk* lets you classify messages according to their severity by associating different "loglevels," or priorities with the messages. You indicate the loglevel with a macro. For example, KERN_INFO, which we saw prepended to some of the earlier print statements, is one of the possible loglevels of the message. The loglevel macro expands to a string, which is concatenated to the message text at compile time; that's why there is no comma between the priority and the format string in the examples below. Here are two examples of *printk* commands, a debug message and a critical message:

```
printk(KERN_DEBUG "Here I am: line %i\n", __LINE__);
printk(KERN_CRIT "I'm trashed; giving up on %p\n", ptr);
```

There are eight possible loglevel strings, which are defined in the header `<linux/kernel.h>`. A *printk* statement with no specified priority defaults to DEFAULT_MESSAGE_LOGLEVEL, an integer value specified in *kernel/printk.c.* The default loglevel value has changed several times during Linux development, so I suggest that you always specify a suitable loglevel.

Based on the loglevel, the kernel prints the message to the current text console: if the priority is less than the integer variable `console_loglevel`, the message is displayed. If both *klogd* and *syslogd* are running on the system, kernel messages are appended to */var/log/messages*, independent of `console_loglevel`.

The variable `console_loglevel` is initialized to DEFAULT_CONSOLE_LOGLEVEL and can be modified through the *sys_syslog* system call. One way to change it is by specifying the *–c* switch when invoking *klogd*, as specified in the *klogd* man page. Note that to change the current value, you must first kill the logger and then restart it with the *–c* option. Alternatively, you can write a program to change the console loglevel. You'll find my version of such a program in *miscprogs/setlevel.c* in the source files provided on the O'Reilly FTP site. The new level is specified as an integer value between 1 and 8, inclusive.

You'll probably want to lower the loglevel after a kernel fault (see "Debugging System Faults"), because the fault-handling code raises the `console_loglevel` to 15, causing every subsequent message to appear on the console. You'll want to raise the loglevel if you are running a 2.0.*x* kernel and want to see your debugging messages. The 2.0 kernel release lowered the MINIMUM_CONSOLE_LOGLEVEL, while old versions of *klogd* tried by default to shut up console messages. If you happen to run an old daemon, the 2.0 kernel will be much quieter than you expect unless you raise the loglevel. That's why *hello.c* had the `<1>` markers; they are there to make sure that messages appear on the console.

Versions of Linux from 1.3.43 on allow for some flexibility in logging policies by letting you send messages to a specific virtual console. By default, the "console" is the current virtual terminal. To select a different virtual terminal to receive messages, you can issue `ioctl(TIOCLINUX)` on any console device. The following program, *setconsole*, can be used to choose which console receives kernel messages; it must be run by the superuser. If you don't feel confident using *ioctl*, you might prefer to skip to the next section and come back to this code after reading the section "ioctl" in Chapter 5, *Enhanced Char Driver Operations.*

```
int main(int argc, char **argv)
{
    char bytes[2] = {11,0}; /* 11 is the TIOCLINUX cmd number */

    if (argc==2) bytes[1] = atoi(argv[1]); /* the chosen console */
    else {
        fprintf(stderr, "%s: need a single arg\n",argv[0]); exit(1);
    }
```

```
        if (ioctl(STDIN_FILENO, TIOCLINUX, bytes)<0) {     /* use stdin */
            fprintf(stderr,"%s: ioctl(stdin, TIOCLINUX): %s\n",
                    argv[0], strerror(errno));
            exit(1);
        }
        exit(0);
    }
```

setconsole uses the special *ioctl* command TIOCLINUX, which implements Linux-specific functions. To use TIOCLINUX, you pass it an argument that is a pointer to a byte array. The first byte of the array is a number that specifies the requested subcommand, and the following bytes are subcommand-specific. In *setconsole*, subcommand 11 is used, and the next byte (stored in bytes[1]) identifies the virtual console. The complete description of TIOCLINUX can be found in *drivers/char/tty_io.c*, in the kernel sources.

How Messages Get Logged

The *printk* function writes messages into a circular buffer that is LOG_BUF_LEN bytes long. It then wakes any process that is waiting for messages, i.e., any process that is sleeping in the *syslog* system call or that is reading */proc/kmesg*. These two interfaces to the logging engine are equivalent. Nonetheless, reading the */proc* file is easier because the file looks like a fifo, from which kernel messages can be read. A simple *cat* can read the messages.

If the circular buffer fills up, *printk* wraps around and starts adding new data to the beginning of the buffer, overwriting the oldest data. The logging process thus loses the oldest data. This problem is negligible compared to the advantages of using such a circular buffer. For example, a circular buffer allows the system to run even without a logging process, while minimizing memory waste. Another feature of the Linux approach to messaging is that *printk* can be invoked from anywhere, even from an interrupt handler, with no limit on how much data can be printed. The only disadvantage is the possibility of losing some data.

If the *klogd* process is running, it retrieves kernel messages and dispatches them to *syslogd*, which in turn checks */etc/syslog.conf* to find out how to deal with them. *syslogd* differentiates between messages according to a "facility" and a "priority"; allowable values for both the facility and the priority are defined in <sys/syslog.h>. Kernel messages are logged by the LOG_KERN facility, at a priority corresponding to the one used in *printk*. If *klogd* isn't running, data remains in the circular buffer until someone reads it or the buffer overflows.

If you want to avoid clobbering your system log with the monitoring messages from your driver, you can either specify the –*f* (file) option to *klogd* to write the messages to a different file, or modify */etc/syslog.conf*. Another possibility is to take the brute-force approach: kill *klogd* and verbosely print messages on an unused virtual terminal,* or issue the command *cat /proc/kmesg* from an unused *xterm*.

Using the Preprocessor to Ease Monitoring

During the early stages of driver development, *printk* can help considerably in debugging and testing new code. When you officially release the driver, on the other hand, you should remove, or at least disable, such print statements. Unfortunately, you're likely to find that as soon as you think you no longer need the messages and remove them, you'll implement a new feature in the driver and want to turn at least one of the messages back on. There are several ways to solve both issues—how to globally enable and disable the messages and how to turn individual messages off and on.

The code I use for most of my messaging is shown below and has the following features:

- Each print statement can be enabled or disabled by removing or adding a single letter to the macro's name.

- All the messages can be disabled at once, by changing the value of the CFLAGS variable before compiling.

- The same print statement can be used in kernel code (the driver) and user-level code (demonstration and test programs).

The code fragment below implements these features and comes directly from the header *scull.h*.

```
#undef PDEBUG                /* undef it, just in case */
#ifdef SCULL_DEBUG
# ifdef __KERNEL__
   /* This one if debugging is on, and kernel space */
#  define PDEBUG(fmt, args...) printk(KERN_DEBUG "scull: " fmt, ## args)
# else
   /* This one for user space */
#  define PDEBUG(fmt, args...) fprintf(stderr, fmt, ## args)
# endif
#else
# define PDEBUG(fmt, args...) /* not debugging: nothing */
#endif

#undef PDEBUGG
#define PDEBUGG(fmt, args...) /* nothing: it's a placeholder */
```

The symbols PDEBUG and PDEBUGG depend on whether or not SCULL_DEBUG is defined, and they behave like a *printf* call.

---

* For example, use `setlevel 8; setconsole 10` to set up tty 10 to display messages.

To simplify the process further, add the following lines to your *Makefile*:

```
# Comment/uncomment the following line to disable/enable debugging
DEBUG = y

ifeq ($(DEBUG),y)
  DEBFLAGS = -O -g -DSCULL_DEBUG # "-O" is needed to expand inlines
else
  DEBFLAGS = -O2
endif

CFLAGS = -D__KERNEL__ -DMODULE -Wall $(DEBFLAGS)
```

The macros shown in this section depend on a *gcc* extension to the ANSI C pre-processor that supports macros with a variable number of arguments. This *gcc* dependency shouldn't be a problem because the kernel proper depends heavily on *gcc* features anyway. In addition, the *Makefile* depends on GNU's *gmake*; the same considerations apply to make it not a problem.

If you're familiar with the C preprocessor, you can expand on the definitions above to implement the concept of a "debug level," defining different levels and assigning an integer (or bitmask) value to each level to determine how verbose it should be.

But every driver has its own features and monitoring needs. The art of good programming is in choosing the best tradeoff between flexibility and efficiency, and I can't tell what is the best for you. Remember that preprocessor conditionals (as well as constant expressions in the code) are executed at compile time, so you must recompile to turn messages on or off. A possible alternative is to use C conditionals, which are executed at run time and therefore permit you to turn messaging on and off during program execution. This ability is a nice feature, but it requires additional processing every time the code is executed, which can affect performance even when the messages are disabled. Sometimes this performance hit is unacceptable.

Personally, I've been satisfied with the macros shown above, although they force me to recompile and reload the module every time I want to add or remove a message.

Debugging by Querying

The previous section described how *printk* works and how it can be used. What it didn't talk about are its disadvantages.

A massive use of *printk* can slow down the system noticeably, because *syslogd* keeps syncing its output files, so every line that is printed causes a disk operation. This is correct from *syslogd*'s perspective. It tries to write everything to disk in case the system crashes right after printing the message; however, you don't want to slow down your system just for the sake of debugging messages. This problem can be solved by prefixing with a dash the name of your logfile as it appears in */etc/syslogd.conf*, but sometimes you don't want to change your config files. Otherwise, you can run a program other than *klogd* (like *cat /proc/kmesg*, as suggested above) but this may not provide a suitable environment for normal system operation.

More often than not, the best way to get relevant information is to query the system when you need the information, instead of continually producing data. In fact, every Unix system provides many tools for obtaining system information: *ps*, *netstat*, *vmstat*, and so on.

There are two techniques available to driver developers for querying the system, namely, creating a file in the */proc* filesystem and using the *ioctl* driver method.

Using the /proc Filesystem

The */proc* filesystem in Linux is not associated with any device—the files living in */proc* are generated by the kernel when they are read. These files are usually text files, so they can be (almost) understood by humans as well as by utility programs. For example, the most common Linux implementation of *ps* gets its information from the */proc* filesystem. The idea of a */proc* virtual filesystem is used by several modern operating systems and works quite successfully.

The current implementation of */proc* provides for the dynamic creation of nodes, allowing user modules to create entry points for easy information retrieval.

To create a full-featured file node within */proc* (one that permits reads, writes, seeks, and so on), you need to define both a `file_operations` structure and an `inode_operations` structure, which are similar in role and shape. Creating such a node is not too different from the creation of a whole char device. I won't deal with this issue here, but if you're interested, you can look in the *fs/proc* source tree for further details.

If the file node is only going to be read, as most of the */proc* files are, there is an easier way to create it, which I'll show here. Unfortunately, this technique is only available in Linux 2.0 or later.

Here is the *scull* code for creating a file called */proc/scullmem*, used to retrieve information about the memory used by *scull*.

```
#include <linux/proc_fs.h>

int scull_read_procmem(char *buf, char **start, off_t offset,
                       int len, int unused)
{
    int i, j, quantum, qset;
    Scull_Dev *d;
```

```
#define LIMIT (PAGE_SIZE-80) /* don't print anymore */
                            /* after this size */
len=0;
for(i=0; i<scull_nr_devs; i++) {
    d=&scull_devices[i];
    quantum=d->quantum;  /* retrieve the features of each device */
    qset=d->qset;
    len += sprintf(buf+len,"\nDevice %i: qset %i, q %i, sz %li\n",
                i, qset, quantum, d->size);
    for (; d; d=d->next) { /* scan the list */
        if (len > LIMIT) return len;
        len += sprintf(buf+len, " item at %p, qset at %p\n",
                    d, d->data);
        if (d->data && !d->next) /* dump only the last item */
                                /* to save space */
        for (j=0; j<qset; j++) {
            if (len > LIMIT) return len;
            if (d->data[j])
                len += sprintf(buf+len," % 4i:%8p\n",
                            j,d->data[j]);
        }
    }
}
return len;
}


struct proc_dir_entry scull_proc_entry = {
        0,                  /* low_ino: the inode--dynamic */
        8, "scullmem",      /* len of name and name */
        S_IFREG | S_IRUGO, /* mode */
        1, 0, 0,            /* nlinks, owner, group */
        0,                  /* size--unused */
        NULL,               /* operations--use default */
        &scull_read_procmem,   /* function used to read data */
        /* nothing more */
    };

    /* this is the last line in init_module */
    proc_register_dynamic(&proc_root, &scull_proc_entry);
```

Filling a */proc* file is easy. Your function receives a free page to be filled with data; it writes into the buffer and returns the length it wrote. Everything else is handled by the */proc* filesystem. The only limitation is that the data being written must be less than **PAGE_SIZE** bytes (the **PAGE_SIZE** macro is defined in the header file <asm/page.h>; it is architecture-dependent, but you can count on at least 4KB).

If you need to write more than one page of data, you must fall back on the full-featured file implementation.

Note that if a process reading your */proc* file issues several *read* calls, each retrieving a few bytes, your driver rewrites the entire buffer each time even though only a small amount of actual data is being read. The extra work can cause performance to suffer and the data to become misaligned because if the data generated by the file is different from one time to the next, subsequent *read* calls will reassemble unrelated parts. In fact, performance is rarely a problem, because every application using the C library reads data in one big chunk. Misalignments, however, are worth worrying about because they sometimes show themselves. After retrieving data, the library calls *read* at least once more—end-of-file is only reported when one *read* call returns 0. If the driver happens to produce more data than before, the extra bytes are returned to user space and do not align with the previous data chunk. We'll encounter the misalignment problem again when we look at */proc/jiq**, in the section "Task Queues" in Chapter 6, *Flow of Time*.

Unregistration of the */proc* node should be performed in *cleanup_module*, by the following statement:

```
proc_unregister(&proc_root, scull_proc_entry.low_ino);
```

The arguments passed to the function are the name of the directory containing the file being destroyed and the file's inode number. Since the inode number is allocated dynamically, it is unknown at compile time and must be read back from the data structure.

The ioctl Method

ioctl, which is discussed in more detail in the next chapter, is a system call that acts on a file descriptor; it receives a "command" number and (optionally) another argument, usually a pointer.

As an alternative to using the */proc* filesystem, you can implement a few *ioctl* commands tailored for debugging. These commands copy relevant data structures from the driver to user space, where you can examine them.

Using *ioctl* this way to get information is somewhat more difficult than using */proc*, because you need another program to issue the *ioctl* and display the results. This program must be written, compiled, and kept in sync with the module you're testing.

There are nonetheless times when this is the best way to get information, because it runs faster than reading */proc*. If some work must be performed on the data before it's written to the screen, retrieving the data in binary form can be more efficient than reading a text file. In addition, *ioctl* doesn't limit the amount of data returned to a single page.

An interesting advantage of the *ioctl* approach is that the debugging commands can be left in the driver even when debugging is disabled. Unlike a */proc* file, which is visible to anyone who looks in the directory (and too many people are likely to wonder "what that strange file is"), undocumented *ioctl* commands are likely to remain unnoticed. In addition, they will still be there should something weird happen to the driver. The only drawback is that the module will be slightly bigger.

Debugging by Watching

Sometimes the problems you're encountering are not that bad and running an application program in user space to examine the way the driver reacts to system calls can help track down minor problems or confirm that the driver is working correctly. For example, I was able to feel confident about *scull* after looking at how its *read* implementation reacted to *read* requests for different amounts of data.

There are various ways to watch a user-space program working. You can run a debugger on it to step through its functions, add print statements, or run the program under *strace*. The last technique is most interesting when the real goal is examining kernel code.

The *strace* command is a powerful tool that shows all the system calls issued by a user-space program. Not only does it show the calls, but it can also show the arguments to the calls, as well as return values in symbolic form. When a system call fails, both the symbolic value of the error (e.g., **ENOMEM**) and the corresponding string (Out of memory) are displayed. *strace* has many command-line options; the most useful are *−t* to display the time *when* each call is executed, *−T* to display the time *spent in* the call, and *−o* to redirect the output to a file. By default, *strace* prints tracing information on stderr.

strace receives information from the kernel itself. This means that a program can be traced regardless of whether it was compiled with debugging support (the *−g* option to *gcc*) or whether it is stripped. You can also attach tracing to a running process, similar to the way a debugger can connect to a running process and control it.

The trace information is often used to support bug reports sent to application developers, but it's also invaluable to kernel programmers. We've seen how driver code executes by making system calls; *strace* allows us to check the consistency of each call's input and output data.

For example, the following screen dump shows the last lines of tracing the command *ls /dev > /dev/scull0*:

```
% strace ls /dev > /dev/scull0
[...]
readdir(3, {d_ino=894, d_name="scull0"}) = 1
```

```
readdir(3, {d_ino=895, d_name="scull1"}) = 1
readdir(3, {d_ino=896, d_name="scull2"}) = 1
readdir(3, {d_ino=897, d_name="scull3"}) = 1
readdir(3, 0x8013000)                    = 0
close(3)                                 = 0
brk(0x8035000)                           = 0x8035000
brk(0x8035000)                           = 0x8035000
brk(0x8025000)                           = 0x8025000
fstat(1, {st_mode=S_IFCHR|0664, st_rdev=makedev(63, 0), ...}) = 0
ioctl(1, TCGETS, 0xbfffffac4)            = -1 EINVAL (Invalid argument)
write(1, "MAKEDEV\nXOR\narp\natibm\naudio\n"..., 4096) = 4000
write(1, "3\nttyr4\nttyr5\nttyr6\nttyr7\nt"..., 96) = 96
write(1, "3\nttys4\nttys5\nttys6\nttys7\nt"..., 535) = 535
_exit(0)                                 = ?
```

It's apparent in the first *write* call that after *ls* finished looking in the target directory, it tried to write 4KB. Strangely (for *ls*), only four thousand bytes were written,
and the operation was retried. However, we know that the *write* implementation
in *scull* writes a single quantum at a time, so we could have expected the partial
write. After a few steps, everything sweeps through, and the program exits successfully.

As another example, let's *read* the *scull* device:

```
% strace wc -c /dev/scull0
[...]
open("/dev/scull0", O_RDONLY)            = 3
fstat(3, {st_mode=S_IFCHR|0664, st_rdev=makedev(63, 0), ...}) = 0
read(3, "MAKEDEV\nXOR\narp\natibm\naudio\n"..., 16384) = 4000
read(3, "3\nttyr4\nttyr5\nttyr6\nttyr7\nt"..., 16384) = 631
read(3, "", 16384)                       = 0
fstat(1, {st_mode=S_IFCHR|0620, st_rdev=makedev(4, 13), ...}) = 0
brk(0x800b000)                           = 0x800b000
ioctl(1, TCGETS, {B38400 opost isig icanon echo ...}) = 0
write(1, "   4631 /dev/scull0\n", 20    4631 /dev/scull0
)    = 20
close(3)                                 = 0
_exit(0)                                 = ?
```

As expected, *read* is able to retrieve only four thousand bytes at a time, but the
total amount of data is the same. It's interesting to note how retries are organized
in this example, as opposed to the previous trace. *wc* is optimized for fast reading
and thus bypasses the standard library, trying to read more data with a single system call. You can see from the **read** lines in the trace how *wc* tried to read 16KB
at a time.

Unix experts can find much useful information in the output of *strace*. If you're
put off by all the symbols, you can limit yourself to watching how the file methods
(*open*, *read*, and so on) work.

Personally, I find the tracing utility most useful for pinpointing run-time errors from system calls. Often the *perror* call in the application or demo program isn't verbose enough to be useful for debugging, and being able to tell exactly which arguments to which system call triggered the error can be a great help.

Debugging System Faults

Even if you've used all the monitoring and debugging techniques, sometimes bugs remain in the driver and the system faults when the driver is executed. When this happens it's important to be able to collect as much information as possible to solve the problem.

Note that "fault" doesn't mean "panic." The Linux code is robust enough to respond gracefully to most errors: a fault usually results in the destruction of the current process, but the system goes on working. The system *can* panic, and it may if a fault happens outside of a process's context, or if some vital part of the system is compromised. But when the problem is due to a driver error, it usually results only in the sudden destruction of the faulty process—the one using the driver. The only unrecoverable damage when a process is destroyed is that some memory allocated to the process's context can be lost; for instance, dynamic lists allocated by the driver through *kmalloc* might be lost. However, since the kernel calls the *close* operation for any open device anyway, your driver can release what was allocated by the *open* method.

We've already said that when kernel code misbehaves, an informative message is printed on the console. The next section explains how to decode and use such messages. Even though they appear rather obscure to the novice, processor dumps are full of interesting information, often sufficient to pinpoint a program bug without the need for additional testing.

Oops Messages

Most bugs show themselves in NULL pointer dereferences or by the use of other incorrect pointer values. The usual outcome of such bugs is an oops message.

Any address used by the processor is a "virtual" address and is mapped to physical addresses through a complex structure of so-called page tables (see "Page Tables" in Chapter 13, *Mmap and DMA*). When an invalid pointer is dereferenced, the paging mechanism fails to map the pointer to a physical address and the processor signals a "page fault" to the operating system. If the address is not valid, the kernel is not able to "page-in" the missing address; it generates an "oops" if this happens while the processor is in supervisor mode. It's interesting to note that the way the kernel deals with faults changed in version 2.1, so that it can handle references to invalid addresses while in supervisor mode. The new implementation is described in the section "Handling Kernel-Space Faults," in Chapter 17, *Recent Developments*.

An oops displays the processor status at the time of the fault, including the contents of the CPU registers, the location of page descriptor tables, and other seemingly incomprehensible information. The message is generated by *printk* statements in the fault handler (*arch/*/kernel/traps.c*) and is dispatched as described earlier in the section "Printk."

Let's look at one such message. Here's how an oops appears on a conventional personal computer (an x86 platform), running Linux 2.0 or newer—version 1.2 has a slightly different layout.

```
Unable to handle kernel paging request at virtual address c202e000
current->tss.cr3 = 012c0000, $r3 = 012c0000
*pde = 00001067
*pte = 00000000
Oops: 0000
CPU:    0
EIP:    0010:[<0202d079>]
EFLAGS: 00010216
eax: 00000041   ebx: 00001000   ecx: 0000004b   edx: 0156b018
esi: 0202e000   edi: 0800aed4   ebp: 01106f90   esp: 01106f6c
ds: 0018   es: 002b   fs: 002b   gs: 002b   ss: 0018
Process cat (pid: 597, process nr: 31, stackpage=01106000)
Stack: 02020018 0202d004 00f992e8 01257440 0800a000 00001000 01257440
       00001000 00f992e8 00120e7a 00f992e8 01257440 0800a000 00001000
       0800a000 00001000 bffffbd8 0010a602 00000003 0800a000 00001000
Call Trace: [<02020018>] [<0202d004>] [<00120e7a>] [<0010a602>]
Code: f3 a5 83 e3 03 89 d9 f3 a4 07 8b 45 14 8d 65 f4 5b 5e 5f 89
```

The message above was generated by running *cat* on a *faulty* module, built deliberately to demonstrate the error. *faulty.c* includes the following code:

```
char faulty_buf[1024];

read_write_t faulty_read (struct inode *inode, struct file *filp,
                          char *buf, count_t count)
{
  printk(KERN_DEBUG "read: inode %p, file %p, buf %p, count %li\n",
         inode, filp, buf, (long)count);
  memcpy_tofs(buf,faulty_buf,count);
  return count;
}
```

Since *read* copies data to user space from its small buffer (`faulty_buf`), we can expect reading the file in small pieces to work. Reading more than one kilobyte at a time, on the other hand, might cross a page boundary, and the *read* will fail if it accesses an invalid page. Indeed, the oops shown earlier happened during a *read* call asking for 4 kilobytes, as shown by the line appearing before the oops message in */var/log/messages* (the default file where *syslogd* stores kernel messages):

```
   read: inode 00f992e8, file 01257440, buf 0800a000, count 4096
```

The same *cat* command doesn't generate an oops on an Alpha because reading 4 kilobytes from `faulty_buf` doesn't cross the page boundary (pages are 8KB on the Alpha and the buffer sits near the beginning of the page). If reading *faulty* doesn't generate an oops message on your system, try using *wc* (word count) instead, or specify an explicit block size to *dd*.

Using ksymoops

The main problem with oops messages is that the hex values are not meaningful for the programmer; they need to be resolved to symbols.

The kernel sources help the developer by including the *ksymoops* utility—but note that the program was missing from version 1.2 of the sources. The tool resolves numeric addresses found in the oops message to kernel symbols, but only for oops messages generated by PCs. Each architecture has its own message format, because the available information is processor-dependent.

ksymoops gets the oops message on standard input and the name of the kernel symbol table on the command line. The symbol table is usually */usr/src/linux/System.map*. The program prints the call trace and program code in a more readable format than the original oops message. The following snapshot was produced by feeding *ksymoops* the oops message shown in the previous section:

```
Trace: 2020018
Trace: 202d004
Trace: 120e7a <sys_read+8a/b0>
Trace: 10a602 <system_call+52/80>

Code: repz movsl %ds:(%esi),%es:(%edi)
Code: andl    $0x3,%ebx
Code: movl    %ebx,%ecx
Code: repz movsb %ds:(%esi),%es:(%edi)
Code: popl    %es
Code: movl    0x14(%ebp),%eax
Code: leal    0xfffffff4(%ebp),%esp
Code: popl    %ebx
Code: popl    %esi
Code: popl    %edi
Code: movl    %eax,(%eax)
```

The code disassembly produced by *ksymoops* shows the instruction that failed and the following ones. It's apparent here—for those who know a little assembler—that the `repz movsl` instruction (REPeat till cx is Zero, MOVe a String of Longs) hit an unmapped page with the source index (`esi`, shown as `0x202e000`). The command *ksyms –m*, used to retrieve module information, shows that the module is mapped to a single page at `0x0202dxxx`, thus confirming that `esi` is out of range.

The decoded call trace still includes two numeric addresses, because the memory area occupied by the *faulty* module isn't described in the system map. The values can be supplemented manually, either by inspecting the output of the *ksyms* command or by grepping for the module name in */proc/ksyms*.

For this particular fault, however, the two addresses don't correspond to code addresses. If you look in *arch/i386/kernel/traps.c*, you'll find that the call trace is extracted from the whole stack dump by using some heuristics to look at the memory layout and distinguish between data values (local variables and function arguments) and return addresses. Only addresses that refer to kernel code and the ones that *might* refer to modules are shown in the call trace. Since module pages contain both code and data, extraneous stack frames can slip through the heuristics, and this is exactly what happened for the two `0x202xxxx` addresses above.

If you'd rather not look for module addresses by hand, the following pipeline can be used to create a new symbol table that encompasses both kernel and module symbols. Whenever you reload the module, you must recreate this symbol table.

```
cat /proc/ksyms /usr/src/linux/System.map | sed 's/ . / /' |\
    awk '{print $1,"T",$2}' | sort -u > /tmp/System.map
```

The pipeline combines the complete system map and the public kernel symbols from */proc/ksyms*; the latter file lists module symbols in the current kernel, in addition to kernel symbols. Such addresses are shown as they appear after *insmod* has relocated the code. Since the two files have different formats, *sed* and *awk* are used to convert all the lines into a suitable format. The map is then sorted, removing duplicates, so that *ksymoops* can use it.

If we rerun *ksymoops*, it extracts the following information from the new symbol table:

```
>>EIP: 202d079 <faulty_read+45/60>
Trace: 2020018 <M_wacom_proto+1fb8/d8e4>
Trace: 202d004 <kmouse_wait+15d8/1608>
Trace: 120e7a <sys_read+8a/b0>
Trace: 10a602 <system_call+52/80>

Code: 202d079 <faulty_read+45/60> repz movsl %ds:(%esi),%es:(%edi)
Code: 202d07b <faulty_read+47/60> andl     $0x3,%ebx
Code: 202d07e <faulty_read+4a/60> movl     %ebx,%ecx
Code: 202d080 <faulty_read+4c/60> repz movsb %ds:(%esi),%es:(%edi)
Code: 202d082 <faulty_read+4e/60> popl     %es
Code: 202d083 <faulty_read+4f/60> movl     0x14(%ebp),%eax
Code: 202d086 <faulty_read+52/60> leal     0xfffffff4(%ebp),%esp
Code: 202d089 <faulty_read+55/60> popl     %ebx
```

```
Code: 202d08a <faulty_read+56/60> popl   %esi
Code: 202d08b <faulty_read+57/60> popl   %edi
Code: 202d08c <faulty_read+58/60> movl   %eax,(%eax)
```

As you can see, creating a modified system map is quite helpful when tracing oops messages related to modules: *ksymoops* can now decode the instruction pointer and the complete call trace. Note also that the format used to show disassembled code is the same as that used by the *objdump* program. *objdump* is a powerful utility; if you want to look at instructions before the one that failed, you can invoke the command *objdump –d faulty.o*.

In the resulting assembly listing of the file, the string `faulty_read+45/60` marks the faulty line. For more information on *objdump* and its command-line options, see the man page for the command.

Even if you build your own modified symbol table, the concern mentioned above regarding the call trace applies: the `0x202xxxx` pointers have been decoded, but are still spurious.

Learning to decode an oops message requires some practice, but it's worth doing. The time spent learning will be quickly repaid. The only issue is where to get the relevant documentation about assembly language, because the Unix syntax for machine instructions is different from the Intel syntax; even if you know PC assembly language, your experience has probably been with Intel-syntax programs. In the bibliography, I give pointers to a pair of documents that can help.

Using oops

Using *ksymoops* is somewhat burdensome. You need the C++ compiler to build it, you must build your own symbol table to fully exploit the capabilities of the program, and you have to merge the original message and the *ksymoops* output to have all the information handy.

If you don't want to go to all that trouble, you can use the *oops* program. *oops* is provided in the source files for this book on the O'Reilly FTP site. It is derived from the original *ksymoops* tool, which is no longer maintained by its author. *oops* is written in C and looks in */proc/ksyms* without requiring the user to build a new symbol table every time a module is loaded.

The program tries to decode all the processor registers and the stack trace to symbolic values. Its disadvantage is that it is more verbose than *ksymoops*, but usually the more information you have available, the sooner you find the bug. Like the original *ksyms*, the program is able to decode oops messages generated on Intel platforms only. Porting to other platforms shouldn't be difficult. The program is released under the GPL like the kernel sources.

Output generated by *oops* is similar to the *ksymoops* output, but more complete. Here is the beginning of its output for the oops shown above—I don't think it's worth showing the entire stack trace because the stack holds nothing interesting in this particular oops message:

```
EIP:    0010:0202d079 <faulty_read+45/60>
EFLAGS: 00010216
eax: 00000041
ebx: 00001000
ecx: 0000004b
edx: 0156b018
esi: 0202e000
edi: 0800aed4
ebp: 01106f90 <%esp+24>
esp: 01106f6c <%esp+0>
ds: 0018   es: 002b   fs: 002b   gs: 002b   ss: 0018
Process cat (pid: 597, process nr: 31, stackpage=01106000)
esp+00: 02020018 <M_wacom_proto+1fb8/d8e4>
esp+04: 0202d004
esp+08: 00f992e8
```

Having the registers and the stack decoded is helpful when you are debugging "real" modules (*faulty* is too short for the difference to be meaningful), and is particularly useful if all the symbols of the module being debugged are exported. It's not unusual for processor registers to point to symbols in the module at the time of the fault, and you can identify them from the output only if the symbol table is exported to */proc/ksyms*.

We can make a complete symbol table available by taking the following steps. First, we won't declare static symbols in the module, since they wouldn't be exported by *insmod*. And second, we can mask the call to *register_symtab* with `#ifdef SCULL_DEBUG` or a similar macro, as shown in the code below, extracted from *scull*'s *init_module* function.

```
#ifndef SCULL_DEBUG
    register_symtab(NULL); /* otherwise, leave global symbols visible */
#endif
```

We saw in "Registering Symbol Tables" in Chapter 2, *Building and Running Modules*, that if the module doesn't register a symbol table, all the global symbols are exported. Although this feature is exploited only if `SCULL_DEBUG` is active, all global symbols should be correctly prefixed to avoid namespace pollution in the kernel (see "Modules Versus Applications" in Chapter 2).

Using klogd

Recent versions of the *klogd* daemon can decode oops messages before they reach the log files. Decoding is performed only by version 1.3 or newer of the daemon and only if *–k /usr/src/linux/System.map* is passed as a command-line option to the daemon. (You can replace *System.map* with another map file.)

A dump of the oops for *faulty*, produced by the new *klogd* and written to the system log, looks like this (note the decoded symbols in the stack trace):

```
EIP:     0010:[<0202d079>]
EFLAGS: 00010216
eax: 00000041   ebx: 00001000   ecx: 0000004b   edx: 00ee2414
esi: 0202e000   edi: 0800aed4   ebp: 0032ff90   esp: 0032ff6c
ds: 0018   es: 002b   fs: 002b   gs: 002b   ss: 0018
Process cat (pid: 861, process nr: 10, stackpage=0032f000)
Stack: 02020018 0202d004 00f992e8 01257c40 0800a000 00001000 01257c40
       00001000 00f992e8 00120e7a 00f992e8 01257c40 0800a000 00001000
       0800a000 00001000 bffffbd8 0010a602 00000003 0800a000 00001000
Call Trace: [<02020018>] [<0202d004>] [sys_read+138/176]
            [system_call+82/128]
Code: f3 a5 83 e3 03 89 d9 f3 a4 07 8b 45 14 8d 65 f4 5b 5e 5f 89
```

I consider the decoding *klogd* a great utility for the average Linux installation to help in debugging the kernel, but we'll see how it is of less use for debugging modules. The message decoded by *klogd* includes most *ksymoops* features and doesn't force the user to compile additional tools or merge two outputs in order to submit a complete bug report should something go wrong with the system. The daemon also correctly decodes the instruction pointer when the oops happens in the kernel proper. It doesn't disassemble the program code, but this is not a problem when the message accompanies a bug report because the binary data is still there, and disassembled code can be generated offline.

Another great feature of the daemon is that it refuses to decode symbols if the symbol table doesn't match the current kernel. If a symbol is decoded on the system log, you can be reasonably sure it is decoded correctly.

However, the tool, despite its usefulness for Linux users, is not that helpful when debugging modules. I personally don't use the decoding options on the computers where I develop my software. The problem with *klogd* is that it doesn't decode symbols in modules; even reading */proc/ksyms* doesn't help, because the daemon is run before the programmer loads the module. The presence of decoded symbols in the log file, then, confuses both *oops* and *ksymoops*, and it's hard to perform additional decoding.

If you want to use *klogd* for debugging your modules, specific support is being added to the newest versions of the daemon, but as I'm writing this, it needs a small kernel patch to be effective.

System Hangs

Although most bugs in kernel code end up as oops messages, sometimes they can completely hang the system. If the system hangs, no message is printed. For example, if the code enters an endless loop, the kernel stops scheduling, and the system doesn't respond to any action, including the magic **Ctrl-Alt-Del** combination.

You have two choices to deal with system hangs—either you need to prevent them beforehand, or you need to be able to debug them after the fact.

You can prevent an endless loop by inserting *schedule* invocations at strategic points. The *schedule* call (as you might guess) invokes the scheduler and thus allows other processes to steal CPU time from the current process. If a process is looping in kernel space due to a bug in your driver, you will be able to *kill* the process, after tracing what is happening.

Inserting *schedule* calls in a driver function creates a new "problem" for the programmer: the function, and all the functions in its call trace, must be reentrant. Under normal circumstances, the driver as a whole is reentrant because different processes can access the device concurrently, but it's not necessary for each function to be reentrant, because the Linux kernel is not preemptible. But if a driver function allows the scheduler to interrupt the current process, a different process might enter the same function. The reentrancy issue is not really important if the *schedule* calls are enabled only during debugging, because you can avoid accessing the driver from two concurrent processes if you know you aren't allowed to. When blocking operations are introduced (in "Writing Reentrant Code" in Chapter 5), the reentrancy problem will be dealt with in more detail.

To debug infinite loops, we can make use of the special functions of the Linux keyboard. By default, the **PrScr** key (keycode 70), if pressed with a modifier key, prints to the current console useful information about the machine's status. This works on both x86 and Alpha systems. The Sparc port of Linux features the same capability, but uses the key marked "Break/Scroll Lock" (keycode 30).

Each of the special functions has a name and is associated with a keypress event, as shown in the following list. The function name appears in parentheses after the key combination.

Shift-PrScr (Show_Memory)
> Prints several lines of information about memory usage, particularly the use of the buffer cache.

Control-PrScr (Show_State)
> Prints one line for each process in the system, with information about the internal process tree. The current process is marked as such.

RightAlt-PrScr (Show_Registers)
> This is the most important key when the system hangs, because it dumps the contents of the processor registers at the time the key is hit. Looking at the instruction pointer and how it changes over time can be extremely useful in understanding where the code is looping, provided there exists a system map for the current kernel.

The name of each function can be passed to *loadkeys* in order to remap the binding to a different key. The keyboard map can be modified at will (it is "policy-free").

The messages printed by these functions appear on the console if `console_loglevel` is high enough. The default level should be high enough, unless you run an old *klogd* and a new kernel. If the messages don't appear, you can raise the loglevel as explained earlier. The definition of "high enough" depends on the kernel version you use. It's 5 for Linux 2.0 and later.

It's important to be sure the loglevel is high enough, because the messages will display on the console even when the computer is hung. The messages are generated at the time of the interrupt and therefore can slip through even if a faulty process is executing a tight loop without releasing the CPU—that is, unless interrupts are disabled, which is both unlikely and unlucky.

Sometimes the system may appear to be hung, but it isn't. This can happen, for example, if the keyboard remains locked in some strange way. These false hangs can be detected by looking at the output of a program you keep running for just this purpose. I have a program that updates the clock on an LED display, and I discovered that the program is also useful as evidence that the scheduler is still working. You can check the scheduler without using external hardware, by implementing a program that flashes the keyboard LEDs, turns on the floppy motor every now and then, or ticks the speaker—conventional beeps are quite annoying and should be avoided, in my opinion. Look for the `KDMKTONE` *ioctl* command instead. A sample program (*misc-progs/heartbeat.c*) that flashes a keyboard LED in a heartbeat fashion is available in the sources on the O'Reilly FTP site.

If the keyboard isn't accepting input, the best thing to do is log into the system through your network in order to kill any offending processes, or reset the keyboard (with *kbd_mode –a*). However, discovering that the hang is only a keyboard lockup is of little use if you don't have a network available to help you recover. If this is the case, you should set up alternative input devices to be able at least to reboot the system cleanly. A shutdown and reboot cycle is easier on your computer than hitting the so-called "big red button," and it saves you from the lengthy *fsck* scanning of your filesystems.

Such alternative input devices can be a joystick or the mouse. There is a *joystick-reboot* daemon on *sunsite.unc.edu*, and the *gpm-1.10* or newer mouse server features a command-line option to enable a similar capability. If the keyboard is erroneously in "raw" mode instead of being locked, you can resort to the tricks described in the documentation of the *kbd* package. I suggest that you read the documentation before the problem arises and it's too late. Another possibility is to configure the *gpm-root* menus to have a "reboot" or "reset keyboard" entry; *gpm-root* is a daemon that responds to control-mouse events in order to draw menus on the screen and perform configurable actions.

Finally, you can hit the "Secure Attention Key" (SAK), a special key meant to recover the system to a usable state. The current Linux versions don't have an entry for the key in the default keyboard map because the implementation is not guaranteed always to succeed. You can nonetheless map SAK to your keyboard by using *loadkeys*. You should also look at the implementation of SAK in the *drivers/char* directory. The comments in the code explain why the key doesn't always work with Linux 2.0, so I won't say any more about it.

If you run 2.1.9 or newer, on the other hand, you'll enjoy having a reliable Secure Attention Key. Moreover, 2.1.43 and newer kernels have a compile-time option to enable a "Magic System Request Key"; I urge you to look in *drivers/char/sysrq.c* and enjoy the new technology.

If your driver really hangs the system, and you don't know where to insert *schedule* calls, the best way to go is to add some print messages and write them to the console (by changing the `console_loglevel` value). It's also wise to mount all your disks read-only (or unmount them) before reproducing the hang. If the disks are read-only or unmounted, there's no risk of damaging the filesystem or leaving it in an inconsistent state. At least you'll avoid the *fsck* pass after resetting the computer. Another possibility is using an NFS-root computer to test new modules. In this case you'll avoid any filesystem corruption, as filesystem coherence is managed by the NFS server, which is not brought down by your device driver.

Using a Debugger

The last resort in debugging modules is using a debugger to step through the code, watching the value of variables and machine registers. This approach is time-consuming and should be avoided whenever possible. Nonetheless, the fine-grained perspective on the code that is achieved through a debugger is sometimes invaluable. In our context, the code being debugged runs in the kernel address space—this makes things harder, because it's impossible to step through the kernel unless you remote-control it. I'll describe remote control last because it's rarely needed when writing modules. Fortunately, it *is* possible to look at variables in the current kernel and to modify them, even without remote control.

Proficient use of the debugger at this level requires some confidence with *gdb* commands, a minimal understanding of assembly code, and the ability to match source code and optimized assembly.

Unfortunately, *gdb* is more useful for dealing with the kernel proper than for debugging modules, and something more is needed to apply the same capabilities to modularized code. This something is the *kdebug* package, which uses the "remote debugging" interface of *gdb* to control the local kernel. I'll introduce *kdebug* after talking about what you can do with the plain debugger.

Using gdb

gdb can be quite useful for looking at the system internals. The debugger must be invoked as though the kernel were an application. In addition to specifying the kernel's filename, you should provide the name of a core file on the command line. A typical invocation of *gdb* looks like the following:

```
gdb /usr/src/linux/vmlinux /proc/kcore
```

The first argument is the name of the uncompressed kernel executable (after you compiled it in */usr/src/linux*). The *zImage* file (sometimes called *vmlinuz*) only exists for the x86 architecture, and is a trick to work around the 640KB limit of real-mode Intel processors; *vmlinux* on the contrary is the uncompressed kernel, on whichever platform you compile your kernel.

The second argument on the *gdb* command line is the name of the core file. Like any file in */proc, /proc/kcore* is generated when it is read. When the *read* system call executes in the */proc* filesystem, it maps to a data-generation function rather than a data-retrieval one; we've already exploited this feature in "Using the /proc Filesystem." *kcore* is used to represent the kernel "executable" in the format of a core file; it is a huge file, because it represents the whole kernel address space, which corresponds to all physical memory. From within *gdb*, you can look at kernel variables by issuing the standard *gdb* commands. For example, `p jiffies` prints the number of clock ticks from system boot to the current time.

When you print data from *gdb*, the kernel is still running, and the various data items have different values at different times; *gdb*, however, optimizes access to the core file by caching data that has already been read. If you try to look at the `jiffies` variable once again, you'll get the same answer as before. Caching values to avoid extra disk access is a correct behavior for conventional core files, but is inconvenient when a "dynamic" core image is used. The solution is to issue the command `core-file /proc/kcore` whenever you want to flush the *gdb* cache; the debugger prepares to use a new core file and discards any old information. You won't, however, always need to issue `core-file` when reading a new datum; *gdb* reads the core in chunks of one kilobyte and caches only chunks it has already referenced.

What you cannot do with plain *gdb* is modify kernel data; the debugger won't try to modify the core file, because it wants to run the program being debugged before accessing its memory image. When debugging a kernel image, issuing the `run` command results in a segmentation fault after a few instructions have executed. For this reason, */proc/kcore* doesn't even implement a *write* method.

If you compile the kernel with debugging support (*–g*), the resulting *vmlinux* file turns out to be a better candidate for use with *gdb* than the same file compiled without *–g*. Note, however, that a huge amount of disk space is needed to compile the kernel with the *–g* option—a version 2.0 kernel image with networking and a minimum set of devices and filesystems occupies more than 11 megs on the PC. Anyway, you can still make the *zImage* file and use it for booting: the debugging information added by *–g* is stripped out when the bootable image is built. If I had enough disk space, I'd always compile with *–g* turned on.

On non-PC computers, the game is different. On the Alpha, `make boot` strips the kernel before creating the bootable image, so you end up with both the *vmlinux* and the *vmlinux.gz* files. The former is useable by *gdb,* and you can boot from the latter. On the Sparc, the kernel (at least the 2.0 kernel) is not stripped by default, so you need to strip it yourself before passing it to *silo* (the Sparc loader) for booting. Neither *milo* (the Alpha loader) nor *silo* can boot an unstripped kernel, due to its size.

When you compile the kernel with –g, and you run the debugger using *vmlinux* together with */proc/kcore, gdb* can return a lot of information about the kernel internals. You can, for example, use commands like `p *module_list`, `p *module_list->next`, and `p *chrdevs[4]->fops` to dump structures. This *sniffing* operation is most interesting if you keep a kernel map and the source code handy.

Another useful task that *gdb* performs on the current kernel is disassembling functions, via the `disassemble` command (which can be abbreviated) or the "examine instructions" (`x/i`) command. The `disassemble` command can take as its argument either a function name or a memory range, while `x/i` takes a single memory address, also in the form of a symbol name. You can invoke, for example, `x/20i` to disassemble 20 instructions. Note that you can't disassemble a module function, because the debugger is acting on *vmlinux,* which doesn't know about your module. If you try to disassemble a module by address, *gdb* is most likely to reply "Cannot access memory at xxxx." For the same reason, you can't look at data items belonging to a module. They can be read from */dev/mem* if you know the address of your variables, but it's hard to make sense out of raw data extracted from system RAM.

If you want to disassemble a module function, you're better off running the *objdump* utility on the module object file. Unfortunately, the tool runs on the disk copy of the file, not the running one; therefore, the addresses as shown by *objdump* will be the addresses before relocation, unrelated to the module's execution environment.

As you see, *gdb* is a useful tool when your aim is to peek into the running kernel, but it lacks some features, the most important being the ability to modify kernel items and to access modules. This hole is filled by the *kdebug* package.

Using kdebug

kdebug can be retrieved from the usual FTP sites under *pcmcia/extras,* but if you want to be sure to retrieve the latest version, you should look at *ftp://hyper.stanford.edu/pub/pcmcia/extras/.* The tool is not actually related to *pcmcia,* but the two packages are written by the same author.

kdebug is a small tool that uses the "remote debugging" interface of *gdb* to talk to the running kernel. A module is loaded into the system, and the debugger is fired up using */dev/kdebug* to access kernel data. *gdb* thinks the device is a serial port that communicates with the "application" being debugged, but it is really only a communication channel for accessing kernel space. Because the module itself is running in kernel space, you can look at kernel-space addresses that you can't access with the plain debugger. As you may have guessed, the module is a char driver, and it uses dynamic assignment of the major number.

The benefit of *kdebug* is that it doesn't force you to patch and recompile anything: neither the kernel nor the debugger. All you need to do is compile and install the package, and then invoke *kgdb*, a script that performs some set-up and calls *gdb* using the new interface to the kernel internals.

Even *kdebug*, however, doesn't provide the ability to step through kernel code or to set breakpoints. This is almost unavoidable, because the kernel must run to keep the system alive, and the only way to step through kernel code is to control the system via a serial line from another computer, as described later. The implementation of *kgdb* nonetheless allows the user to modify data items in the application being debugged (i.e., the current kernel), to call functions by passing them arbitrary parameters, and to access, in a read-write fashion, the address ranges occupied by modules.

That last feature is achieved by adding the module's symbol table to the debugger's internal table using *gdb* commands. This task is performed by the *kgdb* script. *gdb* then knows what address to ask for whenever the user requests access to a particular symbol. The actual access is performed by kernel code in the module. Note, however, that the current version of *kdebug* (1.6) has some problems in mapping symbols to addresses for modularized code. You are better off making some checks with the version you are using by printing the address of a few symbols and comparing them to */proc/ksyms*. If the addresses are mismatched, you can still use numeric values and cast them to the correct type. The following is an example of such a cast:

```
(gdb) p (struct file_operations)(*0x02015cf0)
$16 = {lseek = 0x20152d0 <kmouse_seek>,
read = 0x20154fc <kmouse_read_data>,
write = 0x2015738 <kmouse_write_data>,
readdir = 0, select = 0x201585c <kmouse_select>,
ioctl = 0x20158ec <kmouse_ioctl>,
mmap = 0, open = 0x20152dc <kmouse_open>,
release = 0x2015448 <kmouse_release>, fsync = 0,
fasync = 0x2015a8c <kmouse_fasync>, check_media_change = 0,
revalidate = 0}
```

Another advantage of *kdebug* over plain *gdb* is that it permits you to read the data structures as they change, without the need to flush the debugger's cache; the *gdb* command **set remotecache 0** can be used to disable data caching.

I won't show any more examples of interaction with the tool, because it works like plain *gdb*. Such examples would be trivial for those who know how to use the debugger and obscure for those who don't. Becoming skilled in using a debugger takes time and experience, and I won't undertake the role of teacher.

All in all, *kdebug* is a really good program to have available. Being able to easily modify data structures on the fly is a real win for a developer (and a good way to hang your computer with a single typo). There are times when the tool makes your life easier—for example, during the development of *scull*, I used *kdebug* to reset the usage count for the module to 0, after it got screwed up.* This saved me from the annoyance of having to reboot, log in, and start all my applications running again.

Remote Debugging

The final option for debugging a kernel image is to use the remote-debugging capabilities of *gdb*.

When performing remote debugging, you need two computers: one runs *gdb*, and the other runs the kernel you want to debug. The two computers are linked by a conventional serial line. As you might expect, the controlling *gdb* must be able to understand the binary format of the kernel it controls. If the computers have different architectures, the debugger must be compiled to support its target platform.

As of 2.0, the Intel port of the Linux kernel doesn't support remote debugging, but the Alpha and the Sparc versions do. On the Alpha, you must include support for remote debugging at compile time and enable it at boot time by passing the kernel the command-line argument `kgdb=1`, or just `kgdb`. On the Sparc, support for remote debugging is always included. The boot option `kgdb=ttyx` selects which serial line is used to control the kernel, where *x* is `a` or `b`. If no `kgdb=` option is used, the kernel boots in the normal way.

If remote debugging is enabled on the kernel, a special initialization function is called at boot that sets up the controlled kernel to handle its own breakpoints and then jumps to a breakpoint purposely compiled into the program. This stops normal execution of the kernel and transfers control to the breakpoint-service routine. Such a handler waits to receive commands from *gdb* via the serial line and, when it gets one, executes it. With this setup, the programmer can single-step through the code, set breakpoints, and do all the other nifty things *gdb* usually allows.

On the controlling side, a copy of the target image is needed (let's assume it's called *linux.img*) as well as a copy of any module you want to debug. The following commands must be passed to *gdb*:

---

* The usage count is the very first word of a module's address space, though this fact is undocumented and could change in the future.

`file linux.img`

> The `file` command tells *gdb* which binary file is being debugged. Alternatively, the image filename can be passed on the command line. The file itself must be identical to the kernel running on the other side of the link.

`target remote /dev/ttyS1`

> This command instructs *gdb* to use the remote computer as the target of the debugging session. */dev/ttyS1* is the local serial port used to communicate, and you can specify any device. The *kgdb* script part of the *kdebug* package introduced above, for example, uses `target remote /dev/kdebug`.

`add-symbol-file` *module.o address*

> If you want to debug a module that has been loaded on the controlled kernel, you need a copy of the module object on the controlling system. `add-symbol-file` prepares *gdb* to deal with the module, assuming its code has been relocated to address *address*.

Even though remote debugging can be used with modules, it's quite tricky to do so, since you have to load the module and hit another breakpoint before you can insert a new breakpoint in the module itself. I personally wouldn't use remote debugging to trace a module unless there are major problems with parts of the code that run asynchronously, like interrupt handlers.

CHAPTER FIVE

ENHANCED CHAR DRIVER OPERATIONS

In the chapter about char drivers, we built a complete device driver, which the user can write to and read from. But a real device usually offers more functionality than synchronous *read* and *write*. Now that we're equipped with debugging tools should something go awry, we can safely go ahead and implement new operations.

One of the functionalities that usually complements the need for reading and writing the device is controlling the hardware, and the most common way to perform control operations via a device driver is implementing the *ioctl* method. The alternative is to look at the data flow being written to the device and use special sequences as control commands. Though this latter technique is sometimes used, it should be avoided whenever possible. Nonetheless, I'll describe it later in this chapter in "Device Control Without ioctl."

As I suggested in the previous chapter, the *ioctl* system call offers a device-specific entry point for the driver to issue "commands." *ioctl* is device-specific in that, unlike *read* and other methods, it allows applications to access specific features of the hardware being driven—configuring the device and entering or exiting operating modes. These "control operations" are usually not available through the read/write file abstraction. For example, everything you write to a serial port is transmitted through the port, and you cannot change the baud rate by writing to the device. That is what *ioctl* is for: controlling the I/O channel.

Another important feature of real devices (unlike *scull*) is that data being read or written is exchanged with other hardware, and some synchronization is needed. The concepts of blocking I/O and asynchronous notification fill the gap and are introduced in this chapter by means of a modified *scull* device. The driver uses interaction between different processes to create asynchronous events. As with the original *scull*, you don't need special hardware to test the driver's workings. We *will* definitely deal with real hardware, but not until Chapter 8, *Hardware Management*.

ioctl

The *ioctl* function call in the user space corresponds to the following prototype:

```
int ioctl(int fd, int cmd, ...);
```

The prototype stands out in the list of Unix system calls because of the dots, which usually represent a variable number of arguments. In a real system, however, a system call can't actually have a variable number of arguments. System calls must have a well-defined number of arguments because user programs can access them only through hardware "gates," as outlined in "User Space and Kernel Space" in Chapter 2, *Building and Running Modules.* Therefore, the third argument of *ioctl* is actually a single optional argument, and the dots are simply there to prevent type checking during compilation. The actual nature of the third argument depends on the specific control command being issued (the second argument). Some commands take no arguments, some take an integer value, and some take a pointer to other data. Using a pointer is the way to pass arbitrary data to the *ioctl* call; the device will be able to retrieve any amount of data from user space.

Arguments to the system call are passed to the driver method according to the method declaration:

```
int (*ioctl) (struct inode *inode, struct file *filp,
              unsigned int cmd, unsigned long arg);
```

The `inode` and `filp` pointers are the values corresponding to the file descriptor `fd` passed on by the application and are used in the same way as *read* and *write* use them. The `cmd` argument is passed unchanged, and the optional `arg` argument is passed in the form of an `unsigned long`, regardless of whether it was passed as an integer or a pointer. If the invoking program doesn't pass a third argument, the `arg` value received by the driver operation won't be meaningful.

Since type checking is disabled on the extra argument, the compiler can't warn you if an invalid argument is passed to *ioctl*, and the programmer won't notice the error until run time. This is the only problem I see with the *ioctl* semantics.

As you might imagine, most *ioctl* implementations consist of a `switch` statement that selects the correct behavior according to the `cmd` argument. Different commands have different numeric values, which are usually given symbolic names to simplify coding. The symbolic name is assigned by a preprocessor definition. Custom drivers usually declare such symbols in their header files; *scull.h* declares them for *scull.*

Choosing the ioctl Commands

Before writing the code for *ioctl*, you need to choose the numbers that correspond to commands. Unfortunately, the simple choice of using small numbers starting from 1 and going up doesn't work well.

The command numbers should be unique across the system, in order to prevent errors caused by issuing the right command to the wrong device. Such a mismatch is not unlikely to happen, and a program might find itself trying to change the baud rate of a non-serial-port input stream, like a FIFO or the *kmouse* device. If each *ioctl* number is unique, then the application will get an EINVAL error, rather than succeeding in doing something unintended.

To the aim of uniqueness, every command number can be thought of as consisting of multiple bitfields. The first versions of Linux used 16-bit numbers: the top eight were the "magic" number associated with the device, and the bottom eight were a sequential number, unique within the device. This happened because Linus was "clueless" (his own word) and a better division of bitfields was conceived only later. Unfortunately, few drivers use the new convention, which discourages programmers from sticking to the convention. In my sources, I'll use the new way of defining commands in order to exploit what it offers and to avoid being banned as a heretic by other developers.

To choose *ioctl* numbers for your driver, you should first check *include/asm/ioctl.h* and *Documentation/ioctl-number.txt*. The header defines the bitfields: type (magic number), ordinal number, direction of transfer, and size of argument. The *ioctl-number.txt* file lists the magic numbers used throughout the kernel. The new version of this file (2.0 and later kernels) also lists the reasons why the convention should be used.

Unfortunately, the complete set of macros to split the *ioctl* bit fields was missing from the header files released with Linux 1.2.x. If you want to use the new way, as I do in *scull*, and remain backward-compatible, you should use the lines of code from *scull/sysdep.h*, where I document and fix the problems.

The old, and now deprecated, way of choosing an *ioctl* number was easy: choose a magic 8-bit number, such as "k" (hex 0x6b), and add an ordinal number, like this:

```
#define SCULL_IOCTL1 0x6b01
#define SCULL_IOCTL2 0x6b02
/* .... */
```

If both the application and the driver agree on the numbers, you only need to implement the switch statement in your driver. However, this way of defining *ioctl* numbers, which has its foundations in Unix tradition, shouldn't be used any more in favor of a new convention. I've only shown the old way to give you a taste of what *ioctl* numbers look like.

The new way to define numbers uses four bitfields, which have the following meanings. Any new symbols I introduce in the list below are defined in `<linux/ioctl.h>`.

type

> The magic number. Just choose one number and use it throughout the driver. This field is 8 bits wide (_IOC_TYPEBITS).

number

> The ordinal (sequential) number. It's 8 bits (_IOC_NRBITS) wide.

direction

> The direction of data transfer, if the particular command involves a data transfer. The possible values are _IOC_NONE (no data transfer), _IOC_READ, _IOC_WRITE, and _IOC_READ | _IOC_WRITE (data is transferred both ways). Data transfer is seen from the application's point of view; _IOC_READ means reading *from* the device, so the driver must write to user space. Note that the field is a bitmask, so _IOC_READ and _IOC_WRITE can be extracted using a logical AND operation.

size

> The size of data transfer involved. The width of this field is architecture-dependent and currently ranges from 8 to 14 bits. You can find its value for your specific architecture in the macro _IOC_SIZEBITS. If you intend your driver to be portable, however, you can only count on a size up to 255. It's not mandatory that you use the size field. If you need larger data transfers, you can just ignore it. We'll see soon how this field is used.

The header file <asm/ioctl.h>, which is included by <linux/ioctl.h>, defines macros that help set up the command numbers: _IO(type,nr), _IOR(type,nr,size), _IOW(type,nr,size), and _IOWR(type,nr, size). Each macro corresponds to one of the possible values for the direction of the transfer, while the other bitfields are passed as arguments. The header also defines macros to decode the numbers: _IOC_DIR(nr), _IOC_TYPE(nr), _IOC_NR(nr), and _IOC_SIZE(nr). I won't go into any more detail about these macros, as the header file is clear, and sample code is shown later in this section.

Here is how some *ioctl* commands are defined in *scull*. In particular, these commands set and get the driver's configurable parameters. In the standard macros, the size of the data item that is to be transferred is represented by an instance of the item itself, not sizeof(item), because sizeof is part of the macro expansion.

```
/* Use 'k' as magic number */
#define SCULL_IOC_MAGIC  'k'

#define SCULL_IOCRESET    _IO(SCULL_IOC_MAGIC, 0)

/*
 * S means "Set" through a ptr,
 * T means "Tell" directly with the argument value
 * G means "Get": reply by setting through a pointer
```

```
 * Q means "Query": response is on the return value
 * X means "eXchange": G and S atomically
 * H means "sHift": T and Q atomically
 */
#define SCULL_IOCSQUANTUM _IOW(SCULL_IOC_MAGIC,  1, scull_quantum)
#define SCULL_IOCSQSET    _IOW(SCULL_IOC_MAGIC,  2, scull_qset)
#define SCULL_IOCTQUANTUM _IO(SCULL_IOC_MAGIC,   3)
#define SCULL_IOCTQSET    _IO(SCULL_IOC_MAGIC,   4)
#define SCULL_IOCGQUANTUM _IOR(SCULL_IOC_MAGIC,  5, scull_quantum)
#define SCULL_IOCGQSET    _IOR(SCULL_IOC_MAGIC,  6, scull_qset)
#define SCULL_IOCQQUANTUM _IO(SCULL_IOC_MAGIC,   7)
#define SCULL_IOCQQSET    _IO(SCULL_IOC_MAGIC,   8)
#define SCULL_IOCXQUANTUM _IOWR(SCULL_IOC_MAGIC, 9, scull_quantum)
#define SCULL_IOCXQSET    _IOWR(SCULL_IOC_MAGIC,10, scull_qset)
#define SCULL_IOCHQUANTUM _IO(SCULL_IOC_MAGIC,  11)
#define SCULL_IOCHQSET    _IO(SCULL_IOC_MAGIC,  12)

#define SCULL_IOCHARDRESET _IO(SCULL_IOC_MAGIC, 15) /* debugging tool */

#define SCULL_IOC_MAXNR 15
```

The last command, `HARDRESET`, is used to reset the module's usage count to 0, so the module can be unloaded should something go wrong with the counter. The actual source file also defines all the commands between `IOCHQSET` and `HARDRESET`, although they're not shown here.

I chose to implement both ways of passing integer arguments—by pointer and by explicit value, although by an established convention *ioctl* should exchange values by pointer. Similarly, both ways are used to return an integer number: by pointer or by setting the return value. This works as long as the return value is a positive integer; on return from any system call, a positive value is preserved (as we saw for *read* and *write*), while a negative value is considered an error and is used to set `errno` in user space.

The "exchange" and "shift" operations are not particularly useful for *scull*. I implemented "exchange" to show all the possibilities for the "direction" bitfield, and "shift" to pair "tell" and "query." There are times when atomic* test-and-set operations like these are needed—in particular, when applications need to set or release locks.

The explicit ordinal number of the command has no specific meaning. It is used only to tell the commands apart. Actually, you could even use the same ordinal number for a read command and a write command, since the actual *ioctl* number is different in the "direction" bits. I chose not to use the ordinal number of the command anywhere but in the declaration, so I didn't assign a symbolic value to

---

* A fragment of program code is said to be "atomic" when it will always be executed as though it were a single instruction, without the possibility for anything to happen in between.

it. That's why explicit numbers appear in the definition above. I'm showing you one way to use the command numbers, but you are free to do it differently.

The value of the `cmd` argument is not currently used by the kernel, and it's quite unlikely it will be in the future. Therefore, you could, if you were feeling lazy, avoid the complex declarations above and explicitly declare a set of 16-bit numbers. On the other hand, if you did, you wouldn't benefit from using the bitfields. The header `<linux/kd.h>` is an example of this old-fashioned approach, although it was done that way because it used the technology then available, not out of laziness. Changing it now would require recompiling too many applications.

The Return Value

The implementation of *ioctl* is usually a `switch` statement based on the command number. But what should the `default` selection be when the command number doesn't match a valid operation? The question is controversial. Most kernel functions return `-EINVAL` ("Invalid argument"), which makes sense, because the command argument is indeed not a valid one. The POSIX standard, however, states that if an inappropriate *ioctl* command has been issued, then `-ENOTTY` should be returned. The corresponding message string is "Not a typewriter"—not what the user expects to see. You have to decide whether you want to stick to the standard or to common sense. We'll see later in this chapter why compliance to POSIX requires `ENOTTY`.

The Predefined Commands

Though the *ioctl* system call is most often used to act on devices, a few commands are recognized by the kernel. Note that these commands are decoded *before* your own file operations are called, so if you choose the same number for one of your *ioctl* commands, you won't ever see any request for that command, and the application will ask for something unexpected, due to the collision caused by the non-uniqueness of the *ioctl* number.

The predefined commands are divided into three groups: those issued on any file (regular, device, FIFO, or socket), those that are issued only on regular files, and those specific to the filesystem type; commands in the last group are executed by the implementation of the hosting filesystem (see the *chattr* command). Device-driver writers are only interested in the first group of commands, whose magic number is "T." Looking at the workings of the other groups is left as an exercise to the reader; *ext2_ioctl* is a most interesting function (though easier than you may expect), as it implements the append-only flag and the immutable flag.

The following *ioctl* commands are predefined for any file:

`FIOCLEX`
    Set the close-on-exec flag (File IOctl CLose on EXec).

FIONCLEX

Clear the close-on-exec flag.

FIOASYNC

Set or reset synchronous write for the file. Synchronous write is not yet implemented in Linux; the call exists so that applications asking for synchronous writes can be compiled and run without complaining. If you don't know what synchronous write is, you don't need to worry about it: you won't need it.

FIONBIO

"File IOctl Nonblocking I/O" (described later in "Blocking and Nonblocking Operations"). This call modifies the O_NONBLOCK flag in `filp->f_flags`. The third argument to the system call is used to indicate whether the flag is to be set or cleared. We'll look at the role of the flag later in this chapter. Note that the flag can also be changed by the *fcntl* system call, using the F_SETFL command.

The last item in the list introduced a new system call, *fcntl*, which looks like *ioctl*. In fact, the *fcntl* call is very similar to *ioctl* in that it gets a command argument and an extra (optional) argument. It is kept separate from *ioctl* mainly for historical reasons: when Unix developers faced the problem of "controlling" I/O operations, they decided that files and devices were different. At the time, the only devices were ttys, which explains why -ENOTTY is the standard reply for an incorrect *ioctl* command. The issue is the old one of whether or not to be backwards compatible.

Using the ioctl Argument

The last point we need to cover before looking at the *ioctl* code for the *scull* driver is how to use the extra argument. If it is an integer, it's easy: it can be used directly. If it is a pointer, however, some care must be taken.

When a pointer is used to refer to user space, we must ensure that the user address is valid and that the corresponding page is currently mapped. If kernel code tries to access an address out of range, the processor issues an exception. Exceptions in kernel code are turned to oops messages by every Linux kernel up through 2.0.*x*. A device driver should prevent these faults by verifying that the user-space addresses it is going to access are valid, and it should return an error if they aren't.

One of the new features introduced in Linux 2.1 is exception handling for kernel code. Unfortunately, the correct implementation required non-trivial changes to the driver-kernel interface. This chapter presents a method that is suitable only for older kernels, 1.2.13 to 2.0.*x*, inclusive. The new interface is discussed in "Handling Kernel-Space Faults," in Chapter 17, *Recent Developments*, and the sample code shown there allows your driver to extend the range of supported kernels to 2.1.43 by using some hairy preprocessor macros.

Address verification for kernels 1.*x*.*y* and 2.0.*x* is implemented in the function *verify_area*, whose prototype resides in `<linux/mm.h>`:

```
int verify_area(int mode, const void *ptr, unsigned long extent);
```

The first argument should be either `VERIFY_READ` or `VERIFY_WRITE`, depending on whether the action to be performed is reading the memory area or writing it. The `ptr` argument holds a user-space address, and `extent` is a byte count. If *ioctl*, for instance, needs to read an integer value from user space, `extent` is `sizeof(int)`. If you need to both read and write at the given address, use `VERIFY_WRITE`, as it is a superset of `VERIFY_READ`.

Verifying for reading checks that the address is valid; in addition to this, verifying for writing takes care of read-only and copy-on-write pages. A copy-on-write page is a shared writable page that has never been written by any of the sharing processes; when you verify for writing, *verify_area* performs the "copy-and-make-writable" operation. It's interesting to note that there's no need to check that the page is actually "present" in memory, as valid page faults are correctly managed by the fault handler even when called from kernel code. We've already seen that kernel code can successfully page-fault in "Scull's Memory Usage" in Chapter 3, *Char Drivers*.

Like most functions, *verify_area* returns an integer value: 0 means success, and a negative value signals an error, which should be returned to the caller.

The *scull* source exploits the bitfields in the *ioctl* number to check the arguments before the `switch`:

```
int err = 0, tmp, size = _IOC_SIZE(cmd); /* the size bitfield in cmd */

/*
 * extract the type and number bitfields, and don't decode
 * wrong cmds: return EINVAL before verify_area()
 */
if (_IOC_TYPE(cmd) != SCULL_IOC_MAGIC) return -EINVAL;
if (_IOC_NR(cmd) > SCULL_IOC_MAXNR) return -EINVAL;

/*
 * the direction is a bitmask, and VERIFY_WRITE catches R/W
 * transfers. 'Type' is user-oriented, while
 * verify_area is kernel-oriented, so the concept of "read" and
 * "write" is reversed
 */
if (_IOC_DIR(cmd) & _IOC_READ)
    err = verify_area(VERIFY_WRITE, (void *)arg, size);
else if (_IOC_DIR(cmd) & _IOC_WRITE)
    err = verify_area(VERIFY_READ, (void *)arg, size);
if (err) return err;
```

After calling *verify_area*, the driver can perform the actual transfer. In addition to the *memcpy_tofs* and *memcpy_fromfs* functions, the programmer can exploit two functions that are optimized for the most-used data sizes (1, 2, and 4 bytes, as well as 8 bytes on 64-bit platforms). The functions are defined in <asm/segment.h>.

put_user(datum, ptr)

This is actually a macro that calls the inline function *__put_user*; it expands to a single machine instruction at compile time. Drivers should use *put_user* whenever possible instead of *memcpy_tofs*. Since type checking is not per-formed on macro expansion, you can pass any type of pointer to *put_user*, and it should be a user-space address. The size of the data transfer depends on the type of the ptr argument and is determined at compile time using a special *gcc* pseudo-function that isn't worth showing here. As a result, if ptr is a char pointer, 1 byte is transferred, and so on for 2, 4, and possibly 8 bytes. If the data that is pointed to is not one of the supported sizes, the compiled code calls the function *bad_user_access_length*. If such compiled code is a module, it isn't loadable, as the symbol is not exported.

get_user(ptr)

This macro is used to retrieve a single datum from user space. It behaves exactly like *put_user*, but it transfers data in the opposite direction.

The awkwardly long name of *bad_user_access_length* is meant to build a mean-ingful error message when *insmod* doesn't resolve the symbol. Hopefully, the developer will load and test the module before distributing it to the general public, and will find and fix the error. Conversely, if a driver with an incorrectly sized *put_user* or *get_user* is directly linked into the kernel, *bad_user_access_length* causes a system panic. Although an oops would be a friendlier response than a system panic to a missized data transfer, the aggressive approach has been chosen to strongly discourage such errors.

The *scull* implementation of *ioctl* only transfers the configurable parameters of the device and turns out to be as easy as the following:

```
switch(cmd) {

    #ifdef SCULL_DEBUG
        case SCULL_IOCHARDRESET:
        /*
         * reset the counter to 1, to allow unloading in case
         * of problems. Use 1, not 0, because the invoking file
         * is still to be closed.
         */
            mod_use_count_ = 1;
        /* don't break: fall through */
    #endif

    case SCULL_IOCRESET:
        scull_quantum = SCULL_QUANTUM;
        scull_qset = SCULL_QSET;
        break;
```

```
        case SCULL_IOCSQUANTUM: /* Set: arg points to the value */
            scull_quantum = get_user((int *)arg);
            break;

        case SCULL_IOCTQUANTUM: /* Tell: arg is the value */
            scull_quantum = arg;
            break;

        case SCULL_IOCGQUANTUM: /* Get: arg is pointer to result */
            put_user(scull_quantum, (int *)arg);
            break;

        case SCULL_IOCQQUANTUM: /* Query: return it (it's positive) */
            return scull_quantum;

        case SCULL_IOCXQUANTUM: /* eXchange: use arg as pointer */
            tmp = scull_quantum;
            scull_quantum = get_user((int *)arg);
            put_user(tmp, (int *)arg);
            break;

        case SCULL_IOCHQUANTUM: /* sHift: like Tell + Query */
            tmp = scull_quantum;
            scull_quantum = arg;
            return tmp;

        default:  /* redundant, as cmd was checked against MAXNR */
            return -EINVAL;

    }
    return 0;
```

There are also six entries that act on `scull_qset`. These entries are identical to the ones for `scull_quantum` and are not shown in the example above, to save space.

The six ways to pass and receive arguments look like the following from the caller's point of view (i.e., from user space):

```
int quantum;

ioctl(fd,SCULL_IOCSQUANTUM, &quantum);
ioctl(fd,SCULL_IOCTQUANTUM, quantum);
ioctl(fd,SCULL_IOCGQUANTUM, &quantum);
quantum = ioctl(fd,SCULL_IOCQQUANTUM);
ioctl(fd,SCULL_IOCXQUANTUM, &quantum);
quantum = ioctl(fd,SCULL_IOCHQUANTUM, quantum);
```

If you want to write a module that runs with Linux-1.2, *get_user* and *put_user* can cause you some headaches, because they weren't introduced until the first 1.3

kernels. Before switching to type-independent macros, programmers used functions called *get_user_byte*, etc. The old macros are defined in the 1.3 and 2.0 kernels only if you issue the `#define WE_REALLY_WANT_TO_USE_A_BROKEN_INTERFACE` preprocessor command in advance. However, defining *put_user* for older kernels is a better approach to portability, so *scull/sysdep.h* contains the definition of the good macros in order to run the driver with older kernels without problems.

Device Control Without ioctl

Sometimes controlling the device is better accomplished by writing control sequences to the device itself. This technique is used, for example, in the console driver, where so-called "escape sequences" are used to move the cursor, change the default color, or perform other configuration tasks. The benefit of implementing device control this way is that the user can control the device just by writing data, without needing to use (or sometimes write) programs built just for configuring the device.

For example, the *setterm* program acts on the console (or another terminal) configuration by printing escape sequences. This behavior has the advantage of permitting the remote control of devices. The controlling program can live on a different computer than the controlled device, because a simple redirection of the data stream does the configuration job. You're already used to this with ttys, but the technique is more general.

The drawback of "controlling by printing" is that it adds policy contraints to the device; for example, it is viable only if you are sure that the control sequence can't appear in the data being written to the device during normal operation. This is only partly true for ttys. While a text display is meant to display only ASCII characters, sometimes control characters can slip through in the data being written and can thus affect the console setup. This can happen, for example, when you issue *grep* on a binary file; the extracted lines can contain anything, and you often end up with the wrong font on your console.*

Controlling-by-write *is* definitely the way to go for those devices that don't transfer data, but just respond to commands, like robotic devices.

For instance, one of the drivers I wrote for fun moves a camera on two axes. In this driver, the "device" is simply a pair of old stepper motors, which can't really be read from or written to. The concept of "sending a data stream" to a stepper motor makes little or no sense. In this case, the driver interprets what is being written as ASCII commands and converts the requests to sequences of impulses that manipulate the stepper motors. The commands can be anything like "move

---

* **Ctrl-N** sets the alternate font, which is made up of graphic symbols and thus isn't a friendly font for typing input to your shell; if you encounter this problem, echo a **Ctrl-O** character to restore the primary font.

left by 14 steps," "reach position 100,43," or "lower the default speed." This driver uses the device node in */dev* only as a command channel for the applications. The advantage of direct control for this device is that you can use *cat* to move the camera without writing and compiling special code to issue the *ioctl* calls.

When writing "command-oriented" drivers, there's no reason to implement the *ioctl* method. An additional command in the interpreter is much easier both to implement and to use.

The curious reader can look at the source code for my stepper driver in the directory *stepper* in the source files provided on the O'Reilly FTP site; it's not included here, as I don't consider the code particularly interesting (nor is it particularly high quality).

Blocking I/O

One problem that might arise with *read* is what to do when there's no data *yet*, but we're not at end-of-file.

The default answer is "we must go to sleep waiting for data." This section shows how a process is put to sleep, how it is awakened, and how an application can ask if there is data, without blocking within the *read* call. We'll then apply the same concepts to *write*.

As usual, before I show you the real code, I'll explain a few concepts.

Going to Sleep and Awakening

When a process is waiting for an event (be it input data, the termination of a child process, or whatever else) it should be put to sleep so another process can use the computational resources. You can put a process to sleep by calling one of the following functions:

```
void interruptible_sleep_on(struct wait_queue **q);
void sleep_on(struct wait_queue **q);
```

Processes are then awakened by one of:

```
void wake_up_interruptible(struct wait_queue **q);
void wake_up(struct wait_queue **q);
```

In the preceding functions, the `wait_queue` pointer-pointer is used to refer to an event; we'll discuss it in detail later in "Wait Queues." For now, it will suffice to say that processes are awakened using the same queue that put them to sleep. Thus, you'll need one wait queue for each event that can block processes. If you manage four devices, you'll need four wait queues for blocking-read and four for blocking-write. The preferred place to put such queues is the hardware data structure associated with each device (`Scull_Dev` in our example).

But what's the difference between "interruptible" and plain calls?

sleep_on can't be aborted by a signal, while *interruptible_sleep_on* can. In practice, *sleep_on* is called only by critical sections of the kernel; for example, while waiting for a swap page to be read from disk. The process can't proceed without the page, and interrupting the operation with a signal doesn't make sense. *interruptible_sleep_on*, on the other hand, is used during so-called "long system calls," like *read*. It *does* make sense to kill a process with a signal while it's waiting for keyboard input.

Similarly, *wake_up* wakes any process sleeping on the queue, while *wake_up_interruptible* wakes only interruptible processes.

As a driver writer, you'll call *interruptible_sleep_on* and *wake_up_interruptible*, because a process sleeps in the driver's code only during *read* or *write*. Actually, you could call *wake_up* as well, since no "uninterruptible" processes will sleep on your queue. However, that's not usually done, for the sake of consistency in the source code. (In addition, *wake_up* is also slightly slower than its counterpart.)

Writing Reentrant Code

When a process is put to sleep, the driver is still alive and can be called by another process. Let's consider the console driver as an example. While an application is waiting for keyboard input on tty1, the user switches to tty2 and spawns a new shell. Now both shells are waiting for keyboard input within the console driver, although they sleep on different wait queues: one on the queue associated with tty1 and the other on the queue associated with tty2. Each process is locked within the *interruptible_sleep_on* function, but the driver can still receive and answer requests from other ttys.

Such situations can be handled painlessly by writing "reentrant code." Reentrant code is code that doesn't keep status information in global variables and thus is able to manage interwoven invocation without mixing anything up. If all the status information is process-specific, no interference will ever happen.

If status information is needed, it can either be kept in local variables within the driver function (each process has a different stack page where local variables are stored), or it can reside in `private_data` within the `filp` accessing the file. Using local variables is preferred, because sometimes the same `filp` can be shared between two processes (usually parent and child).

If you need to save large amounts of status data, you can keep the pointer in a local variable and use *kmalloc* to retrieve the actual storage space. In this case you must remember to *kfree* the data, because there's no equivalent to "everything is released at process termination" when you're working in kernel space.

You need to make reentrant any function that calls a flavor of *sleep_on* (or just *schedule*) and any function that can be in its call-trace. If *sample_read* calls *sample_getdata*, which in turn can block, then *sample_read* must be reentrant as well as *sample_getdata*, because nothing prevents another process from calling it while it is already executing on behalf of a process that went to sleep. Moreover, any function that copies data to or from user space must be reentrant, as access to user space might page-fault, and the process will be put to sleep while the kernel deals with the missing page.

Wait Queues

The next question I hear you ask is, "How exactly can I use a wait queue?"

A wait queue is easy to use, although its design is quite subtle and you are not expected to peek at its internals. The best way to deal with wait queues is to stick to the following operations:

- Declare a `struct wait_queue *` variable. You need one such pointer variable for each event that can put processes to sleep. This is the item that I suggested you put in the structure describing hardware features.

- Pass a pointer to this variable as argument to the various *sleep_on* and *wake_up* functions.

It's that easy. For example, let's imagine you want to put a process to sleep when it reads your device and awaken it when someone else writes to the device. The following code does just that:

```
struct wait_queue *wq = NULL; /* must be zeroed at the beginning */

read_write_t sleepy_read (struct inode *inode, struct file *filp,
                          char *buf, count_t count)
{
    printk(KERN_DEBUG "process %i (%s) going to sleep\n",
           current->pid, current->comm);
    interruptible_sleep_on(&wq);
    printk(KERN_DEBUG "awoken %i (%s)\n", current->pid, current->comm);
    return 0; /* EOF */
}

read_write_t sleepy_write (struct inode *inode, struct file *filp,
                           const char *buf, count_t count)
{
    printk(KERN_DEBUG "process %i (%s) awakening the readers...\n",
           current->pid, current->comm);
    wake_up_interruptible(&wq);
    return count; /* succeed, to avoid retrial */
}
```

The code for this device is available as *sleepy* in the example programs and can be tested using *cat* and input/output redirection, as usual.

The two operations listed above are the only ones you are allowed to use with a wait queue. However, I know that some readers might be interested in the internals and grasping them from the sources can be difficult. If you're not interested in more detail, you can skip to the next subsection without missing anything. Note that I talk about the "current" implementation (version 2.0.*x*), but there's nothing forcing kernel developers to stick to that implementation. If a better one comes along, the kernel can easily switch to the new one without bad effects as long as driver writers use the wait queue only through the two legal operations.

The current implementation of `struct wait_queue` uses two fields: a pointer to `struct task_struct` (the waiting process), and a pointer to `struct wait_queue` (the next item in the list). A wait queue is always circular, with the last structure pointing to the first.

The compelling feature of the design is that driver writers never declare or use such a structure; they only pass along pointers and pointer-pointers. Actual structures *do* exist, but only in one place: as a local variable within the function __*sleep_on*, which is called by both the *sleep_on* functions introduced above.

Strange as it appears, this is really a smart choice, because there's no need to deal with allocation and deallocation of such structures. A process sleeps on a single queue at a time, and the data structure describing its sleeping exists in the non-swappable stack page associated with the process.

The actual operations performed when a process is added or removed from a wait queue are schematically represented in Figure 5-1.

Blocking and Nonblocking Operations

There is another point we need to touch on before we look at the implementation of full-featured *read* and *write* methods, and that is the O_NONBLOCK flag in `filp->f_flags`. The flag is defined in <linux/fcntl.h>, which is automatically included by <linux/fs.h> in recent kernels. You should include *fcntl.h* manually if you want your module to compile with 1.2.

The flag gets its name from "open-nonblock," because it can be specified at open time (and originally could only be specified there). The flag is reset by default, because the normal behavior of a process waiting for data is just sleeping. In the case of a blocking operation, the following behavior should be implemented:

- If a process calls *read*, but no data is (yet) available, the process must block. The process is awakened as soon as some data arrives, and that data is returned to the caller, even if there is less than the amount requested in the `count` argument to the method.

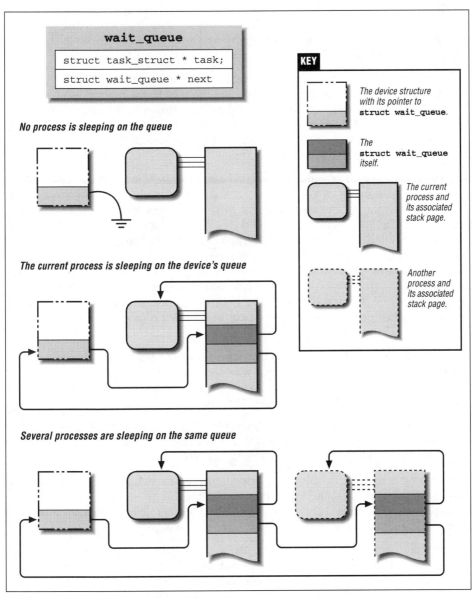

Figure 5-1: *The workings of wait queues*

- If a process calls *write* and there is no space in the buffer, the process must block, and it must be on a different wait queue from the one used for reading.

When some data has been written to the device, and space becomes free in the output buffer, the process is awakened, and the *write* call succeeds, although the data may be only partially written if there isn't room in the buffer for the count bytes that were requested.

Both statements in the previous list assume that there is an input and an output buffer, but every device driver has them. The input buffer is required to avoid losing data that arrives when nobody is reading, and the output buffer is useful for squeezing more performance out of the computer, though it's not strictly compulsory. Data can't be lost on *write*, because if the system call doesn't accept data bytes, they remain in the user-space buffer.

The performance gain of implementing an output buffer in the driver results from the diminished number of context switches and user-level/kernel-level transitions. Without an output buffer (assuming a slow device), only one or a few characters are accepted by each system call, and while one process sleeps in *write*, another process runs (that's one context switch). When the first process is awakened, it resumes (another context switch), *write* returns (kernel/user transition), and the process reiterates the system call to write more data (user/kernel transition); the call blocks, and the loop continues. If the output buffer is big enough, *write* succeeds on the first attempt; data is pushed out to the device at interrupt time, without control ever going back to user space. The choice of a suitable dimension for the output buffer is clearly device-specific.

We didn't use an input buffer in *scull*, because data is already available when *read* is issued. Similarly, no output buffer was used, as data is simply copied to the memory area associated with the device. We'll see the use of buffers in Chapter 9, *Interrupt Handling*, in the section titled "Interrupt-Driven I/O."

The behavior of *read* and *write* is different if O_NONBLOCK is specified. In this case, the calls simply return -EAGAIN if a process calls *read* when no data is available, or if it calls *write* when there's no space in the buffer.

As you might expect, nonblocking operations return immediately, allowing the application to poll for data. Applications must be careful when using the stdio functions when dealing with nonblocking files, because you can easily mistake a nonblocking return for EOF. You always have to check errno.

As you may imagine from its name, O_NONBLOCK is meaningful also in the *open* method. This happens when the call can actually block for a long time; for example, when opening a FIFO that has no writers (yet), or accessing a disk file with a pending lock. Usually, opening a device either succeeds or fails, without the need to wait for external events. Sometimes, however, opening the device requires a long initialization, and you may choose to check O_NONBLOCK, returning immediately with -EAGAIN (try it again) if the flag is set, after spawning device initialization. You might also decide to implement a blocking *open* to support access policies in a way similar to file locks. We'll see one such implementation later in the section "Blocking Open as an Alternative to EBUSY."

Only the *read, write,* and *open* file operations are affected by the nonblocking flag.

A Sample Implementation: scullpipe

The */dev/scullpipe* devices (there are four of them by default) are part of the *scull* module and are used to show how blocking I/O is implemented.

Within a driver, a process blocked in a *read* call is awakened when data arrives; usually the hardware issues an interrupt to signal such an event, and the driver awakens processes while handling the interrupt. The goal of *scull* is different, since you should be able to run *scull* on any computer without requiring any particular hardware—and without any interrupt handler. I chose to use another process to generate the data and wake the reading process; similarly, reading processes are used to wake sleeping writer processes. The resulting implementation is similar to that of a FIFO (or "named pipe") filesystem node, whence the name.

The device driver uses a device structure that embeds two wait queues and a buffer. The size of the buffer is configurable in the usual ways (at compile time, load time, or run time).

```
typedef struct Scull_Pipe {
    struct wait_queue *inq, *outq;   /* read and write queues */
    char *buffer, *end;              /* begin of buf, end of buf */
    int buffersize;                  /* used in pointer arithmetic */
    char *rp, *wp;                   /* where to read, where to write */
    int nreaders, nwriters;          /* number of openings for r/w */
    struct fasync_struct *async_queue; /* asynchronous readers */
} Scull_Pipe;
```

The *read* implementation manages both blocking and nonblocking input and looks like this:

```
read_write_t scull_p_read (struct inode *inode, struct file *filp,
                        char *buf, count_t count)
{
    Scull_Pipe *dev = filp->private_data;

    while (dev->rp == dev->wp) { /* nothing to read */
        if (filp->f_flags & O_NONBLOCK)
            return -EAGAIN;
        PDEBUG("\"%s\" reading: going to sleep\n",current->comm);
        interruptible_sleep_on(&dev->inq);
        if (current->signal & ~current->blocked) /* a signal arrived */
            return -ERESTARTSYS;      /* tell the fs layer to handle it */
        /* otherwise loop */
    }
    /* ok, data is there, return something */
    if (dev->wp > dev->rp)
```

```
            count = min(count, dev->wp - dev->rp);
        else /* the write pointer has wrapped, return data up to dev->end */
            count = min(count, dev->end - dev->rp);
    memcpy_tofs(buf, dev->rp, count);
    dev->rp += count;
    if (dev->rp == dev->end)
        dev->rp = dev->buffer; /* wrapped */

    /* finally, awake any writers and return */
    wake_up_interruptible(&dev->outq);
    PDEBUG("\"%s\" did read %li bytes\n",current->comm, (long)count);
    return count;
}
```

As you can see, I left some PDEBUG statements in the code. When you compile the driver, you can enable messaging to make it easier to follow the interaction of different processes.

The if statement that follows *interruptible_sleep_on* takes care of signal handling. This statement ensures the proper and expected reaction to signals, which is to let the kernel take care of restarting the system call or returning -EINTR (the kernel handles -ERESTARTSYS internally, and what reaches user space is -EINTR instead). We don't want the kernel to do this for blocked signals, though, because we want to ignore them. That is why we check current->blocked and screen out those signals. Otherwise, we pass a -ERESTARTSYS error value back to let the kernel do its work. We'll use the same statement to deal with signal handling for every *read* and *write* implementation.

The implementation for *write* is quite similar to that for *read*. Its only "peculiar" feature is that it never completely fills the buffer, always leaving a hole of at least one byte. Thus when the buffer is empty, wp and rp are equal; when there is data there, they are always different.

```
    read_write_t scull_p_write (struct inode *inode, struct file *filp,
                                const char *buf, count_t count)
    {
        Scull_Pipe *dev = filp->private_data;
        /* left is the free space in the buffer, but it must be positive */
        int left = (dev->rp + dev->buffersize - dev->wp) % dev->buffersize;

        PDEBUG("write: left is %i\n",left);
        while (left==1) { /* empty */
            if (filp->f_flags & O_NONBLOCK)
                return -EAGAIN;
            PDEBUG("\"%s\" writing: going to sleep\n",current->comm);
            interruptible_sleep_on(&dev->outq);
            if (current->signal & ~current->blocked) /* a signal arrived */
              return -ERESTARTSYS; /* tell the fs layer to handle it */
            /* otherwise loop, but recalculate free space */
            left = (dev->rp + dev->buffersize - dev->wp) % dev->buffersize;
        }
```

```
    /* ok, space is there, accept something */
    if (dev->wp >= dev->rp) {
        count = min(count, dev->end - dev->wp); /* up to */
                                               /* end-of-buffer */
        if (count == left) /* leave a hole, even if at e-o-b */
            count--;
    }
    else /* the write pointer has wrapped, fill up to rp-1 */
        count = min(count, dev->rp - dev->wp - 1);
    PDEBUG("Going to accept %li bytes to %p from %p\n",
            (long)count, dev->wp, buf);
    memcpy_fromfs(dev->wp, buf, count);
    dev->wp += count;
    if (dev->wp == dev->end)
        dev ->wp = dev->buffer; /* wrapped */

    /* finally, awake any reader */
    wake_up_interruptible(&dev->inq);  /* blocked in read() */
                                       /* and select() */
    if (dev->async_queue)
        kill_fasync (dev->async_queue, SIGIO); /* asynchr. readers */
    PDEBUG("\"%s\" did write %li bytes\n",current->comm, (long)count);
    return count;
}
```

The device, as I conceived it, doesn't implement blocking *open* and is simpler than a real FIFO. If you want to look at the real thing, you can find it in *fs/pipe.c*, in the kernel sources.

To test the blocking operation of the *scullpipe* device, you can run some programs on it, using input/output redirection as usual. Testing nonblocking activity is trickier, as the conventional programs don't perform nonblocking operations. The *misc-progs* source directory contains the following simple program, called *nbtest*, for testing nonblocking operations. All it does is copy its input to its output, using nonblocking I/O and delaying between retrials. The delay time is passed on the command line and is one second by default.

```
int main(int argc, char **argv)
{
    int delay=1, n, m=0;

    if (argc>1) delay=atoi(argv[1]);
    fcntl(0, F_SETFL, fcntl(0,F_GETFL) | O_NONBLOCK); /* stdin */
    fcntl(1, F_SETFL, fcntl(1,F_GETFL) | O_NONBLOCK); /* stdout */

    while (1) {
        n=read(0, buffer, 4096);
        if (n>=0)
            m=write(1, buffer, n);
        if ((n<0 || m<0) && (errno != EAGAIN))
            break;
        sleep(delay);
```

```
    }
    perror( n<0 ? "stdin" : "stdout");
    exit(1);
}
```

Select

When using nonblocking I/O, applications often exploit the *select* system call, which relies on a device method when it involves device files. This system call is also used to multiplex input from different sources. In the following discussion, I'm assuming that you understand the use of the *select* semantics in user space. Note that version 2.1.23 of the kernel introduced the *poll* system call, thus changing the way the driver method works in order to account for both the system calls.

The implementation of the *select* system call in Linux 2.0 uses a `select_table` structure to keep information about all the files (or devices) being waited for. Once again, you're expected not to look inside the structure (but we'll do it anyway a little later) and are allowed only to call the functions that act on such a structure.

When the *select* method discovers that there's no need to block, it returns 1; when the process should wait, it should "almost" go to sleep. In this case, the correct wait queue is added to the `select_table` structure, and the function returns 0.

The process actually goes to sleep only if no file being selected can accept or return data. This happens in *sys_select*, within *fs/select.c*.

The code for the *select* operation is far easier to write than to describe, and it's high time to show the implementation used in *scull*:

```
int scull_p_select (struct inode *inode, struct file *filp,
                    int mode, select_table *table)
{
    Scull_Pipe *dev = filp->private_data;

    if (mode == SEL_IN) {
        if (dev->rp != dev->wp) return 1; /* readable */
        PDEBUG("Waiting to read\n");
        select_wait(&dev->inq, table); /* wait for data */
        return 0;
    }
    if (mode == SEL_OUT) {
        /*
         * the buffer is full if "wp" is right behind "rp",
         * and the buffer is circular. "left" can't drop
         * to 0, as this would be taken as empty buffer
         */
        int left = (dev->rp + dev->buffersize - dev->wp) %
                    dev->buffersize;
        if (left>1) return 1; /* writable */
```

```
        PDEBUG("Waiting to write\n");
        select_wait(&dev->outq, table); /* wait for free space */
        return 0;
    }
    return 0; /* never exception-able */
}
```

There's no code for the "third form of select," selecting for exceptions. This form is identified by `mode == SEL_EX`, but most of the time you code it as the default case, to be executed when the other checks fail. The meaning of exception events is device-specific, so you can choose whether or not to use them in your own driver. Such a feature will be used only by programs specifically designed to use your driver, but that's exactly its intent. In that respect, it is similar to the device-dependency of the *ioctl* call. In the real world, the main use of exception conditions in *select* is to signal arrival of Out-Of-Band (urgent) data on a network connection, though it is also used in the tty layer and in the pipe/FIFO implementation (you can look for `SEL_EX` in *fs/pipe.c*). Note, however, that other Unix systems don't implement exception conditions for pipes and FIFOs.

The *select* code as shown is missing end-of-file support. When a *read* call is at end-of-file, it should return 0, and *select* must support this behavior by reporting that the device is readable, so the application will actually issue the *read* without waiting forever. With real FIFOs, for example, the reader sees an end-of-file when all the writers close the file, while in *scullpipe* the reader never sees end-of-file. The behavior is different because a FIFO is intended to be a communication channel between two processes, while *scullpipe* is a trashcan where everyone can put data as long as there's at least one reader. Moreover, it makes no sense to reimplement what is already available in the kernel.

Implementing end-of-file as FIFOs do would mean checking `dev->nwriters`, both in *read* and in *select*-for-reading, and acting accordingly. Unfortunately though, if a reader opens the *scullpipe* device before the writer, it sees end-of-file, without having a chance to wait for data. The best way to fix this problem is to implement blocking within *open*, but this task is left as an exercise to the reader.

Interaction with read and write

The purpose of the *select* call is to determine in advance if an I/O operation will block. In that respect, it complements *read* and *write*. *select* is also useful because it lets the driver wait simultaneously for several data streams (but this is not relevant in the case at hand).

A correct implementation of the three calls is fundamental in order to make applications work correctly. Though the following rules have more or less already been stated, I'll summarize them here.

Reading data from the device

If there is data in the input buffer, the *read* call should return immediately, with no noticeable delay, even if less data than requested is available and the driver is sure the remaining data will arrive soon. You can always return less data than you're asked for if this is convenient (we did it in *scull*), provided you return at least one byte. The implementation of bus mice in the current kernel is faulty in this respect, and several programs (like *dd*) fail to correctly read the device.

If there is no data in the input buffer, *read* must block until at least one byte is there, unless O_NONBLOCK is set. A nonblocking *read* returns immediately with a return value of -EAGAIN (although some old versions of SystemV return 0 in this case). *select* must report that the device is unreadable until at least one byte arrives. As soon as there is some data, we fall back to the previous case.

If we are at end-of-file, *read* should return immediately with a return value of 0, independent of O_NONBLOCK. *select* should report that the file is readable.

Writing to the device

If there is space in the output buffer, *write* should return without delay. It can accept less data than the call requested, but it must accept at least one byte. In this case, *select* reports that the device is writable.

If the output buffer is full, *write* blocks until some space is freed, unless O_NONBLOCK is set. A nonblocking write returns immediately, with a return value of -EAGAIN (or conditionally 0, as stated previously for older SystemV reads). *select* should report that the file is not writable. If, on the other hand, the device is not able to accept any more data, *write* returns -ENOSPC ("No space left on device"), independently of O_NONBLOCK.

If the program using the device wants to ensure that the data it queues in the output buffer is actually transmitted, the driver must provide an *fsync* method. For instance, a removable device should have an *fsync* entry point. Never make a *write* call wait for data transmission before returning, even if O_NONBLOCK is clear. This is because many applications use *select* to find out whether a *write* will block. If the device is reported as writable, the call must consistently not block.

Flushing pending output

We've seen how the *write* method doesn't account for all data output needs. The *fsync* function, invoked by the system call of the same name, fills the gap.

If some application will ever need to be assured that data has been sent to the device, the *fsync* method must be implemented. A call to *fsync* should return only when the device has been completely flushed (i.e., the output buffer is empty), even if that takes some time, regardless of whether O_NONBLOCK is set.

The *fsync* method has no unusual features. The call isn't time-critical, so every device driver can implement it to the author's taste. Most of the time, char drivers just have a NULL pointer in their fops. Block devices, on the other hand, always implement the method by calling the general-purpose *block_fsync*, which in turn flushes all the blocks of the device, waiting for I/O to complete.

The Underlying Data Structure

The particular implementation of *select* used in 2.0 kernels is quite efficient and slightly complex. If you're not interested in understanding the secrets of the operating system, you can jump directly to the next section.

First of all, I suggest that you look at Figure 5-2, which represents graphically the steps involved in making a *select* call. Looking at the figure will make it easier to follow the discussion.

The *select* work is performed by the functions *select_wait*, declared inline in <linux/sched.h>, and *free_wait*, defined in *fs/select.c*. The underlying data structure is an array of struct select_table_entry, where each entry is made up of a struct wait_queue and a struct wait_queue **. The former is the actual structure that gets inserted in the wait queue for the device (the one that only exists as a local variable when calling *sleep_on*), while the latter is the "handle" that's needed to remove the current process from the queue when at least one of the selected conditions becomes true—for example, it contains &dev->inq when selecting *scullpipe* for reading (see the earlier example in "Select").

In short, *select_wait* inserts the next free select_table_entry into the specified wait queue. When the system call returns, *free_wait* removes every entry from its own wait queue, using the associated pointer-pointer.

The select_table structure (made up of a pointer to the array of entries and the number of active entries) is declared as a local variable in *do_select*, similar to what happens for __sleep_on. The array of entries, on the other hand, resides in a different page, because it could overflow the stack page for the current process.

If you're having trouble understanding this description, try looking at the source code. Once you understand the implementation, you'll see that it is compact and efficient.

Asynchronous Notification

Though the combination of blocking and nonblocking operations and the *select* method are sufficient for querying the device most of the time, some situations aren't efficiently managed by the techniques we've seen so far. Let's imagine, for example, a process that executes a long computational loop at low priority, but needs to process incoming data as soon as possible. If the input channel is the

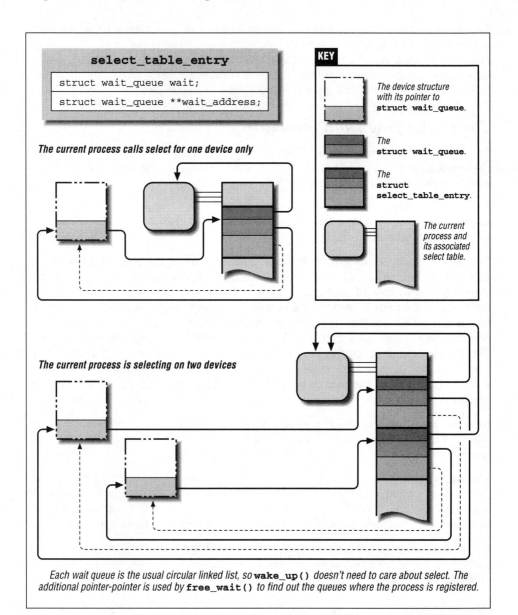

select_table_entry

```
struct wait_queue wait;
struct wait_queue **wait_address;
```

KEY

The device structure with its pointer to struct wait_queue.

The struct wait_queue.

The struct select_table_entry.

The current process and its associated select table.

The current process calls select for one device only

The current process is selecting on two devices

Each wait queue is the usual circular linked list, so wake_up() doesn't need to care about select. The additional pointer-pointer is used by free_wait() to find out the queues where the process is registered.

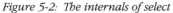

Figure 5-2: The internals of select

keyboard, you are allowed to send a signal to the application (using the "INTR" character, usually **Ctrl-C**), but this signalling ability is part of the tty layer, which isn't attached to general char devices. What we need for asynchronous notification is something different. Furthermore, *any* input data should generate an interrupt, not just **Ctrl-C**.

User programs have to execute two steps to enable asynchronous notification from an input file. First, they specify a process as the "owner" of the file. The user ID of a file's owner is stored in `filp->f_owner` by the *fcntl* system call when an application invokes the `F_SETOWN` command. Additionally, the user programs must set the `FASYNC` flag in the device by means of another *fcntl* in order to actually enable asynchronous notification.

After these two calls have been executed, the input file generates a `SIGIO` signal whenever new data arrives. The signal is sent to the process (or process group, if the value is negative) stored in `filp->f_owner`.

For example, the following lines enable asynchronous notification to the current process for the `stdin` input file:

```
signal(SIGIO, &input_handler); /* the dirty way; /*
                               /* sigaction() is better */
fcntl(0, F_SETOWN, getpid());
oflags=fcntl(0, F_GETFL);
fcntl(0, F_SETFL, oflags | FASYNC);
```

The program named *asynctest* in the sources is a simple program that reads `stdin` as shown. It can be used to test the asynchronous capabilities of *scullpipe*. The program is similar to *cat*, but doesn't terminate on end-of-file; it responds only to input, not to the absence of input.

Note, however, that not all the devices support asynchronous notification, and you can choose not to offer it. Applications usually assume that the asynchronous capability is available only for sockets and ttys. For example, pipes and FIFOs don't support it, at least in the current kernels. Mice offer asynchronous notification (although not in 1.2), because some programs expect a mouse to be able to send `SIGIO` like a tty does.

There is one remaining problem with input notification. When a process receives a `SIGIO`, it doesn't know which input file has new input to offer. If more than one file is enabled to asynchronously notify the process of pending input, the application must still resort to *select* to find out what happened.

The Driver's Point of View

A more relevant topic for us is how the device driver can implement asynchronous signalling. The following list details the sequence of operations from the kernel's point of view:

- When `F_SETOWN` is invoked, nothing happens, except that a value is assigned to `filp->f_owner`.

- When F_SETFL is executed to turn on FASYNC, the driver's *fasync* method is called. This method is called whenever the value of FASYNC is changed in filp->f_flags, to notify the driver of the change so it can respond properly. The flag is zeroed by default when the file is opened. We'll look at the standard implementation of the driver method soon.

- When data arrives, all the processes registered for asynchronous notification must be sent a SIGIO signal.

While implementing the first step is trivial—there's nothing to do on the driver's part—the other steps involve maintaining a dynamic data structure to keep track of the different asynchronous readers; there might be several of these readers. This dynamic data structure, however, doesn't depend on the particular device involved, and the kernel offers a suitable general-purpose implementation so you don't have to rewrite the same code in every driver.

Unfortunately, such an implementation is not included in 1.2 kernels. It's not easy to implement asynchronous notification in a module for older kernel versions, as you have to create your own data structure. The *scull* module, for simplicity, doesn't offer asynchronous notification for older kernels.

The general implementation offered by Linux is based on one data structure and two functions (to be called in the steps described above). The header that declares related material is <linux/fs.h>—nothing new—and the data structure is called struct fasync_struct. As we did with wait queues, we need to insert a pointer to the structure in the device-specific data structure. Actually, we've already seen such a field in the section "A Sample Implementation: scullpipe."

The two functions to call correspond to the following prototypes:

```
int fasync_helper(struct inode *inode, struct file *filp,
                  int mode, struct fasync_struct **fa);
void kill_fasync(struct fasync_struct *fa, int sig);
```

The former is invoked to add or remove files to the list of interested processes when the FASYNC flag changes for an open file, while the latter should be called when data arrives.

Here's how *scullpipe* implements the *fasync* method:

```
int scull_p_fasync (struct inode *inode, struct file *filp, int mode)
{
    Scull_Pipe *dev = filp->private_data;

    return fasync_helper(inode, filp, mode, &dev->async_queue);
}
```

It's clear that all the work is performed by *fasync_helper*. It wouldn't be possible, however, to implement the functionality without a method in the driver, because the helper function needs to access the correct pointer to `struct fasync_struct *` (here `&dev->async_queue`) and only the driver can provide that information.

When data arrives, then, the following statement must be executed to signal asynchronous readers. Since new data for the *scullpipe* reader is generated by a process issuing a *write*, the statement appears in the *write* method of *scullpipe*.

```
if (dev->async_queue)
    kill_fasync (dev->async_queue, SIGIO); /* asynchronous readers */
```

It might appear that we're done, but there's still one thing missing. We must invoke our *fasync* method upon file close to remove the file being closed from the list of active asynchronous readers. While this call is required only if `filp->f_flags` has `FASYNC` set, calling the function anyway doesn't hurt and is the usual implementation. The following lines, for example, are part of the *close* method for *scullpipe*:

```
/* remove this filp from the asynchronously notified filp's */
scull_p_fasync(inode, filp, 0);
```

The data structure underlying asynchronous notification is almost identical to the structure `struct wait_queue`, because both situations involve waiting on an event. The difference is that `struct file` is used in place of `struct task_struct`. The `struct file` in the queue is then used to retrieve `f_owner`, in order to signal the process.

Seeking a Device

The difficult part of the chapter is over, and I'll quickly detail the *lseek* method, which is useful and easy to implement. Note that the prototype of the method changed slightly in 2.1.0, as detailed in "Prototype Differences," in Chapter 17.

The lseek Implementation

I've already stated that if the *lseek* method is missing from the device's operations, the default implementation in the kernel acknowledges seeks from the beginning of file and from the current position, by modifying `filp->f_pos`.

If seeking relative to the end-of-file makes sense for your device, you should offer your own method, which will look like the following code:

```
int scull_lseek (struct inode *inode, struct file *filp,
                off_t off, int whence)
{
    Scull_Dev *dev = filp->private_data;
    long newpos;
```

```
        switch(whence) {
          case 0: /* SEEK_SET */
            newpos = off;
            break;

          case 1: /* SEEK_CUR */
            newpos = filp->f_pos + off;
            break;

          case 2: /* SEEK_END */
            newpos = dev->size + off;
            break;

          default: /* can't happen */
            return -EINVAL;
        }
        if (newpos<0) return -EINVAL;
        filp->f_pos = newpos;
        return newpos;
    }
```

The only device-specific operation here is retrieving the file length from the device. For the *lseek* system call to work correctly, however, the *read* and *write* calls must cooperate by updating `filp->f_pos` whenever data is transferred; they should also use the `f_pos` field to locate the data they transfer. The implementation of *scull* includes these features, as shown in "Read and Write" in Chapter 3.

While the implementation shown above makes sense for *scull*, which handles a well-defined data area, most devices offer a data flow rather than a data area (just think about the serial ports or the keyboard), and seeking doesn't make sense. If this is the case, you can't just refrain from declaring the *lseek* operation, because the default method allows seeking. Instead, you should use the following code:

```
int scull_p_lseek (struct inode *inode, struct file *filp,
                   off_t off, int whence)
{
    return -ESPIPE; /* unseekable */
}
```

The function just shown comes from the *scullpipe* device, which isn't seekable; the error code is translated to "Illegal seek," though the symbolic name means "is a pipe." Since the position-indicator `filp->f_pos` is meaningless for non-seekable devices, neither *read* nor *write* needs to update it during data transfer.

Access Control on a Device File

Offering access control is sometimes vital for the reliability of a device node. Not only should unauthorized users not be permitted to use the device (which is enforced by the filesystem permission bits), but sometimes only one authorized user should be allowed to open the device at a time.

None of the code shown up to now implements any access control in addition to the filesystem permission bits. If the *open* system call forwards the request to the driver, *open* will succeed. I'm now going to introduce a few techniques for implementing some additional checks.

The problem is similar to that of using ttys. In that case, the *login* process changes the ownership of the device node whenever a user logs into the system, in order to prevent intrusion in the tty data flow. However, it's impractical to use a privileged program to change the ownership of a device every time it is opened, just to grant unique access to it.

Every device shown in this section has the same behavior as the bare *scull* device (that is, it implements a persistent memory area); it differs from *scull* only in access control, which is implemented in the *open* and *close* operations.

Single-Open Devices

The brute-force way to provide access control is to permit a device to be opened by only one process at a time (single-openness). I personally dislike this technique, because it inhibits user ingenuity. A user might well want to run different processes on the same device, one reading status information while the other is writing data. Often a handful of simple programs and a shell script can accomplish a lot. In other words, single-openness is more like policy than mechanism (at least to my way of thinking).

Despite my aversion to single-openness, it's the easiest implementation for a device driver, so it's shown here. The source code is extracted from a device called *scullsingle*.

The *open* call refuses access based on a global integer flag:

```
int scull_s_open (struct inode *inode, struct file *filp)
{
    Scull_Dev *dev = &scull_s_device; /* device information */
    int num = NUM(inode->i_rdev);

    if (num > 0) return -ENODEV; /* 1 device only */
    if (scull_s_count) return -EBUSY; /* already open */
    scull_s_count++;
```

```
    /* then, everything else is copied from the bare scull device */

    if ( (filp->f_flags & O_ACCMODE) == O_WRONLY)
        scull_trim(dev);
    filp->private_data = dev;
    MOD_INC_USE_COUNT;
    return 0;              /* success */
}
```

The *close* call, on the other hand, marks the device as no longer busy.

```
void scull_s_release (struct inode *inode, struct file *filp)
{
    scull_s_count--; /* release the device */
    MOD_DEC_USE_COUNT;
    return;
}
```

The best place to put the open flag (`scull_s_count`) is within the device structure (`Scull_Dev` here) because, conceptually, it belongs to the device.

The *scull* driver, however, uses a standalone variable to hold the open flag in
order to use the same device structure and methods as the bare *scull* device and
minimize code duplication.

Restricting Access to a Single User at a Time

A more sensible implementation of access control is granting access to a user only
if nobody else has control of the device. This kind of check is performed *after* the
normal permission checking and can only make access more restrictive than that
specified by the owner and group permission bits. This is the same access policy
as that used for ttys, but it doesn't resort to an external privileged program.

Sensible features are a little trickier to implement than single-open. In this case,
two items are needed, an open count and the uid of the "owner" of the device.
Once again, the best place for such items is within the device structure; the samples use global variables instead, for the reason explained previously for *scullsingle*. The name of the device is *sculluid*.

The *open* call grants access on first open, but remembers the owner of the device.
This means that a user can open the device multiple times, thus allowing cooper-
ating processes to work flawlessly. At the same time, no other user can open it,
thus avoiding external interference. Since this version of the function is almost
identical to the preceding one, only the relevant part is reproduced here:

```
if (scull_u_count &&
    (scull_u_owner != current->uid) &&  /* allow user */
    (scull_u_owner != current->euid) && /* allow whoever did su */
    !suser()) /* still allow root */
        return -EBUSY;    /* -EPERM would confuse the user */
```

```
if (scull_u_count == 0)
    scull_u_owner = current->uid; /* grab it */

scull_u_count++;
```

I made the decision to return **-EBUSY** and not **-EPERM**, even if the code performs permission checks, in order to point a user who is denied access in the right direction. The reaction to "Permission denied" is usually to check the mode and owner of the */dev* file, while "Device Busy" correctly suggests that the user should look for a process already using the device.

The code for *close* is not shown, since all it does is decrement the usage count.

Blocking Open as an Alternative to EBUSY

Returning an error when the device isn't accessible is usually the most sensible approach, but there are situations when you'd prefer to wait for the device.

For example, if a data communication channel is used both to transmit reports on a timely basis (using *crontab*) and for casual usage according to people's needs, it's much better for the timely report to be slightly delayed rather than fail just because the channel is currently busy.

This is one of the choices that the programmer must make when designing a device driver, and the right answer depends on the particular problem being solved.

The alternative to **EBUSY**, as you may have guessed, is to implement blocking *open*.

The *scullwuid* device is a version of *sculluid* that waits for the device on *open* instead of returning **-EBUSY**. It differs from *sculluid* only in the following part of the *open* operation:

```
while (scull_w_count &&
        (scull_w_owner != current->uid) &&  /* allow user */
        (scull_w_owner != current->euid) && /* allow whoever did su */
        !suser()) {
    if (filp->f_flags & O_NONBLOCK) return -EAGAIN;
    interruptible_sleep_on(&scull_w_wait);
    if (current->signal & ~current->blocked) /* a signal arrived */
        return -ERESTARTSYS; /* tell the fs layer to handle it */
    /* else, loop */
}
if (scull_w_count == 0)
    scull_w_owner = current->uid; /* grab it */
scull_w_count++;
```

The *release* method, then, is in charge of awakening any pending process:

```
void scull_w_release (struct inode *inode, struct file *filp)
{
    scull_w_count--;
    if (scull_w_count == 0)
        wake_up_interruptible(&scull_w_wait); /* awake other uid's */
    MOD_DEC_USE_COUNT;
    return;
}
```

The problem with a blocking-open implementation is that it is really unpleasant to the interactive user, who has to keep guessing what is going wrong. The interactive user usually invokes precompiled commands like *cp* and *tar* and can't just add O_NONBLOCK to the *open* call. Someone who's making a backup using the tape drive in the next room would prefer to get a plain "device or resource busy" message, instead of being left to guess why the hard drive is so silent today while *tar* is scanning it.

This kind of problem (different incompatible policies for the same device) is best solved by implementing one device node for each access policy, similar to the way */dev/ttyS0* and */dev/cua0* act on the same serial port in different ways, or */dev/sculluid* and */dev/scullwuid* offer two different policies for accessing a memory area.

Cloning the Device on Open

Another technique to manage access control is creating different private copies of the device depending on the process opening it.

Clearly this is only possible if the device is not bound to a hardware object; *scull* is an example of such a "software" device. The *kmouse* module also uses this technique so that every virtual console appears to have a private pointing device. When copies of the device are created by the software driver, I call them "virtual devices"—just as "virtual consoles" use a single physical tty device.

While a requirement for this kind of access control is unusual, the implementation can be enlightening in showing how easily kernel code can change the applications' perspective of the surrounding world (i.e., the computer). The topic is quite exotic, actually, so if you aren't interested, you can jump directly to the next chapter.

The */dev/scullpriv* device node implements virtual devices within the *scull* package. The *scullpriv* implementation uses the minor number of the process's controlling tty as a key to access the virtual device. You can nonetheless easily modify the sources to use any integer value for the key; each choice leads to a different policy. For example, using the uid leads to a different virtual device for each user, while using a pid key creates a new device for each process accessing it.

The decision to use the controlling terminal is meant to enable easy testing of the device using input/output redirection.

The *open* method looks like the following code. It must look for the right virtual device and possibly create one. The final part of the function is not shown because it is copied from the bare *scull*, which we've already seen.

```
struct scull_listitem {
    Scull_Dev device;
    int key;
    struct scull_listitem *next;
};

struct scull_listitem *scull_c_head;

int scull_c_open (struct inode *inode, struct file *filp)
{
    int key;
    int num = NUM(inode->i_rdev);
    struct scull_listitem *lptr, *prev;

    if (num > 0) return -ENODEV; /* 1 device only */

    if (!current->tty) {
        PDEBUG("Process \"%s\" has no ctl tty\n",current->comm);
        return -EINVAL;
    }
    key = MINOR(current->tty->device);

    /* look for a device in the linked list; if missing create it */
    prev = NULL;
    for (lptr = scull_c_head; lptr && (lptr->key != key);
        lptr = lptr->next)
        prev=lptr;
    if (!lptr) { /* not found */
        lptr = kmalloc(sizeof(struct scull_listitem), GFP_KERNEL);
        if (!lptr)
            return -ENOMEM;
        memset(lptr, 0, sizeof(struct scull_listitem));
        lptr->key = key;
        scull_trim(&(lptr->device)); /* initialize it */
        if (prev)
            prev->next = lptr;
        else
            scull_c_head = lptr; /* the first one */
    }

    /* then, everything else is copied from the bare scull device */
```

The *close* method does nothing special. It could release the device on last close, but I chose not to maintain an open count in order to simplify testing the driver. If the device were released on last close, you wouldn't be able to read the same data after writing to the device unless a background process were to keep it open at least once. The sample driver takes the easier approach of keeping the data, so that at the next *open*, you'll find it there. The devices are released when *cleanup_module* is called.

Here's the *close* implementation for */dev/scullpriv*, which closes the chapter as well.

```
void scull_c_release (struct inode *inode, struct file *filp)
{
    /*
     * Nothing to do, because the device is persistent.
     * A "real" cloned device should be freed on last close
     */
    MOD_DEC_USE_COUNT;
    return;
}
```

Quick Reference

This chapter introduced you to the following symbols and header files:

#include <linux/ioctl.h>

> This header declares all the macros used to define *ioctl* commands. It is currently included by <linux/fs.h>. Linux 1.2 doesn't declare the fancy macros introduced in this chapter; if backward compatibility is needed, I'd suggest looking in *scull/sysdep.h*, which defines the correct symbols for old kernel versions.

_IOC_NRBITS
_IOC_TYPEBITS
_IOC_SIZEBITS
_IOC_DIRBITS

> The number of bits available for the different bit fields of *ioctl* commands. There are also four macros that specify the MASKs and four that specify the SHIFTs, but they're mainly for internal use. _IOC_SIZEBITS is an important value to check, because it changes across architectures.

_IOC_NONE
_IOC_READ
_IOC_WRITE

> The possible values for the "direction" bitfield. "Read" and "write" are different bits and can be ORed to specify read/write. The values are 0-based.

```
_IOC(dir,type,nr,size)
_IO(type,nr)
_IOR(type,nr,size)
_IOW(type,nr,size)
_IOWR(type,nr,size)
```
Macros used to create an *ioctl* command.

```
_IOC_DIR(nr)
_IOC_TYPE(nr)
_IOC_NR(nr)
_IOC_SIZE(nr)
```
Macros used to decode a command. In particular, _IOC_TYPE(nr) is an OR-combination of _IOC_READ and _IOC_WRITE.

```
#include <linux/mm.h>
int verify_area(int mode, const void *ptr,
                unsigned long extent);
```
This function checks that a pointer in the user space is actually usable. *verify_area* deals with page faults and must be called before accessing user space outside of *read* and *write*, whose buffer has already been verified. A non-zero return value signals an error and should be returned to the caller. For the use of *verify_area* and the following macros and functions with the 2.1 kernel see "Accessing User Space" in Chapter 17.

```
VERIFY_READ
VERIFY_WRITE
```
The possible values for the **mode** argument in *verify_area*. VERIFY_WRITE is a superset of VERIFY_READ.

```
#include <asm/segment.h>
void put_user(datum,ptr);
unsigned long get_user(ptr);
```
Macros used to store or retrieve a single datum to or from user space. The number of bytes being transferred depends on `sizeof(*ptr)`. These functions are missing from version 1.2 of the kernel. Look at *scull/sysdep.h* if you want to compile a module under both version 1.2 and 2.0.

```
void put_user_byte(val,ptr);
unsigned char get_user_byte(ptr);
```
These functions and their _word and _long relatives are deprecated. 2.0 and later kernels only declare the functions (which are inline) #ifdef WE_REALLY_WANT_TO_USE_A_BROKEN_INTERFACE. Programmers are strongly urged to invoke *put_user* and *get_user* instead.

```
#include <linux/sched.h>
void interruptible_sleep_on(struct wait_queue **q);
void sleep_on(struct wait_queue **q);
```
Calling either of these functions puts the current process to sleep on a queue. Usually, you'll choose the `interruptible` form to implement blocking read and write.

```
void wake_up(struct wait_queue **q);
void wake_up_interruptible(struct wait_queue **q);
```
These functions wake processes that are sleeping on the queue q. The `_interruptible` form wakes only interruptible processes.

```
void schedule(void);
```
This function selects a runnable process from the run queue. The chosen process can be `current` or a different one. You won't usually call *schedule* directly, as the *sleep_on* functions do it internally.

```
void select_wait(struct wait_queue **wait_address,
                 select_table *p);
```
This function puts the current process into a wait queue without scheduling immediately. It is designed to be used by the *select* method of device drivers. The entire *select* implementation changed in 2.1.23; see "The poll Method" in Chapter 17 for details.

```
#include <linux/fs.h>
SEL_IN
SEL_OUT
SEL_EX
```
One of these symbols is passed as the `mode` argument to the *select* method of the device.

```
int fasync_helper(struct inode *inode, struct file *filp,
                  int mode, struct fasync_struct **fa);
```
This function is a "helper" for implementing the *fasync* device method. The mode argument is the same value that is passed to the method, while `fa` points to a device-specific `fasync_struct *`.

```
void kill_fasync(struct fasync_struct *fa, int sig);
```
If the driver supports asynchronous notification, this function can be used to send a signal to processes registered in `fa`.

## CHAPTER SIX

FLOW OF TIME

A t this point, we know how to write a full-featured char module. We'll deal with kernel resources available to the driver in the next few chapters. I'll start by showing how timing issues are addressed from kernel code. This involves, in ascending order of complexity:

- Knowing the current time

- Delaying operation for a specified amount of time

- Scheduling asynchronous functions to happen after a specified time lapse

Time Intervals in the Kernel

The first point we need to cover is the timer interrupt, which is the mechanism the kernel uses to keep track of time intervals. The timer interrupt is set to a default frequency of HZ, which is an architecture-dependent value defined in <linux/param.h>. Through at least version 2.0 and 2.1.43, Linux defines HZ to be 1024 for the Alpha and 100 for all other platforms.

When the timer interrupt occurs, the jiffies value is incremented. jiffies is thus the number of clock ticks since the operating system was booted; it is declared in <linux/sched.h> as unsigned long volatile, and it will overflow in one and a third years of continuous operation. If you're planning on more than one and a third years of uptime, you'd better buy yourself an Alpha, which won't overflow for half a billion years—it has 64-bit longs. I can't tell you exactly what happens when jiffies overflows, and I haven't got time to wait to find out.

If you change the value of HZ and try to recompile the kernel, you won't notice any difference when you are in user space. Everything works as usual, except that the `jiffies` value increments at a different pace. The more interrupts you generate, the greater the overhead, but the system will be snappier, because the processor is scheduled more often.

I tried a few values on my PC: at 20Hz, the system reacts quite slowly; 100Hz is the default; at 1kHz, the computer is slightly slower, but reasonably responsive; at 10kHz, it is noticeably slow; and at 50kHz, it is unbearable. Note that changing the interrupt frequency also has other side effects, like a different time lag before `jiffies` overflows (in as few as five days with a 10kHz clock frequency) and a different precision in the BogoMips calculation.* Moreover, there are some hard limits that are not written down anywhere. For example, 19 is the smallest possible integer value for the clock frequency on the PC, and similar limits exist on the other supported architectures.

Additionally, you must be really careful when using modules. If you change the definition of HZ, you *must* recompile and reinstall all modules you are using. Everything in the kernel depends on HZ, including modules. I realized this when I couldn't double-click my mouse after I incremented the value of HZ.

All in all, the best approach to the timer interrupt is to keep the default value for HZ, by virtue of our complete trust in the kernel developers, who have certainly chosen the best value. More information about this issue can be retrieved by reading the header `<linux/timex.h>`.

Knowing the Current Time

Kernel code can always retrieve the current time by looking at the value of `jiffies`. Usually the fact that the value represents only the time since the last boot is not relevant to the driver, because its life is limited to the system uptime. Drivers can use the current value of `jiffies` to calculate time intervals across events (I used it to tell double clicks from single clicks in the *kmouse* module). In short, looking at `jiffies` is almost always sufficient when you need to measure time intervals.

It's quite unlikely that a driver will ever need to know the wall-clock time, as this knowledge is usually needed only by user programs like *cron* and *at*. If such a capability is needed, it will be a particular case of device usage, and the driver can be correctly instructed by a user program, which can easily do the conversion from wall-clock time to the system clock.

If your driver really needs the current time, the *do_gettimeofday* function comes to the rescue. The function doesn't tell the current day of the week or anything like

---

* The higher the clock frequency, the coarser the precision, because of interrupt overhead.

that; rather, it fills a **struct timeval** pointer with the usual seconds-microseconds values. It responds to the following prototype:

```
#include <linux/time.h>
void do_gettimeofday(struct timeval *tv);
```

The source states that *do_gettimeofday* has "near microsecond resolution" for all architectures except the Alpha and the Sparc, where it has the same resolution as **jiffies**. The Sparc port has been upgraded in 2.1.34 to support fine-grained time measures. The current time is also available (though with less precision) from the **xtime** variable (a **struct timeval**); however, direct use of this variable is discouraged because you can't atomically access both the **timeval** fields **tv_sec** and **tv_usec**, unless you disable interrupts. Using the **timeval** structure filled by *do_gettimeofday* is much safer.

Unfortunately, *do_gettimeofday* was not exported by Linux 1.2. If you need to know the current time and want to be backward compatible, you should resort to the following version of the function:

```
#if LINUX_VERSION_CODE < VERSION_CODE(1,3,46)
/*
 * kernel headers already declare the function as non-static.
 * We reimplement it with another name, and #define it
 */
extern inline void redo_gettimeofday(struct timeval *tv)
{
    unsigned long flags;

    save_flags(flags);
    cli();
    *tv = xtime;
    restore_flags(flags);
}
#define do_gettimeofday(tv) redo_gettimeofday(tv)
#endif
```

This version is coarser than the real function because it uses only the current value of the **xtime** structure, which is no more fine-grained than **jiffies**. However, it is portable across Linux platforms. The "real" function attains better resolution by querying the real-time clock through architecture-dependent code.

Code for reading the current time is available within the *jit* ("Just In Time") module, in the source files provided on the O'Reilly FTP site. *jit* creates a file called */proc/currentime*, which returns the current time in ASCII when it is read. I chose to use a dynamic */proc* file because it requires less module code—it's not worth creating a whole device just to return two lines of text.

If you use *cat* to read the file multiple times in less than a timer tick, you'll appreciate the difference between **xtime** and *do_gettimeofday*:

```
morgana% cat /proc/currentime /proc/currentime /proc/currentime
gettime: 846157215.937221
xtime:   846157215.931188
jiffies: 1308094
gettime: 846157215.939950
xtime:   846157215.931188
jiffies: 1308094
gettime: 846157215.942465
xtime:   846157215.941188
jiffies: 1308095
```

Delaying Execution

Using the timer interrupt and the value of `jiffies`, it's easy to generate time intervals that are multiples of the timer tick, but for smaller delays, the programmer must resort to software loops, which are introduced last in this section.

Although I'll show you all the fancy techniques, I think it's best to become familiar with timing issues by first looking at simple code, though the first implementations I'm going to show are not the best ones.

Long Delays

If you want to delay execution by a multiple of the clock tick or you don't require strict precision (for example, if you want to delay an integer number of seconds), the easiest implementation (and the most brain-dead) is the following, also known as *busy waiting*:

```
unsigned long j = jiffies + jit_delay * HZ;

while (jiffies < j)
    /* nothing */;
```

This kind of implementation should definitely be avoided.* I'm showing it here because on occasion you might want to run this code to understand better the internals of other code (I'll suggest how to test using busy waiting towards the end of this chapter).

But let's look at how this code works. The loop is guaranteed to work because `jiffies` is declared as `volatile` by the kernel headers and therefore is reread any time some C code accesses it. Though "correct," this busy loop completely locks the computer for the duration of the delay; the scheduler never interrupts a process that is running in kernel space. Since the kernel is non-reentrant in the current implementation, a busy loop in the kernel locks all the processors of an SMP machine.

---

* It is particularly bad on SMP boxes, where it can potentially lock the whole machine.

Still worse, if interrupts happen to be disabled when you enter the loop, `jiffies` won't be updated, and the `while` condition remains true forever. You'll be forced to hit the big red button.

This implementation of delaying code is available, like the following ones, in the *jit* module. The */proc/jit** files created by the module delay a whole second every time they are read. If you want to test the busy wait code, you can read */proc/jitbusy*, which busy-loops for one second whenever its *read* method is called; a command like *dd if=/proc/jitbusy bs=1* delays one second each time it reads a character.

As you may suspect, reading */proc/jitbusy* is terrible for system performance, as the computer can run other processes only once a second.

A better solution that allows other processes to run during the time interval is the following, although this method can't be used in hard real-time tasks or other time-critical situations:

```
while (jiffies < j)
    schedule();
```

The variable `j` in this example and the following ones is the value of `jiffies` at the expiration of the delay and is always calculated as shown for busy waiting.

This loop (which can be tested by reading */proc/jitsched*), still isn't optimal. The system can schedule other tasks; the current process does nothing but release the CPU, but it remains in the run queue. If it is the only runnable process, it will actually run (it calls the scheduler, which selects the same process, which calls the scheduler, which . . .). In other words, the load of the machine (the average number of running processes) will be at least 1, and the idle task (process number 0, also called "swapper" for historical reasons) will never run. Though this issue may seem irrelevant, running the idle task when the computer is idle relieves the processor's workload, decreasing its temperature and increasing its lifetime, as well as the duration of the batteries if the computer happens to be your laptop. Moreover, since the process is actually executing during the delay, it will be accounted for all the time it consumes. You can see this by running *time cat /proc/jitsched*.

Despite its drawbacks, the previous loop can provide a quick and dirty way to monitor the workings of a driver. If a bug in your module locks the system solid, adding a small delay after each debugging *printk* statement ensures that every message you print before the processor hits your nasty bug reaches the system log before the system locks. Without such delays, the messages are correctly printed to the memory buffer, but the system locks before *klogd* can do its job.

Arguably, there is a better way to implement delays. The correct way to put a process to sleep in kernel mode is to set `current->timeout` and sleep on a wait queue. The `timeout` value for the process is compared with `jiffies` every time the scheduler runs. If `timeout` is smaller than or equal to the current time, the process is awakened independent of what happens to its wait queue. If no system event wakes the process and takes it off the queue, the timeout is reached and the scheduler wakes the process.

Here's what such a delay looks like:

```
struct wait_queue *wait = NULL;

current->timeout = j;
interruptible_sleep_on(&wait);
```

It's important to call *interruptible_sleep_on*, not simply *sleep_on*, because the `timeout` value is never checked for non-interruptible processes—sleeping can't be interrupted, even by timing out. Therefore, if you called *sleep_on*, you would have no way to interrupt a sleeping process. You can test the code shown above by reading */proc/jitqueue*.

The `timeout` field is an interesting system resource. It can be used to implement a timeout for blocking system calls, in addition to calculating delays. If your hardware guarantees a response within some predefined time unless an error occurs, the device driver should set the `timeout` value for the process before it goes to sleep. For example, when you request a data transfer from or to mass storage, the disk is expected to honor the request within, say, one second. If you've set the timeout and it is reached, the process is awakened, and the driver can properly handle the missing transfer. If you use this technique, the `timeout` value should be reset to 0 if the process is awakened normally. If the timeout expires, the scheduler resets the field and the driver doesn't need to.

You may have noticed that using a wait queue may be overkill when the aim is just to insert a delay. Actually, you can use `current->timeout` without wait queues, as follows:

```
current->timeout = j;
current->state = TASK_INTERRUPTIBLE;
schedule();
current->timeout = 0; /* reset the timeout */
```

These statements change the status of the process before calling the scheduler. Making the process `TASK_INTERRUPTIBLE` (as opposed to `TASK_RUNNING`), ensures that it won't be run again until its timeout expires (or some other event, like a signal, wakes it). This way of delaying is implemented in */proc/jitself*—its name emphasizes the fact that the reading process is "sleeping by itself," without calling *sleep_on*.

Short Delays

Sometimes a real driver needs to calculate very short delays in order to synchronize with the hardware. In this case, using the `jiffies` value is definitely not the solution.

The kernel function *udelay* serves this purpose.* Its prototype is:

```
#include <linux/delay.h>
void udelay(unsigned long usecs);
```

The function is compiled inline on most supported architectures and uses a software loop to delay execution for the required number of microseconds. This is where the BogoMips value is used: *udelay* uses the integer value `loops_per_second`, which in turn is the result of the BogoMips calculation performed at boot time.

The *udelay* call should be called only for short time lapses, because the precision of `loops_per_second` is only 8 bits and noticeable errors accumulate when calculating long delays. Even though the maximum allowable delay is nearly one second (since calculations overflow for longer delays), the suggested maximum value for *udelay* is 1000 microseconds (one millisecond).

It's also important to remember that *udelay* is a busy-waiting function and that other tasks can't be run during the time lapse. The source is in `<asm/delay.h>`.

There's currently no support in the kernel for delays shorter than a timer tick but longer than one millisecond. This is not an issue, because delays need to be just long enough to be noticed by humans or by the hardware. One hundredth of a second is a suitable precision for human-related time intervals, while one millisecond is a long enough delay for hardware activities. If you *really* need a delay in between, you can easily build a loop around *udelay(1000)*.

Task Queues

One feature many drivers need is to schedule execution of some tasks at a later time without resorting to interrupts. Linux offers two different interfaces for this purpose: task queues and kernel timers. Task queues provide a flexible utility for scheduling execution at a later time, with various meanings for later; they are most useful when writing interrupt handlers, and we'll see them again in "Bottom Halves," in Chapter 9, *Interrupt Handling*. Kernel timers are used to schedule a task to run at a specific time in the future and are dealt with later in this chapter, in "Kernel Timers."

A typical situation in which you might use task queues is for managing hardware that cannot generate interrupts but still allows blocking read. You need to poll the

---

* The u represents the Greek letter "mu" and stands for "micro."

device, while taking care not to burden the CPU with unnecessary operations. Waking the reading process at fixed time intervals (for example, using `current->timeout`) isn't a suitable approach, because each poll would require two context switches and often a suitable polling mechanism can be implemented only outside of a process's context.

A similar problem is giving timely input to a simple hardware device. For example, you might need to feed steps to a stepper motor that is directly connected to the parallel port—the motor needs to be moved by single steps on a timely basis. In this case, the controlling process talks to your device driver to dispatch a movement, but the actual movement should be performed step by step after returning from *write*.

The preferred way to perform such floating operations quickly is to register a task for later execution. The kernel supports task "queues," where tasks accumulate to be "consumed" when the queue is run. You can declare your own task queue and trigger it at will, or you can register your tasks in predefined queues, which are run (triggered) by the kernel itself.

The next section first describes task queues, then introduces predefined task queues, which provide a good start for some interesting tests (and hang the computer if something goes wrong), and finally introduces how to run your own task queues.

The Nature of Task Queues

A task queue is a list of tasks, each task being represented by a function pointer and an argument. When a task is run, it receives a single `void *` argument and returns `void`. The pointer argument can be used to pass along a data structure to the routine, or it can be ignored. The queue itself is a list of structures (the tasks) that are owned by the kernel module declaring and queueing them. The module is completely responsible for allocating and deallocating the structures; static structures are commonly used for this purpose.

A queue element is described by the following structure, copied directly from `<linux/tqueue.h>`:

```
struct tq_struct {
    struct tq_struct *next;        /* linked list of active bh's */
    int sync;                      /* must be initialized to zero */
    void (*routine)(void *);       /* function to call */
    void *data;                    /* argument to function */
};
```

The "bh" in the first comment means *bottom-half*. A bottom-half is "half of an interrupt handler"; we'll discuss this topic thoroughly when we deal with interrupts in "Bottom Halves" in Chapter 9.

Task queues are an important resource for dealing with asynchronous events, and most interrupt handlers schedule part of their work to be executed when task queues are run. On the other hand, some task queues *are* bottom halves, in that their execution is triggered by the *do_bottom_half* function. While I intend for this chapter to make sense even if you don't understand bottom-halves, nonetheless, I do refer to them when necessary.

The most important fields in the data structure shown above are `routine` and `data`. To queue a task for later execution, you need to set both these fields before queueing the structure, while `next` and `sync` should be cleared. The `sync` flag in the structure is used to prevent queueing the same task more than once, as this would corrupt the `next` pointer. Once the task has been queued, the structure is considered "owned" by the kernel and shouldn't be modified.

The other data structure involved in task queues is `task_queue`, which is currently just a pointer to `struct tq_struct`; the decision to `typedef` this pointer to another symbol permits the extension of `task_queue` in the future, should the need arise.

The following list summarizes the operations that can be performed on `struct tq_structs`; all the functions are inlines.

void queue_task(struct tq_struct *task, task_queue *list);
> As its name suggests, this function queues a task. It disables interrupts to prevent race conditions and can be called from any function in your module.

void queue_task_irq(struct tq_struct *task,
                    task_queue *list);
> This function is similar to the previous one, but it can be called only from a non-reentrant function (such as an interrupt handler, whence the name). It is slightly faster than *queue_task* because it doesn't disable interrupts while queueing. If you call this routine from a reentrant function, you risk corruption of the queue due to the unmasked race condition. However, this function does mask against queueing-while-running (queueing a task at the exact place where the queue is being consumed).

void queue_task_irq_off(struct tq_struct *task,
                        task_queue *list);
> This function can be called only when interrupts are disabled. It is faster than the previous two, but doesn't prevent either concurrent-queueing or queueing-while-running race conditions.

void run_task_queue(task_queue *list);
> *run_task_queue* is used to consume a queue of accumulated tasks. You won't need to call it yourself unless you declare and maintain your own queue.

Both *queue_task_irq* and *queue_task_irq_off* have been removed in version 2.1.30 of the kernel, as the speed gain was not worth the effort. See "Task Queues" in Chapter 17, *Recent Developments*, for details.

Before delving into the details of the queues, I'd better explain some of the subtleties that hide behind the scenes. Queued tasks execute asynchronously with respect to system calls; this asynchronous execution requires additional care and is worth explaining first.

Task queues are executed at a *safe time*. Safe here means that there aren't stringent requirements about the execution times. The code doesn't need to be extremely fast, because hardware interrupts are enabled during execution of task queues. Queued functions should be reasonably fast anyway because only hardware interrupts can be dealt with by the system as long as a queue is being consumed.

Another concept related to task queues is that of *interrupt time*. In Linux, interrupt time is a software concept, enforced by the global kernel variable `intr_count`. This variable keeps a count of the number of nested interrupt handlers being executed at any time.*

During the normal computation flow, when the processor is executing on behalf of a process, `intr_count` is 0. When `intr_count` is not 0, on the other hand, the code is asynchronous with the rest of the system. Asynchronous code might be handling a hardware interrupt or a "software interrupt"—a task that is executed independent of any processes, which we'll refer to as running "at interrupt time." Such code is not allowed to perform certain operations; in particular, it cannot put the current process to sleep because the value of the `current` pointer is not related to the software interrupt code being run.

A typical example is code executed on exit from a system call. If for some reason there is a job scheduled for execution, the kernel can dispatch it as soon as a process returns from a system call. This is a "software interrupt," and `intr_count` is incremented before dealing with the pending job. The function being dispatched is at "interrupt time" because the main instruction stream has been interrupted.

When `intr_count` is non-zero, the scheduler can't be invoked. This also means that `kmalloc(GFP_KERNEL)` is not allowed. Only atomic allocations (see "The Priority Argument" in Chapter 7, *Getting Hold of Memory*) can be performed at interrupt time, and atomic allocations are more prone to fail than "normal" allocations.

If code being executed at interrupt time calls *schedule*, an error message like "Aiee: scheduling in interrupt" is printed on the console, followed by the hexadecimal address of the calling instruction. From version 2.1.37 onwards, this message is followed by an oops, to help debug the problem by analyzing the registers. Trying to allocate memory at interrupt time with non-atomic priority generates an error message that includes the caller's address.

---

* Version 2.1.34 of the kernel got rid of `intr_count`. See "Interrupt Management" in Chapter 17 for details on this.

Predefined Task Queues

The easiest way to perform deferred execution is to use the queues that are already maintained by the kernel. There are four of these queues, described below, but your driver can use only the first three. The queues are declared in `<linux/tqueue.h>`, which you should include in your source.

`tq_scheduler`

> This queue is consumed whenever the scheduler runs. Since the scheduler runs in the context of the process being scheduled out, tasks that run in the scheduler queue can do almost anything; they are not executed at interrupt time.

`tq_timer`

> This queue is run by the timer tick. Since the tick (the function *do_timer*) runs at interrupt time, any task within this queue runs at interrupt time as well.

`tq_immediate`

> The immediate queue is run as soon as possible, either on return from a system call or when the scheduler is run, whichever comes first. The queue is consumed at interrupt time.

`tq_disk`

> This queue, not present in version 1.2 of the kernel, is used internally in memory management and can't be used by modules.

The timeline of a driver using a task queue is represented in Figure 6-1. The figure shows a driver that queues a function in `tq_scheduler` from an interrupt handler.

How the examples work

Examples of deferred computation are available in the *jiq* (Just In Queue) module, from which the source in this section has been extracted. This module creates */proc* files that can be read using *dd* or other tools; this is similar to *jit*. The sample module can't run on Linux 1.2 because it uses dynamic */proc* files.

The process reading a *jiq* file is put to sleep until the buffer is full.* The buffer is filled by successive runs of a task queue. Each pass through the queue appends a text string to the buffer being filled; each string reports the current time (in jiffies), the process that is `current` during this pass, and the value of `intr_count`.

For best results, the file should be read in one shot, with the command `dd count=1`; if you use a command like *cat*, the *read* method is invoked several times, and the results overlap, as explained in "Using the /proc Filesystem," in Chapter 4, *Debugging Techniques*.

---

* The buffer of a */proc* file is a page of memory: 4KB or 8KB.

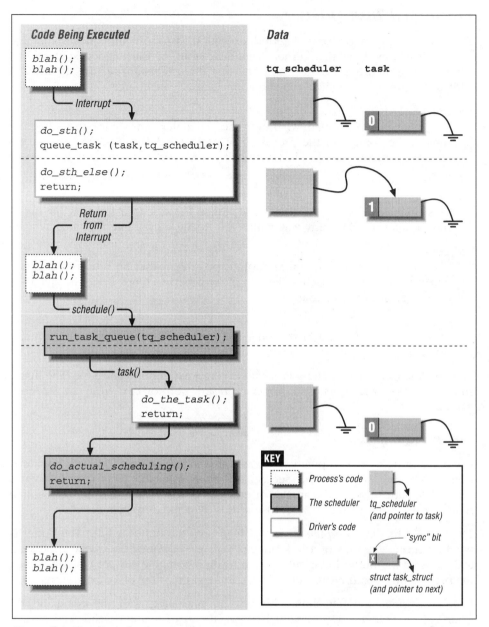

Figure 6-1: Timeline of task-queue usage

The code for filling the buffer is confined to the *jiq_print* function, which executes at each run through the queue being used. The printing function is not interesting and is not worth showing here; instead, let's look at the initialization of the task to be inserted in a queue:

```
struct tq_struct jiq_task; /* global: initialized to zero */

/* this lines are in init_module() */
jiq_task.routine = jiq_print;
jiq_task.data = (void *)&jiq_data;
```

There's no need to clear the **sync** and **next** fields of **jiq_task** because static variables are initialized to 0 by the compiler.

The scheduler queue

The easiest queue to use is **tq_scheduler** because queued tasks are not constrained by being executed at interrupt time.

/proc/jiqsched is a sample file that uses **tq_scheduler**. The *read* function for the file dispatches everything to the task queue, in the following way:

```
int jiq_read_sched(char *buf, char **start, off_t offset,
                   int len, int unused)
{

    jiq_data.len = 0;             /* nothing printed, yet */
    jiq_data.buf = buf;           /* print in this place */
    jiq_data.jiffies = jiffies;   /* initial time */

    /* jiq_print will queue_task() again in jiq_data.queue */
    jiq_data.queue = &tq_scheduler;

    queue_task(&jiq_task, &tq_scheduler); /* ready to run */
    interruptible_sleep_on(&jiq_wait);    /* sleep till completion */

    return jiq_data.len;
}
```

Reading */proc/jiqsched* is interesting, because it shows when the scheduler is run—the value of **jiffies** shown is the value when the scheduler gets invoked. If CPU-bound processes are active on the system, there is a delay between successive runs of the queue; the scheduler won't preempt the processes before several clock ticks have elapsed. Reading the file can thus take several seconds, since the file is roughly 100 lines long (or twice that on the Alpha).

The simplest way to test this situation is to run a process that executes an empty loop. The *load50* program is a load-raising program that executes 50 concurrent busy loops in the user space; you'll find its source in the sample programs. When *load50* is running in the system, *head* extracts the following from */proc/jiqsched*:

```
 time  delta intr_count pid command
1643733   0        0    701 head
1643747  14        0    658 load50
1643747   0        0      3 kswapd
1643755   8        0    655 load50
1643761   6        0    666 load50
1643764   3        0    650 load50
1643767   3        0    661 load50
1643769   2        0    659 load50
1643769   0        0      6 loadmonitor
```

Note that the scheduler queue is run immediately after entering *schedule*, and thus the `current` process is the one that is being scheduled out. That's why the first line in */proc/jiqsched* always represents the process reading the file; it has just gone to sleep and is being scheduled out. Note also that both *kswapd* and *loadmonitor* (a program I run on my system) execute for less than 1 time tick, while *load50* is preempted when its time quantum expires, several clock ticks after it acquires the processor.

When no process is actually running, the current process is always the idle task (process 0, historically called "swapper") and the queue is run either continuously or once every timer tick. The scheduler, and thus the queue, runs continuously if the processor can't be put into a "halted" state; it runs at every timer tick only if the processor is halted by process 0. A halted processor can be awakened only by an interrupt. When this happens, the idle task runs the scheduler (and the associated queue). The following shows the results of *head /proc/jitsched* run on an unloaded system:

```
 time  delta intr_count pid command
1704475   0        0    730 head
1704476   1        0      0 swapper
1704477   1        0      0 swapper
1704478   1        0      0 swapper
1704478   0        0      6 loadmonitor
1704479   1        0      0 swapper
1704480   1        0      0 swapper
1704481   1        0      0 swapper
1704482   1        0      0 swapper
```

The timer queue

Using the timer queue is not too different from using the scheduler queue. The main difference is that, unlike the scheduler queue, the timer queue executes at interrupt time. Additionally, you're guaranteed that the queue will run at the next clock tick, thus overcoming any dependency on system load. The following is what *head /proc/jiqtimer* returned while my system was compiling:

```
 time  delta intr_count pid command
1760712   1        1    945 cc1
1760713   1        1    945 cc1
```

```
1760714   1        1       945 cc1
1760715   1        1       946 as
1760716   1        1       946 as
1760717   1        1       946 as
1760718   1        1       946 as
1760719   1        1       946 as
1760720   1        1       946 as
```

One feature of the current implementation of task queues is that a task can requeue itself in the same queue it is run from. For instance, a task being run from the timer tick can reschedule itself to be run on the next tick. Rescheduling is possible because the head of the queue is replaced with a NULL pointer before consuming queued tasks. This implementation dates back to kernel version 1.3.70. In earlier versions (such as 1.2.13), rescheduling was not possible because the kernel didn't trim the queue before running it. Trying to reschedule a task with Linux 1.2 hangs the system in a tight loop. The ability to reschedule is the only relevant difference in task-queue management from 1.2.13 to 2.0.*x*.

Although rescheduling the same task over and over might appear to be a pointless operation, it is sometimes useful. For example, my own computer moves a pair of stepper motors one step at a time by rescheduling itself on the timer queue until the target has been fulfilled. Another example is the *jiq* module, where the printing function reschedules itself to show each pass through the queues.

The immediate queue

The last predefined queue that can be used by modularized code is the immediate queue. It works like a bottom-half interrupt handler, and thus it must be "marked" with `mark_bh(IMMEDIATE_BH)`. For efficiency, bottom-halves are run only if they are marked. Note that the handler must be marked *after* the call to *queue_task*; otherwise a race condition is created. See "Bottom Halves" in Chapter 9 for more detail.

The immediate queue is the fastest queue in the system—it's executed soonest and is consumed after incrementing `intr_count`. The queue is so "immediate" that if you re-register your task, it is rerun as soon as it returns. The queue is run over and over until it is empty. If you read */proc/jiqimmed*, you'll see that the reason it is so fast is that it keeps control of the CPU during the entire reading process.

The queue is consumed either by the scheduler or as soon as one process returns from its system call. It's interesting to note that the scheduler (at least with the 2.0 kernel) doesn't keep rerunning the immediate queue until it is empty; this happens only when the queue is run on return from a system call. You can see this behavior in the next sample output—the first line of *jiqimmed* shows *head* as the current process, while the next lines don't.

```
 time  delta intr_count pid command
1975640   0      1     1060 head
1975641   1      1        0 swapper
1975641   0      1        0 swapper
1975641   0      1        0 swapper
1975641   0      1        0 swapper
1975641   0      1        0 swapper
1975641   0      1        0 swapper
1975641   0      1        0 swapper
1975641   0      1        0 swapper
```

It's clear that the queue can't be used to delay the execution of a task—it's an "immediate" queue. Instead, its purpose is to execute a task as soon as possible, but at a "safe time." This feature makes it a great resource for interrupt handlers, because it offers them an entry point for executing program code outside of the actual interrupt management routine.

Although */proc/jiqimmed* re-registers its task in the queue, this technique is discouraged in real code; this uncooperative behavior ties up the processor as long as a task is re-registering itself, whith no advantage over completing the work in one pass.

Running Your Own Task Queues

Declaring a new task queue is not difficult. A driver is free to declare a new task queue, or even several of them; tasks are queued just as we've seen with `tq_scheduler`.

Unlike a predefined task queue, a custom queue is not automatically triggered by the kernel. The programmer who maintains a queue must arrange for a way of triggering it.

The following macro declares the queue and needs to be expanded where you want your task queue to be declared:

```
DECLARE_TASK_QUEUE(tq_custom);
```

After declaring the queue, you can invoke the usual functions to queue tasks. The call above pairs naturally with the following:

```
queue_task(&custom_task, &tq_custom);
```

And the following one will run `tq_custom`:

```
run_task_queue(&tq_custom);
```

If you want to experiment with custom queues now, you need to register a function to trigger the queue in one of the predefined queues. Although this may look like a roundabout way to do things, it isn't. A custom queue can be useful whenever you need to accumulate jobs and execute them all at the same time, even if you use another queue to select that "same time."

Kernel Timers

The ultimate resources for time-keeping in the kernel are the timers. Timers are used to dispatch execution of a function (a timer handler) at a particular time in the future. This is different from task queues, in that you can specify *when* in the future your function must be called, whereas you can't tell exactly when a queued task will be executed. On the other hand, kernel timers are similar to task queues in that a function registered in a kernel timer is executed only once—timers aren't cyclic.

There are times when you need to execute operations detached from any process's context, like turning off the floppy motor or terminating another lengthy shutdown operation. In that case, delaying the return from *close* wouldn't be fair to the application program. Using a task queue is also overkill, because a queued task must continually re-register itself while making its time calculations.

A timer is much easier to use. You register your function once and the kernel calls it once when the timer expires. Such a functionality is used often within the kernel proper, but it is sometimes needed by the drivers as well, as in the example of the floppy motor.

Linux uses two kinds of timers, so-called "old timers" and new timers. I'll quickly mention the old timers before showing you how to use the better new timers. The new timers, indeed, are not that new; they were introduced before Linux 1.0.

The old timers consist of 32 static timers. They survive only for compatibility reasons (and because removing them would mean modifying and testing several device drivers).

The data structure underlying the old timers is a bitmask of active timers and an array of timer structures, each containing the pointer to a handling function and the expiration time for the timer. The main problem with the old timers is that each device needing a timer to run a deferred operation has to have a timer number statically assigned to it.

This implementation was acceptable some years ago, when the number of supported devices (and thus the need for timers) was limited, but it is inadequate for current versions of Linux.

I won't show you how to use the old timers; I mentioned them here for the benefit of the curious reader.

The New Timer List

The new timers are organized in a doubly-linked list. This means that you can create as many timers as you want. A timer is characterized by its timeout value (in jiffies) and the function to be called when the timer expires. The timer handler receives an argument, which is stored in the data structure, together with a pointer to the handler itself.

The data structure of a timer looks like the following, which is extracted from `<linux/timer.h>`:

```
struct timer_list {
        struct timer_list *next;        /* never touch this */
        struct timer_list *prev;        /* never touch this */
        unsigned long expires;          /* the timeout, in jiffies */
        unsigned long data;             /* argument to the handler */
        void (*function)(unsigned long); /* handler of the timeout */
};
```

As you can see, the implementation of timers is slightly different from that of task queues, though the nature of the list item is similar. The two data structures aren't quite the same because they were created by two different programmers at almost the same time; one was not copied from the other. Thus, the timer handler takes an argument that is `unsigned long` instead of `void *`, and the handler itself is called `function` instead of `routine`.

The timeout of a timer is a "jiffy" value in that `timer->function` is required to run when `jiffies` is equal to or greater than `timer->expires`. The timeout is an absolute value; it's not relative to the current time and doesn't need to be updated.

Once a `timer_list` structure is initialized, *add_timer* inserts it into a sorted list, which is then looked up more or less 100 times a second (even if the timer tick is more frequent as it sometimes is, to save CPU time).

In short, these are the functions used to act on timers:

void init_timer(struct timer_list * timer);
  This inline function is used to initialize the timer structure. Currently, it zeroes only the `prev` and `next` pointers. Programmers are strongly urged to use this function to initialize a timer and to never explicitly touch the pointers in the structure, in order to be forward-compatible.

void add_timer(struct timer_list * timer);
  This function inserts a timer into the global list of active timers. It's interesting to note that the first implementations of the kernel timers behave differently from the current ones; in Linux 1.2, the function *add_timer* expects `timer->expires` to be relative to the current jiffy count, so it adds `jiffies` to the value before inserting the structure in the global list. This incompatibility is dealt with by *sysdep.h* in the source files.

```
int del_timer(struct timer_list * timer);
```
If a timer needs to be removed from the list before it expires, *del_timer* should be called. When a timer expires, on the other hand, it is automatically removed from the list.

An example of timer usage can be seen in the *jiq* module. The file */proc/jitimer* uses a timer to generate two data lines; the printing function is the same as above for the task queues. The first data line is generated from the *read* call, while the second line is printed by the timer function after 100 jiffies have elapsed.

The code for */proc/jitimer* is the following:

```
struct timer_list jiq_timer;

void jiq_timedout(unsigned long ptr)
{
    jiq_print((void *)ptr);           /* print a line */
    wake_up_interruptible(&jiq_wait); /* awake the process */
}



int jiq_read_run_timer(char *buf, char **start, off_t offset,
                  int len, int unused)
{

    jiq_data.len = 0;          /* prepare the argument for jiq_print() */
    jiq_data.buf = buf;
    jiq_data.jiffies = jiffies;
    jiq_data.queue = NULL;    /* don't requeue */

    init_timer(&jiq_timer);              /* init the timer structure */
    jiq_timer.function = jiq_timedout;
    jiq_timer.data = (unsigned long)&jiq_data;
    jiq_timer.expires = jiffies + HZ; /* one second */

    jiq_print(&jiq_data);    /* print and go to sleep */
    add_timer(&jiq_timer);
    interruptible_sleep_on(&jiq_wait);
    return jiq_data.len;
}
```

Running `head /proc/jitimer` gives the following output:

```
   time  delta intr_count pid command
 2121704   0        0    1092 head
 2121804 100        1       0 swapper
```

It's apparent from the value of `intr_count` in the second line that the timer function runs "at interrupt time."

What can appear strange when using timers is that the timer expires at just the right time, even if the processor is executing in a system call. I suggested earlier that when a process is running in kernel space, it won't be scheduled away; the clock tick, however, is special, and it does all of its tasks independent of the current process. You can try to look at what happens when you read */proc/jitbusy* in the background and */proc/jitimer* in the foreground. Although the system appears to be locked solid by the busy-waiting system call, both the timer queue and the kernel timers continue running.

Quick Reference

This chapter introduced the following symbols:

```
#include <linux/param.h>
HZ
```
> The HZ symbol specifies the number of clock ticks generated per second.

```
volatile unsigned long jiffies
```
> The jiffies variable is incremented once for each clock tick; thus it's incremented HZ times per second.

```
#include <linux/time.h>
void do_gettimeofday(struct timeval *tv);
```
> This function returns the current time. It is not available in version 1.2 of the kernel.

```
#include <linux/delay.h>
void udelay(unsigned long usecs);
```
> The *udelay* function delays an integer number of microseconds. It should be used to wait for no longer than one millisecond.

```
#include <linux/tqueue.h>
void queue_task(struct tq_struct *task, task_queue *list);
void queue_task_irq(struct tq_struct *task,
                    task_queue *list);
void queue_task_irq_off(struct tq_struct *task,
                        task_queue *list);
```
> These functions register a task for later execution. The first function, *queue_task*, can always be called; the second can be called only from non-reentrant functions, and the last one can be called only when interrupts are disabled. Only the first function is available in recent kernels (see "Task Queues" in Chapter 17).

```
void run_task_queue(task_queue *list);
```
This function consumes a task queue.

```
task_queue tq_immediate, tq_timer, tq_scheduler;
```
These predefined task queues are run as soon as possible, after each timer tick, and before the kernel schedules a new process, respectively.

```
#include <linux/timer.h>
void init_timer(struct timer_list * timer);
```
This function initializes a newly allocated `timer`.

```
void add_timer(struct timer_list * timer);
```
This function inserts the `timer` into the global list of pending timers.

```
int del_timer(struct timer_list * timer);
```
del_timer removes a timer from the list of pending timers. If the timer was actually queued, *del_timer* returns 1, otherwise it returns 0.

## CHAPTER SEVEN

GETTING HOLD
OF MEMORY

U ntil now, we have always used *kmalloc* and *kfree* for memory allocation. However, sticking to these functions would be a simplistic approach to managing memory. This chapter describes other allocation techniques. We're not interested yet in how the different architectures actually administer memory. Modules are not involved in issues of segmentation, paging, and so on, since the kernel offers a unified memory-management interface to the drivers. In addition, I won't describe the internal details of memory management in this chapter, but will defer it to "Memory Management in Linux," in Chapter 13, *Mmap and DMA*.

The Real Story of kmalloc

The *kmalloc* allocation engine is a powerful tool, and easily learned due to its similarity to *malloc*. The function is fast—unless it blocks—and it doesn't clear the memory it obtains; the allocated region still holds its previous content. In the next few sections, I'll talk in detail about *kmalloc*, so you can compare it to the memory allocation techniques that I'll discuss later.

The Priority Argument

The first argument to *kmalloc* is the size, which I'll talk about in the next section. The second argument, the priority, is much more interesting, because it causes *kmalloc* to modify its behavior when it has difficulty finding a page.

The most-used priority, GFP_KERNEL, means that the allocation (internally performed by calling *get_free_pages*, which explains the name) is performed on behalf of a process running in kernel space. In other words, this means that the calling function is executing a system call on behalf of a process. Using GFP_KERNEL allows *kmalloc* to delay returning if free memory is under the low-water mark, min_free_pages. In low-memory situations, the function puts the current process to sleep to wait for a page.

The new page can be retrieved in one of several ways. One way is by swapping out another page; since swapping takes time, the process waits for it to complete, while the kernel schedules other tasks. Therefore, every kernel function that calls kmalloc(GFP_KERNEL) should be reentrant. See "Writing Reentrant Code" in Chapter 5, *Enhanced Char Driver Operations*, for more about reentrancy.

GFP_KERNEL isn't always the right priority to use; sometimes *kmalloc* is called from outside a process's context—this happens, for instance, in interrupt handlers, task queues, and kernel timers. In this case, the current process should not be put asleep, and GFP_ATOMIC must be used as *kmalloc* priority. Atomic allocations are allowed to use every free bit of memory, independent of min_free_pages. In fact, the only reason the low-water mark exists is to be able to fulfill atomic requests. The kernel isn't allowed to swap out data or shrink filesystem buffers to fulfill the allocation request, so some real free memory has to be available.

Other priorities are defined for *kmalloc*, but they aren't used often and some of them are used only in internal memory management algorithms. The only other value of some interest is GFP_NFS, which allows the NFS filesystem to shrink the free list slightly below min_free_pages before putting the process to sleep. Needless to say, using GFP_NFS instead of GFP_KERNEL in order to get a "faster" driver degrades overall system performance.

In addition to the conventional priorities, *kmalloc* also recognizes a bitfield: GFP_DMA. The GFP_DMA flag should be used together with GFP_KERNEL or GFP_ATOMIC to allocate pages suitable for Direct Memory Access (DMA). We'll see how to use this flag in "Direct Memory Access" in Chapter 13.

The Size Argument

The kernel manages the system's *physical* memory, which is available only in page-sized chunks. This fact leads to a page-oriented allocation technique to obtain the maximum flexibility from the computer's RAM. A simple linear allocation technique similar to that used by *malloc* wouldn't work; a linear allocation pool is hard to maintain in a page-oriented environment like a Unix kernel. Hole management would soon become a problem, resulting in memory waste and performance penalties.

Linux addresses the problem of managing *kmalloc*'s needs by administering a page pool, so that pages can be added or removed from the pool easily. To be able to fulfill requests for more than PAGE_SIZE bytes, *fs/kmalloc.c* manages lists of page clusters. Each cluster holds a set of *consecutive* pages and is thus suitable for DMA allocations. I won't talk about the low-level details, as the internal structures can change at any time without affecting the allocation semantics or the driver code. As a matter of fact, version 2.1.38 replaced the implementation of *kmalloc* with a completely new one. The 2.0 implementation of memory allocation can be seen in *mm/kmalloc.c*, while the new one lives in *mm/slab.c*. See "Allocation and Deallocation" in Chapter 16, *Physical Layout of the Kernel Source*, for a more complete overview of the 2.0 implementation.

The net result of the allocation policies used by Linux is that the kernel can allocate only certain predefined fixed-sized byte arrays. If you ask for an arbitrary amount of memory, you're likely to get slightly more than you asked for.

The data sizes available are generally "slightly less than a power of two" (while the new implementation manages chunks of memory that are exactly a power of two). If you keep this fact in mind, you'll use memory more efficiently. For example, if you need a buffer of about 2000 bytes and run Linux 2.0, you're better off asking for 2000 bytes, rather than 2048. Requesting exactly a power of two is the worst possible case with any kernel older than 2.1.38—the kernel will allocate twice as much as you requested. This is why *scull* used 4000 bytes per quantum instead of 4096.

You can find the exact values used for the allocation blocks in *mm/kmalloc.c* (or *mm/slab.c*), but remember that they can change again without notice. The trick of allocating less than 4KB works with both the current 2.0 and 2.1 kernels, but it's not guaranteed to be optimal in the future.

In any case, the maximum size that can be allocated by *kmalloc* in Linux 2.0 is slightly less than 32 pages—256KB on the Alpha or 128KB on the Intel and other architectures. The limit is 128KB for any platform with 2.1.38 and newer kernels. If you need more than a few kilobytes, however, there are better ways to obtain memory, as outlined below.

get_free_page and Friends

If a module needs to allocate big chunks of memory, it is better to use a page-oriented technique. Requesting whole pages also has other advantages, which will be introduced later, in "The mmap Device Operation" in Chapter 13.

To allocate pages, the following functions are available:

- *get_free_page* returns a pointer to a new page and zeros the page.

- _ _*get_free_page* is like *get_free_page*, but doesn't clear the page.

- *__get_free_pages* returns a pointer to the first byte of a memory area that is several pages long, but doesn't zero the area.

- *__get_dma_pages* returns the pointer to the first byte of a memory area several pages long; the pages are consecutive in physical memory and suitable for DMA.

The prototypes for the functions, as defined in Linux 2.0, follow:

```
unsigned long get_free_page(int priority);
unsigned long __get_free_page(int priority);
unsigned long __get_dma_pages(int priority,
                              unsigned long order);
unsigned long __get_free_pages(int priority,
                              unsigned long order, int dma);
```

As a matter of fact, all the functions except *__get_free_pages* are either macros or inline functions that ultimately map to *__get_free_pages*.

When a program is done with the pages, it can call one of the following functions. The first function is a macro that falls back on the second:

```
void free_page(unsigned long addr);
void free_pages(unsigned long addr, unsigned long order);
```

If you're writing code to work with both 1.2 and 2.0, it's better *not* to use *__get_free_pages* directly because the way you call it changed twice between version 1.2 and 2.0 of the kernel. Using only *get_free_page* and *__get_free_page* (as well as *free_page*) is safe and portable, and should meet most needs.

As far as DMA is concerned, it has always been a problem to correctly address it with ISA boards, due to several design "peculiarities" of the PC platform. When I introduce DMA in "Direct Memory Access," in Chapter 13, I'll limit the discussion to 2.0 kernels to avoid introducing several portability problems.

The `priority` argument in the allocation functions has the same meaning as it does in *kmalloc*. The `dma` argument to *__get_free_pages* is either zero or non-zero; if it's non-zero, then DMA can be used on the allocated page cluster. `order` is the power of two of the number of pages you are requesting or freeing (i.e., $\log_2 N$). For example, `order` is 0 if you want one page and 3 to get eight pages. If `order` is too big, the page allocation will fail. If you try to free a different number of pages than you allocated, the memory map will probably become corrupted. In current Linux versions, the maximum value of `order` is 5 (corresponding to 32 pages). Anyway, the bigger the order, the more likely it is that the allocation will fail.

It's worth stressing that *get_free_pages* and the other functions can be called at any time, subject to the same rules of priority as we saw for *kmalloc*. The functions can fail to allocate memory in certain circumstances, most often when the priority is `GFP_ATOMIC`. Therefore, the program calling these allocation functions must be written to handle an allocation failure.

It has been said that if you want to live dangerously, you can assume that neither *kmalloc* nor the underlying *get_free_pages* will ever fail when called with a priority of GFP_KERNEL. This is *almost* true, but not completely: my faithful 386, equipped with a spare 4MB of RAM, behaved quite wildly when I was running a "play-it-dangerous" module. Unless you are just programming for fun and have plenty of memory, I'd recommend always checking the allocation results.

Although kmalloc(GFP_KERNEL) sometimes fails when there is no available memory, the kernel does its best to fulfill allocation requests. Therefore, it's easy to degrade system responsiveness by allocating too much memory. For example, you can bring the computer down by pushing too much data into a *scull* device; the system will start crawling while it tries to swap out as much as possible in order to fulfill the *kmalloc* request. Since every resource is being sucked up by the growing device, the computer is soon rendered unusable; at that point you can no longer spawn a new process on your shell. I don't address this issue in *scull*, as it is just a sample module and not a real tool to put into a multiuser system. As a programmer, you must nonetheless be careful, because a module is privileged code, and it can open new security holes in the system (the most likely is a "denial-of-service" hole like the one just outlined).

A scull Using Whole Pages: scullp

Now we're through discussing theory, and I'll show you some code that uses page allocation. *scullp* is a cut-down version of the *scull* module that implements only the bare device—the persistent memory region. Unlike *scull*, *scullp* uses page allocation to retrieve memory; the scullp_order variable defaults to 0 and can be specified at either compile time or load time. The device, when compiled against Linux 1.2, refuses to load if the order is greater than 0, for the reasons outlined above. Only the "safe" single-page allocation function is allowed by *scullp* when run with Linux 1.2.

Although this is a real example, there are only two lines of code worth showing, because the device is really a *scull* device with a single change in the allocation and deallocation functions. The following code shows these lines used to allocate and release pages with a little surrounding context:

```
/* Here's the allocation of a single quantum */
if (!dptr->data[s_pos]) {
    dptr->data[s_pos] = (void *)__get_free_pages(GFP_KERNEL,
                                             dptr->order,0);
    if (!dptr->data[s_pos])
        return -ENOMEM;
    memset(dptr->data[s_pos], 0, PAGE_SIZE << dptr->order);

        /* This code frees a whole quantum-set */
        for (i = 0; i < qset; i++)
```

```
if (dptr->data[i])
    free_pages((unsigned long)(dptr->data[i]),
                dptr->order);
```

At the user level, the perceived difference is primarily a speed improvement. I ran some tests copying 4 megabytes from *scull0* to *scull1* and then from *scullp0* to *scullp1*; the results showed a slight improvement in kernel-space processor usage.

The performance improvement is not dramatic, because *kmalloc* is designed to be fast. The main advantage of page-level allocation isn't actually speed, but rather the more efficient memory usage. Allocating by pages wastes no memory, while using *kmalloc* wastes an unpredictable amount of memory. As a matter of fact, you might remember from "The Underlying Data Structure" in Chapter 5 that select_table is allocated with *__get_free_page*.

But the biggest advantage of *__get_free_page* is that the page is completely yours, and you could, in theory, assemble the pages into a linear area by appropriate tweaking of the page tables. As a result, you can allow a user process to *mmap* memory areas obtained as single unrelated pages. I'll discuss this kind of operation in "The mmap Device Operation," in Chapter 13, where the internals of page tables are covered.

vmalloc and Friends

The next memory allocation function that I'll show you is *vmalloc*, which allocates a contiguous memory region in the *virtual* address space. Although the pages are not necessarily consecutive in physical memory (each page is retrieved with a separate call to *__get_free_page*), the kernel sees them as a contiguous range of addresses. The allocated space is mapped only to the kernel segments and is not visible from user space—not unlike the other allocation techniques. *vmalloc* returns 0 (the NULL address) if an error occurred, otherwise it returns a pointer to a linear memory area of size size.

The prototypes of the function, and its relatives, are the following:

```
void * vmalloc(unsigned long size);
void vfree(void * addr);
void * vremap(unsigned long offset, unsigned long size);
```

Note that *vremap* was renamed *ioremap* in version 2.1. Moreover, Linux 2.1 introduced a new header, <linux/vmalloc.h>, that must be included if you use *vmalloc*.

vmalloc is different from the other memory allocation functions because it returns "high" addresses—addresses that are higher than the top of physical memory. The processor is able to access the returned memory range because *vmalloc* arranged the processor's page tables to access the allocated pages through consecutive "high" addresses. Kernel code can use addresses returned by *vmalloc* just like any other address, but the address used by the program is not the same as the one that appears on the electrical data bus.

Addresses allocated by *vmalloc* can't be used outside of the microprocessor, because they make sense only on top of the processor's paging unit. When a driver needs a real physical address (such as a DMA address, used by peripheral hardware to drive the system's bus), you can't use *vmalloc*. The right time to call *vmalloc* is when you are allocating memory for a large sequential buffer that exists only in software. It's important to note that *vmalloc* has more overhead than _ _*get_ free_pages* because it must both retrieve the memory and build the page tables. Therefore, it doesn't make sense to call *vmalloc* to allocate just one page.

An example of a function that uses *vmalloc* is the *create_module* system call, which uses *vmalloc* to get space for the module being created. The module itself is later copied to the allocated space using *memcpy_fromfs*, after *insmod* has relocated the code.

Memory allocated with *vmalloc* is released by *vfree*, in the same way that *kfree* releases memory allocated by *kmalloc*.

Like *vmalloc*, *vremap* (or *ioremap*) builds new page tables, but unlike *vmalloc*, it doesn't actually allocate any memory. The return value of *vremap* is a virtual address that can be used to access the specified physical address range; the virtual address obtained is eventually released by calling *vfree*.

vremap is most useful for mapping a high-memory PCI buffer to user space. For example, if the frame buffer on the VGA device has been mapped to the address 0xf0000000 (a typical value), *vremap* can be used to build the correct tables for the processor to access it. System initialization builds page tables only to access memory from address 0 up to the the top of physical memory. System initialization does not probe for PCI buffers, but leaves each driver responsible for managing buffers on its own device; PCI issues are explained in more detail in "The PCI Interface," in Chapter 15, *Overview of Peripheral Buses*. On the other hand, you don't need to remap the ISA hole below 1MB, because this memory is accessed by other means, described in the section "Accessing Memory on Device Boards," in Chapter 8, *Hardware Management*.

If your driver is meant to be portable across different platforms, however, you must be careful when using *vremap*. Some platforms are unable to directly map PCI memory regions to the processor address space. This happens, for example, for the Alpha. In this case you can't access remapped regions like conventional memory, and you need to use *readb* and the other I/O functions (see "ISA Memory Below 1M" in Chapter 8). This set of functions is portable across platforms.

There is almost no limit to how much memory *vmalloc* and *vremap* can allocate, although *vmalloc* refuses to allocate more memory than the amount of physical

RAM, in order to detect common errors or typos made by programmers. You should remember, however, that requesting too much memory with *vmalloc* leads to the same problems as it does with *kmalloc*.

Both *vremap* and *vmalloc* are page-oriented (they work by modifying the page tables); thus the relocated or allocated size is rounded up to the nearest page boundary. In addition, *vremap* won't even consider remapping a physical address that doesn't start at a page boundary.

One minor drawback of *vmalloc* is that it can't be used at interrupt time because internally it uses `kmalloc(GFP_KERNEL)` to acquire storage for the page tables. This shouldn't be a problem—if the use of *__get_free_page* isn't good enough for an interrupt handler, then the software design needs some cleaning up.

A scull Using Virtual Addresses: scullv

Sample code using *vmalloc* is provided in the *scullv* module. Like *scullp*, this module is a stripped-down version of *scull* that uses a different allocation function to obtain space for the device to store data.

The module allocates memory 16 pages at a time (128KB on the Alpha, 64KB on the x86). The allocation is done in large chunks to achieve better performance than *scullp* and to show something that takes too long with other allocation techniques to be feasible. Allocating more than one page with *__get_free_pages* is failure-prone, and even when it succeeds, it can be slow. As we saw earlier, *vmalloc* is faster than other functions in allocating several pages, but somewhat slower when retrieving a single page, due to the overhead of page-table building. *scullv* is designed exactly like *scullp*. `order` specifies the "order" of each allocation and defaults to 4. The only difference between *scullv* and *scullp* is in the following code:

```
/* Allocate a quantum using virtual addresses */
if (!dptr->data[s_pos]) {
    dptr->data[s_pos] = (void *)vmalloc(PAGE_SIZE << order);
    if (!dptr->data[s_pos])
        return -ENOMEM;

        /* Release the quantum-set */
        for (i = 0; i < qset; i++)
            if (dptr->data[i])
                vfree(dptr->data[i]);
```

If you compile both modules with debugging enabled, you can look at their data allocation by reading the files they create in */proc*. The following snapshot was taken on my home computer, whose physical addresses go from 0 to 0x1800000 (24MB):

```
morgana.root# cp /bin/cp /dev/scullp0
morgana.root# cat /proc/scullpmem
Device 0: qset 500, order 0, sz 19652
  item at 0063e598, qset at 006eb018
        0: 150e000
        1:  de6000
        2: 10ca000
        3:  e19000
        4:  bd1000

morgana.root# cp /zImage.last /dev/scullv0
morgana.root# cat /proc/scullvmem

Device 0: qset 500, order 4, sz 289840
  item at 0063ec98, qset at 00b3e810
        0: 2034000
        1: 2045000
        2: 2056000
        3: 2067000
        4: 2078000
```

It's apparent from the values shown that *scullp* allocates physical addresses (within 0x1800000), while *scullv* uses virtual addresses (but note that the actual values are different with Linux 2.1, as the organization of the virtual address space was changed—see "Virtual Memory" in Chapter 17, *Recent Developments*).

Playing Dirty

If you really need a huge buffer of consecutive memory, the easiest (and least flexible, but the least prone to fail) way to allocate it is at boot time. Needless to say, a module can't allocate memory at boot time; only drivers directly linked to the kernel can play dirty and allocate the memory.

Allocation at boot time looks like the only way to retrieve a big memory buffer, although I'll introduce an alternative technique (though somewhat worse) in "Allocating the DMA Buffer," in Chapter 13. Allocating the buffer at boot time is "dirty" because it bypasses the kernel's memory management policies. Moreover, it isn't feasible for the average user because it involves replacing the whole kernel. Most Linux users are willing to load a module, but are reluctant to patch and recompile the kernel. While I won't suggest that you use this "allocation technique," it's worth mentioning because it used to be the only way to allocate a DMA-capable buffer in the first Linux versions, before GFP_DMA was introduced.

But let's look at how boot-time allocation works. When the kernel is booted, it gains access to all of the physical memory in the system. It then initializes each of its subsystems by calling that subsystem's initialization function, passing it the current bounds of the free memory area as arguments. Each initialization function can steal part of this area, returning the new lower bound. A driver allocating memory at boot time, therefore, steals consecutive memory from the linear array of available RAM.

This way of allocating memory has several disadvantages, not least the inability to ever free the buffer. After a driver has taken some pages, it has no way of returning them to the pool of free pages; the pool is created after all the physical allocation has taken place, and I don't recommend hacking the data structures internal to memory management. On the other hand, the advantage of this technique is that it makes available an area of consecutive physical memory that is suitable for DMA or whatever else. This is currently the only "safe" way to allocate a buffer of more than 32 consecutive pages, because the maximum value of order that is accepted by *get_free_pages* is 5. If, however, you need many pages and they don't have to be physically contiguous, *vmalloc* is by far the best function to use.

If you are going to resort to grabbing memory at boot time, you must modify *init/main.c* in the kernel sources. You'll find more about *main.c* in Chapter 16, and in "ISA Memory Above 1M" in Chapter 8.

Note that this "allocation" can be performed only in multiples of the page size, though the number of pages doesn't have to be a power of two.

Quick Reference

The functions and symbols related to memory allocation are listed below:

```
#include <linux/malloc.h>
void *kmalloc(unsigned int size, int priority);
void kfree(void *obj);
```
The most frequently used interface to memory allocation.

```
#include <linux/mm.h>
GFP_KERNEL
GFP_ATOMIC
GFP_DMA
```
kmalloc priorities. GFP_DMA is a flag that can be ORed to either GFP_KERNEL or GFP_ATOMIC.

```
unsigned long get_free_page(int priority);
unsigned long __get_free_page(int priority);
unsigned long __get_dma_pages(int priority,
                              unsigned long order);
unsigned long __get_free_pages(int priority,
```

```
                              unsigned long order,
                              int dma);
```
The page-oriented allocation functions. The underscore-prefixed functions don't clear the page(s). Only the former two functions are portable across Linux 1.2 and 2.0, because the latter two behaved differently in 1.2.

```
void free_page(unsigned long addr);
void free_pages(unsigned long addr, unsigned long order);
```
These functions release page-oriented allocations.

```
void * vmalloc(unsigned long size);
void * vremap(unsigned long offset, unsigned long size);
void vfree(void * addr);
```
These functions allocate or free a contiguous *virtual* address space. *vremap* accesses physical memory through virtual addresses (and is called *ioremap* in Linux 2.1), while *vmalloc* allocates free pages. In either case, the pages are released with *vfree*. Linux 2.1 introduced the header <linux/vmalloc.h>, which you must include to use these functions.

## CHAPTER EIGHT

HARDWARE MANAGEMENT

W hile playing with *scull* and similar toys can be a pleasant way to become familiar with the software interface of a Linux device driver, testing a *real* device requires hardware. The driver is the abstraction layer between software concepts and hardware circuitry; as such, it needs to talk with both of them. Up to now, we have examined the internals of software concepts; this chapter should complete the picture by showing you how a driver can access I/O ports and I/O memory, while being portable across Linux platforms.

As usual, I won't bind the sample code to a particular device. However, we can no longer use a memory-based device like *scull*. Instead, the examples in this chapter use the parallel port to show I/O instructions and the standard video buffer of text-mode VGA boards to show memory-mapped I/O.

I chose the parallel port because it offers direct input and output of several bits of information. Data bits written to the device appear on the output pins, and voltage levels on the input pins are directly accessible by the processor. In practice, you have to connect LEDs to the port to actually *see* the results of an I/O operation. The parallel port is easy to program, much easier than the serial port, and almost every computer (even the Alpha) has a parallel port that works like the one in the PC.

As far as memory-mapped I/O is concerned, text-mode VGA is the most standardized memory-mapped device, and almost every computer has a VGA-compatible text mode. Unfortunately, not every Alpha has a VGA video adapter, and the Sparc definitely doesn't, so our VGA-related code won't be as portable as the parallel port example. Also, you'll have to switch the computer to text mode in order to run the sample code, which shouldn't be a serious constraint. The biggest problem with experimenting using VGA memory is that the sample driver will unavoidably trash the foreground virtual console.

Using I/O Ports

In some sense, I/O ports are like memory locations: they can be read and written by means of the same electrical signals that memory chips receive. But they are not exactly the same; port operations talk directly to peripheral devices, which are often less flexible than RAM. In particular, there are 8-bit ports, 16-bit ports, and 32-bit ports, and you can't mix them.*

A C program, therefore, must call different functions to access different size ports. The Linux kernel headers (specifically, the architecture-dependent header `<asm/io.h>`) define the inline functions listed below.

NOTE   From now on, when I use `unsigned` without further type specifications, I am referring to an architecture-dependent definition whose exact nature is not relevant. The functions are almost portable because the compiler automatically casts the values during assignment—their being unsigned helps prevent compilation-time warnings. No information is lost with such casts as long as the programmer assigns sensible values to avoid overflow. I'll stick to this convention of "incomplete typing" for the rest of the chapter.

```
unsigned inb(unsigned port);
void outb(unsigned char byte, unsigned port);
```
Read or write byte ports (8 bits wide). The `port` argument is defined as `unsigned long` for some platforms and `unsigned short` for others. The return type of *inb* is also different across architectures.

```
unsigned inw(unsigned port);
void outw(unsigned short word, unsigned port);
```
These functions access 16-bit ports ("word-wide"); they are not available in the M68k version of Linux because the processor supports byte I/O, but neither word nor long operations.

```
unsigned inl(unsigned port);
void outl(unsigned doubleword, unsigned port);
```
These functions access 32-bit ports. `doubleword` is either declared as `unsigned long` or `unsigned int`, according to the platform.

In addition to the single-shot in and out operations, most processors implement special instructions to transfer a sequence of bytes, words, or longs to and from a

---

* As a matter of fact, sometimes I/O ports *are* arranged like memory, and you can (for example) bind two 8-bit writes into a single 16-bit operation. This applies, for instance, to PC video boards, but in general you can't count on this feature.

single I/O port. These are the so-called "string instructions," which are introduced in "String Operations," later in this chapter.

Note that no 64-bit I/O operations are defined. Even on 64-bit architectures, I/O ports only use a 32-bit data path.

The functions described above are primarily meant to be used by device drivers, but they can also be used from user space (the preprocessor definitions or inline declarations are not protected by #ifdef __KERNEL__). The following conditions should, however, apply in order for *inb* and friends to be used in user-space code:

- The program must be compiled with the *–O* option to force expansion of inline functions.

- *ioperm* or *iopl* must be used to get permission to perform I/O operations on ports. *ioperm* gets permission for individual ports, while *iopl* gets permission for the entire I/O space. Both these functions are Intel-specific.

- The program must run as root to invoke *ioperm*. Alternatively, one of its ancestors must have gained port access running as root.

The sample sources *misc-progs/inp.c* and *misc-progs/outp.c* are a minimal tool for reading and writing 8-bit ports from the command line, in user space. I have run them successfully on my PC. They don't run on other plaftorms due to the missing *ioperm* capability. The programs can be made set-uid, if you want to live dangerously and play with your hardware without acquiring explicit privileges.

Platform Dependencies

If you are looking for porting problems, you'll find that I/O instructions are the most processor-dependent of all computer instructions. As a consequence, much of the source code related to port I/O is platform-dependent.

The Linux system, though portable, isn't completely transparent to processor peculiarities. Most hardware devices are not portable across platforms, and driver writers don't generally address more than two or three architectures in the same module.

You can see one of the incompatibilities, data typing, by looking back at the list of functions, where the arguments are typed differently based on the architectural differences between platforms. For example, a port is unsigned short on the x86 (where the processor supports a 64KB-byte I/O space), but unsigned long on the Alpha, whose ports are just special locations in the same address space as memory; the Alpha, by design, has no I/O address space, and its ports are folded to non-cacheable memory addresses.

I/O typing is one part of the kernel that still needs some cleaning up, although things work correctly now. The best solution to ambiguous typing would be to define an architecture-specific `port_t` type and use `u8`, `u16`, and `u32` for the data items (see "Assigning an Explicit Size to Data Items" in Chapter 10, *Judicious Use of Data Types*). Nobody has taken care of the problem yet, however, as the issue is mostly cosmetic.

Other platform dependencies arise from basic structural differences in the processors and thus are unavoidable. I won't go into detail about the differences, because I assume that you won't be writing a device driver for a particular system without understanding the underlying hardware. Instead, the following is an overview of the capabilities of the supported architectures:

x86

> The architecture supports all the functions described in this chapter.

Alpha

> All the functions are supported, but there are differences in the implementation of port I/O for different Alpha platforms. String functions are implemented in C and defined in *arch/alpha/lib/io.c*. Unfortunately, only word and long string operations are exported in 2.0 kernels till 2.0.29; therefore, *insb* and *outsb* are not available to modules. This problem has been fixed in version 2.0.30 and 2.1.3.

Sparc

> The Sparc doesn't have special I/O instructions. I/O space is memory-mapped and is marked by flags in the page-table entry. The header defines empty functions for *inb* and the other functions to prevent the compiler from complaining when first porting drivers to the Sparc architecture.

M68k

> Only *inb*, *outb*, and their pausing counterparts (see below) are supported. No string functions are defined for the 68000, nor are *readb*, *writeb*, and friends defined.

Mips

> The Mips port supports all the functions. String operations are implemented with tight assembly loops, as the processor lacks machine-level string I/O.

PowerPC

> All the functions except string I/O are supported.

The curious reader can extract more information from the *io.h* files, which sometimes define a few architecture-specific functions in addition to those I describe in this chapter.

It's interesting to note that the Alpha processors don't feature a different address space for ports, even though AXP computers are often shipped with ISA and PCI slots, and both buses feature signal lines to differentiate memory and I/O operations. Alpha-based PCs implement the Intel-compatible I/O abstraction through specific interface chips that translate references to particular memory addresses into I/O port access.

I/O operations on the Alpha are well described in the "Alpha Reference Manual," which is available free from Digital Equipment Corporation. The manual thoroughly describes the I/O issue and tells how the AXP processors divide virtual addresses into "memory-like" and "non-memory-like" regions; the latter are used for memory-mapped I/O.

Pausing I/O

Some platforms—most notably the i386—can have problems when the processor tries to transfer data too quickly to or from the bus. The problems can arise because the processor is over-clocked with respect to the ISA bus, and can show up when the device board is too slow; the solution is to insert a small delay after an I/O instruction if another such instruction follows. If your device misses some data, or if you fear it might miss some, you can use pausing functions in place of the normal ones. The pausing functions are exactly like those listed above, but their names end in _p; they are called *inb_p*, *outb_p*, and so on. For all the supported architectures, when the non-pausing function is defined, the pausing equivalent is defined as well, even in cases where they expand to the same code.

If you want to explicitly insert a small pause in your driver (smaller than you'd get with *udelay*), you can use the explicit SLOW_DOWN_IO statement. This macro expands to instructions that do nothing except delay execution. You might want to insert the statement at critical points in your source. SLOW_DOWN_IO actually executes the same code as that added to *outb* when *outb_p* is expanded.

The definition of SLOW_DOWN_IO (and thus the _p pause) depends on whether SLOW_IO_BY_JUMPING and/or REALLY_SLOW_IO are defined before <asm/io.h> is included. Fortunately, new hardware doesn't require the programmer to deal with these questions, so I won't talk about pausing any more. The interested reader is urged to browse <asm/io.h>. As a driver writer, you should nonetheless remember that SLOW_DOWN_IO is undefined for the Sparc and M68k architectures (though pausing calls like *outb_p* are defined, with the limitations outlined in "Platform Dependencies," earlier in this chapter).

String Operations

The Linux headers define functions to perform string operations, which can be used by some drivers to get better performance than a C-language loop. The Linux implementation for string I/O maps either to a single machine instruction or to a tight loop, or it is missing altogether, depending on the capabilities of the target processor or platform.

The prototypes for string functions are the following:

```
void insb(unsigned port, void *addr, unsigned long count);
void outsb(unsigned port, void *addr, unsigned long count);
```
Read or write count bytes starting at the memory address addr. Data is read from or written to the single port port.

```
void insw(unsigned port, void *addr, unsigned long count);
void outsw(unsigned port, void *addr, unsigned long count);
```
Read or write 16-bit values to a single 16-bit port.

```
void insl(unsigned port, void *addr, unsigned long count);
void outsl(unsigned port, void *addr, unsigned long count);
```
Read or write 32-bit values to a single 32-bit port.

Using the Parallel Port

The parallel port, which we'll use as the test case for our I/O code, is really basic; in fact, I can hardly imagine a simpler interface adapter.

Although most readers probably have parallel port specifications available, I'll summarize them here for your convenience while you're reading the code for the module I'm going to introduce.

Basics of the Parallel Port

The parallel port, in its minimal configuration (I'm not going to deal with ECP and EPP modes) is made up of a few 8-bit ports. Data written to the output ports appears as signal levels on the output pins of the 25-pin connector, and what you read from the input ports is the current logic level at input pins.

The signal levels used in parallel communications are standard TTL levels: 0 and 5 volts, with the logic threshold at about 1.2 volts; you can count on the ports at least meeting the standard TTL LS current ratings, although most modern parallel ports do better in both current and voltage ratings.

WARNING   The parallel connector is not isolated from the computer's internal circuitry, which is useful if you want to connect logic gates directly to the port. But you have to be careful to do the wiring correctly; the parallel port is easily burned when you play with your own custom circuitry. You can choose to use plug-in parallel ports if you fear you'll damage your motherboard.

The bit specifications are outlined in Figure 8-1. You can access 12 output bits and 5 input bits, some of which are logically inverted over the course of their signal path. The only bit with no associated signal pin is bit 4 (0x10) of port 2. We'll make use of this bit in Chapter 9, *Interrupt Handling*.

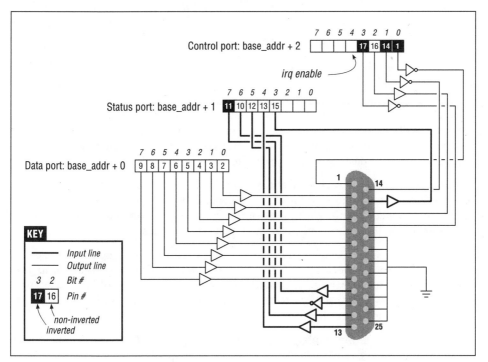

Figure 8-1: The pinout of the parallel port

A Sample Driver

The driver I'm going to introduce is called *short* (Simple Hardware Operations and Raw Tests). All it does is read and write the various 8-bit ports of the parallel interface (or other I/O device). Each device node (with a unique minor number) accesses a different port. The *short* driver doesn't do anything useful; it just isolates for external use a single instruction acting on a port. If you are not used to port I/O, you can use *short* to get familiar with it; you can measure the time it takes to transfer data through a port or play other games.

To watch what happens on the parallel connector, I suggest that you solder a few LEDs to the output pins. Each LED should be connected in series to a 1KB resistor leading to a ground pin. If you connect an output pin to an input pin, you'll generate your own input to be read from the input ports.

If you are going to visualize parallel data by soldering LEDs to a D-type connector, I suggest that you not use pins 9 and 10, as we'll be connecting them together later to run the sample code shown in Chapter 9.

As far as *short* is concerned, */dev/short0* writes data by means of a tight loop that copies user data to the output port, one byte at a time:

```
while (count--)
    outb(*(ptr++), port);
```

You can run the following command to light your LEDs:

```
echo -n any string > /dev/short0
```

Each LED monitors a single bit of the output port. Remember that only the last character written remains steady on the output pin long enough to be perceived by your eyes. For that reason, I suggest that you prevent automatic insertion of a trailing newline by passing the *−n* option to *echo*.

Reading is performed by a similar function, built around *inb* instead of *outb*. In order to read "meaningful" values from the parallel port, you need to have some hardware connected to the input pins of the connector to generate signals. If there is no signal, you'll read an endless stream of identical bytes.

For complete I/O coverage, there are three variations of each *short* device: */dev/short0* performs the loop just shown, */dev/short0p* uses *outb_p* and *inb_p* in place of the "fast" functions, and */dev/short0s* uses the string instructions. There are four such devices, from *short0* to *short3*, and each of them accesses one I/O port. The four ports are consecutive.

When compiled for the Alpha, which doesn't export *insb* or *outsb*, the device *short0s* behaves exactly like *short0*.

Though *short* doesn't perform any "real" hardware control, it can be an interesting test platform for timing the different instructions, and it can help you get started. Everyone interested in writing device drivers surely owns more interesting devices to play with, but the old and silly parallel port can still perform some useful tasks—I personally use it to prepare my coffee after turning on my radio in the morning.

Accessing Memory on Device Boards

The last chapter introduced every possible way to allocate memory from RAM; we'll now deal with another kind of memory that can be present in the computer: memory on expansion boards. Peripherals do have memory on them. Display boards host a frame buffer, video grabbers hold grabbed data, and an Ethernet interface might host received packets in a memory region; additionally, most peripheral boards have some on-board ROM that must be executed by the processor at system boot. All such entities are "memory," in that the processor accesses them through memory instructions. I am limiting the discussion here to the ISA and PCI devices, as they are the most used nowadays.

There are three common kinds of peripheral memory on standard x86 computers: ISA memory in the 640KB–1MB range, ISA memory in the 14MB–16MB range, and PCI memory above the end of physical memory. The addresses used above are physical addresses, the numbers that travel in the computer's address bus, and they have nothing to do with the virtual addresses used by program code (see "vmalloc and Friends" in Chapter 7, *Getting Hold of Memory*). The physical location where I/O memory lives is mainly an historical heritage, as explained later when the three memory ranges are introduced.

Unfortunately (or fortunately, if you prefer good architectural design to easy portability), not every Linux platform supports ISA and PCI; this section is limited to the discussion of those that do.

ISA Memory Below 1M

I've already introduced an "easy" (and broken) way to deal with such memory in "ISA Memory" in Chapter 2, *Building and Running Modules*, where I showed how pointers holding the physical hardware address dereference correctly to the requested I/O memory. Though this technique works on the x86 platforms, it is not portable to all Linux platforms. Pointer dereferencing might be a good choice for small and short-lived projects, but it's not recommended for a production driver.

The recommended interface to I/O memory was introduced into the kernel during the 1.3 development tree and is missing from older kernels. The *sysdep.h* header released with the *short* sample code, however, implements the new semantics for kernel versions back to 1.2.

The new interface consists of a set of macros and function calls that are used in place of pointer dereferencing whenever you need to access I/O memory. Such macros and functions are portable; this means that the same source code will compile and run on different architectures, as long as they host the same peripheral bus.

Most of these macros currently expand to pointer dereferencing when you compile code on your Intel-based PC, but their internal behavior could well change in the future. One such change happened, for example, in the initial switch from 2.0 to 2.1, when Linus decided to change the virtual memory layout. With the new layout, ISA memory can't be accessed in the old-fashioned way described in Chapter 2.

The new interface to I/O memory consists of the following functions:

```
unsigned readb(address);
unsigned readw(address);
unsigned readl(address);
```
> These macros are used to retrieve 8-bit, 16-bit, and 32-bit data values from I/O memory. They are missing from Linux 1.2. The advantage of using macros is the typelessness of the argument: `address` is cast before being used, because the value "is not clearly either an integer or a pointer, and we will accept both" (from *asm-alpha/io.h*). Neither the reading nor the writing functions check the validity of `address`, as they are meant to be as fast as pointer dereferencing (we already know that sometimes they actually expand into pointer dereferencing).

```
void writeb(unsigned value, address);
void writew(unsigned value, address);
void writel(unsigned value, address);
```
> Like the previous functions, these functions (macros) are used to write 8-bit, 16-bit, and 32-bit data items.

```
memset_io(address, value, count);
```
> When you need to call *memset* on I/O memory, this function does what you need, while keeping the semantics of the original *memset.*

```
memcpy_fromio(dest, source, nbytes);
memcpy_toio(dest, source, nbytes);
```
> These functions move blocks of data to and from I/O memory and behave like *memcpy_tofs.* They have been introduced together with the functions above, and they are missing in Linux 1.2. The *sysdep.h* header distributed with the sample drivers fixes the version dependency of the functions and defines them for any kernel from 1.2 on.

The portability of these functions across the supported architectures is currently limited, like that of the port I/O functions. The functions are completely missing from some platforms; on some they are macros that expand to pointer operations, and on others they are real functions.

People like me, accustomed to the flat memory model of our old PCs, might hesitate to bother with a new interface just to access "a region of physical addresses." Actually, getting comfortable with the interface is simply a question of getting some practice using the functions. There's nothing better for gaining confidence than looking at a silly module that just accesses I/O memory. The module I'm going to show you is actually called *silly*, short for "Simple Tool for Unloading and Printing ISA Data."

The module features four device nodes that perform the same task using different data transfer functions. The *silly* devices act as a window over I/O memory, in a way similar to */dev/mem*. You can read and write data, *lseek* to an arbitrary I/O memory address, and *mmap* the region to your process (see "The mmap Device Operation" in Chapter 13, *Mmap and DMA*).

/dev/sillyb, featuring minor number 0, accesses I/O memory with *readb* and *writeb*. The following code shows the implementation for *read*, which remaps the address range 0xA0000–0xFFFFF to file offset 0–0x5FFFF. The *read* function is structured as a `switch` statement over the different access modes; here is the *sillyb* `case`:

```
case M_8:
  while (count) {
      *ptr = readb(add);
      add++; count--; ptr++;
  }
  break;
```

The next two devices are */dev/sillyw* (minor number 1) and */dev/sillyl* (minor number 2). They act exactly like */dev/sillyb*, except that they use 16-bit and 32-bit functions. Here's the *write* implementation of *sillyl*, again part of a `switch`:

```
case M_32:
  while (count >= 4) {
      writel(*(u32 *)ptr, add);
      add+=4; count-=4; ptr+=4;
  }
  break;
```

The last device is */dev/sillycp* (minor number 3), which uses the *memcpy_*io* functions to perform the same task. Here's the core of its *read* implementation:

```
case M_memcpy:
  memcpy_fromio(ptr, add, count);
  break;
```

ISA Memory Above 1M

Some ISA device boards carry on-board memory that is mapped to the physical addresses between 14MB and 16MB. These devices are slowly disappearing, but it's worth introducing how their memory range can be accessed. This discussion, however, only applies to the x86 architecture; I've no information on how the Alpha or other architectures behave with such ISA boards.

In the old days of the 80286 processor, when the physical address space was 20 bits wide (16MB) and all the address lines were present on the ISA bus, almost no computer carried more than 1 or 2 megs of RAM. Why couldn't the expansion board steal some high memory addresses for its buffer? This idea is not new; it's the same concept that led to ISA memory below 1M, and it was later recycled to implement high PCI buffers. The chosen address range for ISA device boards was the top two megs, though most boards just use the top meg.

Nowadays, there are still a few motherboards that can host these old-fashioned boards even when there are more than 14 megs of physical RAM. Correctly handling this memory requires you to play games with the address ranges to avoid ending up with overlapping RAM and bus addresses.

If you have an ISA device with high memory, and you're unlucky enough to have less than 16MB RAM, managing the memory is easy. Your software should behave as though it had a high PCI buffer (see the next section), except that it will be slower, because ISA memory is slow.

If you have an ISA device with high memory and you have 16MB or more, then you're in deep trouble.

One possibility is that your motherboard doesn't correctly support the "ISA hole." In that case, there's nothing you can do to access the on-board memory except change the board or remove some RAM. If, on the other hand, the motherboard handles the ISA hole, you still need to tell the Linux kernel about such memory and do some work to be able to access the rest of your RAM (the range over 16M).

The place where you need to do some hacking to correctly reserve the high ISA memory, while not losing access to the remaining RAM, is in the map of the computer's physical memory. This map is built in *arch/i386/mm/init.c*, within the *mem_init* function. The array `mem_map` holds the relevant information about each memory page; if the bit `PG_reserved` is set for a page, the kernel won't use that page for normal paging activity (i.e., the page is "reserved" and can't be touched). Reserved pages can nonetheless be used by drivers; the range between 640KB and 1MB is marked as "reserved," but it hosts usable device memory.

The following code, inserted in *mem_init*, correctly reserves the memory space between 15MB and 16MB:

```
while (start_mem < high_memory) {
    if (start_mem >= 0xf00000 && start_mem < 0x1000000) {
        /* keep it reserved, and prevent counting as data */
        reservedpages++; datapages--;
    }
    else
        clear_bit(PG_reserved, &mem_map[MAP_NR(start_mem)].flags);
    start_mem += PAGE_SIZE;
}
```

Initially all the memory is marked as "reserved," and the lines shown above take care not to unreserve high I/O memory; the original code only has the **else** branch within the loop shown. Since every reserved page after the end of the kernel code is counted as kernel data, two counters are modified to prevent a mismatching message at boot time. My box, with 32MB and the previous code to access the ISA hole, reports:

```
Memory: 30120k/32768k available (512k kernel code, 1408k reserved,
        728k data)
```

I tested this code with my own Intel box (ISA-hole aware) with kernel 2.0.29. If you are running a different kernel version, you might need to tweak the code—the internal structures related to memory management changed slightly in 2.1 and were different in version 1.2 of the kernel. Hacking with kernel code is unavoidable when you're supporting old-fashioned (and sometimes badly designed) hardware.

High PCI Memory

Accessing high PCI memory is much easier than accessing high ISA memory. High memory on PCI boards is *really* high—higher than any reasonable physical RAM address (at least for the next few years).

As discussed in "vmalloc and Friends" in Chapter 7, a single call to *vremap* (*ioremap* with kernel 2.1) is all it takes to access this memory. If you want to be portable across platforms, however, you should access the remapped memory range only through *readb* and similar functions. This restriction applies because not all platforms are able to directly map PCI buffers in the processor's address space.

Accessing the Text-Mode Video Buffer

While the *silly* module showed you how to access video memory in the 640KB–1MB address range, a more "visible" demo program can help you get comfortable with *readb* and *writeb*. The *silly* module features two more device nodes: */dev/sillytxt* (minor number 4) and */dev/silliest* (minor number 5).

WARNING   Such devices can be used only with a VGA-compatible video board running in text mode; using the devices on systems without a VGA adapter is potentially destructive, like any uncontrolled access to hardware resources.

The first device, *sillytxt*, is just a window on the VGA text buffer. Unlike the other *silly* nodes, it can be the target of output redirection and can be used to overwrite the contents of your console. This is reminiscent of */dev/vcs*, but the *silly* implementation is neither portable nor integrated into the kernel as *vcs* is.

The last device is kind of a joke: it drops the letters off your text screen. Each byte written to the device causes a character on your screen to drop to the bottom of the screen. This device is provided only to show a more complex action on the I/O memory—the same code can be used to operate on a VGA buffer or on other memory, such as network packets or the video data of a frame grabber.

Remember that any modification to the text screen is volatile and interferes with the kernel's own text management. If you really need to access the text buffer from an application, there are better ways to accomplish the task: either through the *ncurses* library or through */dev/vcs*. The *vcs* device is the "Virtual Console Screen," which can be used to retrieve the current snapshot of each virtual console's text buffer or change it. The *vcs* device is documented in its own source: *drivers/char/vc_screen.c* in the kernel source tree. Alternatively, you can look for a description of the device in the latest *man-pages* distribution.

Quick Reference

This chapter introduced the following symbols related to hardware management:

```
#include <asm/io.h>
unsigned inb(unsigned port);
void outb(unsigned char byte, unsigned port);
unsigned inw(unsigned port);
void outw(unsigned short word, unsigned port);
unsigned inl(unsigned port);
void outl(unsigned doubleword, unsigned port);
```
> These functions are used to read and write I/O ports. They can also be called by user-space programs, provided they have the right privileges to access ports. Not all the platforms support all the functions, which depend on underlying hardware design.

```
SLOW_DOWN_IO;
unsigned inb_p(unsigned port);
```
. . .
> The statement SLOW_DOWN_IO is sometimes needed to deal with slow ISA boards on the x86 platform. If a small delay is needed after an I/O operation, you can use the six pausing counterparts of the functions introduced above, whose names end in _p.

```
void insb(unsigned port, void *addr, unsigned long count);
void outsb(unsigned port, void *addr, unsigned long count);
void insw(unsigned port, void *addr, unsigned long count);
void outsw(unsigned port, void *addr, unsigned long count);
```

```
void insl(unsigned port, void *addr, unsigned long count);
void outsl(unsigned port, void *addr, unsigned long count);
```
> The "string functions" are optimized to transfer data from an input port to a region of memory, or the other way round. Such transfers are performed by reading or writing the same port count times.

```
unsigned readb(address);
unsigned readw(address);
unsigned readl(address);
void writeb(unsigned value, address);
void writew(unsigned value, address);
void writel(unsigned value, address);
memset_io(address, value, count);
memcpy_fromio(dest, source, nbytes);
memcpy_toio(dest, source, nbytes);
```
> All of these functions are used to access I/O memory regions, either low ISA memory or high PCI buffers (after calling *vremap*).

CHAPTER NINE

INTERRUPT HANDLING

Interrupts are the ultimate resource for hardware management. We all know that a device uses interrupts to let the software know it is ready to be acted upon. Linux offers a good interface for interrupt handling. In fact, it's so good that writing and installing an interrupt handler is almost as easy as writing any other kernel function. A few caveats nonetheless apply, because the interrupt handler runs asynchronously from the rest of the system.

The sample code in this chapter uses the parallel port to generate real interrupts, as this task can't be accomplished with software-only techniques. Therefore, if you want to run the test programs, you need to plug in the soldering iron, even if you refused to do so for the examples in the last chapter.

To demonstrate interrupt management, we'll use the *short* module from the last chapter. Its name, *short*, actually means *short int* (it is C, isn't it?), to remind us that it handles *int*errupts.

Preparing the Parallel Port

Although the parallel interface is simple, as I've shown in "Using the Parallel Port" in Chapter 8, *Hardware Management*, it can trigger interrupts. This capability is used by the printer to notify the *lp* driver that it is ready to accept the next character in the buffer.

The interface doesn't actually generate interrupts before it's instructed to do so; the parallel standard states that setting bit 4 of port 2 (0x37a, 0x27a, or whatever) enables interrupt reporting. The simple *outb*, which sets the bit, is performed by *short* at module initialization.

After enabling interrupt reporting, the parallel interface generates an interrupt whenever the electrical signal at pin 10 (the so-called "ACK" bit) changes from low to high. The simplest way to force the interface to generate interrupts (short of hooking up a printer to the port) is to connect pins 9 and 10 of the parallel connector. You can use one male 25-pin type D connector and an inch of wire for this purpose.

Pin 9 is the most significant bit of the parallel data byte. If you write binary data to */dev/short0*, you'll generate several interrupts. Writing ASCII text to the port won't generate interrupts, though, because the most significant bit won't be set.

If you want to actually "see" interrupts being generated, writing to the hardware device isn't enough; a software handler must be configured in the system. Currently, Linux-x86 and Linux-Alpha simply acknowledge and ignore any unexpected interrupts.

Installing an Interrupt Handler

Interrupt lines are a precious and often limited resource, particularly when there are only 15 or 16 of them. The kernel keeps a registry of interrupt lines, similar to the registry of I/O ports. A module is allowed to request an interrupt channel (or IRQ, for Interrupt ReQuest) and release it when it's done. The following functions, declared in <linux/sched.h>, implement the interface:

```
int request_irq(unsigned int irq,
                void (*handler)(int, void *, struct pt_regs *),
                unsigned long flags,
                const char *device,
                void *dev_id);
void free_irq(unsigned int irq, void *dev_id);
```

Note that version 1.2 featured different prototypes. See "Version Dependencies of IRQ Handling" later in this chapter for portability issues.

The value returned to the requesting function is 0 to indicate success or a negative error code, as usual. It's not uncommon for the function to return −EBUSY to signal that another driver is already using the requested interrupt line. The arguments to the functions are as follows:

unsigned int irq
> This is the interrupt number. Sometimes the mapping from the Linux number to the hardware number isn't one-to-one. Look, for example, at *arch/ alpha/kernel/irq.c* to see the Alpha mapping. The argument to the kernel functions is the Linux number rather than the hardware number.

```
void (*handler)(int, void *, struct pt_regs *)
```
The pointer to the handling function being installed.

```
unsigned long flags
```
As you might expect, a bitmask of options related to interrupt management.

```
const char *device
```
The string passed to *request_irq* is used in */proc/interrupts* to show the owner of the interrupt (see the next section).

```
void *dev_id
```
This pointer is used for shared interrupt lines. It is a unique identifier, much like a ClientData (the `this` object of C++). The driver is free to use `dev_id` at will. `dev_id` is frequently set to NULL, unless interrupt sharing is in force. We'll see a practical use for `dev_id` later, in "Implementing a Handler."

The bits that can be set in `flags` are:

```
SA_INTERRUPT
```
When set, this indicates a "fast" interrupt handler. When clear, the handler is a "slow" one. The concept of "fast" and "slow" handlers is described under "Fast and Slow Handlers."

```
SA_SHIRQ
```
This bit signals that the interrupt can be shared between devices. The concept of sharing is outlined later in "Interrupt Sharing."

```
SA_SAMPLE_RANDOM
```
This bit indicates that the generated interrupts can contribute to the entropy pool used by */dev/random* and */dev/urandom*. These devices return truly random numbers when read and are designed to help application software choose secure keys for encryption. Such random numbers are extracted from an entropy pool that is contributed to by various random events. If your device generates interrupts at truly random times, you should set this flag. If, on the other hand, your interrupts will be predictable (for example, vertical blanking of a frame grabber), the flag is not worth setting—it wouldn't contribute to system entropy anyway. See the comments in *drivers/char/random.c* for more information.

The interrupt handler can be installed either at driver initialization or when the device is first opened. While installing the interrupt handler from within *init_module* might sound like a good idea, it actually isn't. Because the number of interrupt lines is limited, you don't want to waste them. You can easily end up with more devices in your computer than there are interrupts. If a module requests an IRQ at initialization, it prevents any other driver from using the interrupt, even if the device holding it is never used. Requesting the interrupt at device open, on the other hand, allows a limited sharing of resources.

It is possible, for example, to run the frame grabber on the same interrupt as the modem, as long as you don't use the two devices at the same time. It is quite common for users to load the module for a special device at system boot, even if the device is rarely used. A data acquisition gadget might use the same interrupt as the second serial port. While it's not too hard to avoid connecting to your ISP during data acquisition, being forced to unload a module in order to use the modem is really unpleasant.

The correct place to call *request_irq* is when the device is first opened, *before* the hardware is instructed to generate interrupts. The place to call *free_irq* is the last time the device is closed, *after* the hardware is told not to interrupt the processor any more. The disadvantage of this technique is that you need to keep a per-device open count. Using the module count isn't enough if you control two or more devices from the same module.

Despite what I've just said, *short* requests its interrupt line at load time. I did this so you can run the test programs without having to run an extra process to keep the device open. *short*, therefore, requests the interrupt from within *init_module* instead of doing it in *short_open*, as a real device would.

The interrupt requested by the code below is `short_irq`. The actual assignment of the variable is shown later, as it is not relevant to the current discussion. `short_base` is the base I/O address of the parallel interface being used; register 2 of the interface is written to enable interrupt reporting.

```
if (short_irq >= 0) {
    result = request_irq(short_irq, short_interrupt,
                         SA_INTERRUPT, "short", NULL);
    if (result) {
        printk(KERN_INFO "short: can't get assigned irq %i\n",
               short_irq);
        short_irq = -1;
    }
    else { /* actually enable it--assume this *is* a parallel port */
        outb(0x10,short_base+2);
    }
}
```

The code shows that the handler being installed is a fast handler (`SA_INTERRUPT`), does not support interrupt sharing (`SA_SHIRQ` is missing), and doesn't contribute to system entropy (`SA_SAMPLE_RANDOM` is missing too). The *outb* call then enables interrupt reporting for the parallel port.

The /proc Interface

Whenever a hardware interrupt reaches the processor, an internal counter is incremented, providing a way to check whether the device is working as expected. Reported interrupts are shown in */proc/interrupts*. The following snapshot was taken after an hour and a half uptime of my 486:

```
 0:   537598    timer
 1:    23070    keyboard
 2:        0    cascade
 3:     7930  + serial
 5:     4568    NE2000
 7:    15920  + short
13:        0    math error
14:    48163  + ide0
15:     1278  + ide1
```

The first column is the IRQ number. You can see from the IRQs that are missing that the file shows only interrupts corresponding to installed handlers. For example, the first serial port (which uses interrupt number 4) is not shown, indicating that my modem isn't being used. In fact, even if I'd used the modem earlier, but wasn't using it at the time of the snapshot, it wouldn't show up in the file; the serial ports are well-behaved and release their interrupt handlers when the device is closed. The plus sign that appears in half the records signals a fast interrupt handler.

The */proc* tree contains another interrupt-related file, */proc/stat*; sometimes you'll find one more useful and sometimes you'll prefer the other. */proc/stat* records several low-level statistics about system activity, including (but not limited to) the number of interrupts received since system boot. Each line of *stat* begins with a text string that is the key to the line; the `intr` mark is what we are looking for. The following snapshot was taken half a minute later than the previous one:

```
intr 947102 540971 23346 0 8795 4907 4568 0 15920 0 0 0 0 0 48317 1278
```

The first number is the total of all interrupts, while each of the others represents a single IRQ line, starting with interrupt 0. This snapshot shows that interrupt number 4 has been used 4907 times, even though no handler is *currently* installed. If the driver you're testing acquires and releases the interrupt at each open and close cycle, you may find */proc/stat* more useful than */proc/interrupts*.

Another difference between the two files is that *interrupts* is not architecture-dependent, while *stat* is: the number of fields depends on the hardware underlying the kernel. The number of available interrupts varies from as few as 15 on the Sparc to as many as 72 on the Atari (M68k processor).

The following snapshots show how the files appear inside my Alpha station (which has a total of 16 interrupts, just like my x86 box):

```
 1:        2    keyboard
 5:     4641    NE2000
15:    22909  + 53c7,8xx
```

```
intr 27555 0 2 0 1 1 4642 0 0 0 0 0 0 0 0 22909
```

The most noticeable feature of this snapshot is that the timer interrupt is missing. On the Alpha, the timer interrupt reaches the processor separately from other interrupts and has no IRQ number assigned.

Autodetecting the IRQ Number

One of the most compelling problems for a driver when it is initializing is how to determine which IRQ line is going to be used by the device. The driver needs the information in order to install the correct handler. Even though a programmer could require the user to specify the interrupt number at load time, this is a bad practice, as most of the time the user doesn't know the number, either because he didn't configure the jumpers or because the device is jumperless. Autodetection of the interrupt number is a basic requirement for driver usability.

Sometimes autodetection depends on the knowledge that some devices feature a default behavior which rarely, if ever, changes. In this case, the driver might assume that the default values apply. This is exactly how *short* behaves with the parallel port. The implementation is straightforward, as shown by *short* itself:

```
if (short_irq < 0) /* not yet specified: force the default on */
    switch(short_base) {
      case 0x378: short_irq = 7; break;
      case 0x278: short_irq = 2; break;
      case 0x3bc: short_irq = 5; break;
    }
```

The code assigns the interrupt number according to the chosen base I/O address, while allowing the user to override the default at load time by calling `insmod short short_irq=x`. `short_base` defaults to 0x378, so `short_irq` defaults to 7.

Some devices are more advanced in design and simply "announce" which interrupt they're going to use. In this case, the driver retrieves the interrupt number by reading a status byte from one of the device's I/O ports. When the target device is one that has the ability to tell the driver which interrupt it is going to use, autodetecting the IRQ number just means probing the device, with no additional work required to probe the interrupt.

It's interesting to note here that modern devices supply their interrupt configuration. The PCI standard solves the problem by requiring peripheral devices to declare what interrupt line(s) they are going to use. The PCI standard is discussed in Chapter 15, *Overview of Peripheral Buses.*

Unfortunately, not every device is programmer-friendly, and autodetection might require some probing. The technique is quite simple: the driver tells the device to generate interrupts and watches what happens. If everything goes well, only one interrupt line is activated.

Though probing is simple in theory, the actual implementation might be unclear. We'll look at two ways to perform the task: calling kernel-defined helper functions and implementing our own version.

Kernel-helped probing

The mainstream kernel offers a low-level facility for probing the interrupt number. The facility consists of two functions, declared in `<linux/interrupt.h>` (which also describes the probing machinery):

`unsigned long probe_irq_on(void);`
> This function returns a bitmask of unassigned interrupts. The driver must preserve the returned bitmask and pass it to *probe_irq_off* later. After this call, the driver should arrange for its device to generate at least one interrupt.

`int probe_irq_off(unsigned long);`
> After the device has requested an interrupt, the driver calls this function, passing as argument the bitmask previously returned by *probe_irq_on*. *probe_irq_off* returns the number of the interrupt that was issued after "probe_on." If no interrupts occurred, 0 is returned (thus IRQ 0 can't be probed for, but no custom device can use it on any of the supported architectures anyway). If more than one interrupt occurred (ambiguous detection), *probe_irq_off* returns a negative value.

The programmer should be careful to enable the device *after* the call to *probe_irq_on* and to disable it *before* calling *probe_irq_off*. Additionally, you must remember to service the pending interrupt in your device, after *probe_irq_off*.

The *short* module demonstrates how to use such probing. If you load the module with `probe=1`, the following code is executed to detect your interrupt line, provided pins 9 and 10 of the parallel connector are bound together:

```
int count = 0;
do {
    unsigned long mask;

    mask = probe_irq_on();
    outb_p(0x10,short_base+2); /* enable reporting */
    outb_p(0x00,short_base);   /* clear the bit */
    outb_p(0xFF,short_base);   /* set the bit: interrupt! */
    outb_p(0x00,short_base+2); /* disable reporting */
    short_irq = probe_irq_off(mask);

    if (short_irq == 0) { /* none of them? */
        printk(KERN_INFO "short: no irq reported by probe\n");
        short_irq = -1;
    }
    /*
     * if more than one line has been activated, the result is
     * negative. We should service the interrupt (no need for lpt port)
     * and loop over again. Loop at most five times, then give up
     */
} while (short_irq < 0 && count++ < 5);
if (short_irq < 0)
printk("short: probe failed %i times, giving up\n", count);
```

Probing might be a lengthy task. While this is not true for *short*, probing a frame grabber, for example, requires a delay of at least 20ms (which is ages for the processor), and other devices might take even longer. Therefore, it's best to probe for the interrupt line only once, at module initialization, independently of whether you install the handler at device open (as you should) or within *init_module* (which you shouldn't do anyway).

It's interesting to note that on the Sparc and M68k, probing is unnecessary and therefore isn't implemented. Probing is a hack, and mature architectures are like PCI, which provides all the needed information. As a matter of fact, M68k and Sparc kernels export to the modules stub probing functions that always return 0—every architecture must define the functions, because they are exported by an architecture-independent source file. All the other supported architectures allow probing using the technique just shown.

The problem with *probe_irq_on* and *probe_irq_off* is that they are not exported by early kernel versions. Thus, if you want to write a module that ports back to 1.2, you must implement probing yourself.

Do-it-yourself probing

Probing can be implemented in the driver itself without too much trouble. The *short* module performs do-it-yourself detection of the IRQ line if it is loaded with `probe=2`.

The mechanism is the same as the one described above: enable all unused interrupts, then wait and see what happens. We can, however, exploit our knowledge of the device. Often a device can be configured to use one IRQ number from a set of three or four; probing just those IRQs enables us to detect the right one, without having to test for all possible IRQs.

The *short* implementation assumes that 3, 5, 7, and 9 are the only possible IRQ values. These numbers are actually the values that some parallel devices allow you to select.

The code below probes by testing all "possible" interrupts and looking at what happens. The `trials` array lists the IRQs to try and has 0 as the end marker; the `tried` array is used to keep track of which handlers have actually been registered by this driver.

```
int trials[] = {3, 5, 7, 9, 0};
int tried[]  = {0, 0, 0, 0, 0};
int i, count = 0;

/*
 * install the probing handler for all possible lines. Remember
 * the result (0 for success, or -EBUSY) in order to only free
 * what has been acquired
 */
```

```
for (i=0; trials[i]; i++)
    tried[i] = request_irq(trials[i], short_probing,
                           SA_INTERRUPT, "short probe", NULL);

do {
    short_irq = 0; /* none got, yet */
    outb_p(0x10,short_base+2); /* enable */
    outb_p(0x00,short_base);
    outb_p(0xFF,short_base); /* toggle the bit */
    outb_p(0x10,short_base+2); /* disable */

    /* the value has been set by the handler */
    if (short_irq == 0) { /* none of them? */
        printk(KERN_INFO "short: no irq reported by probe\n");
    }
    /*
     * If more than one line has been activated, the result is
     * negative. We should service the interrupt (but the lpt port
     * doesn't need it) and loop over again. Do it at most 5 times
     */
} while (short_irq <=0 && count++ < 5);

/* end of loop, uninstall the handler */
for (i=0; trials[i]; i++)
    if (tried[i] == 0)
        free_irq(trials[i], NULL);

if (short_irq < 0)
    printk("short: probe failed %i times, giving up\n", count);
```

You might not know in advance what the "possible" IRQ values are. In that case, you'll need to probe all the free interrupts, instead of limiting yourself to a few `trials[]`. To probe for all interrupts, you have to probe from IRQ 0 to IRQ NR_IRQS-1, where NR_IRQS is defined in <asm/irq.h> and is platform-dependent.

Now we are missing only the probing handler itself. The handler's role is to update `short_irq` according to which interrupts are actually received. A zero value in `short_irq` means "nothing yet," while a negative value means "ambiguous." I chose these values to be consistent with *probe_irq_off* and to use the same code to call either kind of probing within *short.c*.

```
void short_probing(int irq, void *dev_id, struct pt_regs *regs)
{
    if (short_irq == 0) short_irq = irq;    /* found */
    if (short_irq != irq) short_irq = -irq; /* ambiguous */
}
```

The arguments to the handler are described later. Knowing that `irq` is the interrupt being handled should be sufficient to understand the function just shown.

Fast and Slow Handlers

As you've seen, I've specified the **SA_INTERRUPT** flag for the *short* interrupt handler, thus asking for a "fast" handler. It's high time to explain what "fast" and "slow" mean. Actually, not all the architectures support different implementations for fast and slow handlers. The Alpha and Sparc ports, for example, service fast and slow handlers in the same way. Versions 2.1.37 and later of the Intel port removed the difference as well, since with the available processing power of modern computers there's no longer any need to differentiate between fast and slow interrupts.

The main difference between the two kinds of interrupt handlers is that fast handlers guarantee atomic processing of interrupts and slow handlers don't (this difference is preserved in the new implementation of interrupt handling). In other words, the "interrupt enable" processor flag is turned off while a fast handler runs, thus preventing any interrupts from being serviced. When a slow handler is invoked, on the other hand, the kernel reenables interrupt reporting in the microprocessor, so other interrupts can be serviced while a slow handler runs.

Another task performed by the kernel before calling the actual interrupt handler, whether slow or fast, is to disable the interrupt line just reported. An IRQ service routine thus doesn't need to be reentrant, to the joy of programmers. On the flip side, even a slow handler should be written to run as fast as possible, in order to avoid losing the next interrupt.

If a new interrupt arrives for a device while a handler is still processing the last interrupt, the new interrupt is lost forever. The interrupt controller doesn't buffer disabled interrupts, whereas the processor does—as soon as *sti* is issued, pending interrupts are serviced. The *sti* function is the "Set Interrupt Flag" processor instruction (introduced in "ISA Memory" in Chapter 2, *Building and Running Modules*).

To summarize the slow and fast executing environments:

* A fast handler runs with interrupt reporting disabled in the microprocessor, and the interrupt being serviced is disabled in the interrupt controller. The handler can nonetheless enable reporting in the processor by calling *sti*.

* A slow handler runs with interrupt reporting enabled in the processor, and the interrupt being serviced is disabled in the interrupt controller.

But there is another difference between fast and slow handlers: the overhead added by the kernel. Slow handlers *are* actually slower because of additional housekeeping on the kernel's side. This implies that frequent interrupts are best serviced by a fast handler. As far as *short* is concerned, several thousand interrupts per second can be generated by copying a large file to */dev/short0*. Thus I chose to use a fast handler to control the amount of overhead being inserted into the system. This split behavior is what has been unified in the newer 2.1 kernels; the overhead is now added to all interrupt handlers.

A good candidate for a slow handler might be a frame grabber. It interrupts the processor 50 or 60 times per second, and a slow handler can choose to copy every frame from the interface board to physical RAM without blocking other system interrupts, such as those generated by serial ports or timer service.

This description should satisfy most readers, though I suspect someone with a taste for hardware and some experience with his or her computer might be interested in going deeper. If you don't care about the internal details, you can skip to the next section.

The internals of interrupt handling on the x86

This description has been extrapolated from *arch/i386/kernel/irq.c* and *include/asm-i386/irq.h* as they appear in the 2.0.*x* kernels; although the general concepts remain the same, the hardware details differ on other platforms and have been slightly modified during 2.1 development.

The lowest level of interrupt handling resides in assembly code declared as macros in *irq.h* and expanded in *irq.c*. Three functions are declared for each interrupt: the slow, the fast, and the bad handlers.

The "bad" handler, the smallest, is the assembler entry point when no C-language handler has been installed for the interrupt. It acknowledges the interrupt to the proper PIC (Programmable Interrupt Controller) device* and disables it, to avoid losing any further processor time due to spurious interrupts. The bad handler is reinstalled by *free_irq* when a driver is done with an interrupt line. The bad handler doesn't increment the counter in */proc/stat*.

It's interesting to note that IRQ probing in both the x86 and the Alpha is based on the behavior of the bad handler. *probe_irq_on* enables all the bad interrupts, without installing a handler; *probe_irq_off* simply checks which interrupts have been disabled since *probe_irq_on*. You can verify this behavior by observing that loading *short* with `probe=1` (kernel-aided probing) doesn't increment the interrupt counters, while loading it with `probe=2` (home-made probing) increments them.

The assembler entry point for slow interrupts saves all the registers on the stack and makes data segments (the DS and ES processor registers) point into the kernel address space (CS has already been set by the processor). The code then acknowledges the interrupt to the PIC, disables notification of new interrupts on the same IRQ line, and issues an *sti* (set interrupt flag). Bear in mind that the processor

---

* Each PC used to be equipped with two interrupt-controller chips, called 8259 chips. These devices don't exist any more, but the same behavior is implemented in modern chipsets.

automatically clears the flag when servicing an interrupt. The slow handler then passes the interrupt number and a pointer to the processor registers to *do_IRQ*, a C function that dispatches the right C-language handler. The `struct pt_regs *` argument that is passed to the interrupt handler in the driver is just a pointer to the position in the stack where the registers are stored.

When *do_IRQ* is finished, *cli* is issued, the specific interrupt is enabled in the PIC, and *ret_from_sys_call* is invoked. This last entry point (*arch/i386/kernel/entry.S*) restores all the registers from the stack, handles any pending bottom half (see "Bottom Halves" later in the chapter) and, if needed, reschedules the processor.

The fast entry point is different in that *sti* is not called prior to jumping to the C code, and not every machine register is saved before calling *do_fast_IRQ*. When the driver's handler is called, the `regs` argument is NULL (because the registers aren't stored on the stack) and interrupts are still disabled.

Finally, the fast handler reenables the interrupt in the 8259, restores the registers that were saved earlier, and returns without passing through *ret_from_sys_call*. Pending bottom halves are not run.

In all kernels up to 2.1.34, both handlers increment `intr_count` before passing control to C code (see "The Nature of Task Queues" in Chapter 6, *Flow of Time*).

Implementing a Handler

So far, we've learned to register an interrupt handler, but not to write one. Actually, there's nothing unusual about a handler—it's ordinary C code.

The only peculiarity is that a handler runs at interrupt time and therefore suffers some restrictions on what it can do. These restrictions are the same as those we saw with task queues. A handler can't transfer data to or from user space, because it doesn't execute in the context of a process. A fast handler, however, can count on being executed atomically and doesn't need to protect itself against race conditions when accessing shared data items. Slow handlers are not atomic in that other interrupts can be serviced while the slow handler is running.

The role of an interrupt handler is to give feedback to its device about interrupt reception and to read or write data according to the meaning of the interrupt being serviced. The first step usually consists of clearing a bit on the interface board; most hardware devices won't generate other interrupts until their "interrupt-pending" bit has been cleared. Some devices don't require this step because they don't have an "interrupt-pending" bit; such devices are a minority, although the parallel port is one of them. For that reason, *short* does not have to clear such a bit.

A typical task for an interrupt handler is awakening processes sleeping on the device if the interrupt signals the event they're waiting for, such as the arrival of new data.

To stick with the frame grabber example, a process could acquire a sequence of images by continuously reading the device; the *read* call blocks after reading each frame, while the interrupt handler awakens the process as soon as a new frame arrives. This assumes that the grabber interrupts the processor to signal successful arrival of each new frame.

The programmer should be careful to write a routine that executes in a minimum of time, independent of its being a fast or slow handler. If a long computation needs to be performed, the best approach is to use a task queue to schedule computation at a safer time (see "Task Queues" in Chapter 6). This is why bottom halves exist (see "Bottom Halves" later in this chapter).

Our sample code in *short* makes use of the interrupt to call *do_gettimeofday* and print the current time to a page-sized circular buffer. It then awakens any reading process (which is actually woken only at the next slow interrupt or the next clock tick, because *short* uses a fast handler).

```
void short_interrupt(int irq, void *dev_id, struct pt_regs *regs)
{
    struct timeval tv;
    do_gettimeofday(&tv);

    /* Write a 16 byte record. Assume PAGE_SIZE is a multiple of 16 */
    short_head += sprintf((char *)short_head,"%08u.%06u\n",
                          (int)(tv.tv_sec % 100000000),
                          (int)(tv.tv_usec));
    if (short_head == short_buffer + PAGE_SIZE)
        short_head = short_buffer; /* wrap */

    wake_up_interruptible(&short_queue); /* wake any reading process */
}
```

This code, though simple, represents the typical job of an interrupt handler.

The node used to read the buffer being filled at interrupt time is */dev/shortint*. This is the only *short* device node that wasn't introduced in Chapter 8. The internals of */dev/shortint* are specifically tailored for interrupt generation and reporting. Writing to the device generates one interrupt every other byte; reading the device gives the time when each interrupt was reported.

If you connect together pins 9 and 10 of the parallel connector, you can generate interrupts by raising the high bit of the parallel data byte. This can be accomplished by writing binary data to */dev/short0* or by writing anything to */dev/shortint.**

The following code implements *read* and *write* for */dev/shortint*:

```
read_write_t short_i_read (struct inode *inode, struct file *filp,
                          char *buf, count_t count)
{
    int count0;

    while (short_head == short_tail) {
        interruptible_sleep_on(&short_queue);
        if (current->signal & ~current->blocked) /* a signal arrived */
            return -ERESTARTSYS; /* tell the fs layer to handle it */
        /* else, loop */
    }
    /* count0 is the number of readable data bytes */
    count0 = short_head - short_tail;
    if (count0 < 0) /* wrapped */
        count0 = short_buffer + PAGE_SIZE - short_tail;
    if (count0 < count) count = count0;

    memcpy_tofs(buf, (char *)short_tail, count);
    short_tail += count;
    if (short_tail == short_buffer + PAGE_SIZE)
        short_tail = short_buffer;
    return count;
}

read_write_t short_i_write (struct inode *inode, struct file *filp,
                const char *buf, count_t count)
{
    int written = 0, odd = filp->f_pos & 1;
    unsigned port = short_base; /* output to the parallel data latch */

    while (written < count)
        outb(0xff * ((++written + odd) & 1), port);

    filp->f_pos += count;
    return written;
}
```

Using Arguments

Though *short* ignores them, three arguments are passed to an interrupt handler: `irq`, `dev_id`, and `regs`. Let's look at the role of each.

---

* The *shortint* device accomplishes its task by alternately writing 0x00 and 0xff to the parallel port.

The interrupt number (`int irq`) can be useful if a single handler manages more than one device and the devices talk on different IRQ lines. For example, a stereoscopic video system might support two frame grabbers using two interrupts. The driver should be able to detect both devices and install a handler to manage both IRQs. The driver can then use the `irq` argument to tell the handler which device caused an interrupt.

For example, if the driver has declared an array of device structures called `hwinfo`, each with an `irq` field, the following code selects the correct device when an interrupt arrives. The driver prefix for this code is `cx`.

```
static void cx_interrupt(int irq, void *dev_id, struct pt_regs *regs)
{
    /* "Cxg_Board" is the data-type of hardware information */
    Cxg_Board *board; int i;

    for (i=0, board=hwinfo; i<cxg_boards; board++, i++)
        if (board->irq==irq)
            break;

    /* now 'board' points to the right hardware description */
    /* .... */
}
```

The second argument, `void *dev_id`, is a sort of ClientData; a `void *` argument is passed to *request_irq*, and this device ID is then passed back as an argument to the handler when the interrupt happens. The `dev_id` argument was introduced in Linux 1.3.70 in order to handle shared interrupts, but it is useful even if no sharing is performed.

Let's assume that the driver in our example has registered its interrupt as follows (where `board->irq` is the interrupt being requested, and `board` is the ClientData):

```
static void cx_open(struct inode *inode, struct file *filp)
{
    Cxg_Board *board = hwinfo + MINOR(inode->i_rdev);
    request_irq(board->irq,cx_interrupt,0,"cx100",board /* dev_id */);
    /*....*/
    return 0;
}
```

Then the handler code can be reduced to the following:

```
static void cx_interrupt(int irq, void *dev_id, struct pt_regs *regs)
{
    Cxg_Board *board=dev_id;

    /* now 'board' points to the right hardware item */
    /* .... */
}
```

The last argument, `struct pt_regs *regs`, is rarely used. It holds a snapshot of the processor's context before the processor entered interrupt code. The registers can be used for monitoring and debugging, and they actually are used for this purpose by *show_regs* (the debugging function spawned by the keyboard interrupt when **RightAlt-PrScr** is pressed—see "System Hangs," in Chapter 4, *Debugging Techniques*).

Enabling and Disabling Interrupts

Sometimes it's useful for a driver to enable and disable interrupt reporting for its own IRQ line. The kernel offers two functions for this purpose, both declared in `<asm/irq.h>`:

```
void disable_irq(int irq);
void enable_irq(int irq);
```

Calling either function updates the mask for the specified `irq` in the PIC.

In practice, when an interrupt is disabled, it isn't reported to the processor even if the hardware is eager to be serviced. For example, "The internals of interrupt handling on the x86" states that the "bad" handler in the x86 implementation disables any interrupt it receives.

But why disable the interrupt? Sticking to the parallel port, let's look at the *plip* network interface. A *plip* device uses the bare-bones parallel port to transfer data. Since only five bits can be read from the parallel connector, they are interpreted as four data bits and a clock/handshake signal. When the first bits of a packet are transmitted by the initiator (the interface sending the packet), the clock line is raised, causing the receiving interface to interrupt the processor. The *plip* handler is then invoked to deal with newly arrived data.

After the device has been alerted, the data transfer proceeds, using the handshake line to clock new data to the receiving interface (this might not be the best implementation, but it is necessary for compatibility with other packet drivers using the parallel port). Performance would be unbearable if the receiving interface had to handle two interrupts for every byte received. The driver therefore disables the interrupt during the reception of the packet.

Similarly, since the handshake line from the receiver to the transmitter is used to acknowledge data reception, the transmitting interface disables its IRQ line during packet transmission.

You should be careful, however, because enabling and disabling the interrupt line cannot be performed from within the handler. This limitation applies because the kernel disables the interrupt before calling the handler and enables it again when the handler is done, as described above. Disabling and enabling the interrupt is nonetheless an interesting option, as long as you do it from within a bottom half (see the next section).

Finally, it's interesting to note that the Sparc implementation defines both the *disable_irq* and *enable_irq* symbols as pointers rather than functions. This trick allows the kernel to assign the pointers at boot time after detecting what flavor of Sparc you're on (the Sun4c and the Sun4m have different IRQ hardware). The C language semantics to use the function are the same on all Linux systems, independent of whether this trick is used or not, and it helps avoid some tedious coding of conditionals.

Bottom Halves

One of the main problems with interrupt handling is how to perform longish tasks within a handler. Linux resolves this problem by splitting the interrupt handler into two halves: the so-called "top half" is the routine you register through *request_irq*, and the "bottom half" ("bh" for short) is a routine that is scheduled by the top half, to be executed later, at a safer time.

But what is a bottom half useful for?

The big difference between the top-half handler and the bottom half is that all interrupts are enabled during execution of the bh—that's why it runs at a "safer" time. In the typical scenario, the top half saves device data to a device-specific buffer, marks its bottom half, and exits: this is very fast. The bh then dispatches newly arrived data to the processes, awakening them if necessary. This setup permits the top half to service a new interrupt while the bottom half is still working. New data arriving before the top half terminates, on the other hand, are lost because the IRQ line is disabled in the interrupt controller.

Every serious interrupt handler is split this way. For instance, when a network interface reports the arrival of a new packet, the handler just retrieves the data and pushes it up to the protocol layer; actual processing of the packet is performed in a bottom half.

This kind of job should be reminiscent of task queues; actually, task queues have evolved from an older implementation of bottom halves. Even version 1.0 of the kernel had bottom halves, while task queues didn't yet exist.

Unlike task queues, which are dynamic, bottom halves are limited in number and predefined in the kernel; this is similar to the old kernel timers. The static nature of bottom halves is not a problem because some of them evolve into a dynamic object by running a task queue. In <linux/interrupt.h>, you'll find the list of available bottom halves; the most interesting of them are discussed below.

The Design of Bottom Halves

The bottom halves exist as an array of function pointers and a bitmask—that's why there are no more than 32 of them. When the kernel is ready to deal with asynchronous events, it calls *do_bottom_half*. We have seen how this happens on return from a system call and on exiting a slow handler; both events occur frequently. The decision to use a bitmask is mainly dictated by performance: checking the bitmask takes only one machine instruction and minimizes overhead.

Whenever some code wants to schedule a bottom half for running, it calls *mark_bh*, which sets a bit in the bitmask variable to queue the corresponding function for execution. A bottom half can be scheduled by an interrupt handler or any other function. When the bottom-half handler is executed, it is automatically unmarked.

Marking bottom halves is defined in `<linux/interrupt.h>` as:

```
void mark_bh(int nr);
```

Here, `nr` is the "number" of the bh to activate. The number is a symbolic constant defined in `<linux/interrupt.h>` that identifies which bit needs to be set in the bitmask. The function that corresponds to each bh is provided by the driver that owns the bottom half. For example, when `mark_bh(KEYBOARD_BH)` is called, the function being scheduled for execution is *kbd_bh*, which is part of the keyboard driver.

Since bottom halves are static objects, a modularized driver won't be able to register its *own* bottom half. There's currently no support for dynamic allocation of bottom halves, and it's unlikely there ever will be, as the immediate task queue can be used instead.

The rest of this section lists some of the most interesting bottom halves. It then describes how the kernel runs a bottom half, which you should understand in order to use bottom halves properly.

Several bottom halves declared by the kernel are interesting to look at, and a few can even be used by a driver, as introduced above. These are the most interesting bottom halves:

IMMEDIATE_BH

> This is the most important bh for driver writers. The function being scheduled consumes a task queue, `tq_immediate`. A driver (like a custom module) that doesn't own a bottom half can use the immediate queue as if it were its own bh. After registering a task in the queue, the driver must mark the bh in order to have its code actually executed; how to do this was introduced in "The immediate queue," in Chapter 6.

TQUEUE_BH

> This bh is activated at each timer tick *if* a task is registered in `tq_timer`. In practice, a driver can implement its own bottom half using `tq_timer`; the timer queue introduced in Chapter 6 (in the section "The timer queue") is a bottom half, but there's no need to call *mark_bh* for it. TQUEUE_BH is always executed *later* than IMMEDIATE_BH.

NET_BH

> Network drivers should mark this queue to notify the upper network layers of events. The bh itself is part of the network layer and not accessible to modules. We'll see how to use it proficiently in "Interrupt-Driven Operation," in Chapter 14, *Network Drivers.*

CONSOLE_BH

> The console performs tty switching in a bottom half. This operation can involve process control. For instance, switching between the X Window system and text mode is controlled by the X server. Moreover, if the keyboard driver asks for a console change, the console switching can't be done during the interrupt. It also can't be done while a process is writing to the console. Using a bh fits the task because bottom halves can be disabled at the driver's will; in this case, `console_bh` is disabled during a console write.*

TIMER_BH

> This bh is marked by *do_timer,* the function in charge of the clock tick. The function that this bh executes is the one that drives the kernel timers. There is no way to use this facility for a driver short of using *add_timer.*

The remaining bottom halves are used by specific kernel drivers. There are no entry points in them for a module, and it wouldn't make sense for there to be any.

Once a bh has been activated, it is executed when *do_bottom_half (kernel/softirq.c)* is invoked, which happens within *return_from_sys_call.* The latter procedure is executed whenever a process exits from a system call or when a slow interrupt handler exits. The bottom halves are not executed on exit from a fast handler; whenever a driver needs fast execution of its bottom half, it should register a slow handler.

ret_from_sys_call is always executed by the clock tick; thus, if a fast handler marks a bh, the actual function will be executed at most 10ms later (less than 1ms later on the Alpha, whose clock tick runs at 1024 Hz).

After a bottom half has run, the scheduler is called if the **need_resched** variable is set; the variable is set by the various *wake_up* functions. The top half can thus leave to the bottom half any work related to awakening processes—they'll be scheduled right away. This is what happens, for example, when a *telnet* packet arrives from the network. *net_bh* awakens *telnetd,* and the scheduler gives it processor time with no additional delays.

---

* The function *disable_bh* can be used by drivers using their own bottom half, as explained in a while.

Writing a Bottom Half

Bottom-half code runs at a safe time—safer than when the top-half handler runs. Nonetheless, some care is necessary because a bh is still at "interrupt time"; intr_count is not 0 because the bottom half executes outside the context of a process. The limitations outlined in "The Nature of Task Queues," in Chapter 6, thus apply to code executing in a bottom half.

The main problem with the bottom halves shown is that they often need to share data structures with the top-half interrupt handler, and race conditions must be prevented. This might mean temporarily disabling interrupt reporting or using locking techniques.

It's quite apparent from the previous list of available bottom halves in "The Design of Bottom Halves" that a new driver implementing a bottom half should attach its code to IMMEDIATE_BH, by using the immediate queue. If your driver is important enough, however, you can even have your own bh number assigned in the kernel itself. Important drivers are a minority, however, and I won't go into detail about them. Three functions exist to deal with privately owned bottom halves: *init_bh*, *enable_bh*, and *disable_bh*. If you're interested, you'll find them in the kernel sources.

Actually, using the immediate queue is no different from managing your own bottom half—the immediate queue *is* a bottom half. When IMMEDIATE_BH is marked, the function in charge of the immediate bottom half just consumes the immediate queue. If your interrupt handler queues its bh handler to tq_immediate and marks the bottom half, the queued task will be called at just the right time. Since in all recent kernels you can queue the same task multiple times without trashing the task queue, you can queue your bottom half every time the top-half handler runs. We'll see this behavior in a while.

Drivers with exotic configurations—multiple bottom halves or other setups that can't easily be handled with a plain tq_immediate—can be satisfied by using a custom task queue. The interrupt handler queues the tasks in its own queue, and when it's ready to run them, a simple queue-consuming function is inserted into the immediate queue. See "Running Your Own Task Queues" in Chapter 6 for details.

Let's now look at the *short* implementation. When loaded with bh=1, the module installs an interrupt handler that uses a bottom half.

short performs split interrupt management as follows: the top half (the handler) saves the current time value in a circular buffer and schedules the bottom half. The bh prints accumulated time values to the text buffer and then awakens any reading process.

The top half turns out to be really simple:

```
void short_bh_interrupt(int irq, void *dev_id, struct pt_regs *regs)
{
    do_gettimeofday(tv_head);
    tv_head++;

    if (tv_head == (tv_data + NR_TIMEVAL) )
        tv_head = tv_data; /* wrap */

    /* Queue the bh. Don't care for multiple queueing */
    queue_task_irq_off(&short_task, &tq_immediate);
    mark_bh(IMMEDIATE_BH);

    short_bh_count++; /* record that an interrupt arrived */
}
```

As expected, this code calls *queue_task* without checking whether the task is aready queued. This behavior doesn't work with Linux 1.2, and if you compile *short* against 1.2 headers, it uses a different handler, which queues the task only when **short_bh_count** is 0.

The bottom half, then, performs the rest of the work. It also records the number of times the top half was invoked before the bottom half was scheduled. The number is always 1 if the top half is a "slow" handler, because pending bottom halves are always run whenever a slow handler exits, as described above.

```
void short_bottom_half(void *unused)
{
    int savecount = short_bh_count;
    short_bh_count = 0; /* we've already been removed from the queue */
    /*
     * The bottom half reads the tv array, filled by the top half,
     * and prints it to the circular text buffer, which is then consumed
     * by reading processes
     */

    /* First write the no. of interrupts that occurred before this bh */

    short_head += sprintf((char *)short_head,
                        "bh after %6i\n", savecount);
    if (short_head == short_buffer + PAGE_SIZE)
        short_head = short_buffer; /* wrap */

    /*
     * Then, write the time values. Write exactly 16 bytes at a time,
     * so it aligns with PAGE_SIZE
     */

    do {
        short_head += sprintf((char *)short_head,"%08u.%06u\n",
                            (int)(tv_tail->tv_sec % 100000000),
```

```
                                (int)(tv_tail->tv_usec));
        if (short_head == short_buffer + PAGE_SIZE)
            short_head = short_buffer; /* wrap */

        tv_tail++;
        if (tv_tail == (tv_data + NR_TIMEVAL) )
            tv_tail = tv_data; /* wrap */

    } while (tv_tail != tv_head);

    wake_up_interruptible(&short_queue); /* awake any reading process */
}
```

Timings taken on my oldish computer show that, using a bottom half, the interval between two interrupts has shrunk from 53 microseconds to 27, since less work is performed in the top-half handler. While the total work needed to handle the interrupt is the same, a faster top half has the advantage that the interrupt remains disabled for a shorter time. This is not an issue for *short* because the *write* function generating interrupts is restarted only after the handler is done, but timing might be relevant for real hardware interrupts.

Here's an example of what you see when loading *short* by specifying bh=1:

```
morgana% echo 1122334455 > /dev/shortint ; cat /dev/shortint
bh after      5
50588804.876653
50588804.876693
50588804.876720
50588804.876747
50588804.876774
```

Interrupt Sharing

A well-known "feature" of the PC is its inability to attach different devices to the same interrupt line. However, Linux 2.0 broke the spell. Even though my ISA hardware manual—a Linux-unaware book—says that "at most one device" can be attached to an IRQ line, the electrical signals don't have these restrictions unless the device hardware is unfriendly by design. The problem is with the software.

Linux software support for sharing was developed for PCI devices, but it works with ISA boards as well. Needless to say, non-PC platforms and buses support interrupt sharing too.

In order to develop a driver that can manage a shared interrupt line, there are some details that need to be considered. As discussed below, some of the features described in this chapter are not available for devices using interrupt sharing. Whenever possible, it's better to support sharing because it presents fewer problems for the final user.

Installing a Shared Handler

Shared interrupts are installed through *request_irq* just like owned ones, but there are two differences:

- The `SA_SHIRQ` bit must be specified in the `flags` argument when requesting the interrupt.

- The `dev_id` argument *must* be unique. Any pointer into the module's address space will do, but `dev_id` definitely cannot be set to `NULL`.

The kernel keeps a list of shared handlers associated with the interrupt, and `dev_id` differentiates between them, like a driver's signature. If two drivers were to register `NULL` as their signature on the same interrupt, things might get mixed up at unload time, causing the kernel to oops when an interrupt arrived. This happened to me when I was first testing with shared handlers (when I just thought "let's add `SA_SHIRQ` to those two drivers").

Under these conditions, *request_irq* succeeds if either the interrupt line is free or both the following conditions are met:

- The previously registered handler specified `SA_SHIRQ` in its `flags`.

- Both the new handler and the old one are fast handlers, or both are slow.

The reasons behind these requirements should be quite apparent: fast and slow handlers live in different environments, and you can't mix them. Similarly, you can't force sharing with a handler that was installed standalone. This condition about fast and slow handlers has been removed in recent 2.1 kernels because the two types now behave in the same way.

Whenever two or more drivers are sharing an interrupt line and the hardware interrupts the processor on that line, the kernel invokes every handler registered for that interrupt, passing each its own `dev_id`. Therefore, a shared handler must be able to recognize its own interrupts.

If you need to probe for your device before requesting the IRQ line, the kernel can't help you. No probing function is available for shared handlers. The standard probing mechanism works if the line being used is free; but if the line is already held by another driver with sharing capabilities, the probe will fail, even if your driver would have worked perfectly.

The only available technique for probing shared lines, then, is the do-it-yourself way. The driver should request every possible IRQ line as a shared handler and then see where interrupts are reported. The difference between that and "Do-it-yourself probing" is that the probing handler must check that the interrupt actually occurred, as it could have been called in response to another device interrupting on a shared line.

Releasing the handler is performed in the normal way using *release_irq*. Here the `dev_id` argument is used to select the correct handler to release from the list of shared handlers for the interrupt. That's why the `dev_id` pointer must be unique.

A driver using a shared handler needs to be careful about one more thing: it can't play with *enable_irq* or *disable_irq*. If it does, things might go haywire for other devices sharing the line. In general, the programmer must remember that his driver doesn't own the IRQ, and its behavior should be more "social" than is necessary if you own the interrupt line.

Running the Handler

As suggested above, when the kernel receives an interrupt, all the registered handlers are invoked. A shared handler must be able to distinguish between interrupts that it needs to handle and interrupts generated by other devices.

Loading *short* with the option `shared=1` installs the following handler instead of the default:

```
void short_sh_interrupt(int irq, void *dev_id, struct pt_regs *regs)
{
    int value;
    struct timeval tv;

    /* If it wasn't short, return immediately */
    value = inb(short_base);
    if (!(value & 0x80)) return;

    /* clear the interrupting bit */
    outb(value & 0x7F, short_base);

    /* the rest is unchanged */

    do_gettimeofday(&tv);
    short_head += sprintf((char *)short_head,"%08u.%06u\n",
                    (int)(tv.tv_sec % 100000000),
                    (int)(tv.tv_usec));
    if (short_head == short_buffer + PAGE_SIZE)
        short_head = short_buffer; /* wrap */

    wake_up_interruptible(&short_queue); /* awake any reading process */
}
```

An explanation is due here. Since the parallel port has no "interrupt-pending" bit to check, the handler uses the ACK bit for this purpose. If the bit is high, the interrupt being reported is for *short*, and the handler clears the bit.

The handler resets the bit by zeroing the high bit of the parallel interface's data port—*short* knows that pins 9 and 10 are connected together. If one of the other devices sharing the IRQ with *short* generates an interrupt, *short* sees that its own line is still inactive and does nothing.

Obviously, a *real* handler does more; in particular, it uses the `dev_id` argument to refer to its own hardware structure.

A full-featured driver probably splits the work into top and bottom halves, but that's easy to add and does not have any impact on the code that implements sharing.

The /proc Interface

Installing shared handlers in the system doesn't affect */proc/stat* (which doesn't even know about handlers). However, */proc/interrupts* changes slightly.

All the handlers installed for the same interrupt number appear on the same line of */proc/interrupts*. The following snapshot was taken on my computer, after I loaded *short* and the driver for my frame grabber as shared handlers:

```
 0:    1153617    timer
 1:      13637    keyboard
 2:          0    cascade
 3:      14697 +  serial
 5:     190762    NE2000
 7:       2094 +  short, + cx100
13:          0    math error
14:      47995 +  ide0
15:      12207 +  ide1
```

The shared interrupt line here is IRQ 7; the active handlers are listed on one line, separated by commas. It's apparent that the kernel is unable to distinguish *short* interrupts from grabber (*cx100*) interrupts.

Interrupt-Driven I/O

Whenever a data transfer to or from the managed hardware might be delayed for any reason, the driver writer should implement buffering. Data buffers help to detach data transmission and reception from the *write* and *read* system calls, and improve overall system performance.

A good buffering mechanism leads to "interrupt-driven I/O," in which an input buffer is filled at interrupt time and is emptied by processes that read the device; an output buffer is filled by processes that write to the device and is emptied at interrupt time.

For interrupt-driven data transfer to happen successfully, the hardware should be able to generate interrupts with the following semantics:

- For input, the device interrupts the processor when new data has arrived and is ready to be retrieved by the system processor. The actual actions to perform depend on whether the device uses I/O ports, memory mapping, or DMA.

- For output, the device delivers an interrupt either when it is ready to accept new data or to acknowledge a successful data transfer. Memory-mapped and DMA-capable devices usually generate interrupts to tell the system they are done with the buffer.

The timing relationships between a *read* or *write* and the actual arrival of data were introduced in "Blocking and Nonblocking Operations," in Chapter 5, *Enhanced Char Driver Operations*. Interrupt-driven I/O introduces the problem of synchronizing concurrent access to shared data items, and therefore all the issues related to race conditions.

Race Conditions

Whenever a variable or other data item is modified at interrupt time, there is the possibility that the driver will operate inconsistently because of race conditions. A race condition happens whenever an operation is not executed atomically, but it still needs to count on data coherence throughout its execution. The "race" therefore is between the non-atomic operation and other code that might be executed in the meantime. Typically, race conditions appear in three situations: implicit calls to *schedule* from within a function, blocking operations, and access to data shared by interrupt code and system calls. The last situation is the most frequent, and that's why race conditions are dealt with in this chapter.

Dealing with race conditions is one of the trickiest aspects of programming, because the related bugs are subtle and very difficult to reproduce, and it's hard to tell when there is a race condition between interrupt code and the driver methods. The programmer must take great care to avoid corruption of data or metadata.

In general, the techniques used to prevent race conditions are implemented in the driver methods, which must be sure to handle the data items correctly if they unexpectedly change. The interrupt handler, on the other hand, doesn't usually need special care, because it operates atomically with respect to the device methods.

Different techniques can be employed to prevent data corruption, and I'm going to introduce the most common ones. I won't show complete code because the best code for each situation depends on the operating mode of the device being driven, and on the programmer's taste.

The most common ways of protecting data from concurrent access are:

*   Using a circular buffer and avoiding shared variables.

*   Temporarily disabling interrupts in the method whenever the shared variables are accessed.

*   Using lock variables, which are atomically incremented and decremented.

Whatever approach you choose, you still need to decide what to do when accessing a variable that can be modified at interrupt time. Such variables can be declared as `volatile`, to prevent the compiler from optimizing access to its value (for example, it prevents the compiler from holding the value in a register for the whole duration of a function). However, the compiler generates horrible code whenever `volatile` variables are involved, so you might choose to resort to *cli* and *sti* instead. The Linux implementation of these functions uses a *gcc* directive to ensure the processor is in a safe state before the interrupt flag is modified.

Using Circular Buffers

Using a circular buffer is an effective way of handling concurrent-access problems: the best way to deal with concurrent access is to perform no concurrent access whatsoever.

The circular buffer uses an algorithm called "producer and consumer"—one player pushes data in and the other pulls data out. Concurrent access is avoided if there is exactly one producer and exactly one consumer. There are two examples of producer and consumer in the *short* module. In one case, the reading process is waiting to consume data that is produced at interrupt time; in the other, the bottom half consumes data produced by the top half.

Two pointers are used to address a circular buffer: `head` and `tail`. `head` is the point at which data is being written and is updated only by the producer of the data. Data is being read from `tail`, which is updated only by the consumer. As I mentioned above, if data is written at interrupt time, you must be careful when accessing `head` multiple times. You should either declare it as `volatile` or disable interrupts before entering race conditions.

The circular buffer runs smoothly, except when it fills up. If that happens, things become hairy, and you can choose among different possible solutions. The *short* implementation just loses data; there's no check for overflow, and if `head` goes beyond `tail`, a whole buffer of data is lost. Some alternative implementations are to drop the last item; overwrite the buffer tail, as *printk* does (see "How Messages Get Logged" in Chapter 4); hold up the producer, as *scullpipe* does; or allocate a temporary extra buffer to back up the main buffer. The best solution depends on the importance of your data and other situation-specific questions, so I won't cover it here.

Although the circular buffer appears to solve the problem of concurrent access, there is still the possibility of a race condition when the *read* function goes to sleep. This code shows where the problem appears in *short*:

```
while (short_head == short_tail) {
    interruptible_sleep_on(&short_queue);
    /* ... */
}
```

When executing this statement, it is possible that new data will arrive *after* the `while` condition is evaluated as true and *before* the process goes to sleep. Information carried in by the interrupt won't be read by the process; the process goes to sleep even though `head != tail`, and it isn't awakened until the next data item arrives.

I didn't implement correct locking for *short* because the source of *short_read* is included in "A Sample Driver" in Chapter 8, and at that point this discussion was not worth introducing. Also, the data involved is not worth the effort.

While the data that *short* collects is not vital, and the likelihood of getting an interrupt in the time lapse between two successive instructions is often negligible, sometimes you just can't take the risk of going to sleep when data is pending.

This problem is general enough to deserve special treatment and is delayed to "Going to Sleep Without Races" later in this chapter, where I'll discuss it in detail.

It's interesting to note that only a producer and consumer situation can be addressed with a circular buffer. A programmer must often deal with more complex data structures to solve the concurrent-access problem. The producer/consumer situation is actually the simplest class of these problems; other structures, such as linked lists, simply don't lend themselves to a circular buffer implementation.

Disabling Interrupts

A commonly used method of acquiring unique access to shared data is to call *cli* to disable interrupt reporting in the processor. Whenever a data item (like a linked list) is modified at interrupt time *and* by a function living in the normal computational flow, interrupts must be disabled by the latter function before it touches shared data.

The race condition in this case is between the instruction reading a shared item and the instruction using the knowledge just acquired. For example, the following loop may fail reading a linked list if the list is modified at interrupt time:

```
for (ptr = listHead; ptr; ptr = ptr->next)
    /* do something */ ;
```

An interrupt may change the value of `ptr` after it has been read but before it is used. If this happens, you'll have problems as soon as you use `ptr` because the current value of the pointer is no longer related to the list.

One possible solution is to disable interrupts for the duration of the critical loop. Although the code for disabling interrupts was introduced in Chapter 2, in the section "ISA Memory," it is worth repeating it here:

```
unsigned long flags;
save_flags(flags);
cli();
/* critical code */
restore_flags(flags);
```

As a matter of fact, in the device methods, the simpler *cli/sti* pair can be used instead because you can count on interrupts being enabled when a process enters a system call. However, you have to use the safer *save_flags/restore_flags* solution in a function that is called by other code, where you can't make any assumptions about the current value of the interrupt flag.

Using Lock Variables

The third approach to shared data variables is to use locks that are accessed through atomic instructions. Whenever one of two unrelated entities (such as an interrupt handler and the *read* system call, or two processors in a Symmetric Multi-Processor computer) need to access a shared data item, it must first acquire the lock. If the lock can't be acquired, it must be waited for.

The Linux kernel exports two sets of functions to deal with locks: bit operations and access to the "atomic" data type.

Bit operations

It's quite common to have single-bit lock variables or to update device status flags at interrupt time—while a process may be accessing them. The kernel offers a set of functions that modify or test single bits atomically. Because the whole operation happens in a single step, no interrupt can interfere.

Atomic bit operations are very fast, as they usually perform the operation using a single machine instruction without disabling interrupts. The functions are architecture-dependent and are declared in `<asm/bitops.h>`. They are guaranteed to be atomic even on SMP computers and are therefore the suggested way to keep coherence across processors.

Unfortunately, data typing in these functions is architecture-dependent as well. Both the `nr` argument and the return value are `unsigned long` for the Alpha and the Sparc and `int` for the other architectures. The following list describes the bit operations as they appear in versions 1.2 through 2.1.37. The list changed in 2.1.38, as detailed in "Bit Operations" in Chapter 17, *Recent Developments*.

```
set_bit(nr, void *addr);
```
> This function sets bit number **nr** in the data item pointed to by **addr**. The function acts on an **unsigned long**, even though **addr** is a pointer to void. The value returned is the previous value of the bit—0 or non-zero.

```
clear_bit(nr, void *addr);
```
> The function clears the specified bit in the **unsigned long** datum that lives at **addr**. Its semantics are the same as *set_bit*.

```
change_bit(nr, void *addr);
```
> This function toggles the bit. Otherwise, it is identical to *set_bit* and *clear_bit*, above.

```
test_bit(nr, void *addr);
```
> This function is the only bit operation that doesn't need to be atomic; it simply returns the current value of the bit.

When these functions are used to access and modify a shared flag, you don't have to do anything except call them. Using bit operations to manage a lock variable that controls access to a shared variable, on the other hand, is more complicated, and deserves an example.

A code segment that needs to access a shared data item tries to atomically acquire a lock using either *set_bit* or *clear_bit*. The usual implementation is shown below; it assumes that the lock lives at bit **nr** of address **addr**. It also assumes that the bit is 0 when the lock is free and non-zero when the lock is busy.

```
/* try to set lock */
while (set_bit(nr, addr) != 0)
    wait_for_a_while();

/* do your work */

/* release lock, and check... */
if (clear_bit(nr, addr) == 0)
    something_went_wrong(); /* already released: error */
```

The downside of accessing shared data this way is that both the contending parties must be able to wait. This is not easily achieved when one of the parties is an interrupt handler.

Atomic integer operations

Kernel programmers often need to share an integer variable between an interrupt handler and other functions. We have just seen how atomic access to bits is not sufficient to guarantee that everything will work well (in the previous case, *cli* must be used anyway if one of the parties is an interrupt handler).

The need to prevent race conditions, actually, is so compelling that the kernel developers devoted an entire header to the problem: `<asm/atomic.h>`. This header is quite recent and is missing in Linux 1.2. It is therefore not available to drivers meant to be backward compatible.

The facility offered by *atomic.h* is much stronger than the bit operations just described. *atomic.h* defines a new data type, `atomic_t`, which can be accessed only through atomic operations.

`atomic_t` is currently defined as `int` on all supported architectures. The following operations are defined for the type and are guaranteed to be atomic with respect to all processors of an SMP computer. The operations are very fast because they compile to a single machine instruction whenever possible.

`void atomic_add(atomic_t i, atomic_t *v);`
> Add i to the atomic variable pointed to by v. The return value is `void`, as most of the time there's no need to know the new value. This function is used by the networking code to update statistics about memory usage in sockets.

`void atomic_sub(atomic_t i, atomic_t *v);`
> Subtract i from *v. The i argument for both these functions is declared as `int` in recent 2.1 kernels, but this change is mainly aesthetic and shouldn't affect source code.

`void atomic_inc(atomic_t *v);`
`void atomic_dec(atomic_t *v);`
> Increment or decrement an atomic variable.

`int atomic_dec_and_test(atomic_t *v);`
> This function was added in version 1.3.84 and is useful for keeping track of usage counts. The return value is 0 only if the variable *v is 0 after being decremented.

As suggested above, `atomic_t` data items must be accessed only through these functions. If you pass an atomic item to a function that expects an integer argument, you'll get a compiler warning. Needless to say, you are allowed to read the current value of an atomic item and to cast atomic variables to other types.

Going to Sleep Without Races

The one race condition that has been omitted so far in this discussion is the problem of going to sleep. It is a problem far more general than interrupt-driven I/O, and an efficient solution requires a little knowledge of the internals of *sleep_on*.

This particular race condition occurs between the time the condition is checked for going to sleep and the actual invocation of *sleep_on*. This test case is the same statement used above, but I feel it is worth showing once again:

```
while (short_head == short_tail) {
    interruptible_sleep_on(&short_queue);
    /* ... */
}
```

If the comparison and the going to sleep must be performed safely, *first* disable interrupt reporting and *then* test the condition and go to sleep. Thus, the variable being tested in the comparison cannot be modified. The kernel allows the process to go to sleep after issuing *cli*. The kernel simply reenables interrupt reporting just before calling *schedule*, after inserting the process into its wait queue.

The code examples introduced here use a **while** loop, which performs signal handling. If a blocked signal is reported to the process, *interruptible_sleep_on* returns, and the test in the **while** statement is performed again. The following is one possible implementation:

```
while (short_head == short_tail) {
    cli();
    if (short_head == short_tail)
        interruptible_sleep_on(&short_queue);
    sti();
    /* .... signal decoding .... */
}
```

If an interrupt happens after the *cli*, the interrupt remains pending while the current process is being put to sleep. By the time the interrupt is eventually reported to the processor, the process is already asleep and can be awakened safely.

In this case, I used *cli/sti* because the sample code is designed to live within the *read* method; the safer *save_flags*, *cli*, and *restore_flags* functions should be used otherwise.

If you don't want to disable interrupt reporting while going to sleep, there is another way to perform the same job (one that Linus likes a lot). Anyway, you can skip the following discussion if you'd like, since it's slightly elaborate.

The idea is that the process can add itself to the wait queue, declare itself to be sleeping, and *then* perform its tests. This is the typical implementation:

```
struct wait_queue wait = { current, NULL };

add_wait_queue(&short_queue, &wait);
do {
    current->state = TASK_INTERRUPTIBLE;
    schedule();
}
while ((short_head == short_tail)
        && !(current->signal & ~current->blocked) );
remove_wait_queue(&short_queue, &wait);

if (current->signal & ~current->blocked) /* a signal arrived */
    return -ERESTARTSYS;
```

This code is somewhat like an unrolling of the internals of *sleep_on*. The `wait` variable is explicitly declared because it is needed to put a process to sleep; this fact was explained in "Wait Queues," in Chapter 5. This example introduced several new symbols:

`current->state`

> This field is a hint for the scheduler. Whenever the scheduler is invoked, it looks at the `state` field of all processes to decide what to do. Each process is free to modify its `state`, but the change won't take effect until the scheduler runs.

```
#include <linux/sched.h>
TASK_RUNNING
TASK_INTERRUPTIBLE
TASK_UNINTERRUPTIBLE
```

> These symbolic names represent the most common values of `current->state`. `TASK_RUNNING` means that the process is running, and the other two mean that it is sleeping.

```
void add_wait_queue(struct wait_queue ** p,
                    struct wait_queue * wait)
void remove_wait_queue(struct wait_queue ** p,
                    struct wait_queue * wait)
void __add_wait_queue(struct wait_queue ** p,
                    struct wait_queue * wait)
void __remove_wait_queue(struct wait_queue ** p,
                    struct wait_queue * wait)
```

> Insert and remove a process from a wait queue. The `wait` argument must point into the process's stack page. The functions with the leading underscores are faster but can only be called when interrupts are disabled (for example, from a fast interrupt handler).

With this background, let's look at what happens when an interrupt arrives. The handler calls `wake_up_interruptible(&short_queue)`; for Linux, this means "set `state` to `TASK_RUNNING`." Therefore, if an interrupt is reported between the `while` condition and the call to *schedule*, the task will already have been marked as running, with no data loss.

If, on the other hand, the process is still "interruptible," *schedule* leaves it sleeping.

It's interesting to note that the *wake_up* call doesn't remove the process from the wait queue. It's *sleep_on* that adds and removes the process from the wait queue. The code must call *add_wait_queue* and *remove_wait_queue* explicitly, because *sleep_on* hasn't been used in this case.

Version Dependencies of IRQ Handling

Not all of the code introduced in this chapter is backward portable to Linux 1.2. I outline here the main differences and suggest how to deal with them. *short* actually compiles and runs equally well with 2.0.*x* and 1.2.13 kernels.

Different Prototypes for request_irq

The way of passing arguments to *request_irq* that I've used throughout this chapter was introduced only with version 1.3.70 of the kernel, when shared handlers appeared.

Previous kernel versions didn't require a `dev_id` argument, and the prototype was slightly simpler:

```
int request_irq(unsigned int irq,
                void (*handler)(int, struct pt_regs *),
                unsigned long flags, const char *device);
```

The new semantics can easily be forced onto the old prototype by using the following macro definitions (note that *free_irq* also had no `dev_id` argument in early versions):

```
#if LINUX_VERSION_CODE < VERSION_CODE(1,3,70)
    /* the preprocessor is able to handle recursive definitions */
#   define request_irq(irq,fun,fla,nam,dev) request_irq(irq,fun,fla,nam)
#   define free_irq(irq,dev)                free_irq(irq)
#endif
```

The macros just discard the extra `dev` argument.

The difference in the handler prototypes is best taken care of with an explicit `#if/#else/#endif` statement. If you use the `dev_id` pointer, the conditional case for old kernels could declare a `NULL` variable, and the body of the handler should be able to deal with a `NULL` device pointer.

One of the *short* examples exemplifies the idea:

```
#if LINUX_VERSION_CODE < VERSION_CODE(1,3,70)
void short_sh_interrupt(int irq, struct pt_regs *regs)
{
    void *dev_id = NULL;
#else
void short_sh_interrupt(int irq, void *dev_id, struct pt_regs *regs)
{
#endif
```

Probing the IRQ Line

The kernel started exporting the probing functions with version 1.3.30. If you want to port your driver to older kernels, you have to implement do-it-yourself probing. The functions themselves exist in all kernels back to 1.2, but they were not available to modularized drivers.

There aren't any other problems porting interrupt handlers.

Quick Reference

These symbols, related to interrupt management, were introduced in this chapter:

```
#include <linux/sched.h>
int request_irq(unsigned int irq, void (*handler)(),
unsigned long flags, const char *device, void *dev_id);
void free_irq(unsigned int irq, void *dev_id);
```
> These calls are used to register and unregister an interrupt handler. Kernels older than 2.0 lack the `dev_id` argument.

```
SA_INTERRUPT
SA_SHIRQ
SA_SAMPLE_RANDOM
```
> Flags for *request_irq*. `SA_INTERRUPT` requests installation of a fast handler (as opposed to a slow one). `SA_SHIRQ` installs a shared handler, and the third flag asserts that interrupt timestamps can be used to generate system entropy.

/proc/interrupts
/proc/stat
> These filesystem nodes are used to report information about hardware interrupts and installed handlers.

```
unsigned long probe_irq_on(void);
int probe_irq_off(unsigned long);
```
> These functions are used by the driver when it has to probe to determine what interrupt line is being used by a device. The result of *probe_irq_on* must be passed back to *probe_irq_off* after the interrupt has been generated. The return value of *probe_irq_off* is the detected interrupt number.

```
void disable_irq(int irq);
void enable_irq(int irq);
```
> A driver can enable and disable interrupt reporting. If the hardware tries to generate an interrupt while interrupts are disabled, the interrupt is lost forever. Calling these functions from a top-half handler has no effect. A driver using a shared handler must not use these functions.

```
#include <linux/interrupt.h>
void mark_bh(int nr);
```
This function marks a bottom half for execution.

```
#include <asm/bitops.h>
set_bit(nr, void *addr);
clear_bit(nr, void *addr);
change_bit(nr, void *addr);
test_bit(nr, void *addr);
```
These functions atomically access bit values; they can be used for flags or lock variables. Using these functions prevents any race condition related to concurrent access to the bit.

```
#include <asm/atomic.h>
typedef int atomic_t;
void atomic_add(atomic_t i, atomic_t *v);
void atomic_sub(atomic_t i, atomic_t *v);
void atomic_inc(atomic_t *v);
void atomic_dec(atomic_t *v);
int atomic_dec_and_test(atomic_t *v);
```
These functions atomically access integer variables. To achieve a clean compile, the `atomic_t` variables must be accessed only through these functions.

```
#include <linux/sched.h>
TASK_RUNNING
TASK_INTERRUPTIBLE
TASK_UNINTERRUPTIBLE
```
The most commonly used values for `current->state`. They are used as hints for *schedule*.

```
void add_wait_queue(struct wait_queue ** p,
                    struct wait_queue * wait)
void remove_wait_queue(struct wait_queue ** p,
                    struct wait_queue * wait)
void __add_wait_queue(struct wait_queue ** p,
                    struct wait_queue * wait)
void __remove_wait_queue(struct wait_queue ** p,
                    struct wait_queue * wait)
```
The lowest-level functions that use wait queues. The leading underscores indicate a lower-level functionality, in which case interrupt reporting must already be disabled in the processor.

CHAPTER TEN

JUDICIOUS USE
OF DATA TYPES

Before we go on to more advanced topics, we need to stop for a quick note on portability issues. The difference between versions 1.2 and 2.0 of Linux lies in the addition of multiplatform capabilities; as a result, most source-level portability problems have been eliminated. This means that a serious Linux driver should be multiplatform as well.

But a core issue with kernel code is being able to both access data items of known length (for example, filesystem data structures or registers on device boards) and to exploit the capabilities of different processors (32-bit and 64-bit architectures, and possibly 16-bit as well).

Several problems encountered by kernel developers while porting x86 code to new architectures have been related to incorrect data typing. Adherence to strict data typing and compiling with the *–Wall –Wstrict-prototypes* flags can prevent most bugs.

Data types used by kernel data are divided into three main classes: standard C types like `int`, explicitly sized types like `u32`, and interface-specific types, like `pid_t`. We are going to see when and how each of the three typing classes should be used. The final sections of the chapter talk about some other typical problems you might run into when porting driver code from the x86 to other platforms.

If you follow the guidelines I provide, your driver will compile and run even on platforms where you are unable to test it.

Use of Standard C Types

While most programmers are accustomed to freely using standard types like `int` and `long`, writing device drivers requires some care to avoid typing conflicts and obscure bugs.

The problem is that you can't use the standard types when you need "a 2-byte filler" or "something representing a 4-byte string" because the normal C data types are not the same size on all architectures. For example, `long` integers and pointers are a different size on the x86 than on the Alpha, as shown by the following screen snapshots:

```
morgana% ./datasize
system/machine: Linux i486
sizeof(char)  =    1
sizeof(short) =    2
sizeof(int)   =    4
sizeof(long)  =    4
sizeof(longlong) = 8
sizeof(pointer) =  4

wolf% ./datasize
system/machine: Linux alpha
sizeof(char)  =    1
sizeof(short) =    2
sizeof(int)   =    4
sizeof(long)  =    8
sizeof(longlong) = 8
sizeof(pointer) =  8

sandra% ./datasize
system/machine: Linux sparc
sizeof(char)  =    1
sizeof(short) =    2
sizeof(int)   =    4
sizeof(long)  =    4
sizeof(longlong) = 8
sizeof(pointer) =  4
```

The *datasize* program is a short program available in the files provided on the O'Reilly FTP site, in the directory *misc-progs*.

While you must be careful when mixing `int` and `long`, sometimes there are good reasons to do so. One such situation is for memory addresses, which are special as far as the kernel is concerned. Although conceptually addresses are pointers, memory administration is better accomplished by using an integer type; the kernel treats physical memory like a huge array, and a memory address is just an index into the array. Furthermore, a pointer is easily dereferenced, and using integers for memory addresses prevents them from being dereferenced, which is what you want. Therefore, addresses in the kernel are `unsigned long`, exploiting the fact that pointers and long integers are always the same size, at least on all the platforms curently supported by Linux. We'll have to wait and see what happens when Linux is ported to a platform breaking this rule.

Assigning an Explicit Size to Data Items

Sometimes kernel code requires data items of a specific size, either to match binary structures* or to align data within structures by inserting "filler" fields.

The kernel offers the following data types for this purpose, all declared in `<asm/types.h>`, which in turn is included by `<linux/types.h>`:

```
u8;    /* unsigned byte (8 bits) */
u16;   /* unsigned word (16 bits) */
u32;   /* unsigned 32-bit value */
u64;   /* unsigned 64-bit value */
```

These data types are accessible only from kernel code (i.e., `__KERNEL__` must be defined before including `<linux/types.h>`). The corresponding signed types exist, but are rarely needed; just replace `u` with `s` in the name if you need them.

If a user-space program needs to use these types, it can prefix the names with a double underscore: `__u8` and the other types are defined independent of `__KERNEL__`. If, for example, a driver needs to exchange binary structures with a program running in user space by means of *ioctl*, the header files should declare 32-bit fields in the structures as `__u32`.

It's important to remember that these types are Linux-specific, and using them hinders porting software to other Unix flavors. There are nonetheless situations where explicit data sizing is needed, and the standard header files (the ones you find on every Unix system) don't declare suitable data types.

You might also note that sometimes the kernel uses conventional types, like `unsigned int`, for items whose dimension is architecture-independent. This is usually done for backward compatibility. When `u32` and friends were introduced in version 1.1.67, the developers couldn't change existing data structures to the new types, because the compiler issues a warning when there is a type mismatch between the structure field and the value being assigned to it.† Linus didn't expect the OS he wrote for his own use to become multi-platform; as a result, old structures are sometimes loosely typed.

---

* This happens when reading partition tables, when executing a binary file, or when decoding a network packet.

† As a matter of fact, the compiler signals type inconsistencies even if the two types are just different names for the same object, like `unsigned long` and `u32` on the PC.

Interface-Specific Types

Most commonly used data types in the kernel have their own `typedef` statement, thus preventing any portability problems. For example, a process identifier (pid) is usually `pid_t` instead of `int`. Using `pid_t` masks any possible difference in the actual data typing. I use the expression "interface-specific" to refer to the programming interface to specific data items.

Other data items that belong to a specific "standard" type can be considered interface-specific as well. A jiffy count, for instance, is always `unsigned long`, independent of its actual size—would you like using `jiffy_t` every so often? I'm concentrating here on the first class of interface-specific types, the ones ending in `_t`.

The complete list of `_t` types appears in `<linux/types.h>`, but the list is rarely useful. When you need a specific type, you'll find it in the prototype of the functions you need to call or in the data structures you use.

Whenever your driver uses functions that require such "custom" types and you don't follow the convention, the compiler issues a warning; if you use the *−Wall* compiler flag and are careful to remove all the warnings, you can feel confident that your code is portable.

The main problem with `_t` data items is that when you need to print them, it's not always easy to choose the right *printk* or *printf* format, and warnings you resolve on one architecture reappear on another. For example, how would you print a `size_t` which is `unsigned long` on some platforms and `unsigned int` on some other?

Whenever you need to print some interface-specific data, the best way to do it is by casting the value to the biggest possible type (usually `long` or `unsigned long`), and then printing it through the corresponding format. This kind of tweaking won't generate errors or warnings because the format matches the type, and you won't lose data bits because the cast is either a null operation or an extension of the item to a bigger data type.

In practice, the data items we're talking about aren't usually meant to be printed, so the issue applies only to debugging messages. Most often, the code needs only to store and compare the interface-specific types, in addition to passing them as arguments to library or kernel functions.

Although `_t` types are the correct solution for most situations, sometimes the right type doesn't exist. This happens for some old interfaces, which haven't yet been cleaned up.

The one ambiguous point I've found in the kernel headers is data typing for I/O functions, which is loosely defined (see the section "Platform Dependencies" in

Chapter 8, *Hardware Management*). The loose typing is mainly there for historical reasons, but it can create problems when writing code. Personally, I often get into trouble by swapping the arguments to *out* functions; if `port_t` were defined, the compiler would pinpoint these errors.

Other Portability Issues

In addition to data typing, there are a few other software issues to keep in mind when writing a driver if you want it to be portable across Linux platforms:

Time intervals

When dealing with time intervals, don't assume that there are 100 jiffies per second. Although this is currently true for Linux-x86, not every Linux platform runs at 100Hz. The assumption can be false even for the x86 if you play with the `HZ` value, and nobody knows what will happen in future kernels. Whenever you calculate time intervals using jiffies, scale your times using `HZ`. For example, to check against a timeout of half a second, compare the elapsed time against `HZ/2`. More generally, the number of jiffies corresponding to `msec` milliseconds is always `msec*HZ/1000`. This detail had to be fixed in many network drivers when porting them to the Alpha; some drivers originally designed for the PC included an explicit jiffy value for the timeout, but the Alpha has a different `HZ` value.

Page size

When playing games with memory, remember that a memory page is `PAGE_SIZE` bytes, not 4KB. Assuming that the page size is 4KB and hard-coding the value is a common error among PC programmers—the Alpha has pages twice as big. The relevant macros are `PAGE_SIZE` and `PAGE_SHIFT`. The latter contains the number of bits to shift an address to get its page number. The number currently is 12 or 13, for 4KB and 8KB pages. The macros are defined in `<asm/page.h>`.

Let's look at a non-trivial situation. If a driver needs 16KB for temporary data, it shouldn't specify an `order` of "2" to *get_free_pages*. You need a portable solution. Using an `#ifdef __alpha__` conditional currently works, but it only accounts for known platforms and would break when another architecture is supported. I'd suggest that you use this code instead:

```
buf = get_free_pages(GFP_KERNEL, 14 - PAGE_SHIFT, 0 /*dma*/);
```

Or, even better:

```
int order = (14 - PAGE_SHIFT > 0) ? 14 - PAGE_SHIFT : 0;
buf = get_free_pages(GFP_KERNEL, order, 0 /*dma*/);
```

Both solutions depend on the knowledge that 16KB is `1<<14`. The quotient of two numbers is the difference of their logarithms (orders), and both `14` and

`PAGE_SHIFT` are orders. The second implementation is better because it prevents passing a negative order to *get_free_pages*; the value of `order` is calculated at compile time with no overhead, and the implementation shown is a safe way to allocate memory for any power of two, independent of `PAGE_SIZE`.

Byte order

Be careful not to make assumptions about byte ordering. Whereas the PC stores multi-byte values low-byte first ("little endian"), most high-level platforms work the other way ("big endian"). While it's true that good programs never depend on byte ordering, sometimes a driver needs to build an integer number out of single bytes or the opposite. In that case, the code should include `<asm/byteorder.h>` and should check whether `__BIG_ENDIAN` or `__LITTLE_ENDIAN` is defined by the header. The leading underscores are missing from the Linux-1.2 header file. You can fix this incompatibility by including *sysdep.h* from the *scull* source after `<asm/byteorder.h>`.

When the byte-order dependency is related to network transmission, the conversion of 16-bit and 32-bit values should be performed using one of the following functions, defined in the same `<asm/byteorder.h>` header:

```
unsigned long    ntohl(unsigned long);
unsigned short   ntohs(unsigned short);
unsigned long    htonl(unsigned long);
unsigned short   htons(unsigned short);
```

These functions, which should be well-known to network programmers, take their name from the phrase "Network TO Host Long" and its equivalents.

Version 2.1.10 of the kernel added cpu-to-little-endian and cpu-to-big-endian conversions, and 2.1.43 expanded on this topic. The new utility functions are described in "Conversion Functions," in Chapter 17, *Recent Developments*.

Data alignment

The last problem worth considering when writing portable code is how to access unaligned data—for example, how to read a 4-byte value stored at an address that isn't a multiple of 4 bytes. PC users often access unaligned data items, but not every architecture permits it. The Alpha, for instance, generates an exception every time the program tries unaligned data transfers. If you need to access unaligned data, use the following macros:

```
#include <asm/unaligned.h>
get_unaligned(ptr);
put_unaligned(val, ptr);
```

These macros are typeless and work for every data item, whether it's 1, 2, 4, or 8 bytes long. The macros are missing from kernels prior to 2.0, but *sysdep.h* defines them for kernel 1.2.

A general rule is to be suspicious of explicit constant values. Usually the code has been parameterized using preprocessor macros to generalize it. Although I can't list every parameterized value here, you'll find the correct hints in the header files.

Unfortunately, however, there are some places where things don't work too well yet; for example, the handling of data sectors on disk. Historically, Linux has been able to deal only with .5KB disk sectors, but fortunately every existing device fits this constraint. The code is currently moving towards the ability to support different sector sizes, but it's hard to find all the places where the half-kilobyte assumption is hardcoded in. The sector-size problem is described further in Chapter 12, *Loading Block Drivers*.

Quick Reference

The following symbols were introduced in this chapter:

```
#include <linux/types.h>
typedef u8;
typedef u16;
typedef u32;
typedef u64;
```
These types are guaranteed to be 8-, 16-, 32-, and 64-bit unsigned integer values. The equivalent signed types exist as well. In user space, you can refer to the types as __u8, __u16, etc.

```
#include <asm/page.h>
PAGE_SIZE
PAGE_SHIFT
```
These symbols define the number of bytes per page for the current architecture and the number of bits in the page offset (12 for 4KB pages and 13 for 8KB pages).

```
#include <asm/byteorder.h>
__LITTLE_ENDIAN
__BIG_ENDIAN
```
Only one of the two symbols is defined, depending on the architecture. Version 1.3.18 and older declared the symbols without the leading underscores (thus conflicting with some of the network headers).

```
#include <asm/byteorder.h>
unsigned long ntohl(unsigned long);
unsigned short ntohs(unsigned short);
unsigned long htonl(unsigned long);
```

```
unsigned short htons(unsigned short);
```
These functions convert long and short data between the network byte order and the host byte order.

```
#include <asm/unaligned.h>
get_unaligned(ptr);
put_unaligned(val, ptr);
```
Some architectures need to protect unaligned data access using these macros. The macros expand to normal pointer dereferencing for architectures that permit you to access unaligned data.

CHAPTER ELEVEN

KERNELD AND ADVANCED MODULARIZATION

In this second part of the book, we'll be discussing more advanced topics than we've seen up to now. Once again, we'll start with modularization. The introduction to modularization in Chapter 2, *Building and Running Modules*, is only part of the story; the *modules* package (whose latest versions are called *modutils* instead) supports some advanced features that are more complex than we needed earlier to get a basic driver up and running.

This chapter talks about the *kerneld* program, version support inside modules (a facility meant to save you from recompiling your modules each time you upgrade your kernel), and support for data persistence across unload and reload of a module. This last capability is available only with version 2.0.0 or later of the *modules* package.

Loading Modules on Demand

To make it easier for users to load and unload modules, and to avoid wasting kernel memory by keeping drivers in core when they are not in use, Linux offers support for automatic loading and unloading of modules. (This support was missing from versions 1.2 and earlier.) To exploit this feature, you need to enable *kerneld* support when you configure the kernel before you compile it. The ability to request additional modules when they are needed is particularly useful for drivers using module stacking.

The idea behind *kerneld* is simple, yet effective. Whenever the kernel tries to access unavailable resources, it notifies the user program instead of simply returning an error. If the daemon succeeds in retrieving the resource, the kernel continues working; otherwise, it returns the error. Virtually any resource can be requested this way: char and block drivers, line disciplines, network protocols, etc.

The mechanism used to achieve demand loading is a modified message queue, used to pass textual information from the kernel to user space and vice versa. For demand loading to work correctly, the user-level daemon must be properly configured, and the kernel code must be prepared to wait for needed modules.

A typical example of a driver that would benefit from demand loading is a generic frame-grabber driver. It can support several different peripherals, while presenting the same external behavior. The distribution will include code for all the supported boards, but only the code for the particular board being used is needed at run time. The developers can thus choose to split the implementation into a general-purpose module defining the software interface and a set of hardware-dependent modules for the low-level operations. After the general-purpose module has detected the type of grabber installed in the system, it can request the correct module for that grabber.

The User-Level Side

The *kerneld* program lives in user space and is responsible for handling requests for new modules from the kernel. It connects to the kernel by creating its own message queue and then goes to sleep waiting for requests.

When a module is requested, the daemon receives a string from the kernel and tries to resolve it. The string can be one of two kinds:

* The name of an object file, like the typical argument to *insmod*. `floppy` is an example of such a name; in this case, the daemon looks for the file *floppy.o* and loads it.

* A more generic identifier, like `block-major-2`, which specifies the block driver with major number 2—the floppy driver once again. This kind of string is the most common, because the kernel usually knows only the numeric identifier of a resource. When you try to use a block device, for example, the kernel knows the device only by its major number; it would be a waste to implement a different hook for each block driver just to be able to ask for them by name.

Clearly, in the latter case, there must some way to map the module's "id" to its actual name. This association is not performed by *kerneld* itself, but rather by *modprobe*, which is called by *kerneld*. *modprobe*, helped by *depmod*, deals with the details of module loading; *kerneld* itself is responsible only for communicating with the kernel and spawning external tasks. All of these programs are distributed within the *modules* package. *depmod* is a utility that creates Makefile-like dependencies for modules, while *modprobe* is an alternative to *insmod* that can correctly load a stack of modules. For example, the *ppp* module stacks on (in other words, uses symbols from) *slhc*, the "Serial Line Header Compression" module. *insmod ppp* fails unless *slhc* is already loaded; *modprobe ppp*, on the other hand, succeeds, provided that *depmod –a* was invoked to build the dependency rules after the modules were installed.

Another difference between *insmod* and *modprobe* is that the latter doesn't look for modules in the current directory, but only in the default directories under */lib/modules*. This is because the program is meant to be a system utility rather than an interactive tool; you can add your own directories to the default set by specifying them in */etc/modules.conf* .

/etc/modules.conf is a text file used to customize the *modules* package. It is the file responsible for associating names like `block-major-2` to `floppy`. Note that versions of the *modules* package prior to 2.0 looked for */etc/conf.modules* instead; the name is still supported for compatibility reasons, but deprecated in favor of the more standardized name *modules.conf*.

The syntax of *modules.conf* is well described by the man page for the *depmod* and *modprobe* commands; I feel, nonetheless, that it's worth mentioning the meaning of a few important directives here. I'll use the following lines as an example:

```
# sample lines for /etc/modules.conf
keep
path[misc]=~rubini/driverBook/src/*
options short irq=1
alias eth0 ne
```

The first line shown is a comment; `path[misc]` states where to look for miscellaneous modules—and `keep` says to add custom paths to the default paths instead of replacing them. The `option` directive says to always specify `irq=1` when loading *short*, and the `alias` line says that when `eth0` needs to be loaded, the relevant file is called *ne.o* (the driver for the ne2000 interface). Lines like `alias block-major-2 floppy` are not actually needed, because *modprobe* already knows all the official major numbers for devices and these "foreseeable" `alias` commands are predefined in the program.

A correct setup of module demand loading, then, reduces to adding lines to */etc/modules.conf*, as *kerneld* relies on *modprobe* for the actual loading operation.

The Kernel-Level Side

In order to request loading and unloading of a module, kernel code can use the functions defined in `<linux/kerneld.h>`, all of which are inline definitions that do the actual work by passing arguments to *kerneld_send*. This function is a flexible engine for communication with *kerneld* and lives in *ipc/msg.c*, where you can browse it if you are interested.

I won't go into the details of *kerneld_send* here, because the following calls, defined in `<linux/kerneld.h>`, are more than enough to enable you to exploit demand loading:

`int request_module(const char *name)`
> This function can be called whenever a module is needed. The **name** argument is either the filename of the module or an id-type string that will be resolved in user space. The function returns after loading has completed successfully (or has failed). *request_module* can be invoked only from the context of a process, because the current process will be put to sleep waiting for the module to be loaded. Any module that is demand loaded is automatically unloaded shortly after its usage count drops to zero.

`int release_module(const char *name, int waitflag)`
> Ask for immediate unloading of a module. The **waitflag**, if not zero, says that the function must wait for unload to terminate before returning. If **waitflag** is zero, the function can be called at interrupt time—for what it's worth.

`int delayed_release_module(const char *name)`
> Ask for delayed module unloading. The function always returns immediately. Its effect is that the module **name** is unloaded shortly after its usage count drops to zero, even if it was not being loaded by *kerneld*.

`int cancel_release_module(const char *name)`
> This function cancels the effect of *delayed_release_module*, without preventing automatic unloading of demand-loaded modules, at least in the current implementation. It's unlikely you'll need this function, which is mentioned here mainly for completeness.

The return value of *kerneld_send*, and thus of all the functions just listed, is negative if errors are detected in kernel space. If everything goes well in the kernel, the return value is set to the exit value of the user-space program performing the required action. The exit value is zero for success and a number between 1 and 255 for an error.

The good news with *kerneld_send* is that the function exists (and is exported to modules) even in kernels configured for no *kerneld* support; it just returns **-ENOSYS**. A module writer can therefore always call the functions shown, unless you run kernel 1.2, because all this machinery was introduced in 1.3.57.

Let's now try to use the demand-loading functions in practice. To this end, we'll use two modules called *master* and *slave*, distributed in the directory *misc-modules*, in the source files provided on the O'Reilly FTP site. We'll also use *slaveD.o* to test delayed unloading, and *slaveH.o* to load the module by hand and unload it automatically.

In order to run this test code without installing the modules, I added the following lines to my own */etc/modules.conf*:

```
keep
path[misc]=~rubini/driverBook/src/misc-modules
```

The slave modules are just empty files, and the master module looks like the following:

```
#include <linux/kerneld.h>

int init_module(void)
{
    int r[3]; /* results */

    r[0]=request_module("slave");
    r[1]=request_module("slaveD");
    r[2]=request_module("unexists");
    printk("master: loading results are %i, %i, %i\n",
            r[0],r[1],r[2]);
    return 0; /* success */
}

void cleanup_module(void)
{
    int r[4]; /* results */

    r[0]=release_module("slave", 1 /* wait */);
    r[1]=release_module("slaveH", 1 /* wait */);
    r[2]=delayed_release_module("slaveD");
    r[3]=release_module("unexists", 1 /* wait */);
    printk("master: unloading results are %i, %i, %i, %i\n",
            r[0],r[1],r[2],r[3]);
}
```

At load time, *master* tries to load two modules and one that doesn't exist. The *printk* messages appear on the console unless you've changed the console loglevel. This is what happens in a system configured for *kerneld* support when the daemon is active:

```
morgana.root# depmod -a
morgana.root# insmod master
master: loading results are 0, 0, 255
morgana.root# cat /proc/modules
slaveD              1          0 (autoclean)
slave               1          0 (autoclean)
master              1          0
isofs               5          1 (autoclean)
```

Both the return value from *request_module* and the */proc/modules* file (described in "Initialization and Shutdown" in Chapter 2) show that the slave modules have been correctly loaded. The return value of 255 for `unexists`, on the other hand, means that the user program failed with exit code 255 (or –1, since it's one byte only).

We'll see shortly what happens at unload time, but first let's load *slaveH* by hand:

```
morgana.root# insmod slaveH
morgana.root# cat /proc/modules
slaveH             1            0
slaveD             1            0 (autoclean)
slave              1            0 (autoclean)
master             1            0
isofs              5            1 (autoclean)
morgana.root# rmmod master
master: unloading results are 0, 0, 0, 255
morgana.root# cat /proc/modules
slaveD             1            0 (autoclean)
isofs              5            1 (autoclean)
morgana.root# sleep 60; cat /proc/modules
isofs              5            1 (autoclean)
```

The result shows that everything but the unloading of **unexists** went well, and *slaveD* was unloaded after some time.

Despite the various facilities offered, you'll find that most of the time *request_module* will suffice for your needs, without requiring you to deal with module unloading; in fact, unloading actually happens by default for unused modules. Most of the time, you won't even need to check the function's return value, because the module is needed for some functionality it offers. The following implementation is more convenient than checking the return value of *request_module*:

```
if ( (ptr = look_for_feature()) == NULL) /* if feature is missing */
    request_module(modname);             /*    try lo load it */
if ( (ptr = look_for_feature()) == NULL) /* if still missing */
    return -ENODEV;                      /*    error */
```

Version Control in Modules

One of the main problems with modules is their version dependency, which was introduced in "Version Dependency," in Chapter 2. The need to recompile the module against the headers of each version being used can become a real pain when you run several custom modules, and recompiling is not even possible if you run a commercial module distributed in binary form.

Fortunately, the kernel developers found a flexible way to deal with version problems. The idea is that a module is incompatible with a different kernel version only if the software interface offered by the kernel has changed. The software interface, then, can be represented by a function prototype and the exact definition of all the data structures involved in the function call. Finally, a CRC algorithm can be used to map all the information about the software interface to a single 32-bit number.*

The issue of version dependence is thus handled by mangling the name of each symbol exported by the kernel to include the checksum of all the information related to that symbol. This information is obtained by parsing the header files and extracting the information from them. This facility is optional and can be enabled at compilation time.

For example, the symbol `printk` is exported to modules as something like `printk_R12345678` when version support is enabled, where `12345678` is the hex representation of the checksum of the software interface used by the function. When a module is loaded into the kernel, *insmod* (or *modprobe*) can accomplish its task only if the checksum added to each symbol in the kernel matches the one added to the same symbol in the module.

But let's see what happens in both the kernel and the module when version support is enabled:

- In the kernel itself, the symbol is not modified. The linking process happens in the usual way, and the symbol table of the *vmlinux* file looks the same as before.

- The public symbol table is built using the versioned names, and this is what appears in */proc/ksyms*.

- The module must be compiled using the mangled names, which appear in the object files as undefined symbols.

- The loading program matches the undefined symbols in the module with the public symbols in the kernel, thus using version information.

The previous scenario is, however, valid only if both the kernel and the module are built to support versioning; if either one uses the original symbol names, *insmod* drops the version information and tries to match the kernel version declared by the module and the one exported by the kernel, in the way described in "Version Dependency" in Chapter 2.

Using Version Support in Modules

While kernel code is already prepared to (optionally) export versioned symbols, the module source needs to be prepared to support the option. Version control can be inserted in one of two places: in the *Makefile* or in the source itself. Since the documentation of the *modules* package describes how to do it in the *Makefile*,

---

* Actually, the incompatibility between SMP and non-SMP modules isn't detected by the CRC algorithm, because a lot of interface functions are `inline` and compile differently on SMP and non-SMP machines, even if they feature the same checksum. You must be very careful not to mix SMP modules with conventional modules.

I'll show you how to do it in the C source. The *master* module used to demonstrate how *kerneld* works is able to support versioned symbols. The capability is automatically enabled if the kernel used to compile the module exploits version support.

The main facility used to mangle symbol names is the header `<linux/modversions.h>`, which includes preprocessor definitions for all the public kernel symbols. After the header is included, whenever the module uses a kernel symbol, the compiler sees the mangled version. The definitions in *modversions.h* are effective only if `MODVERSIONS` is defined in advance.

In order to enable versioning in the module if it has been enabled in the kernel, we must make sure that `CONFIG_MODVERSIONS` has been defined in `<linux/autoconf.h>`. That header controls what features are enabled (compiled) in the current kernel. Each `CONFIG_` macro defined states that the corresponding option is active.

The initial part of *master.c*, therefore, consists of the following lines:

```
#include <linux/autoconf.h> /* retrieve the CONFIG_* macros */
#if defined(CONFIG_MODVERSIONS) && !defined(MODVERSIONS)
#   define MODVERSIONS /* force it on */
#endif

#ifdef MODVERSIONS
#   include <linux/modversions.h>
#endif
```

When compiling the file against a versioned kernel, the symbol table in the object file refers to versioned symbols, which match the ones exported by the kernel itself. The following screenshot shows the symbol names stored in *master.o*. In the output of *nm*, "T" means "text," "D" means "data," and "U" means "undefined." The last tag denotes symbols that the object file references but doesn't declare.

```
morgana% nm master.o
000000b0 T cleanup_module
00000000 T init_module
00000000 D kernel_version
         U kerneld_send_R7d428f45
         U printk_Rad1148ba
morgana% egrep 'printk|kerneld_send' /proc/ksyms
00131b40 kerneld_send_R7d428f45
0011234c printk_Rad1148ba
```

Since the checksum added to the symbol names in *master.o* includes the whole interface related to *printk* and *kerneld_send*, the module is compatible with a wide range of kernel versions. If, however, the data structures related to either function get modified, *insmod* will refuse to load the module because of its incompatibility with the kernel.

Exporting Versioned Symbols

The situation not covered by the previous discussion is what happens when a module exports symbols to be used by other modules. If we rely on version information to achieve module portability, we'd like to be able to add a CRC code to our own symbols. This subject is slightly trickier than just linking to the kernel, because we need to export the mangled symbol name to other modules; we need a way to build the checksums.

The task of parsing the header files and building the checksums is performed by *genksyms*, a tool released with the *modules* package. This program receives the output of the C preprocessor on its own standard input and prints a new header file on standard output. The output file defines the checksummed version of each symbol exported by the original source file. The output of *genksyms* is usually saved with a *.ver* suffix; I'll follow the same practice.

To show you how symbols are exported, I've created two dummy modules called *export.c* and *import.c*. *export* exports a simple function called *export_function*, which is used by the second module, *import.c*. This function receives two integer arguments and returns their sum—we are not interested in the function, but rather in the linking process.

The *Makefile* in the *misc-modules* directory has a rule to build an *export.ver* file from *export.c*, so that the checksummed symbol for *export_function* can be used by the *import* module:

```
ifdef MODVERSIONS
export.o import.o: export.ver
endif

export.ver: export.c
        $(CC) -I$(INCLUDEDIR) -E -D__GENKSYMS__ $^ | genksyms > $@
```

These lines demonstrate how to build *export.ver* and add it to the dependencies of both object files, but only if **MODVERSIONS** is defined. A few lines added to *Makefile* take care of defining **MODVERSIONS** if version support is enabled in the kernel, but they are not worth showing here.

The source file, then, must declare the right preprocessor symbols for every conceivable preprocessor pass: the input to *genksyms* and the actual compilation, both with version support enabled and with it disabled. Moreover, *export.c* should be able to autodetect version support in the kernel, as *master.c* does. The following lines show you how to do this successfully:

```
#ifndef EXPORT_SYMTAB
#  define EXPORT_SYMTAB  /* need this one 'cause we export symbols */
#endif

#include <linux/autoconf.h>  /* retrieve the CONFIG_* macros */
#if defined(CONFIG_MODVERSIONS) && !defined(MODVERSIONS)
```

```
#    define MODVERSIONS
#endif

/*
 * Include the versioned definitions for both kernel symbols and our
 * symbol, *unless* we are generating checksums (__GENKSYMS__
 * defined)
 */
#if defined(MODVERSIONS) && !defined(__GENKSYMS__)
#    include <linux/modversions.h>
#    include "export.ver"     /* redefine "export_function" */
                             /* to include CRC */

#endif
```

The code, though hairy, has the advantage of leaving the *Makefile* in a clean state. Passing the correct flags from *make*, on the other hand, involves writing long command lines for the various cases, which I won't do here.

The simple *import* module calls *export_function* by passing the numbers 2 and 2 as arguments; the expected result is therefore 4. The following example shows that *import* actually links to the versioned symbol of *export* and calls the function. The versioned symbol appears in */proc/ksyms*.

```
morgana.root# insmod export
morgana.root# grep export /proc/ksyms
0202d024 export_function_R2eb14c1e        [export]
morgana.root# insmod import
import: my mate tells that 2+2 = 4
morgana.root# cat /proc/modules
import          1          0
export          3     [import]          0
```

Persistent Storage Across Unload/Load

Once we've equipped ourselves with *kerneld* and version support, using modules turns out to be more flexible than using linked-in drivers. There's only one argument against modularization: if a driver is loaded by *kerneld* and then configured (via *ioctl* or other means), it must be reconfigured the next time it is loaded into the kernel. While load-time configuration can be specified once and for all in */etc/modules.conf*, run-time configuration becomes volatile when demand loading is heavily used. The user can be disappointed by finding that device configuration has been lost after a coffee break. What we need is a technique for persistently storing relevant information while the module is unloaded.

In fact, the *modules* package offers this kind of capability starting with version 2.0.0 (*modules-2.0.0*).

The actual code has not yet been integrated into the official kernels, but it is likely it will be accepted in Linus' sources. Currently, to enable support for persistent storage, you need to apply a patch that is distributed in the *modules* package; the patch adds a few lines to `<linux/kerneld.h>`.

In practice, the idea behind persistent storage of module information is straightforward: kernel code can use the same *kerneld* engine that loads and unloads modules to transfer information to and from user space. The daemon then uses a general-purpose database to manage information storage.

The reason for implementing persistent storage in user space instead of in the kernel is to simplify the code. While a kernel-only implementation can be designed, accessing a database file from kernel space requires replication in non-swappable kernel memory of library code that is already available at no cost in user space.

The proposed implementation in *kerneld* uses the *gdbm* library for the database. Using an on-disk database is optional. If you use the database, you'll get persistence across system boot; if the database is not used, you'll get persistence only for the lifetime of your *kerneld* process.

The following functions are defined in `<linux/kerneld.h>` to access the persistent-storage facility:

```
int set_persist(char *key, void *value, size_t length);
int get_persist(char *key, void *value, size_t length);
```

The arguments to the functions are a unique textual `key` to identify the data item in the database and the item itself, in the familiar form of a pointer and a length. The `key` argument must be unique within the whole system. This allows each module to keep its keys apart by prepending the module's name to the keys, but it also allows different modules to share configuration variables if that is needed for any reason.

The possible return values are the same as for other functions calling *kerneld_send*: 0 for success, negative to signal a kernel-space error, and positive to signal a user-space error. The return value can usually be ignored because *get_persist* doesn't modify `value` if there is an error, and nothing can be done if *set_persist* can't save the value.

Since a recent *kerneld* daemon supports the new feature, a module can choose to include definitions for *set_persist* and *get_persist* without patching *kerneld.h* in the kernel. But be careful about forward compatibility. The patch distributed in *modules* is a proposal; the internals of persistent storage may change before being included in the official kernel source.

We have seen that the main reason for using persistent storage is to avoid reconfiguring a module each time it is loaded into a running kernel. While this is particularly important for run-time configuration of demand-loaded modules, it is an interesting option for load-time configuration as well, because updating */etc/modules.conf* can be tricky for the average user.

Another possible use for persistent storage is to keep track of the system's hardware configuration to avoid unneeded probing. Probing for hardware is a risky operation. It can misconfigure other hardware, particularly ISA devices, because ISA doesn't offer a generalized way to scan the system bus as PCI does. (This issue is thoroughly described in Chapter 15, *Overview of Peripheral Buses.*)

The following sample code shows how a hypothetical module called *psm* (Persistent Storage Module) can avoid unnecessary probing. To simplify the discussion, this example supports at most one device.

```
int psm_base = 0;   /* base I/O port, settable at load time */

int init_module(void)
{
    if (psm_base == 0) { /* not set at load time */
        get_persist("psm_base", &psm_base, sizeof(int));
        if (psm_check_hw(psm_base) != 0)
            psm_base == 0;  /* old value no longer valid: probe */
    }
    else
        if (psm_check_hw(psm_base) != 0)
            return -ENODEV; /* not where specified */

    if (psm_base == 0)
        psm_base = psm_probe(); /* return base port or 0 if not found */
    if (psm_base == 0)
        return -ENODEV; /* no device found */

    set_persist("psm_base", &psm_base, sizeof(int)); /* found: save it */
}
```

The code probes for hardware only if no base port has been specified at load time and if the previous port is no longer valid. If a device is found, the base port is saved for later use.

When the driver can support multiple devices, one possible solution to the problem of detecting newly added hardware is to define a **psm_newhw** variable that the user can set at load time if new devices have been added to the system. If this is implemented, the user is instructed to use `insmod psm_newhw=1` when new hardware is there. If **psm_newhw** is not zero, *init_module* tries to probe for new devices, while using the saved information in the normal case. A change in the base address of a device is already handled in the code shown above and doesn't need user intervention at load time.

Quick Reference

This chapter introduced the following kernel symbols:

/etc/modules.conf
> The configuration file for *modprobe* and *depmod*. It is used to configure demand loading and is described in the man pages for the two programs.

```
#include <linux/kerneld.h>
int request_module(const char *name);
int release_module(const char *name, int waitflag);
int delayed_release_module(const char *name);
int cancel_release_module(const char *name);
```
> These functions perform demand loading of modules by means of the *kerneld* daemon.

```
#include <linux/autoconf.h>
CONFIG_MODVERSIONS
```
> This macro is defined only if the current kernel has been compiled to support versioned symbols.

```
#ifdef MODVERSIONS
#include <linux/modversions.h>
```
> This header, which exists only if `CONFIG_MODVERSIONS` is valid, contains the versioned names for all the symbols exported by the kernel.

`EXPORT_SYMTAB`
> If version support is used, this macro must be defined if your module uses *register_symtab* to export symbols of its own.

`__GENKSYMS__`
> This macro is defined by *make* when preprocessing files to be read by *genksyms* to build new version codes. It is used to conditionally prevent inclusion of `<linux/modversions.h>` when building new checksums.

```
int set_persist(char *key, void *value, size_t length);
int get_persist(char *key, void *value, size_t length);
```
> Support for persistent storage of module data relies on these two functions, which are defined in `<linux/kerneld.h>`.

CHAPTER TWELVE

LOADING BLOCK DRIVERS

As outlined in "Classes of Devices and Modules," in Chapter 1, *An Introduction to the Linux Kernel*, Unix device drivers are not limited to char drivers. This chapter introduces the second main class of device drivers—block drivers. A block-oriented device is one that transfers data only in blocks (for example, the floppy disk or the hard drive), where the hardware block is usually called a "sector." The word "block," on the other hand, will be used to denote a software concept: the driver often uses 1KB blocks even if the sector size is 512 bytes.

In this chapter, we'll build a full-featured block driver called *sbull*, short for "Simple Block Utility for Loading Localities." This driver is similar to *scull* in that it uses the computer's memory as the hardware device. In other words, it's a RAM-disk driver. *sbull* can be executed on any Linux computer (although I have been able to test it only on a limited set of platforms).

If you need to write a driver for a real block device, the information in Chapter 8, *Hardware Management*, and Chapter 9, *Interrupt Handling*, should be used to supplement this chapter.

Registering the Driver

Like a char driver, a block driver in the kernel is identified by a major number. The functions used to register and unregister the driver are:

```
int register_blkdev(unsigned int major, const char *name,
                    struct file_operations *fops);
int unregister_blkdev(unsigned int major, const char *name);
```

The meaning of the arguments is the same as for char drivers, and dynamic assignment of the major number can be performed in the same way. Therefore, the *sbull* device registers itself just like *scull*:

```
result = register_blkdev(sbull_major, "sbull", &sbull_fops);
if (result < 0) {
    printk(KERN_WARNING "sbull: can't get major %d\n",sbull_major);
    return result;
}
if (sbull_major == 0) sbull_major = result; /* dynamic */
major = sbull_major; /* Use 'major' later on to save typing */
```

The `fops` argument to *register_blkdev* is similar to the one we used for char drivers. The operations for *read, write,* and *fsync,* however, need not be driver-specific. The general functions *block_read, block_write,* and *block_fsync* are always used in place of the driver-specific functions. In addition, *check_media_change* and *revalidate* make sense for a block driver, and both are defined in `sbull_fops`.

The `fops` structure used in *sbull* is:

```
struct file_operations sbull_fops = {
    NULL,            /* lseek: default */
    block_read,
    block_write,
    NULL,            /* sbull_readdir */
    NULL,            /* sbull_select */
    sbull_ioctl,
    NULL,            /* sbull_mmap */
    sbull_open,
    sbull_release,
    block_fsync,
    NULL,            /* sbull_fasync */
    sbull_check_change,
    sbull_revalidate
};
```

General read and write operations are used to achieve better performance. The speed-up is achieved through buffering, which is not available to char drivers. Block drivers can be buffered because their data serves the computer's file hierarchy, and is never accessed directly by the applications, while data belonging to char drivers is.

However, when the buffer cache cannot satisfy a read request or pending writes must be flushed to the physical disk, the driver must be called to perform the actual data transfer. The `fops` structure doesn't carry an entry point other than *read* and *write*, so an additional structure, `blk_dev_struct`, is used to deliver requests for actual data transfer.

This structure is defined in `<linux/blkdev.h>` and has several fields, but only the first field needs to be set by the driver.

This is the definition of the structure as found in 2.0 kernels:

```
struct blk_dev_struct {
    void (*request_fn)(void);
    struct request * current_request;
    struct request   plug;
    struct tq_struct plug_tq;
};

extern struct blk_dev_struct blk_dev[MAX_BLKDEV];
```

When the kernel needs to spawn an I/O operation for the *sbull* device, it calls the function `blk_dev[sbull_major].request_fn`. The initialization function for this module should therefore set this field to point to its own request function. The remaining fields of the structure are used internally by the kernel functions and macros; you don't need to explicitly refer to them in your code.

The relationship between a block-driver module and the kernel is shown in Figure 12-1.

In addition to `blk_dev`, several other arrays hold information about block drivers. These arrays are indexed by major, and sometimes also minor, number. They are declared and described in *drivers/block/ll_rw_block.c*.

`int blk_size[][];`
> This array is indexed by the major and minor numbers. It describes the size of each device, in kilobytes. If `blk_size[major]` is NULL, no checking is performed on the size of the device (i.e., the kernel might request data transfers past end-of-device).

`int blksize_size[][];`
> The size of the block used by each device, in bytes. Like the previous one, this two-dimensional array is indexed by both major and minor numbers. If `blksize_size[major]` is a null pointer, a block size of BLOCK_SIZE (currently 1KB) is assumed. The block size for the device *must* be a power of two, because the kernel uses bit-shift operators to convert offsets to block numbers.

`int hardsect_size[][];`
> Like the others, this data structure is indexed by the major and minor numbers. The default value for the hardware sector size is 512 bytes. Up to and including version 2.0.*x*, variable sector sizes aren't really supported, because some kernel code still assumes that the sector size is half a kilobyte; it's nonetheless very likely that variable sector size will be truly implemented in version 2.2.

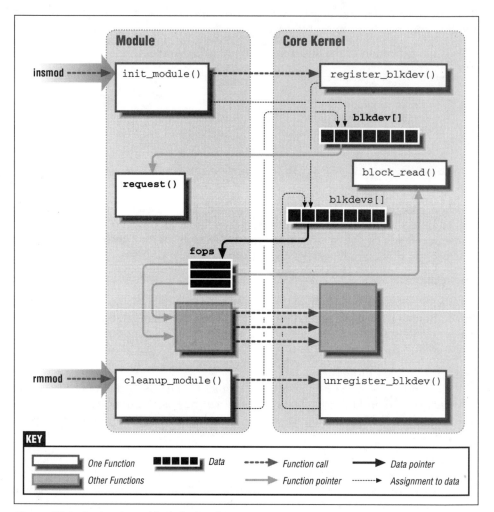

Figure 12-1: Registering a block device driver

`int read_ahead[];`

> This array is indexed by the major number and defines the number of sectors to be read in advance by the kernel when a file is being read sequentially. Reading data before a process asks for it helps system performance and overall throughput. A slower device should specify a bigger read-ahead value, while fast devices will be happy even with a smaller value. The bigger the read-ahead value, the more memory the buffer cache uses. There is one read-ahead value for each major number, and it applies to all its minor numbers. The value can be changed via the driver's *ioctl* method; hard-disk drivers usually set it to 8 sectors, which corresponds to 4KB.

The *sbull* device allows you to set these values at load time, and they apply to all the minor numbers of the sample driver. The variable names and their default values in *sbull* are as follows:

`size=2048` *(kilobytes)*
Each ramdisk created by *sbull* takes two megabytes of RAM.

`blksize=1024` *(bytes)*
The software "block" used by the module is one kilobyte, like the system default.

`hardsect=512` *(bytes)*
The *sbull* sector size is the usual half-kilobyte value. Changing `hardsect` is disabled because, as mentioned above, other sector sizes aren't supported. If you try to change it anyway, by removing the security check in *sbull/sbull.c*, be prepared to experience severe memory corruption unless variable sector-size support has been added by the time you try it.

`rahead=2` *(sectors)*
Since the RAM disk is a fast device, the default read-ahead value is small.

The *sbull* device also allows you to choose the number of devices to install. `devs`, the number of devices, defaults to 2, resulting in a default memory usage of 4 megs—2 disks at 2 megs each.

The implementation of *init_module* for the *sbull* device is as follows (excluding registration of the major number and error recovery):

```
blk_dev[major].request_fn = sbull_request;
read_ahead[major] = sbull_rahead;
result = -ENOMEM; /* for the possible errors */

sbull_sizes = kmalloc(sbull_devs * sizeof(int), GFP_KERNEL);
if (!sbull_sizes)
    goto fail_malloc;
for (i=0; i < sbull_devs; i++) /* all the same size */
    sbull_sizes[i] = sbull_size;
blk_size[major]=sbull_sizes;

sbull_blksizes = kmalloc(sbull_devs * sizeof(int), GFP_KERNEL);
if (!sbull_blksizes)
    goto fail_malloc;
for (i=0; i < sbull_devs; i++) /* all the same blocksize */
    sbull_blksizes[i] = sbull_blksize;
blksize_size[major]=sbull_blksizes;
 sbull_hardsects = kmalloc(sbull_devs * sizeof(int), GFP_KERNEL);
if (!sbull_hardsects)
    goto fail_malloc;
for (i=0; i < sbull_devs; i++) /* all the same hardsect */
    sbull_hardsects[i] = sbull_hardsect;
hardsect_size[major]=sbull_hardsects;
```

The corresponding cleanup function looks like this:

```
for (i=0; i<sbull_devs; i++)
    fsync_dev(MKDEV(sbull_major, i)); /* flush the devices */

blk_dev[major].request_fn = NULL;
read_ahead[major] = 0;
kfree(blk_size[major]);
blk_size[major] = NULL;
kfree(blksize_size[major]);
blksize_size[major] = NULL;
kfree(hardsect_size[major]);
hardsect_size[major] = NULL;
```

Here, the call to *fsync_dev* is needed to free all references to the device that the kernel keeps in various caches. Actually, *fsync_dev* is the engine that operates behind *block_fsync*, which is the *fsync* "method" for block devices.

The Header File blk.h

Since (for the most part) block drivers are device-independent, the kernel developers tried to simplify driver code by concentrating most of the common code in one header, `<linux/blk.h>`. Therefore, every block driver should include that header. The most important function defined in `<linux/blk.h>` is *end_request*, which is declared as `static`. Having it be `static` allows different drivers to have a correctly defined *end_request*, without each needing to write its own implementation.

In Linux 1.2, the header should be included as `<linux/../../ drivers/block/blk.h>`. The reason for this is that custom block drivers were not supported until later, and the header was originally local to the *drivers/block* source directory.

Actually, the *blk.h* header is quite unusual, as it defines several symbols based on the symbol `MAJOR_NR`, which must be declared by the driver *before* it includes the header. Once again, this shows that *blk.h* was not designed with custom drivers in mind.

If you look at *blk.h*, you'll see that several device-dependent symbols are declared according to the value of `MAJOR_NR`, which is expected to be known in advance. However, if the major number is dynamically assigned, the driver has no way to know its assigned number in advance and cannot correctly define `MAJOR_NR`. If `MAJOR_NR` is undefined, *blk.h* can't set up some of the macros used in *end_request*. Therefore, in order for a custom driver to benefit from the general-purpose *end_request* function and to avoid reimplementing it, the driver should define `MAJOR_NR` and a few other symbols *before* including *blk.h*.

The following list describes the symbols in `<linux/blk.h>` that must be defined in advance; at the end of the list, the code used in *sbull* is shown.

MAJOR_NR

> This symbol is used to access a few arrays, in particular `blk_dev` and `blk-size_size`. A custom driver like *sbull*, which is unable to assign a constant value to the symbol, should `#define` it to the variable holding the major number. For *sbull*, this is `sbull_major`.

DEVICE_NAME

> The name of the device being created. This string is used in printing error messages from within *end_request*.

DEVICE_NR(kdev_t device)

> This symbol is used to extract the ordinal number of the physical device from the `kdev_t` device number. The value of this macro can be `MINOR(device)` or another expression, according to the convention used to assign minor numbers to devices and partitions. The macro should return the same device number for all partitions on the same physical device—that is, `DEVICE_NR` represents the disk number, not the partition number. This symbol is used to declare `CURRENT_DEV`, which can be used within *request_fn* to determine which hardware device owns the minor number accessed by a transfer request. Partitionable devices are introduced later in the section "Partitionable Devices."

DEVICE_INTR

> This symbol is used to declare a pointer variable that refers to the current bottom-half handler. The macros `SET_INTR(intr)` and `CLEAR_INTR` are used to assign the variable. Using multiple handlers is convenient when the device can issue interrupts with different meanings. This topic is discussed later in "Interrupt-Driven Block Drivers."

TIMEOUT_VALUE
DEVICE_TIMEOUT

> `TIMEOUT_VALUE` expresses a timeout as a jiffy count. This timeout value is associated with one of the old timers, specifically, timer number `DEVICE_TIMEOUT`. A driver can use a timer to detect error conditions by invoking a callback when a data transfer takes too long. However, since the old timers consist of a static array of preassigned timers (see "Kernel Timers" in Chapter 6, *Flow of Time*), a custom driver can't use them. I've left both symbols undefined in *sbull* and implemented the timeout using the new timers.

DEVICE_NO_RANDOM

> By default, the function *end_request* contributes to system entropy (the amount of collected "randomness"), which is used by */dev/random*. If the device isn't able to contribute significant entropy to the random device,

DEVICE_NO_RANDOM should be defined. */dev/random* was introduced in "Installing an Interrupt Handler," in Chapter 9, where **SA_SAMPLE_RANDOM** was explained.

DEVICE_OFF(kdev_t device)

The *end_request* function calls this macro when it's done. In the floppy driver, for example, it calls a function that is in charge of updating the timer used for motor spin-down. The string **DEVICE_OFF** can be defined to nothing if the device is not turned off. *sbull* doesn't use **DEVICE_OFF**.

DEVICE_ON(kdev_t device)
DEVICE_REQUEST

These functions are not actually used in the Linux headers, and a driver doesn't have to define them. Most official Linux drivers declare these symbols and use them internally, but I don't use them in *sbull*.

The *sbull* driver declares the symbols in the following way:

```
#define MAJOR_NR sbull_major /* force definitions on in blk.h */
int sbull_major; /* must be declared before including blk.h */

#define DEVICE_NR(device) MINOR(device) /* has no partition bits */
#define DEVICE_NAME "sbull"             /* name for messaging */
#define DEVICE_INTR sbull_intrptr       /* pointer to the bottom half */
#define DEVICE_NO_RANDOM                /* no entropy to contribute */

#define DEVICE_OFF(d) /* do-nothing */

#if LINUX_VERSION_CODE < 0x10324 /* 1.3.36 */
#   include <linux/../../drivers/block/blk.h>
#else
#   include <linux/blk.h>
#endif

#include "sbull.h"        /* local definitions */
```

The *blk.h* header uses the macros listed above to define some additional macros usable by the driver. I'll describe those macros in the following sections.

Handling Requests

The most important function in a block driver is the request function, which performs the low-level operations related to reading and writing data. This section introduces the design of such a procedure.

When the kernel schedules a data transfer, it queues the "request" in a list, ordered so that it maximizes system performance. The linked list of requests is then passed to the driver's request function, which should perform the following tasks for each request in the linked list:

- Check the validity of the current request. This task is performed by the macro INIT_REQUEST, defined in *blk.h*.

- Perform the actual data transfer. The CURRENT variable (macro, actually) can be used to retrieve the details of the outstanding request. CURRENT is a pointer to struct request, whose fields are described in the next section.

- Clean up the current request. This operation is performed by *end_request*, a static function whose code resides in *blk.h*. The driver passes the function a single argument, which is 1 in case of success and 0 in case of failure. When *end_request* is called with an argument of zero, an "I/O error" message is delivered to the system logs (via *printk*).

- Loop back to the beginning, to consume the next request. A goto, a surrounding for(;;), or a surrounding while(1) can be used, at the programmer's will.

In practice, the code for the request function is structured like this:

```
void sbull_request(void)
{
    while(1) {
        INIT_REQUEST;
        printk("request %p: cmd %i sec %li (nr. %li), next %p\n",
                CURRENT,
                CURRENT->cmd,
                CURRENT->sector,
                CURRENT->current_nr_sectors,
                CURRENT->next);
        end_request(1); /* success */
    }
}
```

Although this code does nothing but print messages, running this function provides good insight into the basic design of data transfer. The only unclear part of the code at this point should be the exact meaning of CURRENT and its fields, which I'll describe in the next section.

My first *sbull* implementation contained exactly the empty code just shown. I managed to make a filesystem on the "nonexistent" device and use it for a while, as long as data remained in the buffer cache. Looking at the system logs while running a verbose request function like this one can help you understand how the buffer cache works.

This empty-and-verbose function can still be run in *sbull* by defining the symbol SBULL_EMPTY_REQUEST at compile time. If you want to understand how the kernel handles different block sizes, you can experiment with blksize= on the *insmod* command line. The empty request function uncovers the internal kernel workings by printing the details of each request. You *might* also play with hardsect=, but currently this is disabled because it's dangerous (see "Registering the Driver" at the beginning of this chapter).

The code in a request function doesn't explicitly issue `return()`, because `INIT_REQUEST` does it for you when the list of pending requests is exhausted.

Performing the Actual Data Transfer

In order to build a working data transfer for *sbull*, let's look at how the kernel describes a request within a `struct request`. The structure is defined in `<linux/blkdev.h>`. By accessing the fields in `CURRENT`, the driver can retrieve all the information needed to transfer data between the buffer cache and the physical block device.

`CURRENT` is a macro that is used to access the current request (the one to be serviced first). As you might guess, `CURRENT` is a short form of `blk_dev[MAJOR_NR].current_request`.

The following fields of the current request carry useful information for the request function:

`kdev_t rq_dev;`
> The device accessed by the request. The same request function is used for every device managed by the driver. A single request function deals with all the minor numbers; `rq_dev` can be used to extract the minor device being acted upon. Although Linux 1.2 called this field `dev`, you can access this field through the macro `CURRENT_DEV`, which is portable to any kernel version in the range we are addressing.

`int cmd;`
> This field is either `READ` or `WRITE`.

`unsigned long sector;`
> The first sector the request refers to.

`unsigned long current_nr_sectors;`
`unsigned long nr_sectors;`
> The number of sectors (the size) of the current request. The driver should refer to `current_nr_sectors` and ignore `nr_sectors` (which is listed here just for completeness). See the next section, "Clustered Requests," for more detail.

`char *buffer;`
> The area in the buffer cache to which data should be written (`cmd==READ`) or from which data should be read (`cmd==WRITE`).

`struct buffer_head *bh;`
> The structure describing the first buffer in the list for this request. We'll use this field in "Clustered Requests."

There are other fields in the structure, but they are primarily meant for internal use in the kernel; the driver is not expected to use them.

The implementation for the working request function in the *sbull* device is show below. In the following code, `sbull_devices` is like `scull_devices`, introduced in "The open Method" in Chapter 3, *Char Drivers*.

```c
void sbull_request(void)
{
    Sbull_Dev *device;
    u8 *ptr;
    int size;

    while(1) {
        INIT_REQUEST;

        /* Check if the minor number is in range */
        if (DEVICE_NR(CURRENT_DEV) > sbull_devs) {
            static int count = 0;
            if (count++ < 5)  /* print the message at most 5 times */
                printk(KERN_WARNING
                            "sbull: request for unknown device\n");
            end_request(0);
            continue;
        }

        /* pointer to device structure, from the global array */
        device = sbull_devices + DEVICE_NR(CURRENT_DEV);
        ptr = device->data + CURRENT->sector * sbull_hardsect;
        size = CURRENT->current_nr_sectors * sbull_hardsect;
        if (ptr + size > device->data + sbull_blksize*sbull_size) {
            static int count = 0;
            if (count++ < 5)
                printk(KERN_WARNING
                            "sbull: request past end of device\n");
            end_request(0);
            continue;
        }

        switch(CURRENT->cmd) {
          case READ:
            /* from sbull to buffer */
            memcpy(CURRENT->buffer, ptr, size);
            break;
          case WRITE:
            /* from buffer to sbull */
            memcpy(ptr, CURRENT->buffer, size);
            break;
          default:
            /* can't happen */
            end_request(0);
            continue;
        }
```

```
            end_request(1); /* success */
    }
}
```

Since *sbull* is just a RAM disk, its "data transfer" reduces to a *memcpy* call. The only "strange" feature of the function is the conditional statement that limits it to reporting five errors. This is intended to avoid clobbering the system logs with too many messages, since `end_request(0)` already prints an "I/O error" message when the request fails. The `static` counter is a standard way to limit message reporting and is used several times in the kernel.

Clustered Requests

Each iteration of the loop in the request function above transfers a number of sectors—usually the number of sectors that equals a "block" of data, according to the use of such data. For instance, swapping is performed `PAGE_SIZE` bytes at a time, while an extended-2 filesystem transfers 1KB blocks.

Although a block is the most convenient data size for I/O, you can get a significant performance boost by clustering the reading or writing of adjacent blocks. In this context, "adjacent" refers to the location of blocks *on the disk*, while "consecutive" refers to consecutive *memory* areas.

There are two advantages to clustering adjacent blocks. First, clustering speeds up the transfer (for example, the floppy driver assembles adjacent blocks and transfers a whole track at a time). It can also save memory in the kernel by avoiding allocation of redundant `request` structures.

You can, if you want, completely ignore clustering. The skeletal request function shown above works flawlessly, independent of clustering. If you want to exploit clustering, on the other hand, you need to deal in greater detail with the internals of `struct_request`.

Unfortunately, all kernels I know of (up to at least 2.1.51) don't perform clustering for custom drivers, just for internal drivers like SCSI and IDE. If you aren't interested in the internals of the kernel, you can skip the rest of this section. On the other hand, clustering might be available to modules in the future, and it is an interesting way to increase data-transfer performance by reducing inter-request delays for adjacent sectors.

Before I describe how a driver can exploit clustered requests, let's look at what happens when a request is queued.

When the kernel requests the transfer of a data block, it scans the linked list of active requests for the target device. If the new block is adjacent on the disk to a block that has already been requested, the new block is clustered to the first block; the existing request is enlarged without creating a new one.

Unfortunately, the fact that the contents of two data buffers are adjacent on disk doesn't necessarily mean that they are consecutive in memory. This observation, plus the need to efficiently manage the buffer cache, led to the creation of a `buffer_head` structure. One `buffer_head` is associated with each data buffer.

A "clustered" request, then, is a single `request_struct` that refers to a linked list of `buffer_head` structures. The *end_request* function takes care of this problem, and that's why the request function shown earlier works independent of clustering. In other words, *end_request* either cleans up the current request and prepares to service the next one, or prepares to deal with the next buffer in the same request. Clustering is therefore transparent to the device driver that doesn't care about it; the *sbull* function above is such an example.

A driver may want to benefit from clustering by dealing with the whole linked list of buffer heads at each pass through the loop in its *request_fn* function. To do this, the driver should refer to both `CURRENT->current_nr_sectors` (the field I already used above in *sbull_request*) and `CURRENT->nr_sectors`, which contains the number of adjacent sectors that are clustered in the "current" list of `buffer_head`s.

The current buffer head is `CURRENT->bh`, while the data block is `CURRENT->bh->b_data`. The latter pointer is cached in `CURRENT->buffer` for drivers like *sbull* that ignore clustering.

Request clustering is implemented in *drivers/block/ll_rw_block.c*, in the function *make_request*; however, as suggested above, clustering is performed only for a few drivers (floppy, IDE, and SCSI), according to their major number. I've been able to see how clustering works by loading *sbull* with `major=34` because 34 is `IDE3_MAJOR`, and I don't have the third IDE controller on my system.*

The following list summarizes what needs to be done when scanning a clustered request. `bh` is the buffer head being processed—the first in the list. For every buffer head in the list, the driver should carry out the following sequence of operations:

- Transfer the data block at address `bh->b_data`, of size `bh->b_size` bytes. The direction of the data transfer is `CURRENT->cmd`, as usual.

- Retrieve the next buffer head in the list: `bh->b_reqnext`. Then detach the buffer just transferred from the list, by zeroing its `b_reqnext`—the pointer to the new buffer you just retrieved.

- Tell the kernel you're done with the previous buffer, by calling `mark_buffer_uptodate(bh,1); unlock_buffer(bh);`. These calls guarantee that the buffer cache is kept sane, without wild pointers lying

---

* While this is a handy trick to play dirty games on one's home computer, I strongly discourage doing it in a production driver.

around. The "1" argument to `mark_buffer_uptodate` indicates success; if the transfer failed, substitute "0".

* Loop back to the beginning to transfer the next adjacent block.

When you are done with the clustered request, `CURRENT->bh` must be updated to point to the first buffer that was "processed but not unlocked." If all the buffers in the list were processed and unlocked, `CURRENT->bh` can be set to `NULL`.

At this point, the driver can call *end_request*. If `CURRENT->bh` is valid, the function unlocks it before moving to the next buffer—this is what happens for non-clustered operation, where *end_request* takes care of everything. If the pointer is `NULL`, the function just moves to the next request.

A full-featured implementation of clustering appears in *drivers/block/floppy.c*, while a summary of the operations required appears in *end_request*, in *blk.h*. Neither *floppy.c* nor *blk.h* are easy to understand, but the latter is a better place to start.

How Mounting Works

Block devices differ from char devices and normal files in that they can be mounted on the computer's filesystem. This is different from the normal access through a `struct file`, where the structure is bound to a specific process and exists only from *open* to *close*. When a filesystem is mounted, there's no process holding a `filp`.

When the kernel mounts a device in the filesystem, it invokes the normal *open* method to access the driver. However, in this case the `filp` argument to *open* is a dummy variable, almost a placeholder, whose only meaningful field is `f_mode`. The remaining fields hold random values and should not be used. The value of `f_mode` tells the driver whether the device is to be mounted read-only (`f_mode == FMODE_READ`) or read/write (`f_mode == (FMODE_READ|FMODE_WRITE)`). A dummy variable is used instead of a `file` structure because a real `struct file` would be released at process termination, while a mounted filesystem survives after the *mount* command has done its job.

At mount time, the only thing that is invoked in the driver is the *open* method. While the disk is mounted, the kernel invokes the *read* and *write* methods in the device (which map to `request_fn`) to manage files in the filesystem. The driver can't tell if `request_fn` is servicing a process (like *fsck*) or the filesystem layer of the kernel.

As far as *umount* is concerned, it just flushes the buffer cache and calls the *release* (*close*) driver method. Since there is no meaningful `filp` to pass to `fops->release`, the kernel uses `NULL`.

Thus, when you implement *release*, you should set up the driver to handle a NULL filp pointer. On the other hand, if you were to use filp, you would be able to run *mkfs* and *fsck*, which use filp to access the device, and you would also be able to *mount* the device, but *umount* would oops because of the NULL pointer.

Since the *release* implementation of a block driver can't use filp-> private_data to access device information, it uses inode->i_rdev to differentiate between devices instead. This is how *sbull* implements *release*:

```
void sbull_release (struct inode *inode, struct file *filp)
{
    Sbull_Dev *dev = sbull_devices + MINOR(inode->i_rdev);

    dev->usage--;
    MOD_DEC_USE_COUNT;
}
```

Other driver functions don't care about the filp problem because they aren't involved with mounted filesystems. For example, *ioctl* is issued only by processes that explicitly *open* the device.

The ioctl Method

Like char devices, block devices can be acted on by using the *ioctl* system call. The only relevant difference between the two implementations is that block drivers share a number of common *ioctl* commands that most drivers are expected to support.

The commands that block drivers usually handle are the following, declared in <linux/fs.h>:

BLKGETSIZE
> Retrieve the size of the current device, expressed as the number of sectors. The value of arg passed by the system call is a pointer to a long value and should be used to copy the size to a user-space variable. This *ioctl* command is used, for instance, by *mkfs* to know the size of the filesystem being created.

BLKFLSBUF
> Literally, "flush buffers." The implementation of this command is the same for every device and is shown later with the sample code for the whole *ioctl* method.

BLKRAGET
> Used to get the current read-ahead value for the device. The current value should be written to user space as a long item using the pointer passed to *ioctl* in arg.

BLKRASET

Set the read-ahead value. The user process passes the new value in `arg`.

BLKRRPART

Reread the partition table. This command is meaningful only for partitionable devices, introduced later in "Partitionable Devices."

BLKROSET
BLKROGET

These commands are used to change and check the read-only flag for the device. They are implemented by the macro `RO_IOCTLS(kdev_t dev, unsigned long where)` because the code is device-independent. The macro is defined in *blk.h*.

HDIO_GETGEO

Defined in `<linux/hdreg.h>` and used to retrieve the disk geometry. The geometry should be written to user space in a `struct hd_geometry`, which is declared in *hdreg.h* as well. *sbull* shows the general implementation for this command.

The `HDIO_GETGEO` command is the most commonly used of a series of `HDIO_` commands, all defined in `<linux/hdreg.h>`. The interested reader can look in *ide.c* and *hd.c* for more information about these commands.

The major drawback to the commands just listed is that they are defined in the "old" way (see "Choosing the ioctl Commands" in Chapter 5, *Enhanced Char Driver Operations*), and thus the macros for the bitfields can't be used to simplify coding—each command should implement its own *verify_area*. However, if a driver needs to define its own commands to exploit particular features of the device, you are free to use the "new" way of defining commands.

The *sbull* device supports only the general commands above, because implementing device-specific commands is no different from the implementation of commands for char drivers. The *ioctl* implementation for *sbull* is shown below; it should help you understand the commands listed above.

```
int sbull_ioctl (struct inode *inode, struct file *filp,
                 unsigned int cmd, unsigned long arg)
{
    int err, size;
    struct hd_geometry *geo = (struct hd_geometry *)arg;

    PDEBUG("ioctl 0x%x 0x%lx\n", cmd, arg);
    switch(cmd) {

      case BLKGETSIZE:
        /* Return the device size, expressed in sectors */
        if (!arg) return -EINVAL; /* NULL pointer: not valid */
        err=verify_area(VERIFY_WRITE, (long *) arg, sizeof(long));
```

```
    if (err) return err;
    put_user ( 1024 * sbull_sizes[MINOR(inode->i_rdev)]
                / sbull_hardsects[MINOR(inode->i_rdev)],
                (long *) arg);
    return 0;

  case BLKFLSBUF: /* flush */
    if (!suser()) return -EACCES; /* only root */
    fsync_dev(inode->i_rdev);
    invalidate_buffers(inode->i_rdev);
    return 0;

  case BLKRAGET: /* return the readahead value */
    if (!arg)  return -EINVAL;
    err = verify_area(VERIFY_WRITE, (long *) arg, sizeof(long));
    if (err) return err;
    put_user(read_ahead[MAJOR(inode->i_rdev)],(long *) arg);
    return 0;

  case BLKRASET: /* set the readahead value */
    if (!suser()) return -EACCES;
    if (arg > 0xff) return -EINVAL; /* limit it */
    read_ahead[MAJOR(inode->i_rdev)] = arg;
    return 0;

  case BLKRRPART: /* re-read partition table: can't do it */
    return -EINVAL;

  RO_IOCTLS(inode->i_rdev, arg); /* the default RO operations */

  case HDIO_GETGEO:
    /*
     * get geometry: we have to fake one...  trim the size to a
     * multiple of 64 (32KB): tell we have 16 sectors, 4 heads,
     * whatever cylinders. Tell also that data starts at sector 4.
     */
    size = sbull_size * 1024 / sbull_hardsect;
    size &= ~0x3f; /* multiple of 64 */
    if (geo==NULL) return -EINVAL;
    err = verify_area(VERIFY_WRITE, geo, sizeof(*geo));
    if (err) return err;
    put_user(size >> 6, &geo->cylinders);
    put_user(       4, &geo->heads);
    put_user(      16, &geo->sectors);
    put_user(       4, &geo->start);
    return 0;
}

return -EINVAL; /* unknown command */
}
```

The PDEBUG statement at the beginning of the function has been left in so that when you compile the module, you can turn on debugging to see which *ioctl* commands are invoked on the device.

For example, with the *ioctl* commands shown, you can use *fdisk* on *sbull*. This is a sample short session I had on my own system:

```
morgana.root# fdisk /dev/sbull0

Command (m for help): p

Disk /dev/sbull0: 4 heads, 16 sectors, 64 cylinders
Units = cylinders of 64 * 512 bytes

      Device Boot  Begin   Start     End Blocks   Id  System

Command (m for help): w
The partition table has been altered!

Calling ioctl() to re-read partition table.
Syncing disks.
```

The following messages appeared on my system log during the session:

```
Oct 29 10:22:08 morgana kernel: sbull: ioctl 0x301 0xbffffc74
Oct 29 10:22:15 morgana kernel: sbull: ioctl 0x125f 0x2
Oct 29 10:22:15 morgana kernel: sbull: revalidate for dev 0
```

The first *ioctl* is HDIO_GETGEO, invoked at *fdisk* startup, and the second is BLKR-RPART. The *sbull* implementation for the latter command just calls the revalidate function, which in turn prints the last message in the printout just shown (see "revalidate" later in this chapter).

Removable Devices

When we discussed char drivers, we ignored the final two file operations in the fops structure, because they exist only for the sake of removable block devices. It's now time to look at them; *sbull* isn't actually removable, but it pretends to be, and therefore it implements the methods.

The operations I'm talking about are *check_media_change* and *revalidate*. The former is used to find out if the device has changed since the last access, and the latter re-initializes the driver's status after a disk change.

As far as *sbull* is concerned, the data area associated with a device is released half a minute after its usage count drops to zero. Leaving the device unmounted (or closed) long enough simulates a disk change, and the next access to the device allocates a new memory area.

This kind of "timely expiration" is implemented using a kernel timer.

check_media_change

The checking function receives `kdev_t` as a single argument that identifies the device. The return value is 1 if the medium has been changed and 0 otherwise. A block driver that doesn't support removable devices can avoid declaring the function by setting `fops->check_media_change` to NULL.

It's interesting to note that when the device is removable, but there is no way to know if it changed, returning 1 is a safe choice. This is the behavior of the IDE driver when dealing with removable disks.

The implementation in *sbull* returns 1 if the device has already been removed from memory due to the timer expiration, and 0 if the data is still valid. If debugging is enabled, it also prints a message to the system logger; the user can thus check when the method is called by the kernel.

```
int sbull_check_change(kdev_t i_rdev)
{
    int minor = MINOR(i_rdev);
    Sbull_Dev *dev = sbull_devices + minor;

    if (minor >= sbull_devs) /* paranoid */
        return 0;

    PDEBUG("check_change for dev %i\n",minor);

    if (dev->data)
        return 0; /* still valid */
    return 1; /* expired */
}
```

revalidate

The validation function is called when a disk change is detected. It is also called by the various *stat* system calls implemented in version 2.1 of the kernel. The return value is currently unused; to be safe, return 0 to indicate success and a negative error code in case of error.

The action performed by *revalidate* is device-specific, but *revalidate* usually updates the internal status information to reflect the new device.

In *sbull*, the *revalidate* method tries to allocate a new data area if there is not already a valid area.

```
int sbull_revalidate(kdev_t i_rdev)
{
    Sbull_Dev *dev = sbull_devices + MINOR(i_rdev);

    PDEBUG("revalidate for dev %i\n",MINOR(i_rdev));
    if (dev->data)
```

```
        return 0;
    dev->data = vmalloc(dev->size);
    if (!dev->data)
        return -ENOMEM;
    return 0;
}
```

Extra Care

Drivers for removable devices should also check for a disk change when the device is opened; the kernel automatically calls its *check_disk_change* function at *mount* time, but not at *open* time.

Some programs, however, directly access disk data without mounting the device: *fsck, mcopy,* and *fdisk* are examples of such programs. If the driver keeps status information about removable devices in memory, it should call the *check_disk_change* function when the device is first opened. The kernel function falls back on the driver methods (*check_media_change* and *revalidate*), so nothing special has to be implemented in *open* itself.

Here is the *sbull* implementation of *open*, which takes care of the case where there's been a disk change:

```
int sbull_open (struct inode *inode, struct file *filp)
{
    Sbull_Dev *dev; /* device information */
    int num = MINOR(inode->i_rdev);

    if (num >= sbull_devs) return -ENODEV;
    dev = sbull_devices + num;

    /* revalidate on first open and fail if no data is there */
    if (!dev->usage) {
        check_disk_change(inode->i_rdev);
        if (!dev->data)
            return -ENOMEM;
    }
    dev->usage++;
    MOD_INC_USE_COUNT;
    return 0;            /* success */
}
```

Nothing else needs to be done in the driver for a disk change. Data is corrupted anyway if a disk is changed while its open count is greater than zero. The only way the driver can prevent this from happening is for the usage count to control the door lock, in those cases where the physical device supports it. Then *open* and *close* can disable and enable the lock appropriately.

Partitionable Devices

If you try to create partitions with *fdisk*, you'll find out that there's something wrong with them. The *fdisk* program calls the partitions */dev/sbull01*, */dev/sbull02*, and so on, but those names don't exist on the filesystem. Indeed, the base *sbull* device is a byte array with no entry points to provide access to subregions of the data area, so partitioning *sbull* doesn't work.

In order to be able to partition a device, we must assign several minor numbers to each physical device. One number is used to access the whole device (for example, */dev/hda*), and the others are used to access the various partitions (such as */dev/hda1*). Since *fdisk* creates partition names by adding a numerical suffix to the whole-disk device name, we'll follow the same naming convention in our next block driver.

The device I'm going to introduce in this section is called *spull*, because it is a "Simple Partitionable Utility." The device resides in the *spull* directory and is completely detached from *sbull*, even though they share a lot of code.

In the char driver *scull*, different minor numbers were able to implement different behaviors, so that a single driver could show several different implementations. Differentiating according to the minor number is not possible with block devices, and that's why *sbull* and *spull* are kept separate. The inability to differentiate devices according to the minor number is a basic feature of block drivers, as several of the data structures and macros are defined only as a function of the major number.

As far as porting is concerned, it's worth noting that partitionable modules can't be loaded into the 1.2 kernel versions, because the symbol *resetup_one_dev* (introduced later in this section) wasn't exported to modules. Before SCSI disk support was modularized, nobody ever considered partitionable modules.

The device nodes I'm going to introduce are called pd, for "partitionable disk." The four whole devices (also called "units") are thus called *dev/pda* through */dev/pdd*; each device supports at most 15 partitions. Minor numbers have the following meaning: the least significant four bits represent the partition number (where 0 is the whole device), and the most significant four bits represent the unit number. This convention is expressed in the source file by the following macros:

```
#define SPULL_SHIFT 4                          /* max 16 partitions  */
#define SPULL_MAXNRDEV 4                        /* max 4 device units */
#define DEVICE_NR(device) (MINOR(device)>>SPULL_SHIFT)
#define DEVICE_NAME "pd"                        /* name for messaging */
```

The Generic Hard Disk

Every partitionable device needs to know how it is partitioned. The information is available in the partition table, and part of the initialization process consists of decoding the partition table and updating the internal data structures to reflect the partition information.

This decoding isn't easy, but fortunately, the kernel offers "Generic Hard Disk" support usable by all block drivers, which considerably reduces the amount of code needed in the driver for handling partitions. Another advantage of the generic support is that the driver writer doesn't need to understand how the partitioning is done, and new partitioning schemes can be supported in the kernel without requiring changes to driver code.

A block driver that wants to support partitions should include <linux/genhd.h> and should declare a `struct gendisk` structure. All such structures are arranged in a linked list, whose head is the global pointer `gendisk_head`.

Before we go further, let's look at the fields in `struct gendisk`. You'll need to understand them in order to exploit generic device support.

`int major`
> The major number identifies the device driver that the structure refers to.

`const char *major_name`
> The base name for devices belonging to this major number. Each device name is derived from this name by adding a letter for each unit and a number for each partition. For example, "hd" is the base name that is used to build */dev/hda1* and */dev/hdb3*. The base name should be at most five characters long, because *add_partition* builds the full name of the partition in an eight-byte buffer, and the letter that identifies the unit, the partition number, and the `'\0'` terminator have to be appended. The name for *spull* is `pd` ("Partitionable Disk").

`int minor_shift`
> The number of bit-shifts needed to extract the drive number from the device minor number. In *spull* the number is 4. The value in this field should be consistent with the definition of the macro `DEVICE_NR(device)` (see "The Header File blk.h" earlier in this chapter). The macro in *spull* expands to `device>>4`.

`int max_p`
> The maximum number of partitions. In our example, `max_p` is 16, or more generally, `1 << minor_shift`.

`int max_nr`

The maximum number of units. In *spull*, this number is 4. The result of the maximum number of units shifted by `minor_shift` should fit in the available range of minor numbers, which is currently 0–255. The IDE driver can support both many drives and many partitions per drive because it registers several major numbers to work around the small range of minor numbers.

`void (*init)(struct gendisk *)`

The initialization function for the driver, which is called after initializing the device and before the partition check is performed. I'll describe this function in more detail below.

`struct hd_struct *part`

The decoded partition table for the device. The driver uses this item to determine what range of the disk's sectors are accessible through each minor number. The driver is responsible for allocation and deallocation of this array, which most drivers implement as a static array of `max_nr << minor_shift` structures. The driver should initialize the array to zero before the kernel decodes the partition table.

`int *sizes`

This field points to an array of integers. The array holds the same information as `blk_size`. The driver is responsible for allocating and deallocating the data area. Note that the partition check for the device copies this pointer to `blk_size`, so a driver handling partitionable devices doesn't need to allocate the latter array.

`int nr_real`

The number of real devices (units) that exist. This number must be less than or equal to `max_nr`.

`void *real_devices`

This pointer is used internally by each driver that needs to keep additional private information (this is similar to `filp->private_data`).

`void struct gendisk *next`

A link in the list of generic hard disks.

The design of partition checking is best suited to drivers directly linked to the kernel image, so I'll start by introducing the basic structure of the kernel code. Later I'll introduce the way the *spull* module handles its partitions.

Partition Detection in the Kernel

At boot time, *init/main.c* calls the various initialization functions. One of those functions, *start_kernel*, initializes all drivers by calling *device_setup*. This function in turn calls *blk_dev_init* and then checks the partition information of all registered generic hard disks. Any block driver that finds at least one of its devices registers the driver's `genhd` structure in the kernel list so its partitions will be correctly detected.

A partitionable driver, therefore, should declare its own `struct genhd`. The structure looks like the following:

```
struct gendisk my_gendisk = {
    MAJOR_NR,          /* Major number */
    "my",              /* Major name */
    6,                 /* Bits to shift to get real from partition */
    1 << 6,            /* Number of partitions per real */
    MY_MAXNRDEV,       /* Maximum number of devices */
    my_geninit,        /* Init function */
    my_partitions,     /* hd_struct array, filled at partition check */
    my_sizes,          /* Block sizes */
    0,                 /* Number of units: updated by init code */
    NULL,              /* "real_devices" pointer: use at will */
    NULL               /* next: updated by the lines shown below */
};
```

In the initialization function for the driver, then, the structure is queued on the main list of partitionable devices.

The initialization function of a driver that is linked to the kernel is the equivalent of *init_module*, even though it is called in a different way. The function must enclose the following two lines, to take care of queueing the structure:

```
my_gendisk.next = gendisk_head;
gendisk_head = &my_gendisk;
```

By inserting the structure into the linked list, these simple lines are all that's needed in the driver's entry point for all its partitions to be properly recognized and configured.

Additional setup can be performed by *my_geninit*. In the example shown above, the function fills the "number of units" field to reflect the actual hardware setup of the computer system. After *my_geninit* terminates, *gendisk.c* performs the actual partition detection for all the disks (the units). You can see the partitions being detected at system boot because *gendisk.c* prints `Partition check:` on the system console, followed by all the partitions it finds on the available generic hard disks.

You can modify the previous code by delaying allocation of both `my_sizes` and `my_partitions` until the *my_geninit* function. This saves a small amount of kernel memory because the arrays can be as small as `nr_real << minor_shift`, whereas static arrays must be `max_nr << minor_shift` bytes long. The typical savings, however, are a few hundred bytes per physical unit.

Partition Detection in Modules

A modularized driver differs from a driver linked to the kernel in that it can't benefit from the centralized initialization. Instead, it should handle its own setup. There's no two-step initialization for a module, so the `gendisk` structure for *spull* has a `NULL` pointer in its `init` function pointer:

```
struct gendisk spull_gendisk = {
    0,                    /* Major no., assigned after dynamic retreival */
    "pd",                 /* Major name */
    SPULL_SHIFT,          /* Bits to shift to get real from partition */
    1 << SPULL_SHIFT,     /* Number of partitions per real */
    SPULL_MAXNRDEV,       /* Maximum no. of devices */
    NULL,                 /* No init function (isn't called, anyways) */
    NULL,                 /* Partition array, allocated by init_module */
    NULL,                 /* Block sizes, allocated by init_module */
    0,                    /* Number of units: set by init_module */
    NULL,                 /* "real_devices" pointer: not used */
    NULL                  /* Next */
};
```

It is also unnecessary to register the `gendisk` structure in the global linked list of generic disks.

The file *gendisk.c* is prepared to handle a "late" initialization like the one needed by modules by exporting the function *resetup_one_dev*, which scans the partitions for a single physical device. The prototype for *resetup_one_dev* is:

```
void resetup_one_dev(struct gendisk *dev, int drive);
```

You can see from the name of the function that it is meant to *change* the setup information for a device. The function was designed to be called by the BLKR-RPART implementation within *ioctl*, but it can also be used for the initial setup of a module.

When a module is initialized, it should call *resetup_one_dev* for each physical device it is going to access so that the partition information can be stored in `my_gendisk->part`. The partition information is then used in the *request_fn* function of the device.

In *spull*, the *init_module* function includes the following code in addition to the usual instructions. It allocates the arrays needed for partition check and initializes the whole-disk entries in the arrays.

```
/* Prepare the 'size' array and zero it. */
spull_sizes = kmalloc( (spull_devs << SPULL_SHIFT) * sizeof(int),
                GFP_KERNEL);
if (!spull_sizes)
    goto fail_malloc;
```

```
    /* Start with zero-sized partitions, and correctly sized units */
    memset(spull_sizes, 0, (spull_devs << SPULL_SHIFT) * sizeof(int));
    for (i=0; i< spull_devs; i++)
        spull_sizes[i<<SPULL_SHIFT] = spull_size;
    blk_size[MAJOR_NR] = spull_gendisk.sizes = spull_sizes;

    /* Allocate the partitions, and refer the array in spull_gendisk. */
    spull_partitions = kmalloc( (spull_devs << SPULL_SHIFT) *
                                sizeof(struct hd_struct), GFP_KERNEL);
    if (!spull_partitions)
        goto fail_malloc;

    memset(spull_partitions, 0, (spull_devs << SPULL_SHIFT) *
            sizeof(struct hd_struct));
    /* fill whole-disk entries */
    for (i=0; i < spull_devs; i++) {
        /* start_sect is already 0, and sects are 512 bytes long */
        spull_partitions[i << SPULL_SHIFT].nr_sects = 2 * spull_size;
    }
    spull_gendisk.part = spull_partitions;

#if 0
    /*
     * Well, now a *real* driver should call resetup_one_dev().
     * Avoid it here, as there's no allocated data in spull yet.
     */
    for (i=0; i< spull_devs; i++) {
        printk(KERN INFO "Spull partition check: ");
        resetup_one_dev(&spull_gendisk, i);
    }
#endif
```

It's interesting to note that *resetup_one_dev* prints partition information by repeatedly calling:

```
printk(" %s:", disk_name(hd, minor, buf));
```

That's why *spull* would print a leading string. It's meant to add some context to the information that gets stuffed into the system log.

When a partitionable module is unloaded, the driver should arrange for all the partitions to be flushed, by calling *fsync_dev* for every supported major/minor pair. Moreover, if the **gendisk** structure was inserted in the global list, it should be removed—note that *spull* didn't insert itself, for the reasons outlined above.

The cleanup function for *spull* is:

```
for (i = 0; i < (spull_devs << SPULL_SHIFT); i++)
    fsync_dev(MKDEV(spull_major, i)); /* flush the devices */
blk_dev[major].request_fn = NULL;
read_ahead[major] = 0;
kfree(blk_size[major]); /* which is gendisk->sizes as well */
```

```
blk_size[major] = NULL;
kfree(spull_gendisk.part);
```

Partition Detection Using Initrd

If you want to mount your root filesystem from a device whose driver is available only in modularized form, you must use the *Initrd* facility offered by modern Linux kernels. I won't introduce *Initrd* here; this subsection is aimed at readers who know about *Initrd* and wonder how it affects block drivers.

When you boot a kernel with *Initrd*, it establishes a temporary running environment before it mounts the real root filesystem. Modules are usually loaded from within the ramdisk being used as the temporary root file system.

Since the *Initrd* process is run after all boot-time initialization is complete (but before the real root filesystem has been mounted), there's no difference between loading a normal module and one living in the *Initrd* ramdisk. If a driver can be correctly loaded and used as a module, all Linux distributions that have *Initrd* available can include the driver on their installation disks without requiring you to hack in the kernel source.

The Device Methods for spull

In addition to initialization and cleanup, there are other differences between partitionable devices and non-partitionable devices. Basically, the differences are due to the fact that if the disk is partitionable, the same physical device can be accessed using different minor numbers. The mappings from the minor number to the physical position on the disk is stored by *resetup_one_dev* in the `gendisk->part` array. The code below includes only those parts of *spull* that differ from *sbull*, because most of the code is exactly the same.

First of all, *open* and *close* must keep track of the usage count for each device. Since the usage count refers to the physical device (unit), the following assignment is used for the `dev` variable:

```
Spull_Dev *dev = spull_devices + DEVICE_NR(inode->i_rdev);
```

The `DEVICE_NR` macro used here is the one that must be declared before `<linux/blk.h>` is included.

While almost every device method works with the physical device, *ioctl* should access specific information for each partition. For example, *mkfs* should be told the size of each partition, not the size of the whole device. Here is how the `BLKGETSIZE` *ioctl* command is affected by the change from one minor number per device to multiple minor numbers per device. As you might expect, `spull_gendisk->part` is used as the source of the partition size.

```
case BLKGETSIZE:
    /* Return the device size, expressed in sectors */
    if (!arg) return -EINVAL; /* NULL pointer: not valid */
    err=verify_area(VERIFY_WRITE, (long *) arg, sizeof(long));
    if (err) return err;
    size = spull_gendisk.part[MINOR(inode->i_rdev)].nr_sects;
    put_user (size, (long *) arg);
    return 0;
```

The other *ioctl* command that is different for partitionable devices is **BLKRRPART**. Re-reading the partition table makes sense for partitionable devices and is equivalent to revalidating a disk after a disk change:

```
case BLKRRPART: /* re-read partition table: fake a disk change */
    return spull_revalidate(inode->i_rdev);
```

The function *spull_revalidate* in turn calls *resetup_one_dev* to rebuild the partition table. First, however, it must clear any previous information—otherwise, trailing partitions would still appear at the end of the partition table in case the new one contains fewer partitions than before.

```
int spull_revalidate(kdev_t i_rdev)
{
    /* first partition, # of partitions */
    int part1 = (DEVICE_NR(i_rdev) << SPULL_SHIFT) + 1;
    int npart = (1 << SPULL_SHIFT) -1;

    /* first clear old partition information */
    memset(spull_gendisk.sizes+part1, 0, npart*sizeof(int));
    memset(spull_gendisk.part +part1, 0, npart*sizeof(struct hd_struct));

    /* then fill new info */
    printk(KERN_INFO "Spull partition check: ");
    resetup_one_dev(&spull_gendisk, DEVICE_NR(i_rdev));
    return 0;
}
```

But the major difference between *sbull* and *spull* is in the request function. In *spull*, the request function needs to use the partition information in order to correctly transfer data for the different minor numbers.

Information in **spull_gendisk->part** is used to locate each partition on the physical device. **part[minor]->nr_sects** is the partition size, and **part[minor]->start_sect** is its offset from the beginning of the disk. The request function eventually falls back to the whole-disk implementation.

Here are the relevant lines in *spull_request*:

```
/* the sector size is 512 bytes */
ptr = device->data +
        512 * (spull_partitions[minor].start_sect + CURRENT->sector);
size = CURRENT->current_nr_sectors * 512;
```

```
if (CURRENT->sector + CURRENT->current_nr_sectors >
        spull_gendisk.part[minor].nr_sects) {
    printk(KERN_WARNING "spull: request past end of device\n");
    end_request(0);
    continue;
}
```

The number of sectors is multiplied by 512, the sector size (which is hardwired in *spull*), to get the size of the partition in bytes.

Interrupt-Driven Block Drivers

When a driver controls a real hardware device, operation is usually interrupt-driven. Using interrupts helps system performance by releasing the processor during I/O operations. In order for interrupt-driven I/O to work, the device being controlled must be able to transfer data asynchronously and to generate interrupts.

When the driver is interrupt-driven, the request function spawns a data transfer and returns immediately without calling *end_request*. However, the kernel doesn't consider a request fulfilled unless *end_request* has been called. Therefore, the top-half or the bottom-half interrupt handler calls *end_request* when the device signals that the data transfer is complete.

Neither *sbull* nor *spull* can transfer data without using the system microprocessor; however, *spull* is equipped with the capability of faking interrupt-driven operation by specifying the `irq=1` option at load time. When `irq` is not zero, the driver uses a kernel timer to delay fulfillment of the current request. The length of the delay is the value of `irq`: the greater the value, the longer the delay.

The request function for an interrupt-driven device instructs the hardware to perform the transfer and then return. The *spull* function performs the usual error checks and then calls *memcpy* to transfer the data (this is the task that a real driver performs asynchronously). It then delays acknowledgment until interrupt time:

```
void spull_irqdriven_request(void)
{
    Spull_Dev *device;
    u8 *ptr;
    int size, minor, devnr;
    /*
     * Check for errors and start data transfer for the current request.
     * The spull ramdisk performs the transfer right ahead,
     * but delays acknolegment using a kernel timer.
     */
    while(1) {
        INIT_REQUEST;

        devnr = DEVICE_NR(CURRENT_DEV);
        minor = MINOR(CURRENT_DEV);
```

```
                  /* then the core of the function is unchanged.... */


                  /* ... and this is how the function completes: xfer now ... */
                  switch(CURRENT->cmd) {
                    case READ:
                      memcpy(CURRENT->buffer, ptr, size);
                      break;
                    case WRITE:
                      memcpy(ptr, CURRENT->buffer, size);
                      break;
                    default: /* should't happen */
                      end_request(0);
                      continue;
                  }

                  /* ... and wait for the timer to expire--no end_request(1) */
                  spull_timer.expires = jiffies + spull_irq;
                  add_timer(&spull_timer);
                  return;
              }
          }
```

New requests can accumulate while the device is dealing with the current one, but the kernel doesn't call the request function for the driver if it is already dealing with a request. That's why the function just shown doesn't check for double invocation.

It's the responsibility of the interrupt handler to set up for the next data transfer after the last one is complete. To avoid code duplication, the handler usually calls the request function, which should therefore be able to run at interrupt time (see "The Nature of Task Queues" in Chapter 6).

In our sample module, the role of the interrupt handler is performed by the function invoked when the timer expires. That function calls *end_request* and schedules the next data transfer by calling the request function.

```
/* this is invoked when the timer expires */
void spull_interrupt(unsigned long unused)
{
    /*
     * arg to end_request(), default to success, a real device might
     * signal a failure, if it detects one
     */
    int fulfilled = 1;

    end_request(fulfilled);    /* done one */

    if (CURRENT) /* more of them? */
        spull_irqdriven_request();  /* schedule the next */
}
```

Note that this interrupt handler calls the request function to schedule the next operation. This means that in this case the request function must be able to run at interrupt time.

If you try to run the interrupt-driven flavor of the *spull* module, you'll barely notice the added delay. The device is almost as fast as it was before because the buffer cache avoids most data transfers between memory and the physical device. If you want to perceive how a slow device behaves, you can specify a bigger value for `irq=` when loading *spull*.

Quick Reference

The most important functions and macros used in writing block drivers are summarized below. To save space, however, I'm not listing the fields of `struct request` or `struct genhd`, and I'm omitting the predefined *ioctl* commands.

```
int register_blkdev(unsigned int major, const char *name,
                    struct file_operations *fops);
int unregister_blkdev(unsigned int major, const char *name);
```
These functions are in charge of device registration in *init_module* and device removal in *cleanup_module*.

```
struct blk_dev_struct blk_dev[MAX_BLKDEV];
```
This array is used for request passing between the kernel and the driver. `blk_dev[major].request_fn` should be assigned at load time to point to the "request function for the current request."

```
int read_ahead[];
```
Read-ahead values for every major number. A value of 8 is reasonable for devices like hard disks; the value should be greater for slower media.

```
int blksize_size[][];
int blk_size[][];
int hardsect_size[][];
```
These two-dimensional arrays are indexed by major and minor number. The driver is responsible for allocating and deallocating the row in the matrix associated with its major number. The arrays represent the size of device blocks in bytes (it usually is 1KB), the size of each minor device in kilobytes (not blocks), and the size of the hardware sector in bytes. Currently, sector sizes other than 512 are not supported, despite the fact that there's a hook in the code.

MAJOR_NR
DEVICE_NAME
DEVICE_NR(kdev_t device)
DEVICE_INTR
#include <linux/blk.h>

These macros must be defined by the driver *before* it includes the header, as most of the header uses them.

struct request *CURRENT

This macro points to the current request. The request structure describes a data chunk to be transferred and is used by the *request_fn* for the current driver.

#include<linux/gendisk.h>
struct genhd;

The generic hard disk allows Linux to support partitionable devices easily.

void resetup_one_dev(struct gendisk *genhd, int drive);

This function scans the partition table of the disk and rewrites genhd->part to reflect the new partitioning.

## CHAPTER THIRTEEN

MMAP AND DMA

This chapter introduces the internals of Linux memory management and memory mapping. It also describes how "Direct Memory Access" (DMA) is used by device drivers. Although you might object that DMA belongs more to hardware handling than to the software interface, I feel it more related to memory management than to hardware control.

This chapter is quite advanced; most driver writers won't need to go so deep into the system internals. Nonetheless, understanding how memory works will help you design a driver that makes effective use of the system's capabilities.

Memory Management in Linux

Rather than describing the theory of memory management in operating systems, this section tries to pinpoint the main features of the Linux implementation of the theory. This section is mainly informative and skipping over it shouldn't prevent you from understanding the later topics that are more implementation-oriented.

Page Tables

When a program looks up a virtual address, the processor splits the address into bitfields. Each bitfield is used as an index into an array, called a *page table*, to retrieve either the address of the next table or the address of the physical page that holds the virtual address.

The Linux kernel manages three levels of page tables in order to map virtual addresses to physical addresses. This might appear strange at first. As most PC programmers are aware, the x86 hardware implements only two levels of page table. In fact, most 32-bit processors supported by Linux implement two levels, but the kernel implements three anyway.

The use of three levels in a processor-independent implementation allows Linux to support both two-level and three-level processors (such as the Alpha) without clobbering the code with a lot of #ifdef statements. This kind of "conservative coding" doesn't lead to additional overhead when the kernel runs on two-level processors, because the compiler actually optimizes out the unused level.

But let's look for a moment at the data structures used to implement paging. To follow the discussion, you should remember that most data items used for memory management are kept internally as unsigned long, because they represent addresses that are not meant to be dereferenced.

The list below summarizes the implementation of the three levels in Linux, and Figure 13-1 depicts them:

- A "PaGe Directory" (PGD) is the top-level page table. The PGD is an array of pgd_t items, each of which points to a second-level page table. Each process has its own page directory. You can think of the page directory as a page-aligned array of pgd_ts.

- The second-level table is called a "Page Mid-level Directory," or PMD. The PMD is a page-aligned array of pmd_t items. A pmd_t is a pointer to the third-level page table. Two-level processors, such as the x86 and the Sparc-4c, have no physical PMD; they declare their PMD as an array with a single element, whose value is the PMD itself—we'll see in a while how this is handled in C and how the compiler optimizes this level away.

- What comes next is called simply a "Page Table." Once again, it is a page-aligned array of items, each of which is called a "Page Table Entry." The kernel uses the pte_t type for the items. A pte_t contains the physical address of the data page.

The types introduced in this list are defined in <asm/page.h>, which must be included by every source file that plays with paging.

The kernel doesn't need to worry about doing page-table lookups during normal program execution, because they are done in hardware. Nonetheless, the kernel must arrange things so the hardware can do its work. It must build the page tables and look them up whenever the processor reports a page fault; that is, whenever a virtual address needed by the processor is not present in memory.

The following symbols are used to access the page tables. Both <asm/page.h> and <asm/pgtable.h> must be included for all of them to be accessible.

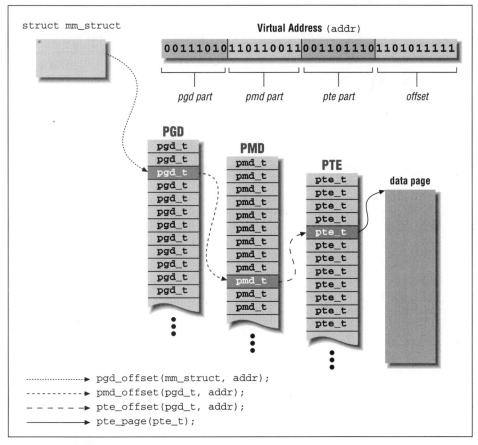

Figure 13-1: The three levels of Linux page tables

`PTRS_PER_PGD`

`PTRS_PER_PMD`

`PTRS_PER_PTE`

> The size of each table. Two-level processors set `PTRS_PER_PMD` to 1, to avoid dealing with the middle level.

`unsigned long pgd_val(pgd_t pgd)`

`unsigned long pmd_val(pmd_t pmd)`

`unsigned long pte_val(pte_t pte)`

> These three macros are used to retrieve the `unsigned long` value from the typed data item. The macros help in using strict data typing in source code without introducing computational overhead.

```
pgd_t * pgd_offset(struct mm_struct * mm,
                    unsigned long address)
pmd_t * pmd_offset(pgd_t * dir, unsigned long address)
pte_t * pte_offset(pmd_t * dir, unsigned long address)
```
These inline functions* are used to retrieve the pgd, pmd, and pte entries associated with address. Page-table lookup begins with a pointer to struct mm_struct. The pointer associated with the memory map of the current process is current->mm. The pointer to kernel space is described by &init_mm, which isn't exported to modules because they don't need it. Two-level processors define pmd_offset(dir,add) as (pmd_t *)dir, thus folding the pmd over the pgd. Functions that scan page tables are always declared as inline, and the compiler optimizes out any pmd lookup.

```
unsigned long pte_page(pte_t pte)
```
This function extracts the address of a physical page from its page-table entry. Using pte_val(pte) wouldn't work, because microprocessors use the low bits of the pte to store additional information about the page. The bits are not part of the actual address, and *pte_page* is needed to extract the real address from the page table.

```
pte_present(pte_t pte)
```
This macro returns a boolean value that indicates whether the data page is currently in memory. This is the most used of several functions that access the low bits in the pte—the bits that are discarded by *pte_page*. It's interesting to note that while physical pages can be present or not, page tables are always present (in the current Linux implementation). This simplifies the kernel code because *pgd_offset* and friends never fail; on the other hand, even a process with a "resident storage size" of zero keeps its page tables in real RAM.

Just seeing the list of these functions is not enough for you to be proficient in the Linux memory management algorithms; real memory management is much more complex and must deal with other complications, like cache coherence. The list above should nonetheless be sufficient to give you a feel for how page management is implemented; you can get more information from the *include/asm* and *mm* subtrees of the kernel source.

Virtual Memory Areas

While paging sits at the lowest level of memory management, something more is necessary before you can use the computer's resources efficiently. The kernel needs a higher-level mechanism to handle the way a process sees its memory.

---

* As a matter of fact, on the Sparc the functions are not inline, but rather real extern functions, which are not exported to modularized code. Therefore you won't be able to use these functions in a module running on the Sparc, but you won't usually need to.

This mechanism is implemented in Linux by means of "Virtual Memory Areas," which I'll refer to as "areas" or "VMAs."

An area is a homogeneous region in the virtual memory of a process, a contiguous range of addresses featuring the same permission flags. It corresponds loosely to the concept of a "segment," although it is better described as "a memory object with its own properties." The memory map of a process is made up of: an area for program code (text); one each for data, BSS (uninitialized data),* and the stack; and one for each active memory mapping. The memory areas of a process can be seen by looking in */proc/pid/maps*. */proc/self* is a special case of */proc/pid*, as it always refers to the current process. As an example, here are three different memory maps, to which I added short comments after a sharp sign:

```
morgana.root# head /proc/1/maps /proc/self/maps
==> /proc/1/maps <==                           #### "init" is a.out on my x86
00000000-00003000 r-xp 00000400 03:01 30818    # hda1:/bin/init--text
00003000-00004000 rwxp 00003400 03:01 30818    # hda1:/bin/init--data
00004000-0000c000 rwxp 00000000 00:00 0        # zero-mapped bss
5ffff000-6009a000 rwxp 00000000 03:01 26621    # hda1:/lib/libc.so.4.7.2
6009a000-600c9000 rwxp 00000000 00:00 0
bfffd000-c0000000 rwxp ffffe000 00:00 0        # zero-mapped stack

==> /proc/self/maps <==                        ####    "head" is ELF on my x86
08000000-08002000 r-xp 00000000 03:01 16778    # hda1:/bin/head--text
08002000-08003000 rw-p 00001000 03:01 16778    # hda1:/bin/head--data
08003000-0800a000 rwxp 00000000 00:00 0        # zero-mapped bss
40000000-40005000 r-xp 00000000 03:01 26863    # /lib/ld-linux.so.1.7.3--text
40005000-40006000 rw-p 00004000 03:01 26863    # /lib/ld-linux.so.1.7.3--data
40006000-40007000 rw-p 00000000 00:00 0
40008000-40080000 r-xp 00000000 03:01 27025    # /lib/libc.so.5.0.9--text
40080000-40085000 rw-p 00077000 03:01 27025    # /lib/libc.so.5.0.9--data
40085000-400b8000 rw-p 00000000 00:00 0
bfffe000-c0000000 rwxp fffff000 00:00 0        # zero-mapped stack

morgana.root# rsh wolf head /proc/self/maps  #### alpha-axp: static ecoff
000000011fffe000-0000000120000000 rwxp 0000000000000000 00:00 0     # stack
0000000120000000-0000000120014000 r-xp 0000000000000000 08:03 2844  # text
0000000140000000-0000000140002000 rwxp 0000000000014000 08:03 2844  # data
0000000140002000-0000000140008000 rwxp 0000000000000000 00:00 0     # bss
```

The fields in each line are:

> *start-end perm offset major:minor inode.*

perm represents a bit mask including the read, write, and execute permissions; it represents what the process is allowed to do with pages belonging to the area. The last character in the field is either **p** for "private" or **s** for "shared."

---

* The name *BSS* is an historical relic, from an old assembly operator meaning "Block Started by Symbol." The BSS segment of executable files isn't stored on disk, and the kernel maps the zero-page to the BSS address range.

Each field in */proc/*/maps* corresponds to a field in `struct vm_area_struct`, and is described in the list below.

A driver that implements the *mmap* method needs to fill a VMA structure in the address space of the process mapping the device. The driver writer should therefore have at least a minimal understanding of VMAs in order to use them.

Let's look at the most important fields in `struct vm_area_struct` (defined in `<linux/mm.h>`). These fields may be used by device drivers in their *mmap* implementation. Note that the kernel maintains lists and trees of VMAs to optimize area lookup, and several fields of `vm_area_struct` are used to maintain this organization. VMAs can't be created at will by a driver, or the structures will break. The main fields of VMAs are the following:

`unsigned long vm_start;`
`unsigned long vm_end;`
> A VMA describes virtual addresses between `vma->vm_start` and `vma->vm_end`. These fields are the first two fields shown in */proc/*/maps*.

`struct inode * vm_inode;`
> If the area is associated with an inode (such as a disk file or a device node), this field is a pointer to the inode. Otherwise, it is `NULL`.

`unsigned long vm_offset;`
> The offset of the area in the inode. When a file or device is mapped, this is the file position (`filp->f_pos`) of the first byte mapped in this area.

`struct vm_operations_struct *vm_ops;`
> `vma->vm_ops` indicates that the memory area is a kernel "object" like the `struct file` we have been using throughout the book. The area declares the "methods" to act on its contents, and this field is used to list the methods.

Like `struct vm_area_struct`, the `vm_operations_struct` is defined in `<linux/mm.h>`; it includes the operations listed below. These operations are the only ones needed to handle the process's memory needs, and they are listed in the order they are declared. The prototypes shown are for 2.0; the minor changes from 1.2.13 are described in each entry. Later in this chapter, some of these functions will be implemented, and they will be described more completely at that point.

`void (*open)(struct vm_area_struct *vma);`
> After the kernel creates a VMA, it opens it. When an area is copied, the child inherits its operations from the father and the new area is opened via `vm_ops->open`. When *fork* copies the areas of the existing process to the new one, for example, `vm_ops->open` is called to open all the maps. Whenever *mmap* executes, on the other hand, the area is created *before* `file->f_ops->mmap` is called, and no `vm_ops->open` gets invoked.

```
void (*close)(struct vm_area_struct *vma);
```
When an area is destroyed, the kernel calls its *close* operation. Note that there's no usage count associated with VMAs; the area is opened and closed only once.

```
void (*unmap)(struct vm_area_struct *vma,
              unsigned long addr, size_t len);
```
The kernel calls this method to "unmap" part or all of an area. If the entire area is unmapped, then the kernel calls `vm_ops->close` as soon as `vm_ops->unmap` returns.

```
void (*protect)(struct vm_area_struct *vma, unsigned long,
                size_t, unsigned int newprot);
```
Currently not used. The handling of permission (protection) bits doesn't depend on the area itself.

```
int (*sync)(struct vm_area_struct *vma, unsigned long,
            size_t, unsigned int flags);
```
This method is called by the *msync* system call to save a dirty memory region to the storage medium. The return value is expected to be 0 to indicate success and negative if there was an error. Kernel version 1.2 used `void` as the return value for this method because the function was not expected to fail.

```
void (*advise)(struct vm_area_struct *vma, unsigned long,
               size_t, unsigned int advise);
```
Currently not used.

```
unsigned long (*nopage)(struct vm_area_struct *vma,
                        unsigned long address,
                        int write_access);
```
When a process tries to access a page that belongs to a valid VMA, but that is currently not in memory, the *nopage* method is called if it is defined for the related area. The method returns the (physical) address of the page. If the method isn't defined for the area, an empty page is allocated by the kernel. It's unusual for drivers to implement *nopage*, because regions mapped by a driver are usually completely mapped in the system's physical addresses. Version 1.2 of the kernel features a different prototype for *nopage* and a different semantic as well. The third argument, `write_access`, counts as "no-share"—a non-zero value means the page must be owned by the current process, while zero means that sharing is possible.

```
unsigned long (*wppage)(struct vm_area_struct *vma,
                        unsigned long address,
                        unsigned long page);
```
This method handles "write-protected" page faults but is currently unused. The kernel handles any attempts to write over a protected page without

invoking the area-specific callback. Write-protect faults are used to implement copy-on-write. A private page can be shared across processes until one process writes to it. When that happens, the page is cloned, and the process writes on its own copy of the page. If the whole area is marked as read-only, a SIGSEGV is sent to the process, and the copy-on-write is not performed.

```
int (*swapout)(struct vm_area_struct *vma,
                unsigned long offset, pte_t *page_table);
```
This method is called when a page is selected for swap-out. The offset argument is the file offset: virt_address - vma->vm_start + vma->vm_offset. A return value of 0 signals success; any other value signals an error. In case of error, the process owning the page is sent a SIGBUS. In version 1.2, the function returned void because it was never expected to fail. The method usually writes useful information to *page_table, so it can be retrieved at swap-in. Such information can be, for example, the offset in the swap device.

```
pte_t (*swapin)(struct vm_area_struct *,
                unsigned long offset, unsigned long entry);
```
This method is used to retrieve a page from swap space. The offset argument is relative to the area (as above for *swapout*), while entry is the current pte for the page—if *swapout* saved some information in the entry, that information can now be used to retrieve the page.

It's unlikely a driver will ever need to implement *swapout* or *swapin*, because drivers usually map pages of I/O memory, not regular memory. I/O pages are physical addresses that are accessed like memory but map to the device hardware instead of to RAM. I/O memory regions are either marked as "reserved" or live above the top of physical memory, so they never get swapped out—swapping I/O memory wouldn't make much sense anyway.

The Memory Map

There is a third data structure related to memory management in Linux. While VMAs and page tables organize the virtual address space, the *physical* address space is summarized in the *memory map*.

The kernel needs a description of the current usage of physical memory. Since memory can be considered as an array of pages, the information is organized in an array. If you need information about a page, you just use its physical address to access the memory map. Here are the symbols used by the kernel code to access the memory map:

```
typedef struct { /* ... */ } mem_map_t;
extern mem_map_t mem_map[];
```
The map itself is an array of mem_map_ts. Each physical page in the system, including kernel code and kernel data, has an entry in mem_map.

PAGE_OFFSET

> This macro represents the virtual address in the kernel address space to which physical addresses are mapped. PAGE_OFFSET must be considered whenever "physical" addresses are used. What the kernel considers to be a physical address is actually a virtual address, offset by PAGE_OFFSET from the real physical address—the one that is used in the electrical address lines outside the CPU. Through Linux 2.0.*x*, PAGE_OFFSET was zero for the PC and nonzero for most other platforms. Version 2.1.0 changed the PC implementation so it now uses offset-mapping as well. Mapping physical space to high virtual addresses has sound advantages as far as kernel code is concerned, but the topic is beyond the scope of this book.

int MAP_NR(addr);

> Whenever a program needs to access the memory map, MAP_NR returns the index in the mem_map array associated with addr. The addr argument can either be an unsigned long or a pointer. Since the macro is used several times by critical memory management functions, it performs no validity checking on addr; the calling code must make its own checks when needed.

((nr << PAGE_SHIFT) + PAGE_OFFSET)

> No standardized function or macro exists to translate a map number into a physical address. If you ever need the inverse function of MAP_NR, this clause will work.

The memory map is used to maintain some low-level information about each memory page. The exact definition of the memory map structure changed several times during kernel development; you don't need to understand the details because drivers aren't expected to look inside the map.

If, however, you are interested in looking at the internals of page management, the header <linux/mm.h> includes a long comment that explains the meaning of the fields in mem_map_t.

The mmap Device Operation

Memory mapping is one of the most interesting features of modern Unix systems. As far as drivers are concerned, memory mapping can be used to provide user programs with direct access to device memory.

For example, a simple ISA frame grabber holds image data in its own memory, either in the 640KB–1MB address range or in the "ISA hole," the range between 14MB and 16MB (see "Accessing Memory on Device Boards" in Chapter 8, *Hardware Management*). While copying image data to conventional (and faster) RAM is a suitable approach for casual grabbing, if the user program needs to access the current image frame every now and then, an *mmap* approach is better suited to the task.

Mapping a device means associating a range of user-space addresses to device memory. Whenever the program reads or writes in the assigned address range, it is actually accessing the device.

As you might suspect, not every device lends itself to the *mmap* abstraction; it makes no sense, for instance, for serial ports and other stream-oriented devices. Another limitation of *mmap* is that mapping is `PAGE_SIZE`-grained. The kernel can dispose of virtual addresses only at the level of page tables; therefore, the mapped area must be a multiple of `PAGE_SIZE` and must live in physical memory starting at an address that is a multiple of `PAGE_SIZE`. The kernel accomodates for size-granularity by making a region slightly bigger if its size isn't a multiple of the page size. Alignment issues are usually handled by mucking with `vma->vm_offset`, but this can't be done for drivers—mapping a device reduces to accessing physical pages, which must be page-aligned.

These limits are not a big constraint for drivers, because the program accessing the device is device-dependent anyway. It needs to know how to make sense of the memory region being mapped, so the `PAGE_SIZE` alignment is not a problem. A bigger constraint exists when you plug ISA boards into an Alpha computer, because ISA memory is accessed only as a scattered set of 8-bit, 16-bit, or 32-bit items, and there's no direct mapping from ISA addresses to Alpha addresses. In this case, you can't use *mmap* at all. The inability to perform direct mapping of ISA addresses to Alpha addresses is due to the incompatible data transfer specifications of the two systems. While the Alpha can issue only 32-bit and 64-bit memory accesses, ISA can do only 8-bit and 16-bit transfers, and there's no way to transparently map one protocol onto the other. As a consequence, you can't use *mmap* at all with ISA boards plugged into an Alpha computer.

There are sound advantages to using *mmap* when it's feasible to do so. For instance, a program like the X server transfers a lot of data from video memory; mapping the graphic display to user space dramatically improves the throughput, as opposed to an *lseek/write* implementation. Another typical example is a program controlling a PCI device. Most PCI peripherals map their control registers to a memory address, and a demanding application might prefer to have direct access to the registers, instead of repeatedly having to call *ioctl* to get its work done.

The *mmap* method is part of the `file_operations` structure and is invoked when the *mmap* system call is issued. With *mmap*, the kernel performs a good deal of work before the actual method is invoked, and therefore the prototype of the method is quite different from that of the system call. This is unlike calls such as *ioctl* and *select*, where the kernel does not do a lot of work before calling the method.

The system call is declared as follows (as described in the *mmap(2)* manual page):

```
mmap (caddr_t addr, size_t len, int prot, int flags, int fd,
      off_t offset)
```

On the other hand, the file operation is declared as:

```
int (*mmap) (struct inode *inode, struct file *filp,
             struct vm_area_struct *vma);
```

The `inode` and `filp` arguments in the method are the same as those introduced in Chapter 3, *Char Drivers*, while **vma** contains the information about the virtual address range that is used to access the device. Therefore, the driver only has to build suitable page tables for the address range and, if necessary, replace `vma->vm_ops` with a new set of operations.

A Simple Implementation

Most implementations of *mmap* for device drivers perform a linear mapping of some I/O memory living on the peripheral device. Both */dev/mem* and */dev/audio* are examples of this kind of remapping. The following code comes from *drivers/char/mem.c* and shows how this task is performed in a typical module called *simple* (Simple Implementation Mapping Pages with Little Enthusiasm):

```
#include <linux/mm.h>

int simple_mmap(struct inode *inode, struct file *filp,
                struct vm_area_struct *vma)
{
/* int remap_page_range(virt_add, phys_add, size, protection); */
    if (remap_page_range(vma->vm_start, vma->vm_offset,
                         vma->vm_end-vma->vm_start, vma->vm_page_prot))
        return -EAGAIN;
    vma->vm_inode = inode;
    inode->i_count++;
    return 0;
}
```

It's clear that the core of the operation is performed by *remap_page_range*, which is exported to modularized drivers because it does just the right job for most mapping needs.

Maintaining the Usage Count

The main problem with the implementation shown above is that the driver doesn't maintain a connection with the mapped area. While this is not a problem with */dev/mem*, which is an integral part of the kernel, a module has to have a way to keep its usage count up-to-date. A program can call *close* on the file descriptor and still access the memory-mapped region. However, if closing the file descriptor leads to the module's usage count dropping to zero, the module might be unloaded, even though it is still being used via *mmap*.

Trying to warn the module's user about the problem is an insufficient workaround, because it's not unlikely that *kerneld* will be used to load and unload your module. The daemon automatically removes modules when their usage count drops to zero, and you just can't warn *kerneld* to be careful about *mmap*.

The solution to this problem is to override the default **vma->vm_ops** with operations that keep track of the usage count. The code is quite simple—a complete *mmap* implementation for a modularized */dev/mem* looks like the following:

```
static struct vm_operations_struct simple_vm_ops = {
    simple_vma_open,
    simple_vma_close, /* no more fields */
    };

void simple_vma_open(struct vm_area_struct * area)
{ MOD_INC_USE_COUNT; }

void simple_vma_close(struct vm_area_struct * area)
{ MOD_DEC_USE_COUNT; }

int simple_mmap(struct inode *inode, struct file *filp,
            struct vm_area_struct *vma)
{
/* int remap_page_range(virt_add, phys_add, size, protection); */
    if (remap_page_range(vma->vm_start, vma->vm_offset,
                    vma->vm_end-vma->vm_start, vma->vm_page_prot))
        return -EAGAIN;
    if (vma->vm_ops)
        return -EINVAL; /* Hmm... shouldn't happen */
    vma->vm_ops = &simple_vm_ops;
    MOD_INC_USE_COUNT; /* open(vma) wasn't called this time */
    vma->vm_inode = inode;
    inode->i_count++;
    return 0;
}
```

This code relies on the fact that the kernel initializes the **vm_ops** field in the newly created area to **NULL** before calling **f_op->mmap**. The code just shown checks the current value of the pointer as a safety measure, should something change in future kernels.

The implementation shown exploits the notion that both *open(vma)* and *close(vma)* are used as a complement to the default implementation. The driver methods don't need to replicate the standard code that opens and closes memory areas; the driver is just implementing additional management.

It's interesting to note that the *swapin* and *swapout* methods for VMAs work the other way—the `vm_ops->swap*` operations defined by the driver replace the default implementation with something completely different instead of adding to it.

Supporting the mremap System Call

The *mremap* system call is used by applications to change the bounding addresses of a mapped region. If the driver wants to be able to deal with *mremap*, the previous implementation won't work correctly, because there's no way for the driver to know that the mapped region has changed.

The Linux implementation of *mremap* doesn't notify the driver of changes in the mapped area. Actually, it *does* notify the driver if the size of the area is reduced via the *unmap* method, but no callback is issued if the area increases in size.

The basic idea behind notifying the driver of a reduction is that the driver (or the filesystem mapping a regular file to memory) needs to know when a region is unmapped in order to take the proper action, like flushing pages to disk. Growth of the mapped region, on the other hand, isn't really meaningful for the driver, unless the program invoking *mremap* accesses the new virtual addresses. In real life, it's quite common to map regions that are never used (unused sections of program code, for example). The Linux kernel, therefore, doesn't notify the driver if the mapped region grows, because the *nopage* method will take care of pages one at a time as they are actually accessed.

In other words, the driver isn't notified when a mapping grows because *nopage* will do it later, without having to use memory before it is actually needed. This optimization is mostly aimed at regular files, whose mapping uses real RAM.

The *nopage* method, therefore, must be implemented if you want to support the *mremap* system call. But once you have *nopage*, you can choose to use it extensively to avoid calling *remap_page_range* from `fops->mmap`; this is shown in the next code fragment. In this implementation of *mmap*, the device method only replaces `vma->vm_fops`. The *nopage* method takes care of "remapping" one page at a time and returning its address.

An implementation of */dev/mem* supporting *mremap* (and not supporting the usage count, to save space) looks like the following:

```
static struct vm_operations_struct simple_vm_ops = {
    NULL, NULL, NULL, NULL, NULL, NULL, simple_nopage,
    };

unsigned long simple_nopage(struct vm_area_struct *vma,
                        unsigned long address, int write)
{
pgd_t *pgd; pmd_t *pmd; pte_t *pte;
```

```
    /* int remap_page_range(virt_add, phys_add, size, protection); */
    remap_page_range(address & PAGE_MASK,
                    address - vma->vm_start + vma->vm_offset,
                    PAGE_SIZE, vma->vm_page_prot);
    /* now return its address to the caller */
    pgd = pgd_offset(current->mm, address);
    pmd = pmd_offset(pgd, page);
    pte = pte_offset(pmd, page);
    return pte_page(*pte);          /* this is the physical address */
    }

    int simple_mmap(struct inode *inode, struct file *filp,
                    struct vm_area_struct *vma)
    {
        vma->vm_ops = &simple_vm_ops;
        vma->vm_inode = inode;
        inode->i_count++;
        return 0;
    }
```

If the *nopage* method is left **NULL**, kernel code that handles page faults maps the zero-page to the faulty virtual address. The zero-page is a copy-on-write page that reads as zero and that is used, for example, to map the BSS segment. Therefore, if a process extends a mapped region by calling *mremap*, and the driver hasn't implemented *nopage*, you'll end up with zero pages instead of a segmentation fault.

Note that the implementation shown is highly suboptimal; it would be better if the memory method directly returned the physical address, bypassing *remap_page_range*. Unfortunately, a correct implementation of such a technique involves several details that will be clarified only later in this chapter. Moreover, the implementation shown above doesn't work with kernel 1.2 because the prototype of *nopage* changed between version 1.2 and 2.0. I won't deal with 1.2 kernels throughout this section.

Remapping Specific I/O Regions

All the examples we've seen so far are reimplementations of */dev/mem*; they remap physical addresses to user space—or at least, that's what they think they do. The typical driver, however, wants to map only the small address range that applies to its peripheral device, not all of memory.

To be able to customize the */dev/mem* implementation for a specific driver, we need to look further into the internals of *remap_page_range*. The full prototype of the function is:

```
    int remap_page_range(unsigned long virt_add, unsigned long phys_add,
                        unsigned long size, pgprot_t prot);
```

The value returned by the function is the usual zero or a negative error code. Let's look at the exact meaning of the function's arguments:

`unsigned long virt_add`

> The virtual address where remapping should begin. The function builds page tables for the virtual address range between `virt_add` and `virt_add+size`.

`unsigned long phys_add`

> The physical address to which the virtual address should be mapped. The address is "physical" in the sense outlined above. The function affects physical addresses from `phys_add` to `phys_add+size`.

`unsigned long size`

> The dimension, in bytes, of the area being remapped.

`pgprot_t prot`

> The "protection" requested for the new page. The driver doesn't need to modify the protection, and the argument found in `vma->vm_page_prot` can be used unchanged. If you're curious, you can find additional information in `<linux/mm.h>`.

In order to map to user space only a subset of the whole memory range, the driver needs to play with the offsets. The following lines will do the trick for a driver mapping a region of `simple_region_size` bytes, beginning at physical address `simple_region_start`:

```
unsigned long off = vma->vm_offset;
unsigned long physical = simple_region_start + off + PAGE_OFFSET;
unsigned long vsize = vma->vm_end - vma->vm_start;
unsigned long psize = simple_region_size - off;

if (off & (PAGE_SIZE-1))
    return -ENXIO; /* need aligned offsets */
if (vsize > psize)
    return -EINVAL; /*  spans too high */
remap_page_range(vma_>vm_start, physical, vsize, vma->vm_page_prot);
```

In addition to calculating the offsets, the code above introduces two checks for error conditions. The first check refuses to map to user space a location that is unaligned in physical space. Since only whole pages can be remapped, the mapped region can only be offset by multiples of the page size. `ENXIO` is the usual error code returned in this case; it expands to "no such device or address."

The second check reports an error when the program tries to map more memory than is available in the I/O region of the target device. In this code, `psize` is the physical I/O size that is left after the offset has been specified, and `vsize` is the requested size of virtual memory; the function refuses to map addresses that extend beyond the allowed memory range.

Note that if the process calls *mremap*, it can extend its mapping. A "very pedantic" driver might want to prevent this from happening; the only way to do that is to implement the `vma->nopage` method. The following implementation of that method is the simplest:

```
unsigned long simple_pedantic_nopage(struct vm_area_struct *vma,
                                     unsigned long address,
                                     int write_access);
{ return 0; /* send a SIGBUS */}
```

If a *nopage* method returns 0 instead of a valid physical address, a `SIGBUS` (bus error) is sent to the current process (the one that experienced the page fault). If the driver doesn't have *nopage* implemented, the process gets the zero-page at the requested virtual address; this is often acceptable, as *mremap* is a rarely-used system call and mapping the zero-page to user space has no security implications.

Remapping RAM

In Linux, a page of physical addresses is marked as "reserved" in the memory map to indicate that it is not available for memory management. On the PC, for example, the range between 640KB and 1MB is marked as "reserved," as are the pages that host the kernel code itself.

An interesting limitation of *remap_page_range* is that it gives access only to reserved pages and physical addresses above the top of physical memory. Reserved pages are locked in memory and are the only ones that can be safely mapped to user space; this limitation is a basic requrement for system stability.*

Therefore, *remap_page_range* won't allow you to remap conventional addresses—which includes the ones you obtain by calling *get_free_page*. Nonetheless, the function does everything that a hardware driver needs it to, because it can remap high PCI buffers and ISA memory—both the first megabyte of memory and, if the change outlined in "ISA Memory Above 1M" in Chapter 8 is applied, the ISA hole at 15MB. When using *remap_page_range* with non-reserved pages, on the other hand, the default *nopage* handler maps the zero-page at the virtual address being accessed.

This behavior can be seen by running *mapper*, one of the sample programs in *misc-programs* in the files provided on the O'Reilly FTP site. *mapper* is a simple tool that can be used to quickly test the *mmap* system call; it maps read-only parts of a file based on the command-line options and dumps the mapped region to standard output. The session below, for instance, shows that */dev/mem* doesn't

---

* When a page becomes part of a process's memory map, its usage count must be incremented, because at *munmap* time, it will be decremented. This kind of locking can't be performed on live RAM pages, as it would prevent normal system operation (like swapping and allocation/deallocation).

map the physical page located at address 64KB (the host computer in this examples is a PC, but the result would be the same on other platforms):

```
morgana.root# ./mapper /dev/mem 0x10000 0x1000 | od -Ax -t x1
mapped "/dev/mem" from 65536 to 69632
000000 00 00 00 00 00 00 00 00 00 00 00 00 00 00 00 00
*
001000
```

The inability of *remap_page_range* to deal with RAM suggests that a device like *scullp* can't easily implement *mmap*, because its device memory is conventional RAM, not I/O memory.

Two workarounds exist to get around the unavailability of *remap_page_range* for RAM. One is a "bad" workaround and the other is a clean one.

Playing with the reserved bit

The bad approach involves setting the `PG_reserved` bit in `mem_map[MAP_NR(page)].flags` for the pages you want to map to user space. This reserves the pages, and once they have been reserved, *remap_page_range* works as desired. The code to set the flag is short and easy, but I won't show it here, because the other solution is more interesting. Needless to say, the reserved bit must definitely be cleared before releasing the page.

There are two reasons why this isn't a good approach. First, pages marked as reserved are never touched by memory management. The kernel identifies them at system boot, before data structures are initialized, so that they are completely unavailable for any other use. On the other hand, any page allocated through *get_free_page*, *vmalloc*, or some other means *is* handled by the memory subsystem. Even though the 2.0 kernel won't panic if you reserve extra pages at run time, doing so might cause problems in the future and is discouraged. You might, nonetheless, want to try this quick-and-dirty technique to see how it works.

The second reason that reserving pages isn't a good approach is that reserved pages don't count as part of the total system memory, and a user is likely to be concerned if the amount of system RAM varies from one session to the next—users often monitor the amount of free memory, and total memory is displayed along with free memory.

Implementing the nopage method

A better way to map real RAM to user space is to use `vm_ops->nopage` to deal with page faults one at a time. A sample implementation is part of the *scullp* module, introduced in Chapter 7, *Getting Hold of Memory*.

scullp is the page-oriented char device. Because it is page-oriented, it can implement *mmap* on its memory. The code implementing memory mapping uses some of the concepts introduced earlier in "Memory Management in Linux."

Before examining the code, let's look at the design choices that affect the *mmap* implementation in *scullp.*

The device updates the usage count for the module.
> To avoid problems with module unloading, the *open* and *close* methods for memory areas are implemented to keep track of module usage.

The device updates the usage count for the pages.
> This is a strict requirement to keep the system stable; failure to update the count will lead to a system crash. Each page has its own usage count; when it drops to zero, the page is inserted in the list of free pages. Whenever an active map is destroyed, the kernel decrements the usage count of associated RAM pages. Therefore, the driver must increment the usage count of each page it maps (note that the count won't be zero before *nopage* increments it, because the page has already been allocated by `fops->write`).

scullp doesn't release device memory as long as the device is mapped.
> This is a matter of policy rather than a requirement, and it is different from the behavior of *scull* and similar devices, which are truncated to a length of zero when opened for writing. Refusing to free a mapped *scullp* device allows a process to overwrite regions actively mapped by another process, so you can test and see how processes and device memory interact. To avoid releasing a mapped device, the driver must keep a count of active mappings; the **vmas** field in the device structure is used for this purpose.

Memory mapping is only performed when the scullp `order` *parameter is zero.*
> The parameter controls how *get_free_pages* is invoked (see the section "get_ free_ page and Friends" in Chapter 7). This choice is dictated by the internals of *get_free_pages*—the allocation engine exploited by *scullp.* In order to maximize allocation performance, the Linux kernel maintains a list of free pages for each allocation order, and only the page count of the first page in a cluster is incremented by *get_free_pages* and decremented by *free_pages.* The *mmap* method is disabled for a *scullp* device if the allocation order is greater than zero, because *nopage* deals with single pages rather than clusters of pages.

The last choice is mostly intended to keep the code simple. It *is* possible to correctly implement *mmap* for multipage allocations by playing with the usage count of the pages, but it would only add to the complexity of the example without introducing any interesting information.

If code is intended to map RAM according to the rules outlined above, it needs to implement *open*, *close*, and *nopage*, and also needs to access mem_map.

This implementation of *scullp_mmap* is very short, because it relies on the *nopage* function to do all the interesting work:

```
int scullp_mmap(struct inode *inode, struct file *filp,
                struct vm_area_struct *vma)
{
    /* refuse to map if order is not 0 */
    if (scullp_devices[MINOR(inode->i_rdev)].order)
        return -ENODEV;
    if (vma->vm_offset & (PAGE_SIZE-1))
        return -ENXIO; /* need aligned offsets */

    /* don't do anything here: "nopage" will fill the holes */
    vma->vm_ops = &scullp_vm_ops;
    vma->vm_inode = inode;
    inode->i_count++;
    scullp_vma_open(vma);
    return 0;
}
```

The purpose of the leading conditionals is to avoid mapping unaligned offsets and devices whose allocation order is not 0. At the end, vm_ops->open is called to update the usage count for the module and the count of active mappings for the device.

open and *close* just keep track of these counts and are defined as:

```
void scullp_vma_open(struct vm_area_struct *vma)
{
    ScullP_Dev *dev = scullp_devices + MINOR(vma->vm_inode->i_rdev);

    dev->vmas++;
    MOD_INC_USE_COUNT;
}

void scullp_vma_release(struct vm_area_struct *vma)
{
    ScullP_Dev *dev = scullp_devices + MINOR(vma->vm_inode->i_rdev);

    dev->vmas--;
    MOD_DEC_USE_COUNT;
}
```

Since the module creates four different *scullp* devices and there's no pri-vate_data pointer available for memory areas, *open* and *close* retrieve the *scullp* device associated with the vma by extracting the minor number from the inode structure. The minor number is used to offset the scullp_devices array of device structures to obtain a pointer to the right structure.

Most of the work is then performed by *nopage*. Whenever the process page faults, the function must retrieve the physical address of the page being referenced and return it to the caller. The method can count on page alignment of the address argument, if that is needed. In the *scullp* implementation, address is used to calculate an offset into the device; the offset is then used to look up the correct page in the *scullp* memory tree.

```
unsigned long scullp_vma_nopage(struct vm_area_struct *vma,
                                unsigned long address, int write)
{
    unsigned long offset = address - vma->vm_start + vma->vm_offset;
    ScullP_Dev *ptr, *dev = scullp_devices +
                            MINOR(vma->vm_inode->i_rdev);
    void *pageptr = NULL; /* default to "missing" */

    if (offset >= dev->size) return 0; /* out of range: send SIGBUS */

    /*
     * Now retrieve the scullp device from the list, then the page.
     * Don't want to allocate: I'm too lazy. If the device has holes,
     * the process receives a SIGBUS when accessing the hole.
     */
    offset >>= PAGE_SHIFT; /* offset is a number of pages */
    for (ptr = dev; ptr && offset >= dev->qset;) {
        ptr = ptr->next;
        offset -= dev->qset;
    }
    if (ptr && ptr->data) pageptr = ptr->data[offset];
    if (!pageptr) return 0; /* hole or end-of-file: SIGBUS */

    /* got it, now increment the count */
    atomic_inc(&mem_map[MAP_NR(pageptr)].count);
    return (unsigned long)pageptr;
}
```

The last line increments the usage count for the page; the count is declared as atomic_t and therefore lends itself to being updated with an atomic operation. As a matter of fact, in this specific situation, an atomic update isn't strictly required, because the page is already in use, and there's no race condition with interrupt handlers or other asynchronous code.

The *scullp* device now works as expected, as you can see in this sample output from the *mapper* utility:

```
morgana% ls -l /dev > /dev/scullp
morgana% ./mapper /dev/scullp 0 140
mapped "/dev/scullp" from 0 to 140
total 13
-rwxr-xr--   1 root      root          11969 Jul 18  1994 MAKEDEV*
lrwxrwxrwx   1 root      root              4 Oct 23 20:28 XOR -> null
```

```
morgana% ./mapper /dev/scullp 8192 100
mapped "/dev/scullp" from 8192 to 8292
 disk      22,  75 Jul 18  1994 hd1b11
brw-rw----  1 root      disk      22,  76 Jul 18  1994 hd1b12
```

Remapping Virtual Addresses

Although it's rarely necessary to remap virtual addresses, it's interesting to see how a driver can map a virtual address to user space using *mmap*. By virtual address, I mean an address returned by *vmalloc*; that is, a virtual address mapped in the kernel page tables. The code in this section is taken from *scullv*, which is the module that works like *scullp* but allocates its storage through *vmalloc*.

Most of the *scullv* implementation is exactly like the one we've just seen for *scullp*, except that there is no need to check the **order** of allocation. The reason for this is that *vmalloc* allocates its pages one at a time, because single-page allocations are far more likely to succeed than multi-page allocations. Therefore, the usage count problem doesn't apply to *vmalloc*ed space.

Most of the work of *vmalloc* is building page tables to access allocated pages as a continuous address range. The *nopage* method, on the other hand, must return a physical address to the caller. Therefore, the *nopage* implementation for *scullv* must scan the page tables to retrieve the physical address associated with the page.

The function is identical to the one we saw for *scullp*, except at the end. This code excerpt only includes the part of *nopage* that differs from *scullp*:

```
unsigned long scullv_vma_nopage(struct vm_area_struct *vma,
                                unsigned long address, int write)
{
    void *pageptr = NULL;
    unsigned long page;
    pgd_t *pgd; pmd_t *pmd; pte_t *pte;


    /*
     * After scullv lookup, "page" is now the address of the page
     * needed by the current process. Since it's a vmalloc address,
     * first retrieve the unsigned long value to be looked up
     * in page tables.
     */
    page = VMALLOC_VMADDR(pageptr);

    pgd = pgd_offset(init_mm_ptr, page);
    pmd = pmd_offset(pgd, page);
    pte = pte_offset(pmd, page);
    page = pte_page(*pte);       /* this is the physical address */

    /* now increment the count and return */
```

```
        atomic_inc(&mem_map[MAP_NR(page)].count);
        return page;
}
```

The page tables are looked up using the functions introduced at the beginning of this chapter. The page directory used for this purpose is stored in the memory structure for kernel space, init_mm.

The macro VMALLOC_VMADDR(pageptr) returns the correct unsigned long value to be used in a page table lookup from a *vmalloc* address. Note that a simple cast of the value wouldn't work on the x86 with kernels older than 2.1, due to a glitch in memory management. Memory management for the x86 changed in version 2.1.1 and VMALLOC_VMADDR is now defined as the identity function, as it has always been for the other platforms.

The last point to cover is how init_mm is accessed, since, as I stated earlier, it is not exported to modules. Actually, *scullv* has to do some extra work to retrieve the pointer to init_mm, as explained below.

In practice, init_mm is not needed by conventional modules, because they are not expected to interact with memory management; they simply call the allocation and deallocation functions. Implementations like *mmap* for *scullv* are very unusual. The code shown in this subsection is not actually needed to drive hardware; I introduced it only to support with real code the discussion about page tables.

While we are at it, however, I want to show you how *scullv* obtains the address of init_mm. The code relies on the fact that process 0 (the so-called idle task) lives in the kernel, and its page directory describes the kernel address space. To reach the idle task's data structures, *scullv* scans the linked list of processes until it finds process 0.

```
static struct mm_struct *init_mm_ptr;

static void retrieve_init_mm_ptr(void)
{
    struct task_struct *p;

    for (p = current ; (p = p->next_task) != current ; )
        if (p->pid == 0)
            break;

    init_mm_ptr = p->mm;
}
```

This function is invoked by fops->mmap, because *nopage* only runs after a call to *mmap*.

Based on the discussion above, you might also want to map addresses returned by *vremap* (or *ioremap* if you are using Linux 2.1) to user space. This mapping is easily accomplished because you can use *remap_page_range* directly, without implementing methods for virtual memory areas. In other words, *remap_page_range* is already usable for building new page tables that map I/O memory to user space; there's no need to look in the kernel page-tables built by *vremap* as we did in *scullv*.

Direct Memory Access

Direct Memory Access, or DMA, is the advanced topic that completes our overview of memory issues. DMA is the hardware mechanism that allows peripheral components to transfer their I/O data directly to and from main memory, without the need for the system processor to be involved in the transfer.

To exploit the DMA capabilities of its hardware, the device driver needs to be able to correctly set up the DMA transfer and synchronize with the hardware. Unfortunately, because of its hardware nature, DMA is very system-dependent. Each architecture has its own techniques to manage DMA transfers, and the programming interface is different for each. The kernel can't offer a unified interface, either, because a driver can't abstract too much from the underlaying hardware mechanisms. In this chapter, I describe how DMA works with ISA devices and PCI peripherals, as these are currently the most common peripheral interface architectures.

However, I won't go into much detail about ISA. The ISA implementation of DMA is unnecessarily complicated and not often used in modern peripherals. Nowadays, the ISA bus is used mainly for dumb peripheral interfaces, as hardware manufacturers who need DMA capability tend to use the PCI bus.

Overview of a DMA Data Transfer

Before introducing the programming details, let's review how a DMA transfer takes place, considering only input transfers to simplify the discussion.

Data transfer can be triggered in two ways: either the software asks for data (via a function such as *read*) or the hardware asynchronously pushes data to the system.

In the first case, the steps involved can be summarized as follows:

*   When a process calls *read*, the driver method allocates a DMA buffer and instructs the hardware to transfer its data. The process is put to sleep.

- The hardware writes data to the DMA buffer and raises an interrupt when it's done.

- The interrupt handler gets the input data, acknowledges the interrupt, and awakens the process, which is now able to read data.

Sometimes DMA is used asynchronously. This happens, for example, with those data acquisition devices that go on pushing data even if nobody is reading it. In this case, the driver should maintain a buffer so that a subsequent *read* call will return all the accumulated data to user space. The steps involved in this kind of transfer are slightly different:

- The hardware raises an interrupt to announce that new data has arrived.

- The interrupt handler allocates a buffer and tells the hardware where to transfer its data.

- The peripheral device writes the data to the buffer and raises another interrupt when it's done.

- The handler dispatches the new data, wakes any relevant process, and takes care of housekeeping.

The processing steps in both cases above emphasize that efficient DMA handling relies on interrupt reporting. While it is possible to implement DMA with a polling driver, it wouldn't make sense, as a polling driver would waste the performance benefits that DMA offers over the easier processor-driven I/O.

Another relevant item introduced here is the DMA buffer. To exploit Direct Memory Access, the device driver must be able to allocate a special buffer, suited to DMA. Note that most drivers allocate their buffer at initialization time and use it until shutdown—the word "allocate" in the lists above therefore means "get hold of the previously allocated buffer."

Allocating the DMA Buffer

The main problem with the DMA buffer is that when it is bigger than one page, it must occupy contiguous pages in physical memory, because the device transfers data using the ISA or PCI system bus, both of which carry physical addresses. It's interesting to note that this constraint doesn't apply to the Sbus (see "Sbus" in Chapter 15, *Overview of Peripheral Buses*), which uses virtual addresses on the peripheral bus.

Although DMA buffers can be allocated either at system boot or at run time, modules can only allocate their buffers at run time. Chapter 7 introduced these techniques: "Playing Dirty" talks about allocation at system boot while "The Real Story of kmalloc" and "get_free_page and Friends" describe allocation at run time. If you use *kmalloc* you must specify GFP_DMA priority, bitwise-ORed with either GFP_KERNEL or GFP_ATOMIC.

It is `GFP_DMA` that requires the memory space to be suitable for DMA transfers. The kernel guarantees that DMA-capable buffers have two features. First, the physical addresses must be consecutive when *get_free_page* returns more than one page (but this is always true, independent of `GFP_DMA`, because the kernel arranges free memory in clusters of consecutive pages). And second, when `GFP_DMA` is set, the kernel guarantees that only addresses lower than `MAX_DMA_ADDRESS` are returned. The macro `MAX_DMA_ADDRESS` is set to 16MB on the PC, to deal with the ISA constraints described later.

As far as PCI is concerned, there's no `MAX_DMA_ADDRESS` limit, and a PCI device driver should avoid setting `GFP_DMA` when allocating its buffers.

Do-it-yourself allocation

We have seen how *get_free_pages* (and therefore *kmalloc*) can't return more than 128KB (or, more generally, 32 pages) of consecutive memory space. But the request is prone to fail even when the allocated buffer is less than 128KB bytes, because system memory becomes fragmented over time.*

When the kernel cannot return the requested amount of memory, or when you need more than 128KB (a common requirement for PCI frame grabbers, for example), an alternative to returning `-ENOMEM` is to allocate memory at boot time or reserve the top of physical RAM for your buffer. I described allocation at boot time in "Playing Dirty" in Chapter 7, but it is not available to modules. Reserving the top of RAM is accomplished by passing a `mem=` argument to the kernel. For example, if you have 32 megs, the argument `mem=31M` keeps the kernel from using the top megabyte. Your module could later use the following code to gain access to such memory:

```
dmabuf = vremap( 0x1F00000 /* 31MB */, 0x100000 /* 1MB */);
```

My own implementation of allocating DMA buffers is available as an *allocator.c* module (with an accompanying header). You can find a version in the sample files within *src/misc-modules*; and the latest version is always available from my own ftp site, *ftp://ftp.systemy.it/pub/develop*. You could also look for the *bigphysarea* kernel patch, which is meant to accomplish the same goal as my allocator.

---

* The word *fragmentation* is usually applied to disks, to express the idea that files are not stored consecutively on the magnetic medium. The same concept applies to memory, where each virtual address space gets scattered throughout physical RAM, and it becomes difficult to retrieve consecutive free pages when a DMA buffer is requested.

Bus Addresses

When dealing with DMA, the device driver has to talk to hardware connected to the interface bus, which uses physical addresses, whereas program code uses virtual addresses.

As a matter of fact, the situation is slightly more complicated than that. DMA-based hardware uses *bus*, rather than *physical*, addresses. While ISA and PCI addresses are the same as physical addresses on the PC, this is not true for every platform. Sometimes the interface bus is connected through bridge circuitry that maps I/O addresses to different physical addresses.

The Linux kernel provides a portable solution by exporting the following functions, defined in `<asm/io.h>`:

```
unsigned long virt_to_bus(volatile void * address);
void * bus_to_virt(unsigned long address);
```

The *virt_to_bus* conversion must be used when the driver needs to send address information to an I/O device (such as an expansion board or the DMA controller), while *bus_to_virt* must be used when address information is received from hardware connected to the bus.

If you look at code that relies on the *allocator* engine described earlier, you'll find a sample use of these functions. The code relies also on *vremap* because of the context:

```
/* the allocator returns a physical address */
dev->dmabuffer = allocator_allocate_dma(kilobytes, GFP_KERNEL);
/* map it in the virtual address space */
dev->dmavbuffer = vremap(dev->dmabuffer, kilobytes*1024);

/* ... */

/* pass the address to the device */
writel(virt_to_bus(dev->dmavbuffer,
                    dev->registers + DEV_DMA_ADDRESS);
```

Although they are not related to DMA, the kernel exports two additional functions that perform address conversion and are worth knowing about:

```
unsigned long virt_to_phys(volatile void * address);
void * phys_to_virt(unsigned long address);
```

These functions convert virtual addresses to physical addresses; they are needed when the program code needs to talk to a Memory Management Unit (MMU) or other hardware connected to the address lines of the processor. On the PC platform the two pairs of functions accomplish the same task; keeping them as separate functions is nonetheless important, both for code clarity and portability.

DMA for ISA devices

The ISA bus allows for two kinds of DMA transfers: "native" DMA uses standard DMA-controller circuitry on the mainboard to drive the signal lines on the ISA bus; ISA-busmaster DMA, on the other hand, is completely controlled by the peripheral device. The latter type of DMA is rarely used and doesn't deserve discussion here because it is similar to DMA for PCI devices, at least from the driver's point of view. An example of an ISA busmaster is the 1542 SCSI controller, whose driver is *drivers/scsi/aha1542.c* in the kernel sources.

As far as "native" DMA is concerned, there are three entities involved in a DMA data transfer on the ISA bus:

The 8237 DMA controller (DMAC)
> The controller holds information about the DMA transfer, such as the direction, the memory address, and the size of the transfer. It also contains a counter that tracks the status of ongoing transfers. When the controller receives a DMA request signal, it gains control of the bus and drives the signal lines so the device can read or write its data.

The peripheral device
> The device must activate the DMA request signal when it's ready to transfer data. The actual transfer is managed by the DMAC; the hardware device sequentially reads or writes data onto the bus when the controller strobes the device. The device usually raises an interrupt when the transfer is over.

The device driver
> The driver has little to do: it provides the DMA controller with the direction, RAM address, and size of the transfer. It also talks to its peripheral to prepare it for transferring the data and responds to the interrupt when the DMA is over.

The original DMA controller used in the PC could manage four "channels." Each channel is associated with one set of DMA registers, so that four devices can store their DMA information in the controller at the same time. Newer PCs contain the equivalent of two DMAC devices:* the second controller (the master) is connected to the system processor, and the first (the slave) is connected to channel 0 of the second controller.†

The channels are numbered from 0 to 7; channel 4 is not available to ISA peripherals because it is used internally to "cascade" the slave controller onto the master. The available channels are thus 0–3 on the slave (the 8-bit channels) and 5–7 on

---

* These circuits are now part of the motherboard's chipset, but a few years ago they were two separate 8237 chips.

† The original PCs had only one controller; the second was added in 286-based platforms. However, the second controller is connected as the master because it handles 16-bit transfers, while the first transfers only 8 bits at a time and is there for backward-compatibility.

the master (the 16-bit channels*). The size of any DMA transfer, as stored in the controller, is a 16-bit number representing the number of bus cycles. The maximum transfer size is therefore 64KB for the slave controller and 128KB for the master.

Since the DMA controller is a system-wide resource, the kernel helps deal with it. It uses a DMA registry to provide a request and free mechanism for the DMA channels and a set of functions to configure channel information in the DMA controller.

Registering DMA usage

You should be used to kernel registries—we've already seen them for I/O ports and interrupt lines. The DMA channel registry is similar to the others. After `<asm/dma.h>` has been included, the following functions can be used to obtain and release ownership of a DMA channel:

```
int request_dma(unsigned int channel, const char *name);
void free_dma(unsigned int channel);
```

The **channel** argument is a number between 0 and 7 or, more precisely, a positive number less than **MAX_DMA_CHANNELS**. On the PC, **MAX_DMA_CHANNELS** is defined as 8, to match the hardware. The **name** argument is a string identifying the device. The specified name appears in the file */proc/dma*, which can be read by user programs.

The return value from *request_dma* is 0 for success and **-EINVAL** or **-EBUSY** if there was an error. The former means that the requested channel is out of range, and the latter means that another device is holding the channel.

I recommend that you take the same care with DMA channels as with I/O ports and interrupt lines; requesting the channel at *open* time is much better than requesting it from *init_module*. Delaying the request allows some sharing between drivers; for example, your sound card and your analog I/O interface can share the DMA channel, as long as they are not used at the same time.

I also suggest that you request the DMA channel *after* you've requested the interrupt line and that you release it *before* the interrupt. This is the conventional order for requesting the two resources; following the convention avoids possible deadlocks. Note that every device using DMA needs an IRQ line as well, otherwise it couldn't signal the completion of data transfer.

In a typical case, the code for *open* looks like the following, which refers to a hypothetical **dad** module (DMA Acquisition Device). The **dad** device as shown uses a fast interrupt handler without support for shared IRQ lines.

---

* Two bytes are transferred at each bus I/O cycle.

```
int dad_open (struct inode *inode, struct file *filp)
{
    struct dad_device *my_device;

    /* ... */
    if ( (error = request_irq(my_device.irq, dad_interrupt,
                                SA_INTERRUPT, "dad", NULL)) )
        return error; /* or implement blocking open */

    if ( (error = request_dma(my_device.dma, "dad")) ) {
        free_irq(my_device.irq, NULL);
        return error; /* or implement blocking open */
    }
    /* ... */
    return 0;
}
```

The *close* implementation that matches the *open* just shown looks like this:

```
void dad_close (struct inode *inode, struct file *filp)
{
    struct dad_device *my_device;

    /* ... */
    free_dma(my_device.dma);
    free_irq(my_device.irq, NULL);
    /* ... */
}
```

As far as */proc/dma* is concerned, here's how the file looks on a system with the sound card installed:

```
merlino% cat /proc/dma
 1: Sound Blaster8
 4: cascade
```

It's interesting to note that the default sound driver gets the DMA channel at system boot and never releases it. The *cascade* entry shown is a placeholder, indicating that channel 4 is not available to drivers, as explained previously.

Talking to the DMA controller

After registration, the main part of the driver's job consists of configuring the DMA controller for proper operation. This task is not trivial, but fortunately the kernel exports all the functions needed by the typical driver.

The driver needs to configure the DMA controller either when *read* or *write* is called, or when preparing for asynchronous transfers. This latter task is performed either at *open* time or in response to an *ioctl* command, depending on the driver and the policy it implements. The code shown here is the code that is typically called by the *read* or *write* device methods.

This subsection provides a quick overview of the internals of the DMA controller so you will understand the code introduced here. If you want to learn more, I'd urge you to read `<asm/dma.h>`
 and some hardware manuals describing the PC architecture. In particular, I don't deal with the issue of 8-bit vs. 16-bit data transfers. If you are writing device drivers for ISA device boards, you should find the relevant information in the hardware manuals for the devices.

The information that must be loaded into the controller is made up of three items: the RAM address, the number of atomic items that must be transferred (in bytes or words), and the direction of the transfer. To this end, the following functions are exported by `<asm/dma.h>`:

`void set_dma_mode(unsigned int channel, char mode);`
> Indicates whether the channel must read from the device (`DMA_MODE_READ`) or write to it (`DMA_MODE_WRITE`). A third mode exists, `DMA_MODE_CASCADE`, which is used to release control of the bus. Cascading is the way the first controller is connected to the top of the second, but it can also be used by true ISA bus-master devices. I won't discuss bus-mastering here.

`void set_dma_addr(unsigned int channel, unsigned int addr);`
> Assigns the address of the DMA buffer. The function stores the 24 least-significant bits of `addr` in the controller. The `addr` argument must be a *bus* address (see "Bus Addresses").

`void set_dma_count(unsigned int channel,`
`                   unsigned int count);`
> Assigns the number of bytes to transfer. The `count` argument represents bytes for 16-bit channels as well; in this case, the number *must* be even.

In addition to these functions, there are a number of housekeeping facilities that must be used when dealing with DMA devices:

`void disable_dma(unsigned int channel);`
> A DMA channel can be disabled within the controller. The channel should be disabled before the DMAC is configured, to prevent improper operation (the controller is programmed via 8-bit data transfers, and thus none of the previous functions is executed atomically).

`void enable_dma(unsigned int channel);`
> This function tells the controller that the DMA channel contains valid data.

`int get_dma_residue(unsigned int channel);`
> The driver sometimes needs to know if a DMA transfer has been completed. This function returns the number of bytes that are still to be transferred. The return value is 0 after a successful transfer and is unpredictable (but not 0) while the controller is working. The unpredictability reflects the fact that the residue is a 16-bit value, which is obtained by two 8-bit input operations.

`void clear_dma_ff(unsigned int channel)`
> The function clears the DMA flip-flop. The flip-flop is used to control access to 16-bit registers. The registers are accessed by two consecutive 8-bit operations, and the flip-flop is used to select the least-significant byte (when it is clear) or the most-significant byte (when it is set). The flip-flop automatically toggles when 8 bits have been transferred; the programmer must clear the flip-flop once before accessing the DMA registers.

Using these functions, a driver can implement a function like the following to prepare for a DMA transfer:

```
int dad_dma_prepare(int channel, int mode, unsigned int buf,
                    unsigned int count)
{
    unsigned long flags;

    save_flags(flags);
    cli();
    disable_dma(channel);
    clear_dma_ff(channel);
    set_dma_mode(channel, mode);
    set_dma_addr(channel, virt_to_bus(buf));
    set_dma_count(channel, count);
    enable_dma(channel);
    restore_flags(flags);

    return 0;
}
```

A function like the next one, then, is used to check for successful completion of DMA:

```
int dad_dma_isdone(int channel)
{
    return (get_dma_residue(channel) == 0);
}
```

The only thing that remains to be done is to configure the device board. This device-specific task usually consists of reading or writing a few I/O ports. Devices differ in significant ways. For example, some devices expect the programmer to tell the hardware how big the DMA buffer is, and sometimes the driver has to read a value that is hardwired into the device. For configuring the board, the hardware manual is your only friend.

DMA and PCI Devices

The PCI implementation of DMA is much easier to handle than the ISA version.

PCI supports multiple bus-masters, and DMA reduces to bus-mastering. The device that needs to read or write main memory simply requests control of the bus and then directly controls the electrical signals. The PCI implementation is more elaborate at the hardware level and easier to manage in the device driver.

Programming a DMA transfer with PCI consists of the following steps:

Allocating a buffer
> The DMA buffer must be physically contiguous in memory, but there's no 16MB addressability limit. A call to *get_free_pages* is sufficient; there's no need to specify `GFP_DMA` in the priority. If you really need it, you can resort to the (deprecated) aggressive allocation technique described ealier in "Allocating the DMA Buffer."

Talking to the device
> The expansion device must be told about the DMA buffer. This usually means writing the address and size of the buffer to a few device registers. Sometimes the DMA size is dictated by the hardware device, but the issue is device-dependent. The address passed to PCI devices must be a bus address.

As you can see, there's no general code used to program DMA for a PCI device. A typical implementation looks like the following one, but every device is different, and the amount of configurable information varies greatly between devices.

```
int dad_dma_prepare_pci(int mode, unsigned long buf,
                        unsigned int count)
{
    unsigned long addr = virt_to_bus(buf);


    writeb(DAD_CMD_DISABLEDMA, DAD_COMMAND);
    writeb(mode, DAD_COMMAND); /* either DAD_CMD_RD or DAD_CMD_WR */
    writel(addr, DAD_DMA_BUFFER);
    writel(count>>2, DAD_DMA_COUNT); /* each transfer is 32 bits */
    writeb(DAD_CMD_ENABLEDMA, DAD_COMMAND);

    return 0;
}
```

Quick Reference

This chapter introduced the following symbols related to memory handling. The list doesn't include the symbols introduced in the first section, as that section is a huge list in itself and those symbols are rarely useful to device drivers.

`#include <linux/mm.h>`
> All the functions and structures related to memory management are prototyped and defined in this header.

```
int remap_page_range(unsigned long virt_add,
                     unsigned long phys_add,
                     unsigned long size,
                     pgprot_t prot);
```
This function sits at the heart of *mmap*. It maps `size` bytes of physical addresses, starting at `phys_addr`, to the virtual address `virt_add`. The protection bits associated with the virtual space are specified in `prot`.

```
#include <asm/io.h>
unsigned long virt_to_bus(volatile void * address);
void * bus_to_virt(unsigned long address);
unsigned long virt_to_phys(volatile void * address);
void * phys_to_virt(unsigned long address);
```
These functions convert between virtual and physical addresses. *Bus* addresses must be used to talk to peripheral devices, *phys* addresses to talk to MMU circuits.

/proc/dma
This file contains a textual snapshot of the allocated channels in the DMA controllers. PCI-based DMA is not shown, as each board works independently, without the need to allocate a channel in the DMA controller.

```
#include <asm/dma.h>
```
This header defines or prototypes all the functions and macros related to DMA. It must be included to use any of the following symbols.

```
int request_dma(unsigned int channel, const char *name);
void free_dma(unsigned int channel);
```
These functions access the DMA registry. Registration must be performed before using ISA DMA channels.

```
void set_dma_mode(unsigned int channel, char mode);
void set_dma_addr(unsigned int channel, unsigned int addr);
void set_dma_count(unsigned int channel,
                   unsigned int count);
```
These functions are used to program DMA information in the DMA controller. `addr` is a bus address.

```
void disable_dma(unsigned int channel);
void enable_dma(unsigned int channel);
```
A DMA channel must be disabled during configuration. These functions change the status of the DMA channel.

```
int get_dma_residue(unsigned int channel);
```
If the driver needs to know how a DMA transfer is proceeding, it can call this function, which returns the number of data transfers that are yet to be completed. After successful completion of DMA, the function returns 0; the value is unpredictable while data is being transferred.

```
void clear_dma_ff(unsigned int channel)
```
The DMA flip-flop is used by the controller to transfer 16-bit values by means of two 8-bit operations. It must be cleared before sending any data to the controller.

CHAPTER FOURTEEN
NETWORK DRIVERS

We are now through discussing char and block drivers and are ready to move on to the fascinating world of networking. Network interfaces are the third standard class of Linux devices, and this chapter describes how they interact with the rest of the kernel.

A network interface doesn't exist in the filesystem the way char and block devices do. Instead, it deals with packet transmission and reception at the kernel level, without being bound to an open file in a process.

The role of a network interface within the system is similar to that of a mounted block device. A block device registers its features in the `blk_dev` array and other kernel structures, and it then "transmits" and "receives" blocks on request, by means of its *request_fn* function. Similarly, a network interface must register itself in specific data structures in order to be invoked when packets are exchanged with the outside world.

There are a few important differences between mounted disks and packet-delivery interfaces. To begin with, a disk exists as a node in the */dev* directory, while a network interface doesn't appear in the filesystem. But the most important difference between the two is that while the disk *is asked* to send a buffer towards the kernel, the net device *asks* to push incoming packets towards the kernel.

The network subsystem of the Linux kernel is designed to be completely protocol-independent. This applies to both networking protocols (IP vs. IPX or other protocols) and hardware protocols (Ethernet vs. Token-Ring, etc.). Interaction between a network driver and the kernel proper deals with one network packet at a time; this allows protocol issues to be hidden neatly from the driver and the physical transmission to be hidden from the protocol.

301

This chapter describes how the network interfaces fit in with the rest of the Linux kernel and shows a memory-based modularized network interface, which is called (you guessed it) *snull*. To simplify the discussion, the interface uses the Ethernet hardware protocol and transmits IP packets. The knowledge you acquire from examining *snull* can be readily applied to protocols other than IP, and switching from Ethernet to another hardware protocol requires only that you have some knowledge of the physical protocol being used.

Another limitation of the *snull* interface is that it won't compile with Linux 1.2. Once again, this choice is meant to keep code simple and to avoid adding boring conditionals to *snull*'s source. Nonetheless, this chapter outlines portability problems related to network drivers.

This chapter doesn't talk about IP numbering schemes, network protocols, or other general networking concepts. Such topics are not of concern to the driver writer, and it's impossible to offer a satisfactory overview of networking technology in less than a few hundred pages. The interested reader is urged to refer to other books describing networking issues.

Before discussing network devices, I'd like to remind you that the atomic data item of a network transaction is called an *octet* and is made up of eight data bits. I'll refer to it that way throughout the chapter. Network documentation doesn't ever use the term "byte."

How snull Is Designed

This section discusses the design concepts that led to the *snull* network interface. Although this information might appear to be of marginal use, failing to understand this driver might lead to problems while playing with the sample code.

The first, and most important, design decision is that the sample interfaces should remain independent of real hardware, just like most of the sample code used in this book. This constraint led to something that resembles the loopback interface.

Another feature of *snull* is that it is an IP interface. This is a consequence of the internal workings of the interface. Real interfaces don't depend on the protocol being transmitted, and this limitation of *snull* doesn't affect the sample code shown in this chapter, which is protocol-independent. The only effect of the IP constraint is on address assignment—we'll assign IP addresses to the sample interfaces.

Assigning IP Numbers

The *snull* module creates two interfaces. These interfaces are different from a simple loopback in that whatever you transmit through one of the interfaces loops back to the other one, not to itself. It looks like you have two external links, but actually your computer is replying to itself.

Unfortunately, this effect can't be accomplished through IP-number assignment alone, as the kernel wouldn't send out a packet through interface A that was directed to its own interface B. Instead, it would use the loopback channel without passing through *snull*. To be able to establish a communication through the *snull* interfaces, the source and destination addresses need to be modified during data transmission. In other words, packets sent through one of the interfaces should be received by the other, but the receiver of the outgoing packet shouldn't be recognized as the local host. The same applies to the source address of received packets.

To achieve this kind of "hidden loopback," the *snull* interface toggles the least significant bit of the third octet of both the source and destination addresses. The net effect is that packets sent to network A (connected to `sn0`, the first interface) appear on the `sn1` interface as packets belonging to network B.

To avoid dealing with too many numbers, let's assign symbolic names to the IP numbers involved:

- `snullnet0` is the class C network that is connected to the `sn0` interface. Similarly, `snullnet1` is the network connected to `sn1`. The addresses of these networks should differ only in the least significant bit of the third octet.

- `local0` is the IP address assigned to the `sn0` interface; it belongs to `snullnet0`. The address associated with `sn1` is `local1`. `local0` and `local1` must differ in both their third and fourth octets.

- `remote0` is a host in `snullnet0`, and its fourth octet is the same as that of `local1`. Any packet sent to `remote0` will reach `local1` after its class C address has been modified by the interface code. The host `remote1` belongs to `snullnet1` and its fourth octet is the same as that of `local0`.

The operation of the *snull* interfaces is depicted in Figure 14-1, where the host-name associated to each interface is printed near the interface name.

Here are possible values for the network numbers. Once you put these lines in */etc/networks*, you can call your networks by name. The values were chosen from the range of numbers reserved for private use.

```
snullnet0      192.168.0.0
snullnet1      192.168.1.0
```

The following are possible host numbers to put into */etc/hosts*:

```
192.168.0.88    local0
192.168.0.99    remote0
192.168.1.99    local1
192.168.1.88    remote1
```

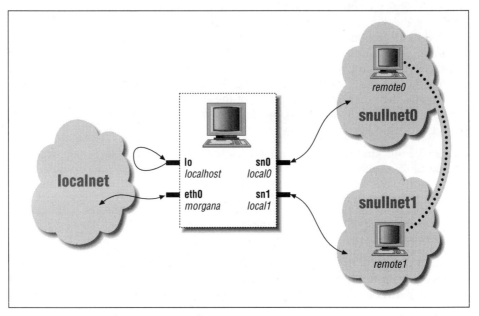

Figure 14-1: How a host sees its interfaces

Be careful, however, if your computer is already connected to a network. The numbers you choose might be real Internet or intranet numbers and assigning them to your interfaces will prevent communication with the real hosts. Also, although the numbers I showed above are not real Internet numbers, they could already be used by your private network if it lives behind a firewall.

Whatever numbers you choose, you can correctly set up the interfaces for operation by issuing the following commands:

```
morgana% ifconfig sn0 local0
morgana% route add -net snullnet0 sn0
morgana% ifconfig sn1 local1
morgana% route add -net snullnet1 sn1
```

At this point, the "remote" end of the interface can be reached. This screenshot shows how my host reaches `remote0` and `remote1` through *snull*.

```
morgana% ping -c 2 remote0
64 bytes from 192.168.0.99: icmp_seq=0 ttl=64 time=1.6 ms
64 bytes from 192.168.0.99: icmp_seq=1 ttl=64 time=0.9 ms
2 packets transmitted, 2 packets received, 0% packet loss

morgana% ping -c 2 remote1
64 bytes from 192.168.1.88: icmp_seq=0 ttl=64 time=1.8 ms
64 bytes from 192.168.1.88: icmp_seq=1 ttl=64 time=0.9 ms
2 packets transmitted, 2 packets received, 0% packet loss
```

Note that you won't be able to reach any other host belonging to the two networks because the packet is discarded by your computer after the address has
been modified and the packet has been received.

The Physical Transport of Packets

As far as data transport is concerned, the *snull* interfaces belong to the Ethernet
class. The sample code uses the Ethernet support provided by the kernel. This
saves us from having to implement some boring details related to network devices.

I'm using Ethernet because the vast majority of existing networks—at least the
segments that a workstation connects to—are based on Ethernet technology, be it
10base2, 10baseT, or 100baseT. Additionally, the kernel offers some generalized
support for Ethernet devices, and there's no reason to refuse to use it. The advantage of being an Ethernet device is so evident that even the *plip* interface (the
interface that uses the printer ports) declares itself as an Ethernet device.

The last advantage of using the Ethernet setup for *snull* is that you can run *tcpdump* on the interface. However, if you want to do that, you need to arrange for
the interfaces to be called `ethx` instead of `snx`. The *snull* module is already prepared to declare itself as `ethx`. If `eth=1` is specified on the *insmod* command
line, this behavior is selected. If you forget to request `eth` naming for *snull*, *tcpdump* refuses to dump the interface, returning an `unknown physical layer
type` error.

Another design decision for the *snull* interface is to deliver only the IP protocol
and to limit the discussion in this chapter to IP. Note, however, that the interface
driver *per se* doesn't depend on the low-level protocol being delivered; a network
driver doesn't peek at the packets it transfers. The issue of multi-protocol transmission is detailed later in "Non-Ethernet Headers."

As a matter of fact, the *snull* code does snoop in the packets, and even modifies
them, because it is required for the code to work. The code modifies the source,
destination, and checksum in the IP header of each packet without checking
whether it actually conveys IP information. This quick-and-dirty data modification
destroys non-IP packets. If you want to deliver other protocols through *snull*, you
must modify the module's source code. However, it's unlikely that this need will
arise, because everyone who owns a Linux box runs IP, while other protocols are
optional.

Connecting to the Kernel

We'll start looking at the structure of network drivers by dissecting the *snull*
source. Keeping the source code for several drivers handy might help you follow
the discussion. Personally, I suggest *loopback.c*, *plip.c*, and *3c509.c*, in order of

increasing complexity. Keeping *skeleton.c* handy might help as well, although this sample driver doesn't actually run. All these files live in *drivers/net*, within the kernel source tree.

Module Loading

When a driver module is loaded into a running kernel, it requests resources and offers facilities; there's nothing new in that. And there's also nothing new in the way resources are requested. The driver should probe for its device and its hardware location (I/O ports and IRQ line)—but without registering them—as described in "Installing an Interrupt Handler" in Chapter 9, *Interrupt Handling*. The way a network driver is registered by its *init_module* function is different from char and block drivers. Instead of asking for a major number, the driver inserts a data structure for each newly detected interface into a global list of network devices.

Each interface is described by a **struct device** item. The structures for **sn0** and **sn1**, the two *snull* interfaces, are declared like this:

```
char snull_names[16]; /* two eight-byte buffers */
struct device snull_devs[2] = {
    {
        snull_names,  /* name--set at load time */
        0, 0, 0, 0,   /* shmem addresses */
        0x000,        /* ioport */
        0,            /* irq line */
        0, 0, 0,      /* various flags: init to 0 */
        NULL,         /* next ptr */
        snull_init,   /* init function, fill other fields with NULLs */
    },
    {
        snull_names+8,/* name--set at load time */
        0, 0, 0, 0,   /* shmem addresses */
        0x000,        /* ioport */
        0,            /* irq line */
        0, 0, 0,      /* various flags: init to 0 */
        NULL,         /* next ptr */
        snull_init,   /* init function, fill other fields with NULLs */
    }
};
```

Note that the first field, the name, points to a static buffer, which will be filled at load time. In this way, the interface name can be chosen later, as explained below. In case you are tempted to use an explicit buffer in the structure, like **"01234567"**, I warn you that the code won't work reliably. This is because the compiler collapses duplicate strings; you end up with a single buffer and two pointers to it. Moreover, the compiler could even choose to store constant strings in read-only memory: not what you want.

I won't completely describe **struct device** until the next section, because it is a huge structure, and it won't help to have it dissected so early. I prefer to use the structure in the driver and explain each field as it is used.

The previous code fragment makes explicit use of the **name** and **init** fields of **struct device**. **name**, the first **struct device** field, holds the interface name (the string identifying the interface). The driver can hardwire a name for the interface or it can allow dynamic assignment, which works like this: if the first character of the name is either the null character or a blank, device registration uses the first available **eth***n* name. Thus, the first Ethernet interface is called **eth0**, and the others follow in numeric order. The *snull* interfaces are called **sn0** and **sn1** by default. However, if **eth=1** is specified at load time, *init_module* uses dynamic assignment. The default names are assigned by *init_module*:

```
if (!snull_eth) { /* call them "sn0" and "sn1" */
    memcpy(snull_devs[0].name, "sn0", 4);
    memcpy(snull_devs[1].name, "sn1", 4);
} else { /* use automatic assignment */
    snull_devs[0].name[0] = snull_devs[1].name[0] = ' ';
}
```

The **init** field is a function pointer. Whenever you register a device, the kernel asks the driver to initialize itself. Initialization means probing for the physical interface and filling the **device** structure with the proper values, as described in the following section. If initialization fails, the structure is not linked to the global list of network devices. This peculiar way of setting things up is most useful during system boot; every driver tries to register its own devices, but only devices that exist are linked to the list. This is different from char and block drivers, which are organized as a two-level tree, indexed by major and minor numbers.

Since the real initialization is performed elsewhere, *init_module* has little to do, and a single statement does it:

```
for (i=0; i<2; i++)
    if ( (result = register_netdev(snull_devs + i)) )
        printk("snull: error %i registering device \"%s\"\n",
               result, snull_devs[i].name);
    else device_present++;
```

Initializing Each Device

Probing for the device should be performed in the **init** function for the interface, which is often called the "probe" function. The single argument received by **init** is a pointer to the device being initialized, while its return value is either 0 or a negative error code, usually **-ENODEV**.

No real probing is performed for the *snull* interface, because it is not bound to any hardware. When you write a real driver for a real interface, the rules for probing char devices apply: check the I/O ports before using them and don't write to them during the probe. Also, you should avoid registering I/O ports and interrupt lines at this point. Real registration should be delayed until device open time; this is particularly important if interrupt lines are shared with other devices. You don't want your interface to be called every time another device triggers an IRQ line just to reply "no, it's not mine."

Actually, device probing at load time is discouraged for ISA devices because it is potentially dangerous—the ISA architecture is notoriously fault-intolerant. For this reason, most network drivers refuse to probe for their hardware when loaded as modules, and the kernel proper probes only for the first network interface, without performing any hardware tests after one network device has been detected. Usually `dev->base_addr`, the base I/O address for the current device, determines what to do:

- If `dev->base_addr` is a valid I/O address for the device, that value should be used without probing any other I/O locations. This happens, for example, when the value is assigned at load time.

- If `dev->base_addr` is zero, probing for the device is acceptable. A user can thus request a probe by setting the I/O address to zero at load time.

- Otherwise, no probing should be performed. The kernel uses a value of `0xffe0` to prevent probing, but any invalid address will do. It's up to the driver to silently reject invalid addresses in `base_addr`. A module should, by default, set the address to an impossible value in order to prevent undesired probing. Note that looking for PCI devices is always safe because it does not involve probing (see Chapter 15, *Overview of Peripheral Buses*).

As you may have noticed, this way of controlling probing using a load-time setting is the same technique that we used in *skull*.

On exit from `dev->init`, the `dev` structure should be filled with correct values. Filling the structure is the main role of the initialization routine. Fortunately, the kernel takes care of some Ethernet-wide defaults, through the function *ether_setup*, which fills `struct device`.

The core of *snull_init* is:

```
ether_setup(dev); /* assign some of the fields */

dev->open            = snull_open;
dev->stop            = snull_release;
dev->set_config      = snull_config;
dev->hard_start_xmit = snull_tx;
dev->do_ioctl        = snull_ioctl;
dev->get_stats       = snull_stats;
dev->rebuild_header  = snull_rebuild_header;
```

```
/* keep the default flags, just add NOARP */
dev->flags          |= IFF_NOARP;
```

The single unusual feature of the code is setting IFF_NOARP in the flags. This specifies that the interface cannot use ARP, the "Address Resolution Protocol." ARP is a low-level Ethernet protocol; every real Ethernet interface is ARP-aware and therefore won't set this flag. It's interesting to note that an interface can work without ARP. For example, the *plip* interface is an Ethernet-like interface without ARP support, like *snull.* This topic is discussed in detail later in "Address Resolution," while the device structure is dissected in the next section.

I'd like to introduce now another struct device field, priv. Its role is similar to that of the private_data pointer that we used for char drivers. Unlike fops->private_data, this priv pointer is allocated at initialization time, instead of open time, because the data item pointed to by priv includes the statistics for the interface. It's important that statistical information is always available, even when the interface is down, because users may want to display the statistics at any time by calling *ifconfig.* The memory wasted by allocating priv during initialization instead of on open is irrelevant because most probed interfaces are constantly up and running in the system. The *snull* module declares a snull_priv data structure to be used for priv. The structure includes struct enet_statistics, which is the standard place to hold interface statistics.

The following lines in *snull_init* allocate dev->priv:

```
dev->priv = kmalloc(sizeof(struct snull_priv), GFP_KERNEL);
if (dev->priv == NULL)
    return -ENOMEM;
memset(dev->priv, 0, sizeof(struct snull_priv));
```

Module Unloading

Nothing special happens when the module is unloaded. The *cleanup_module* function simply unregisters the interfaces from the list, after releasing memory associated with the private structure:

```
void cleanup_module(void)
{
    int i;

    for (i=0; i<2; i++) {
        kfree(snull_devs[i].priv);
        unregister_netdev(snull_devs + i);
    }
    return;
}
```

Modularized and Non-Modularized Drivers

While there is no notable difference between modularized and non-modularized char and block drivers, that's not the case for network drivers.

When a driver is distributed as part of the mainstream Linux kernel, it doesn't declare its own `device` structures; the structures declared in *drivers/net/Space.c* are used instead. *Space.c* declares a linked list of all the network devices, both driver-specific structures like `plip1` and general-purpose `eth` devices. Ethernet drivers don't care about their `device` structures at all, because they use the general-purpose structures. Such general `eth` device structures declare *ethif_probe* as their `init` function. A programmer inserting a new Ethernet interface in the mainstream kernel only needs to add a call to the driver's initialization function to *ethif_probe*. Authors of non-`eth` drivers, on the other hand, insert their `device` structures in *Space.c*. In both cases only the source file *Space.c* has to be modified if the driver must be linked to the kernel proper.

At system boot, the network initialization code loops through all the `device` structures and calls their probing (`dev->init`) functions by passing them a pointer to the device itself. If the probe function succeeds, *Space.c* initializes the `device` structure. This way of setting up drivers permits incremental assignment of devices to the names `eth0`, `eth1`, and so on, without changing the `name` field of each device.

When a modularized driver is loaded, on the other hand, it declares its own `device` structures (as we have seen in this chapter), even if the interface it controls is an Ethernet interface.

The curious reader can learn more about interface initialization by looking at *Space.c* and *net_init.c*. This introduction to driver setup is meant only to stress the importance of the `init` device method. If a driver module were to contain a prefilled device structure, it wouldn't fit the initialization technique of the mainstream kernel and wouldn't be forward-compatible if some new field were introduced in `struct device`.

The device Structure in Detail

The `device` structure is at the very core of network drivers and deserves a complete description. At a first reading, however, you can skip this section, because you don't need a thorough understanding of the structure to get started. This list describes all the fields, but more to provide a reference rather than to be memorized. The rest of this chapter briefly describes each field as soon as it is used in the sample code, so you don't need to keep referring back to this section.

struct device can be conceptually divided into two parts: "visible" and "invisible." The visible part of the structure is made up of the fields that are explicitly assigned in static device structures, like the two items appearing in *snull* and shown above. The remaining fields are used internally. Some are accessed by drivers (for example, the ones that are assigned at initialization time), while some shouldn't be touched. This section is complete up to kernel version 2.0.30.

The Visible Head

The first part of struct device is composed of the following fields, in this order:

char *name;

> The name of the device. If the first character of the name is zero (the NUL character) or a blank, *register_netdev* assigns it the name ethn, with a suitable numeric *n*.

unsigned long rmem_end;
unsigned long rmem_start;
unsigned long mem_end;
unsigned long mem_start;

> These fields hold the beginning and ending addresses of the shared memory used by the device. If the device has different receive and transmit memory, the mem fields are used for transmit memory and the rmem fields for receive memory. mem_start and mem_end can be specified on the kernel command line at system boot, and their value is retrieved by *ifconfig*. The rmem fields are never referenced outside of the driver itself. By convention, the end fields are set so that end - start is the amount of available on-board memory.

unsigned long base_addr;

> The I/O base address. This field, like the previous ones, is assigned during device probe. The *ifconfig* command can be used to display or modify the current value. The base_addr can be explicitly assigned on the kernel command line at system boot or at load time.

unsigned char irq;

> The assigned interrupt number. The value of dev->irq is printed by *ifconfig* when interfaces are listed. This value can usually be set at boot or load time and modified later using *ifconfig*.

unsigned char start;
unsigned char interrupt;

> These fields are binary flags. start is usually set at device open and cleared at close, and it is non-zero when the interface is ready to operate. interrupt is used to tell higher levels of code that an interrupt has arrived for the interface and is being serviced.

`unsigned long tbusy;`

> This field indicates "Transmission Busy." It should be non-zero whenever the driver can't accept a new packet for transmission (i.e., all of the output buffers are full). A `long` type is used instead of `char` because atomic bit operations are sometimes used to avoid race conditions. Note that in version 1.2 of the kernel, `tbusy` was indeed an 8-bit field, so a backward-portable driver should take care of this issue. Atomic bit operations were introduced in "Using Lock Variables," in Chapter 9.

`struct device *next;`

> Used to maintain the linked list; this field shouldn't be touched by the driver.

`int (*init)(struct device *dev);`

> The initialization function. This field is usually the last one explicitly listed in a `device` structure.

The Hidden Fields

The `device` structure includes several additional fields, which are usually assigned at device initialization. Some of these fields convey information about the interface, while some exist only for the benefit of the driver (i.e., they are not used by the kernel); there are also other fields, most notably the device methods, that are part of the kernel-driver interface.

I'm going to list the three groups separately, independent of the actual order of the fields, which is not significant.

Interface information

Most of the information about the interface is correctly set up by the function *ether_setup*. Ethernet cards can rely on this general-purpose function for most of these fields, but the `flags` and `dev_addr` fields are device-specific and must be explicitly assigned at initialization time.

Some non-Ethernet interfaces can use helper functions similar to *ether_setup*. *driver/net/net_init*.c exports *tr_setup* (token ring) and *fddi_setup*. If your device doesn't fall into one of these classes, you'll need to assign all of these fields by hand.

`unsigned short hard_header_len;`

> The "hardware header length" is the number of octets that lead the transmitted packet before the IP header, or other protocol information. The value of `hard_header_len` is 14 for Ethernet interfaces.

`unsigned short mtu;`

The "maximum transfer unit." This field is used by the network layer during packet transmission. Ethernet has an MTU of 1500 octets.

`__u32 tx_queue_len;`

The maximum number of frames that can be queued on the device's transmission queue. This value is set to 100 by *ether_setup*, but you can change it. For example, *plip* uses 10 to avoid wasting system memory (*plip* has a lower throughput than a real Ethernet interface).

`unsigned short type;`

The hardware type of the interface. The `type`field is used by ARP to determine what kind of hardware address the interface supports. Ethernet interfaces set this to ARPHRD_ETHER—*ether_setup* does this for you.

`unsigned char addr_len;`
`unsigned char broadcast[MAX_ADDR_LEN];`
`unsigned char dev_addr[MAX_ADDR_LEN];`

The Ethernet address length is six octets (we are referring to the hardware id of the interface board), and the broadcast address is made up of six `0xff` octets; *ether_setup* arranges for these values to be correct. The device address, on the other hand, must be read from the interface board in a device-specific way, and the driver should copy it to `dev_addr`. The hardware address is used to generate correct Ethernet headers before the packet is handed over to the driver for transmission. The *snull* device doesn't use a physical interface, and it invents its own hardware address.

`unsigned short family;`

The address family for the interface, most often `AF_INET`. The interface doesn't usually need to look at this field or assign a value to it.

`unsigned short pa_alen;`

Protocol Address Length; set to four octets for `AF_INET`. The interface doesn't need to modify this number.

`unsigned long pa_addr;`
`unsigned long pa_brdaddr;`
`unsigned long pa_mask;`

The three addresses that characterize the interface: the interface address, the broadcast address, and the net mask. These values are protocol-specific (i.e., they are "protocol addresses"); they are IP addresses if `dev->family` is AF_INET. These fields are assigned by *ifconfig* and are read-only for the driver.

`unsigned long pa_dstaddr;`
> Point-to-point interfaces like plip and *ppp* use this field to record the IP number of the other side of the link. Like the previous fields, this field is read-only.

`unsigned short flags;`
> Interface flags. The `flags` field includes the following bit values. The `IFF_` prefix stands for "InterFace Flags." Some flags are managed by the kernel, and some are set by the interface at initialization time to assert various capabilities (or inabilities) of the interface. The valid flags are:

> `IFF_UP`
>> The kernel turns this flag on when the interface is active. The flag is read-only for the driver.

> `IFF_BROADCAST`
>> This flag states that the broadcast address of the interface is valid. Ethernet boards support broadcast.

> `IFF_DEBUG`
>> Debug mode. This flag can be used to control the verbosity of your *printk* calls or for other debugging purposes. Although no official driver currently uses this flag, it can be set and reset by user programs via *ioctl*, and your driver can use it. The *misc-progs/netifdebug* program can be used to turn the flag on and off.

> `IFF_LOOPBACK`
>> This flag should be set only in the loopback interface. The kernel checks for `IFF_LOOPBACK` instead of hardwiring the `lo` name as a special interface.

> `IFF_POINTOPOINT`
>> The initialization function for point-to-point interfaces should set this flag. For example, *plip* sets it. The *ifconfig* utility can also set or clear the flag. When `IFF_POINTOPOINT` is set, `dev->pa_dstaddr` should refer to the other end of the link.

> `IFF_NOARP`
>> Conventional network interfaces can convey ARP packets. If the interface can't perform ARP, it must set this flag. For example, point-to-point interfaces don't need to run ARP, which would only convey additional traffic without retrieving useful information. *snull* runs without ARP capabilities, so it sets the flag.

> `IFF_PROMISC`
>> This flag is set to get promiscuous operation. By default, Ethernet interfaces use a hardware filter to ensure that they receive only broadcast packets and packets directed to that interface's hardware address. Packet sniffers like *tcpdump* set promiscuous mode on the interface in order to retrieve all packets that travel on the interface's transmission medium.

IFF_MULTICAST

> This flag is set by interfaces that are capable of multicast transmission. *ether_setup* sets IFF_MULTICAST by default, so if your driver does not support multicasting, it must clear the flag at initialization time.

IFF_ALLMULTI

> This flag tells the interface to receive all multicast packets. The kernel sets it when the host performs multicast routing, only if IFF_MULTICAST is set. IFF_ALLMULTI is read-only for the interface. Both IFF_MULTICAST and IFF_ALLMULTI were defined as far back as 1.2, but were unused at the time. We'll see them used later in the section "Multicasting."

IFF_MASTER
IFF_SLAVE

> These flags are used by the load equalization code. The interface driver doesn't need to know about them.

IFF_NOTRAILERS
IFF_RUNNING

> These flags are unused in Linux, but exist for BSD compatibility.

When a program changes IFF_UP, the *open* or *close* device method is called. When IFF_UP or any other flag is modified, the *set_multicast_list* method is invoked. If the driver needs to perform some action because of a modification in the flags, it must take that action in *set_multicast_list*. For example, when IFF_PROMIS is set or reset, the on-board hardware filter must be notified. The responsibilities of this device method are outlined later in the section "Multicasting."

The device methods

As happens with the char and block drivers, each network device declares the functions that act on it. Operations that can be performed on network interfaces are listed below. Some of the operations can be left NULL and some are usually untouched because *ether_setup* assigns suitable methods to them.

Device methods for a network interface can be divided into two groups: fundamental and optional. Fundamental methods include those that are needed to be able to use the interface; optional methods implement more advanced functionalities that are not strictly required. The following are the fundamental methods:

int (*open)(struct device *dev);

> Open the interface. The interface is opened whenever *ifconfig* activates it. The *open* method should register any system resource it needs (I/O ports, IRQ, DMA, etc.), turn on the hardware, and increment the module usage count.

```
int (*stop)(struct device *dev);
```
Stop the interface. The interface is stopped when it is brought down; operations performed at open time should be reversed.

```
int (*hard_start_xmit) (struct sk_buff *skb,
                           struct device *dev);
```
Hardware Start Transmission. This method requests the transmission of a packet. The packet is contained in a socket buffer (sk_buff) structure. Socket buffers are introduced below.

```
int (*rebuild_header) (void *buf, struct device *dev,
                  unsigned long raddr,
                  struct sk_buff *skb);
```
This function is used to rebuild the hardware header before a packet is transmitted. The default function used by Ethernet devices uses ARP to fill the packet with missing information. The *snull* driver implements its own method because ARP doesn't run on **sn** interfaces. (ARP is explained later in this chapter.) The arguments to *rebuild_header* are the pointer to the hardware header, the device, the "router address" (the packet's initial destination), and the buffer being transmitted.

```
int (*hard_header) (struct sk_buff *skb, struct device *dev,
                  unsigned short type, void *daddr,
                  void *saddr, unsigned len);
```
Hardware Header. This function builds the hardware header from the source and destination hardware addresses that were previously retrieved; its job is to organize the information passed to it as arguments. *eth_header* is the default function for Ethernet-like interfaces, and *ether_setup* assigns this field accordingly. The order of the arguments shown applies to kernel 2.0 and later, while it was different in 1.2. This change is transparent to an Ethernet driver because it inherits the *eth_header* implementation; other drivers might want to deal with the difference to stay backward-compatible with 1.2.

```
struct enet_statistics* (*get_stats)(struct device *dev);
```
Whenever an application needs to get statistics for the interface, this method is called. This happens, for example, when *ifconfig* or *netstat –i* is run. A sample implementation for *snull* is introduced later, in "Statistical Information."

```
int (*set_config)(struct device *dev, struct ifmap *map);
```
Change the interface configuration. This method is the entry point for configuring the driver. The I/O address for the device and its interrupt number can be changed at run time using *set_config*. This capability can be used by the system administrator if the interface cannot be probed for. This method is described later in "Run-Time Configuration."

The remaining device operations are those that I consider optional. The arguments passed to some of them changed several times during the transition from Linux 1.2 to Linux 2.0. If you are writing a driver that you want to work with both versions of the kernel, you might want to implement these operations only for versions starting with 2.0.

```
int (*do_ioctl) (struct device *dev, struct ifreq *ifr,
                 int cmd);
```
Perform interface-specific *ioctl* commands. Implementation of those commands is described later in "Custom ioctl Commands." The prototype shown works with all the kernels from 1.2 onward. The corresponding field in `struct device` can be left as `NULL` if the interface doesn't need any interface-specific commands.

```
void (*set_multicast_list)(struct device *dev);
```
This method is called when the multicast list for the device changes and when the flags change. The argument passing was different in version 1.2. See "Multicasting" for further details and a sample implementation.

```
int (*set_mac_address)(struct device *dev, void *addr);
```
This function can be implemented if the interface supports the ability to change its *hardware* address. Most interfaces either don't support this ability or use the default *eth_mac_addr* implementation. This prototype was different in version 1.2 as well.

```
#define HAVE_HEADER_CACHE
void (*header_cache_bind) (struct hh_cache **hhp,
                           struct device *dev,
                           unsigned short htype,
                           __u32 daddr);
void (*header_cache_update) (struct hh_cache *hh,
                             struct device *dev,
                             unsigned char *  haddr);
```
These functions and the macro were missing in Linux 1.2. Ethernet drivers don't need to concern themselves with `header_cache` issues because *eth_setup* arranges for default methods to be used.

```
#define HAVE_CHANGE_MTU
int (*change_mtu)(struct device *dev, int new_mtu);
```
This function is in charge of taking action if there is a change in the MTU (Maximum Transfer Unit) for the interface. Both the function and the macro were missing in Linux 1.2. If the driver needs to do anything particular when the MTU is changed, it should declare its own function, otherwise the default will do the right thing. *snull* has a template for the function if you are interested.

Utility fields

The remaining `struct device` data fields are used by the interface to hold useful status information. Some of the fields are used by *ifconfig* and *netstat* to provide the user with information about the current configuration. An interface should thus assign values to these fields.

`unsigned long trans_start;`
`unsigned long last_rx;`
> Both of these fields are meant to hold a value in jiffies. They are currently unused, but the kernel might use these timing hints in the future. The driver is responsible for updating these values when transmission begins and when a packet is received. The `trans_start` field can also be used by the driver to detect a lockup. The driver can check for timeouts against `trans_start` while waiting a "transmission done" interrupt.

`void *priv;`
> The equivalent of `filp->private_data`. The driver owns this pointer and can use it at will. Usually the private data structure includes a `struct enet_statistics` item. The field was used earlier in "Initializing Each Device."

`unsigned char if_port;`
> This field is used to record which hardware port is being used by the interface (e.g., BNC, AUI, TP). The `if_port` field is for the use of the driver, and any numerical value can be assigned at will.

`unsigned char dma;`
> The DMA channel being used by the device. This field is used by the `SIOCGIFMAP` *ioctl* command.

`struct dev_mc_list *mc_list;`
`int mc_count;`
> These two fields are used in handling multicast transmission. `mc_count` is the count of items in `mc_list`. See "Multicasting" for further details.

There are other fields in `struct device`, but they are not used by the driver.

Opening and Closing

Our driver can probe for the interface at module load time or at kernel boot. The next step is to assign an address to the interface so the driver can exchange data through it. Opening and closing an interface is performed by the *ifconfig* command.

When *ifconfig* is used to assign an address to the interface, it performs two tasks. First, it assigns the address by means of `ioctl(SIOCSIFADDR)` (Socket I/O Control Set InterFace ADDRess). Then it sets the `IFF_UP` bit in `dev->flag` by means of `ioctl(SIOCSIFFLAGS)` (Socket I/O Control Set InterFace FLAGS) to turn the interface on.

As far as the device is concerned, `ioctl(SIOCSIFADDR)` sets `dev->pa_addr`, `dev->family`, `dev->pa_mask`, and `dev->pa_brdaddr`, but no driver function is invoked—the task is device-independent, and the kernel performs it. The latter command (`ioctl(SIOCSIFFLAGS)`), though, calls the *open* method for the device.

Similarly, when the interface is shut down, *ifconfig* uses `ioctl(SIOCSIFFLAGS)` to clear `IFF_UP`, and the *stop* method is called.

Both device methods return 0 in case of success and the usual negative value in case of error.

As far as the actual code is concerned, the driver has to perform the same tasks as the char and block drivers do. *open* requests any system resources it needs and tells the interface to come up; *stop* shuts down the interface and releases system resources.

One last step is needed if the driver isn't going to use shared interrupts (for example, if it is to be compatible with older kernels). The kernel exports an `irq2dev_map` array, which is addressed by the IRQ number and holds void pointers; the driver might want to use that array to map the interrupt number to a pointer to **struct device**. This is the only way to support more than one interface from within a single driver without using the `dev_id` argument of the interrupt handler.

Additionally, the hardware address needs to be copied from the board to `dev->dev_addr` before the interface can communicate with the outside world. The hardware address can be assigned at probe time or at open time at the driver's will. The *snull* software interface assigns it from within *open*; it just fakes a hardware number using two ASCII strings. The first byte of the address is the null character (as explained later in "Address Resolution").

The resulting *open* code looks like the following:

```
int snull_open(struct device *dev)
{
    int i;

    /* request_region(), request_irq(), ....  (like fops->open) */

#if 0
    /*
     * We have no irq line, otherwise this assignment can be used to
     * grab a non-shared interrupt. To share interrupt lines use
```

```
     * the dev_id argument of request_irq. Seel snull_interrupt below.
     */
    irq2dev_map[dev->irq] = dev;
#endif

    /*
     * Assign the hardware address of the board: use "\0SNULx", where
     * x is 0 or 1. The first byte is '\0': a safe choice with regard
     * to multicast.
     */
    for (i=0; i < ETH_ALEN; i++)
        dev->dev_addr[i] = "\0SNUL0"[i];
    dev->dev_addr[ETH_ALEN-1] += (dev - snull_devs); /* the number */

    dev->start = 1;
    dev->tbusy = 0;
    MOD_INC_USE_COUNT;
    return 0;
}
```

As you can see, a few fields are modified in the **device** structure. **start** states
that the interface is ready, and **tbusy** asserts that the transmitter is not busy (i.e.,
the kernel can send out a packet).

The *stop* method just reverses the operations of *open*, and for this reason, the function implementing *stop* is usually called *close*.

```
int snull_release(struct device *dev)
{
    /* release ports, irq and such--like fops->close */

    dev->start = 0;
    dev->tbusy = 1; /* can't transmit any more */
    MOD_DEC_USE_COUNT;
    /* if irq2dev_map was used, zero the entry here */
    return 0;
}
```

Packet Transmission

The most important tasks performed by network interfaces are data transmission
and reception. I'll start with transmission because it is slightly easier to understand.

Whenever the kernel needs to transmit a data packet, it calls the
hard_start_transmit method to put the data on an outgoing queue. Each packet
handled by the kernel is contained in a socket buffer structure (**struct
sk_buff**), whose definition is found in <linux/skbuff.h>. The structure gets
its name from the Unix abstraction used to represent a network connection, the
socket. Even if the interface has nothing to do with sockets, each network packet

belongs to a socket in the higher network layers, and the input/output buffers of any socket are lists of **struct sk_buff** structures. The same **sk_buff** structure is used to host network data throughout all the Linux network subsystems, but a socket buffer is just a packet as far as the interface is concerned.

A pointer to **sk_buff** is usually called **skb**, and I'm going to follow this practice both in the sample code and in the text.

The socket buffer is a complex structure, and the kernel offers a number of functions to act on it. The functions are described later in "The Socket Buffers"—for now a few basic facts about **sk_buff** are enough for us to write a working driver. Also, I prefer to show how things work before delving into boring details.

The socket buffer passed to *hard_start_xmit* contains the physical packet, complete with the transmission-level headers. The interface doesn't need to modify the data being transmitted. **skb->data** points to the packet being transmitted, and **skb->len** is its length, in octets.

The *snull* packet transmission code is listed below; the physical transmission machinery has been isolated in another function because every interface driver must implement it according to the specific hardware being driven.

```
int snull_tx(struct sk_buff *skb, struct device *dev)
{
    int len, retval=0;
    char *data;

    if (dev->tbusy) {               /* shouldn't happen */
        retval = -EBUSY;
        goto tx_done;
    }
    if (skb == NULL) {
        PDEBUG("tint for %p\n",dev);
        dev_tint(dev);              /* we are ready to transmit */
        return 0;
    }
    dev->tbusy = 1;                 /* transmission is busy */

    len = ETH_ZLEN < skb->len ? skb->len : ETH_ZLEN;  /* minimum len */
    data = skb->data;
    dev->trans_start = jiffies;   /* save the timestamp */

    /* actual deliver of data is device-specific, and not shown here */
    snull_hw_tx(data, len, dev);

  tx_done:
    dev_kfree_skb(skb, FREE_WRITE);  /* release it */

    return retval;                   /* zero == done; nonzero == fail */
}
```

The transmission function thus performs only some sanity checks on the packet and transmits the data through the hardware-related function. `dev->tbusy` is cleared when an interrupt signals a "transmission done" condition.

Packet Reception

Receiving data from the network is trickier than transmitting it because an `sk_buff` must be allocated and handed off to the upper layers from within an interrupt handler—the best way to receive a packet is through an interrupt, unless the interface is a purely software one like *snull* or the loopback interface. While it is possible to write polling drivers, and a few exist in the official kernel as well, interrupt-driven operation is much better, both in data throughput and in computational demands. Since the vast majority of network interfaces is interrupt-driven, I won't talk about the polling implementation, which just exploits kernel timers.

The implementation of *snull* separates the hardware details from the device-independent housekeeping. The function *snull_rx* is thus called after the hardware has received the packet and it is already in the computer's memory. *snull_rx* therefore receives a pointer to the data and the length of the packet. The function's sole responsiblity is to send the packet and some additional information to the upper layers of networking code. This code is independent of the way the data pointer and length are obtained.

```
void snull_rx(struct device *dev, int len, unsigned char *buf)
{
    struct sk_buff *skb;
    struct snull_priv *privp = (struct snull_priv *)dev->priv;
    /*
     * The packet has been retrieved from the transmission
     * medium. Build an skb around it, so upper layers can handle it
     */

    skb = dev_alloc_skb(len+2);
    if (!skb) {
        printk("snull rx: low on mem\n");
        return;
    }
    memcpy(skb_put(skb, len), buf, len);

    /* Write metadata, and then pass to the receive level */
    skb->dev = dev;
    skb->protocol = eth_type_trans(skb, dev);
    skb->ip_summed = CHECKSUM_UNNECESSARY; /* don't check it */
    privp->stats.rx_packets++;
    netif_rx(skb);
    return;
}
```

The function is sufficiently general to act as a template for any network driver, but some explanation is necessary before you can reuse this code fragment with confidence.

Note that the buffer allocation function wants to know the data length. This avoids wasting memory when calling *kmalloc*. The allocation function is called with atomic priority by *dev_alloc_skb*, which can therefore be used safely at interrupt time. The kernel offers other interfaces to socket-buffer allocation, but they are not worth introducing here; socket buffers are explained in detail in "The Socket Buffers," later in this chapter.

Once there is a valid `skb` pointer, the packet data is copied into the buffer by calling *memcpy*; the *skb_put* function updates the end-of-data pointer in the buffer and returns a pointer to the newly created space.

Unfortunately, there isn't enough information in the packet's headers to correctly handle the network layer—the `dev` and `protocol` fields must be assigned before the buffer is passed upstairs. Then we need to specify how checksumming is to be performed on the packet (*snull* does not perform any checksums). The possible policies for `skb->ip_summed` are:

CHECKSUM_HW

>   The board performs checksums in hardware. An example of a hardware checksum is the Sparc HME interface.

CHECKSUM_NONE

>   Checksums are done completely in software. This is the default in newly allocated buffers.

CHECKSUM_UNNECESSARY

>   Don't do any checksums. This is the policy in *snull* and in the loopback interface.

The checksumming options and `ip_summed` are missing from the 1.2 kernel versions.

Finally, the driver updates its statistics counter to record that a packet has been received. The statistics structure is made up of several fields; the most important are `rx_packets` and `tx_packets`, which contain the number of packets received and transmitted. All the fields are thoroughly described later in "Statistical Information."

The last step in packet reception is performed by *netif_rx*, which hands off the socket buffer to the upper layers.

Interrupt-Driven Operation

Most hardware interfaces are controlled by means of an interrupt handler. The interface interrupts the processor to signal one of two possible events: a new packet has arrived or transmission of an outgoing packet is complete. This generalization doesn't always apply, but it does account for all the problems related to asynchronous packet transmission. PLIP and PPP are examples of interfaces that don't fit this generalization. They deal with the same events, but the low-level interrupt handling is slightly different.

The usual interrupt routine can tell the difference between a new-packet-arrived interrupt and a done-transmitting notification by checking a status register found on the physical device. The *snull* interface works similarly, but its status word lives in dev->priv. The interrupt handler for a network interface looks like this:

```
void snull_interrupt(int irq, void *dev_id, struct pt_regs *regs)
{
    int statusword;
    struct snull_priv *privptr;
    /*
     * As usual, check the "device" pointer for shared handlers.
     * Then assign "struct device *dev"
     */
#if 0
    /* This is the way to do things for non-shared handlers */
    struct device *dev = (struct device *)(irq2dev_map[irq]);
#else
    /* Otherwise use this SA_SHIRQ-safe approach */
    struct device *dev = (struct device *)dev_id;
    /* ... and check with hw if it's really ours */
#endif

    if (!dev /*paranoid*/ ) return;
    dev->interrupt = 1; /* lock */
    /* retrieve statusword: real netdevices use inb() or inw() */
    privptr = (struct snull_priv *)(dev->priv);
    statusword = privptr->status;
    if (statusword & SNULL_RX_INTR) {
        /* send it to snull_rx for handling */
        snull_rx(dev, privptr->packetlen, privptr->packetdata);
    }
    if (statusword & SNULL_TX_INTR) {
        /* a transmission is over: tell we are no longer busy */
        privptr->stats.tx_packets++;
        dev->tbusy = 0;
        mark_bh(NET_BH);
    }
    dev->interrupt = 0; /* release lock */
    return;
}
```

The handler's first task is to retrieve a pointer to the correct `struct device`. You can either use `irq2dev_map[]` (assuming you assigned a value to it at open time) or the `dev_id` pointer received as an argument. If you want the driver to run with kernels older than 1.3.70, you must use `irq2dev_map[]` because `dev_id` is not available in earlier versions.

The interesting part of this handler deals with the "transmission done" situation. The interface acknowledges that transmission is over by clearing `dev->tbusy` and marks the network bottom-half routine. When *net_bh* is actually run, it tries to send any pending packet.

Packet reception, on the other hand, doesn't need any special interrupt handling. Calling *snull_rx* is all that's required.

In practice, when *netif_rx* is called by the receiving function, the only real operation it performs is marking *net_bh*. In other words, the kernel does all the network-related work in a bottom-half handler. Therefore, a network driver should always declare its interrupt handler as slow because the bottom half will be executed sooner (see "The Design of Bottom Halves" in Chapter 9).

The Socket Buffers

We've now discussed most of the issues related to network interfaces. The next few sections explain in more detail how the `sk_buff` structure is designed. They introduce both the main fields of the structure and the functions used to act on the socket buffers.

Although there is no strict need to understand the internals of `sk_buff`, the ability to look at its contents can be helpful when you are tracking down problems and when you are trying to optimize the code. For example, if you look in *loopback.c*, you'll find an optimization based on knowledge of the `sk_buff` internals.

I'm not going to describe the whole structure here, just the fields that might be used from within a driver. If you want to see more, you can look at `<linux/skbuff.h>`, where the structure is defined and the functions are prototyped. Additional details about how the fields and functions are used can be easily retrieved by grepping in the kernel sources.

The Important Fields

For our purposes, the important fields in the structure are those a driver writer might need. They are listed here in no particular order.

`struct device *dev;`
> The device receiving or sending this buffer.

```
__u32 saddr;
__u32 daddr;
__u32 raddr;
```
Source address, destination address, and router address, used by the IP proto-col. `raddr` represents the first hop the packet must take to reach its destina-tion. These fields are set before the packet is transmitted and need not be assigned when it is received. An outgoing packet reaching the *hard_start_xmit* method already has a suitable hardware header set up that reflects the "first hop" information.

```
unsigned char *head;
unsigned char *data;
unsigned char *tail;
unsigned char *end;
```
These pointers are used to address the data in the packet. `head` points to the beginning of the allocated space, `data` is the beginning of the valid octets (and is usually slightly greater than `head`), `tail` is the end of the valid octets, and `end` points to the maximum address `tail` can reach. Another way to look at it is that the *available* buffer space is `skb->end - skb->head`, and the *currently used* data space is `skb->tail - skb->data`. This clever way to deal with memory areas was implemented only during 1.3 development. This is the main reason why *snull* hasn't been ported to compile with Linux 1.2.

```
unsigned long len;
```
The length of the data itself (`skb->tail - skb->head`).

```
unsigned char ip_summed;
```
This field is set by the driver on incoming packets and is used in TCP/UDP checksumming. It was described earlier in "Packet Reception."

```
unsigned char pkt_type;
```
This field is used internally for the delivery of incoming packets. The driver is responsible for setting it to `PACKET_HOST` (this packet is for me), `PACKET_BROADCAST`, `PACKET_MULTICAST`, or `PACKET_OTHERHOST` (no, this packet is not for me). Ethernet drivers don't modify `pkt_type` explicitly because *eth_type_trans* does it for them.

```
union { unsigned char *raw; [...] } mac;
```
Like `pkt_type`, the field is used to deal with incoming packets and must be set at packet reception. The function *eth_type_trans* takes care of it for Ether-net drivers. Non-Ethernet drivers should set the `skb->mac.raw` pointer as shown later in "Non-Ethernet Headers."

The remaining fields in the structure are not particularly interesting. They are used to maintain lists of buffers, to account for memory belonging to the socket that owns the buffer, and so on.

Functions Acting on Socket Buffers

Network devices that use a `sock_buff` act on the structure by means of the official interface functions. There are many functions that operate on socket buffers; here are the most interesting ones:

`struct sk_buff *alloc_skb(unsigned int len, int priority);`
`struct sk_buff *dev_alloc_skb(unsigned int len);`

> Allocate a buffer. The *alloc_skb* function allocates a buffer and initializes both `skb->data` and `skb->tail` to `skb->head`. The *dev_alloc_skb* function (which is missing from Linux 1.2) is a shortcut that calls *alloc_skb* with `GFP_ATOMIC` priority and reserves 16 bytes between `skb->head` and `skb->data`. This data space can be used to "push" hardware headers.

`void kfree_skb(struct sk_buff *skb, int rw);`
`void dev_kfree_skb(struct sk_buff *skb, int rw);`

> Free a buffer. The *kfree_skb* call is used internally by the kernel. A driver should use *dev_kfree_skb*, which correctly handles buffer locking, in case the socket owning the buffer needs to use it again. In both functions, the `rw` argument is either `FREE_READ` or `FREE_WRITE`. The value is used to keep track of memory for the socket. Outgoing buffers should be released with `FREE_WRITE` and incoming buffers with `FREE_READ`.

`unsigned char *skb_put(struct sk_buff *skb, int len);`

> This inline function updates the `tail` and `len` fields of the `sk_buff` structure; it is used to add data to the end of the buffer. The function's return value is the previous value of `skb->tail` (in other words, it points to the data space just created). Some drivers use the return value by invoking `ins(ioaddr, skb_put(...))` or `memcpy(skb_put(...), data, len)`. This function and the following ones are not available when building modules for Linux 1.2.

`unsigned char *skb_push(struct sk_buff *skb, int len);`

> This function decrements `skb->data` and increments `skb->len`. It is similar to `skb_put`, except that data is added to the beginning of the packet instead of the end. The return value points to the data space just created.

`int skb_tailroom(struct sk_buff *skb);`

> This function returns the amount of space available for putting data in the buffer. If a driver puts more data into the buffer than it can hold, the system panics. Although you might object that a *printk* would be sufficient to tag the error, memory corruption is so harmful to the system that the developers decided to take definitive action. In practice, you shouldn't need to check the available space if the buffer has been correctly allocated. Since drivers usually get the packet size before allocating a buffer, only a severely broken driver will put too much data in the buffer, and a panic might be seen as due punishment.

`int skb_headroom(struct sk_buff *skb);`
> Returns the amount of space available in front of `data`, i.e., how many octets one can "push" to the buffer.

`void skb_reserve(struct sk_buff *skb, int len);`
> This function increments both `data` and `tail`. The function can be used to reserve headroom before filling the buffer. Most Ethernet interfaces reserve two bytes in front of the packet; thus the IP header is aligned on a 16-byte boundary, after a 14-byte Ethernet header. *snull* does it as well, although the instruction was not shown in "Packet Reception" to avoid introducing extra concepts at that point.

`unsigned char * skb_pull(struct sk_buff *skb, int len);`
> Remove data from the head of the packet. The driver won't need to use this function, but it is included here for completeness. It decrements `skb->len` and increments `skb->data`; this is how the Ethernet header is stripped from the beginning of incoming packets.

The kernel defines several other functions that act on socket buffers, but they are meant to be used in higher layers of networking code, and the driver won't need them.

Address Resolution

One of the most compelling issues of Ethernet communication is the association between hardware addresses (the interface's unique id) and IP numbers. Most protocols have a similar problem, but I'm going to pinpoint only the Ethernet-like case here. I'll try to offer a complete description of the issue, so I'm going to show three situations: ARP, Ethernet headers without ARP (like *plip*), and non-Ethernet headers.

Using ARP with Ethernet

The usual way to deal with address resolution is by using ARP, the Address Resolution Protocol. Fortunately, ARP is managed by the kernel, and an Ethernet interface doesn't need to do anything special to support ARP. As long as `dev->addr` and `dev->addr_len` are correctly assigned at open time, the driver doesn't need to worry about resolving IP numbers to physical addresses; *ether_setup* assigns the correct device methods to `dev->hard_header` and `dev->rebuild_header`.

When a packet is built, the Ethernet header is laid out by `dev->hard_header`, and it is filled later by `dev->rebuild_header`, which uses the ARP protocol to map unknown IP numbers to addresses. The driver writer doesn't need to know the details of this process to build a working driver.

Overriding ARP

Simple point-to-point network interfaces like *plip* might benefit from using Ethernet headers, while avoiding the overhead of sending ARP packets back and forth. The sample code in *snull* falls into this class of network devices. *snull* cannot use ARP because the driver changes IP addresses in packets being transmitted, and ARP packets exchange IP addresses as well.

If your device wants to use the usual hardware header without running ARP, you need to override the default **dev->rebuild_header** method. This is how *snull* implements it, as a simple function made up of three statements:

```
int snull_rebuild_header(void *buff, struct device *dev,
                         unsigned long dst, struct sk_buff *skb)
{
    struct ethhdr *eth = (struct ethhdr *)buff;

    memcpy(eth->h_source, dev->dev_addr, dev->addr_len);
    memcpy(eth->h_dest, dev->dev_addr, dev->addr_len);
    eth->h_dest[ETH_ALEN-1]    ^= 0x01;   /* dest is us xor 1 */
    return 0;
}
```

As a matter of fact, there's no actual need to specify the contents of **eth->h_source** and **eth->h_dest**, because the values are used only for the physical delivery of the packet, and a point-to-point link is guaranteed to deliver the packet to its destination independent of the hardware addresses. The reason *snull* rebuilds the headers is to show you how a *rebuild* function should be implemented for a real network interface when *eth_rebuild_header* can't be used.

When a packet is received by the interface, the hardware header is used only by *eth_type_trans*. We have already seen this call in *snull_rx*:

```
skb->protocol = eth_type_trans(skb, dev);
```

The function extracts the protocol identifier (**ETH_P_IP** in this case) from the Ethernet header; it also assigns **skb->mac.raw**, removes the hardware header from packet data, and sets **skb->pkt_type**. This last item defaults to **PACKET_HOST** at **skb** allocation (which indicates that the packet is directed to this host), but it can be changed to one of the other values according to the Ethernet destination address.

If your interface is a point-to-point link, you won't enjoy receiving unexpected multicast packets. To avoid this, you must remember that a destination address whose first octet has 0 as the least significant bit (LSB) is directed to a single host (i.e., it is either **PACKET_HOST** or **PACKET_OTHERHOST**). The *plip* driver uses 0xfc as the first octet of its hardware address, while *snull* uses 0x00. Both addresses result in a working Ethernet-like point-to-point link.

Non-Ethernet Headers

This section briefly describes how hardware headers can be used to encapsulate relevant information. If you need to know the details, you can extract them from the kernel sources or the technical documentation for the particular transmission medium. We have just seen that the hardware header contains some information in addition to the destination address, the most important being the communication protocol.

However, not all information has to be provided by every protocol. A point-to-point link like *plip* or *snull* could avoid transferring the whole Ethernet header without losing generality. The *hard_header* device method receives the delivery information—both protocol-level and hardware addresses—from the kernel. It also receives the 16-bit protocol number. IP, for example, is identified by `ETH_P_IP`. The driver is expected to correctly deliver both the packet data and the protocol number to the receiving host. A point-to-point link could omit addresses from its hardware header, transferring only the protocol number, because delivery is guaranteed independent of the source and destination addresses. An IP-only link could even avoid transmitting any hardware header whatsoever. In both cases, all the work can be performed by *hard_header*, leaving *rebuild_header* nothing to do except return 0.

When the packet is picked up at the other end of the link, the receiving function is expected to correctly set `skb->protocol`, `skb->pkt_type`, and `skb->mac.raw`.

`skb->mac.raw` is a char pointer used by the address-resolution mechanism implemented in higher layers of the networking code (for instance, *net/ipv4/arp.c*). It must point to a machine address that matches `dev->type`. The possible values for the device type are defined in `<linux/if_arp.h>`; Ethernet interfaces use `ARPHRD_ETHER`. For example, here is how *eth_type_trans* deals with the Ethernet header for received packets:

```
skb->mac.raw=skb->data;
skb_pull(skb,dev->hard_header_len);
```

In the simplest case (a point-to-point link with no headers), `skb->mac.raw` can point to a static buffer containing the hardware address of this interface, `protocol` can be set to `ETH_P_IP`, and `packet_type` can be left with its default value of `PACKET_HOST`.

Load-Time Configuration

There are a couple of standard keywords that users expect to have available for configuring the interface. Any new network module is expected to follow the standard:

`io=`
> Sets the I/O port's base address for the interface. If more than one interface is installed in the system, a comma-separated list can be specified.

`irq=`
> Sets the interrupt number. More than one value can be specified, as above.

In other words, a Linux user who has two **own_eth** interfaces installed will expect to load the module with a command line like:

```
insmod own_eth.o io=0x300,0x320 irq=5,7
```

Both the `io=` and the `irq=` options probe for the interface if 0 is specified as a value. A user can thus force probing by specifying `io=0`. Most drivers usually probe for one interface if the user doesn't specify any option, but sometimes probing is disallowed for modules (see the comments in *ne.c* about probing for NE2000 devices).

The device driver should arrange for the behavior just described. The typical implementation for ISA devices looks like the following, assuming the driver supports up to four interfaces:

```
static unsigned int io[] = {0, ~0, ~0, ~0}; /* probe the first */
static unsigned int irq[] = {0, 0, 0, 0};   /* probe if unknown */

int init_module(void)
{
 i, found = 0;

    /* too high I/O addresses are not valid ones */
    for (i=0; io[i]<0x1000 /* 4KB */ && i<4;  i++) {
        /* the device-specific function below is boolean */
        found += own_eth_register(io[i], irq[i]);
    }
    return found ? 0 : -ENODEV;
}

/* device-specific registration function */
int own_eth_register(unsigned int iobase, unsigned int irq)
{
    if (!iobase) /* if iobase is 0, then probe for a device */
        iobase = own_eth_probe_iobase();
    if (!iobase)
        return 0; /* not found */
    if (!irq) /* if irq is 0, probe for it */
        irq = own_eth_probe_irq(iobase)
    return own_eth_init(iobase, irq);
}
```

This code probes for one board by default and always tries to autodetect the interrupt, but the user can change this behavior. For example, `io=0,0,0` probes for three boards.

In addition to using `io` and `irq`, the driver writer is free to add other load-time configuration variables. There is no established naming standard.

Run-Time Configuration

A user might occasionally want to change the interface configuration at run time. If, for example, the IRQ number can't be probed for, the only way to have it properly configured is through a trial-and-error technique. A user-space program can retrieve the device's current configuration or set a new configuration by invoking *ioctl* on an open socket. The *ifconfig* application, for instance, uses *ioctl* to set the I/O port for an interface.

We saw earlier how one of the methods defined for network interface is *set_config*. The method is used to set or change some interface features at run time.

When a program asks for the current configuration, the kernel extracts the information from `struct device` without notifying the driver; on the other hand, when a new configuration is passed to the interface, the *set_config* method is called so the driver can check the values being passed and take appropriate action. The driver method responds to the following prototype:

```
int (*set_config)(struct device *dev, struct ifmap *map);
```

The `map` argument points to a copy of the structure passed by the user program; the copy is already in kernel space, so the driver doesn't need to call *memcpy_from_fs*.

The fields of `struct ifmap` are:

```
unsigned long mem_start;
unsigned long mem_end;
unsigned short base_addr;
unsigned char irq;
unsigned char dma;
```
These fields correspond to the fields in `struct device`.

```
unsigned char port;
```
This field corresponds to `if_port`, as found in `dev`. The meaning of `map->port` is device-specific.

The *set_config* device method is called when a process issues `ioctl(SIOCSIFMAP)` (Socket I/O Control Set InterFace MAP) for the device. The process should issue `ioctl(SIOCGIFMAP)` (Socket I/O Control Get InterFace MAP) before trying to force new values on, so the driver will just look for mismatches between `struct dev` and `struct ifmap`. Any fields in `map` that are not used by the driver can be skipped. For instance, a network device not using DMA ignores `map->dma`.

The *snull* implementation is designed to show how the driver can behave with respect to configuration changes. None of the fields has any physical sense for the *snull* driver. But for the sake of illustration, the code prohibits changes to the I/O address, allows changes to the IRQ number, and ignores other options in order to show how the changes are acknowledged, refused, or ignored.

```
int snull_config(struct device *dev, struct ifmap *map)
{
    if (dev->flags & IFF_UP) /* can't act on a running interface */
        return -EBUSY;

    /* Don't allow changing the I/O address */
    if (map->base_addr != dev->base_addr) {
        printk(KERN_WARNING "snull: Can't change I/O address\n");
        return -EOPNOTSUPP;
    }

    /* Allow changing the IRQ */
    if (map->irq != dev->irq) {
        dev->irq = map->irq;
        /* request_irq() is delayed to open-time */
    }

    /* ignore other fields */
    return 0;
}
```

The return value of the method is used as the return value for the outstanding *ioctl* system call, and `-EOPNOTSUPP` is returned for drivers that don't implement *set_config*.

If you are curious about how the interface configuration is accessed from user space, look in `misc-progs/netifconfig.c`, which can be used to play with *set_config*. Here is the output from a sample run:

```
morgana.root# ./netifconfig sn0
sn0: mem=0x0-0x0, io=0x0, irq=0, dma=0, port=0
morgana.root# ./netifconfig sn0 irq=4
./netifconfig: ioctl(SIOCSIFMAP): Device or resource busy
morgana.root# ifconfig sn0 down
morgana.root# ./netifconfig sn0 irq=4 tell
sn0: mem=0x0-0x0, io=0x0, irq=4, dma=0, port=0
morgana.root# ./netifconfig eth0
eth0: mem=0x0-0x0, io=0x300, irq=5, dma=0, port=0
morgana.root# ./netifconfig eth0 io=0x400
./netifconfig: ioctl(SIOCSIFMAP): Operation not supported on transport
endpoint
```

Custom *ioctl* Commands

We have seen that the *ioctl* system call is implemented for sockets; SIOCSIFADDR and SIOCSIFMAP are examples of "socket *ioctl*s." Now let's see how the third argument of the system call is used by networking code.

When the *ioctl* system call is invoked on a socket, the command number is one of the symbols defined in <linux/sockios.h>, and the function *sock_ioctl* directly invokes a protocol-specific function (where "protocol" refers to the main network protocol being used; for example, IP or AppleTalk).

Any *ioctl* command that is not recognized by the protocol layer is passed to the device layer. These device-related *ioctl* commands accept a third argument from user space, a struct ifreq *; this structure is defined in <linux/if.h>. The SIOCSIFADDR and SIOCSIFMAP commands actually work on the ifreq structure. The extra argument to SIOCSIFMAP, although defined as ifmap, is just a field of ifreq.

In addition to using the standardized calls, each interface can define its own *ioctl* commands. The *plip* interface, for example, allows the interface to modify its internal timeout values via *ioctl*. The *ioctl* implementation for sockets recognizes 16 commands as private to the interface: SIOCDEVPRIVATE through SIOCDEVPRIVATE+15.

When one of these commands is recognized, dev->do_ioctl is called in the relevant interface driver. The function receives the same struct ifreq * pointer that the general-purpose *ioctl* function uses:

```
int (*do_ioctl)(struct device *dev, struct ifreq *ifr, int cmd);
```

The ifr pointer points to a kernel-space address that holds a copy of the structure passed by the user. After *do_ioctl* returns, the structure is copied back to user space; the driver can thus use the private commands to both receive and return data.

The device-specific commands can choose to use the fields in struct ifreq, but they already convey a standardized meaning, and it's unlikely that the driver can adapt the structure to its needs. The field ifr_data is a caddr_t item (a pointer) that is meant to be used for device-specific needs. The driver and the program used to invoke its *ioctl* commands should agree about the use of ifr_data. For example, *pppstats* uses device-specific commands to retrieve information from the *ppp* interface driver.

It's not worth showing an implementation of *do_ioctl* here, but with the information in this chapter and the kernel examples, you should be able to write one when you need it. Note, however, that the *plip* implementation uses ifr_data incorrectly and should not be used as an example for an *ioctl* implementation.

Statistical Information

The last method a driver needs is *get_stats*. This method returns a pointer to the statistics for the device. Its implementation is pretty easy:

```
struct enet_statistics *snull_stats(struct device *dev)
{
    struct snull_priv *priv = (struct snull_priv *)dev->priv;
    return &priv->stats;
}
```

The real work needed to return meaningful statistics is distributed throughout the driver, where the various fields are updated. The following list shows the most interesting fields in `struct enet_statistics`.

int rx_packets;
int tx_packets;
> These fields hold the total number of incoming and outgoing packets successfully transferred by the interface.

int rx_errors;
int tx_errors;
> The number of erroneous receptions and transmissions. Receive errors can be the result of bad checksums, wrong packet sizes, or other problems. Transmit errors are less common and are due mainly to cable problems.

int rx_dropped;
int tx_dropped;
> The number of packets dropped during reception and transmission. Packets are dropped when there's no memory available for packet data. `tx_dropped` is rarely used.

The structure has several more fields, which can be used to detail the kind of errors that happened during transmission or reception. The interested reader is urged to look at the structure's definition in <linux/if_ether.h>.

Multicasting

A "multicast" packet is a network packet meant to be received by more than one host, but not by all hosts.

This functionality is obtained by assigning special hardware addresses to groups of hosts. Packets directed to one of the special addresses should be received by all the hosts in that group. In the case of Ethernet, a multicast address has the least significant bit of the first address octet set in the destination address, while every device board has the bit clear in its own hardware address.

The tricky part of dealing with host-groups and hardware addresses is performed by applications and the kernel, and the interface driver doesn't need to deal with these problems.

Transmission of multicast packets is a simple problem because they look exactly like any other packet. The interface transmits them over the communication medium without looking at the destination address. It's the kernel that has to assign a correct hardware destination address; the *rebuild_header* device method, if defined, doesn't need to look in the data it arranges.

Receiving multicast packets, on the other hand, needs some cooperation from the device. The hardware should notify the operating system whenever an "interesting" multicast packet is received, i.e., a packet whose destination address identifies a group of hosts that includes this interface. This means that the hardware filter should be programmed to tell some multicast destination addresses from the others. The filter is the unit that matches the destination address of the network packets against its own hardware address during normal operation of the interface.

Typically, hardware belongs to one of three classes, as far as multicasting is concerned:

- Interfaces that cannot deal with multicasting. These interfaces either receive packets directed specifically to their hardware address (plus broadcast packets), or they receive every packet. They can receive multicast packets only by receiving every packet, thus overwhelming the operating system with a huge number of "uninteresting" packets. You don't usually count these interfaces as multicast-capable, and the driver won't set `IFF_MULTICAST` in `dev->flags`.

  Point-to-point interfaces are a special case, as they always receive every packet without performing any hardware filtering.

- Interfaces that can tell multicast packets from other packets (host-to-host or broadcast). These interfaces can be instructed to receive every multicast packet and let the software determine if this host is a valid recipient. The overhead introduced in this case is acceptable, as the number of multicast packets on a typical network is low.

- Interfaces that can perform hardware detection of multicast addresses. These interfaces can be passed a list of multicast addresses for which packets are to be received, and they will ignore other multicast packets. This is the optimum case for the kernel, because it doesn't waste processor time dropping "uninteresting" packets received by the interface.

The kernel tries to exploit the capabilities of high-level interfaces and to support at its best the third device class, which is the most versatile. Therefore, the kernel notifies the driver whenever the list of valid multicast addresses is changed, and it passes the new list to the driver so it can update the hardware filter according to the new information.

Kernel Support for Multicasting

Here is a summary of the data structures and functions related to driver multicast capabilities:

`void (*dev->set_multicast_list)(struct device *dev);`

> This device method is called whenever the list of machine addresses associated with the device changes. It is also called when `dev->flags` is modified, because some flags also require you to reprogram the hardware filter. The method receives a pointer to `struct device` as an argument and returns `void`. A driver not interested in implementing this method can leave the field set to NULL.

`struct dev_mc_list *dev->mc_list;`

> This is a linked list of all the multicast addresses associated with the device. The actual definition of the structure is introduced at the end of this section.

`int dev->mc_count;`

> The number of items in the linked list. This information is somewhat redundant, but checking `mc_count` against 0 is a useful shortcut over checking the list.

IFF_MULTICAST

> Unless the driver sets this flag in `dev->flags`, the interface won't be asked to handle multicast packets. The *set_multicast_list* method will nonetheless be called when `dev->flags` changes.

IFF_ALLMULTI

> This flag is set in `dev->flags` by the networking software to tell the driver to retrieve all multicast packets from the network. This happens when multicast-routing is enabled. If the flag is set, `dev->mc_list` shouldn't be used to filter multicast packets.

IFF_PROMISC

> This flag is set in `dev->flags` when the interface is put into promiscuous mode. Every packet should be received by the interface, independent of `dev->mc_list`.

The last bit of information needed by the driver developer is the definition of `struct dev_mc_list`, which lives in `<linux/netdevice.h>`.

```
struct dev_mc_list {
    struct dev_mc_list *next;        /* next address in the list */
    char dmi_addr[MAX_ADDR_LEN];     /* hardware address */
    unsigned short dmi_addrlen;      /* len in octets of the address */
    unsigned short dmi_users;        /* usage count of the structure */
};
```

Since multicasting and hardware addresses are independent of the actual transmission of packets, this structure is portable across network implementations, and

each address is identified by a string of octets and a length, just like
`dev->dev_addr`.

A Typical Implementation

The best way to describe the design of *set_multicast_list* is to show you some
pseudocode.

The following function is a typical implementation of the function in a full-featured (`ff`) driver. The driver is full-featured in that the interface it controls has a
complex hardware packet filter, which can hold a table of multicast addresses to
be received by this host. The maximum size of the table is `FF_TABLE_SIZE`.

All the functions prefixed with `ff_` are placeholders for hardware-specific operations.

```
void ff_set_multicast_list(struct device *dev)
{
    struct dev_mc_list *mcptr;

    if (dev->flags & IFF_PROMISC) {
        ff_get_all_packets();
        return;
    }
    if (dev->flags & IFF_ALLMULTI || dev->mc_count > FF_TABLE_SIZE) {
        ff_get_all_multicast_packets();
        return;
    }
    if (dev->mc_count == 0) {
        ff_get_only_own_packets();
        return;
    }
    ff_clear_mc_list();
    for (mc_ptr = dev->mc_list; mc_ptr; mc_ptr = mc_ptr->next)
        ff_store_mc_address(mc_ptr->dmi_addr);
    ff_get_packets_in_multicast_list();
}
```

This implementation can be simplified if the interface cannot store a multicast
table in the hardware filter for incoming packets. In that case, `FF_TABLE_SIZE`
reduces to 0 and the last four lines of code are not needed.

Nowadays, interface boards often can't store a multicast list. This is not a big problem, though, because the upper layers of networking code will take care of dropping unwanted packets.

As I suggested earlier, even interfaces that can't deal with multicast packets need
to implement the *set_multicast_list* method to be notified about changes in
`dev->flags`. I call this a "non-featured" (`nf`) implementation. The
implementation is very simple, as shown by the following code:

```
void nf_set_multicast_list(struct device *dev)
{
    if (dev->flags & IFF_PROMISC)
        nf_get_all_packets();
    else
        nf_get_only_own_packets();
}
```

Dealing with `IFF_PROMISC` is important, because otherwise the user won't be able to run *tcpdump* or any other network analyzers. If the interface runs a point-to-point link, on the other hand, there's no need to implement *set_multicast_list* at all, because they receive every packet anyway.

Quick Reference

This section provides a reference for the concepts introduced in this chapter. It also explains the role of each header file that a driver needs to include. The list of fields in the `device` and `sk_buff` structures, however, are not repeated here.

`#include <linux/netdevice.h>`
> This header hosts the definition of `struct device` and includes a few other headers that are needed by network drivers.

`void netif_rx(struct sk_buff *skb);`
> This function can be called at interrupt time to notify the kernel that a packet has been received and encapsulated into a socket buffer.

`#include <linux/if.h>`
> Included by *netdevice.h*, this file declares the interface flags (`IFF_` macros) and `struct ifmap`, which has a major role in the *ioctl* implementation for network drivers.

`#include <linux/if_ether.h>`
`ETH_ALEN`
`ETH_P_IP`
`struct ethhdr;`
`struct enet_statistics;`
> Included by *netdevice.h*, *if_ether.h* defines all the `ETH_` macros used to represent octet lengths (like the address length) and network protocols (like IP). It also defines the structures `ethhdr` and `enet_statistics`. Note that `enet_statistics`, despite its name and the header in which it is defined, is used by all interfaces, not just Ethernet ones.

```
#include <linux/skbuff.h>
```
The definition of `struct sk_buff` and related structures, as well as several inline functions to act on the buffers. This header is included by *netdevice.h*.

```
#include <linux/etherdevice.h>
void ether_setup(struct device *dev);
```
This function sets most device methods to the general-purpose implementation for Ethernet drivers. It also sets `dev->flags` and assigns the next available `ethx` name to `dev->name` if the first character in the name is a blank space or the null character.

```
unsigned short eth_type_trans(struct sk_buff *skb,
                              struct device *dev);
```
When an Ethernet interface receives a packet, this function can be called to set `skb->pkt_type`. The return value is a protocol number that is usually stored in `skb->protocol`.

```
#include <linux/sockios.h>
SIOCDEVPRIVATE
```
This is the first of 16 *ioctl* commands that can be implemented by each driver for its own private use. All the network *ioctl* commands are defined in *sockios.h*.

## CHAPTER FIFTEEN

OVERVIEW OF PERIPHERAL BUSES

While Chapter 8, *Hardware Management*, introduced the lowest levels of hardware control, this chapter provides an overview of the higher-level bus architectures. A bus is made up of both an electrical interface and a programming interface. In this chapter, I'm going to deal with the programming interface.

This chapter covers a number of bus architectures. However, the primary focus is on the kernel functions that access PCI peripherals, because these days the PCI bus is the most commonly used peripheral bus, and the one that is best supported by the kernel.

The PCI Interface

Although many computer users think of PCI (Peripheral Component Interconnect) as a way of laying out electrical wires, it is actually a complete set of specifications defining how different parts of a computer should interact.

The PCI specification covers most issues related to computer interfaces. I'm not going to cover it all here; in this section I'm mainly concerned with how a PCI driver can find its hardware and gain access to it. The probing techniques discussed in "Automatic and Manual Configuration" in Chapter 2, *Building and Running Modules*, and "Autodetecting the IRQ Number" in Chapter 9, *Interrupt Handling*, can be used with PCI devices, but the specification offers an alternative to probing.

The PCI architecture was designed as a replacement for the ISA standard, with three main goals: to get better performance when transferring data between the computer and its peripherals, to be as platform-independent as possible, and to simplify adding and removing peripherals to the system.

The PCI bus achieves better performance by using a higher clock rate than ISA; its clock runs at 25 or 33 MHz (its actual rate being a sub-multiple of the system clock), and a 66 MHz extension is upcoming. Moreover, it is equipped with a 32-bit data bus, and a 64-bit extension has been included in the specification. Platform independence is often a goal in the design of a computer bus, and it's an especially important feature of PCI, because the PC world has always been dominated by processor-specific interface standards.

What is most relevant to the driver writer, however, is the support for autodetection of interface boards. PCI devices are jumperless (unlike most ISA peripherals) and are automatically configured at boot time. The device driver, then, must be able to access configuration information in the device in order to complete initialization. This happens without the need to perform any probing.

PCI Addressing

Each peripheral is identified by a *bus* number, a *device* number, and a *function* number. While the PCI specification permits a system to host up to 256 buses, PCs have only one. Each bus hosts up to 32 devices, and each device can be a multi-function board (such as an audio device with an accompanying CD-ROM drive) with a maximum of 8 functions. Each function can be identified by one 16-bit key or two 8-bit keys. The Linux kernel uses the latter approach.

The hardware circuitry of each peripheral board answers queries pertaining to three address spaces: memory locations, I/O ports, and configuration registers. The first two address spaces are shared by all the devices on a PCI bus (i.e., when you access a memory location, all the devices see the bus cycle at the same time). The configuration space, on the other hand, exploits "geographical addressing;" each slot has a private enable wire for configuration transactions, and the PCI controller accesses one board at a time with no address collision. As far as the driver is concerned, memory and I/O are accessed in the usual ways via *inb*, *memcpy*, etc. Configuration transactions, on the other hand, are performed by calling specific kernel functions to access configuration registers. As far as interrupts are concerned, every PCI device has 4 interrupt pins, whose routing to the processor IRQ lines is the responsibility of the motherboard; PCI interrupts can be shared by design, so that even a processor with a limited number of IRQ lines can host many PCI interface boards.

The I/O space in a PCI bus uses a 32-bit address bus (leading to 4GB of I/O ports), while the memory space can be accessed with either 32-bit or 64-bit addresses. Addresses are supposed to be unique to one device, but it's possible for two devices to map erroneously to the same address, making it impossible to access either one. The good news is that every memory and I/O address region offered by the interface board can be remapped by means of configuration transactions. This is the mechanism by which the devices can be initialized at boot time to avoid address collisions. The addresses to which these regions are currently mapped can be read from the configuration space, so the Linux driver can access its devices without probing. Once the configuration registers have been read, the driver can safely access its hardware.

The PCI configuration space consists of 256 bytes for each device function, and the layout of the configuration registers is standardized. Four bytes of the configuration space hold a unique function ID, so the driver can identify its device by looking for the specific ID for that peripheral.* In summary, each device board is geographically addressed to retrieve its configuration registers; this information can be used to identify the board and take further action.

It should be clear from this description that the main innovation of the PCI interface standard over ISA is the configuration address space. Therefore, in addition to the usual driver code, a PCI driver needs the ability to access configuration space.

For the remainder of this chapter, I'll use the word "device" to refer to a device function, because each function in a multi-function board acts as an independent entity. When I refer to a device I mean the tuple "bus number, device number, function number." As I mentioned earlier, each tuple is represented in Linux by two 8-bit numbers.

Boot Time

Let's look at how PCI works, starting from system boot, since that's when the devices are configured.

When power is applied to a PCI device, the hardware shuts down. In other words, the device will only respond to configuration transactions. At power on, the device has no memory and no I/O ports mapped in the computer's address space; every other device-specific feature, like the interrupt lines, is disabled as well.

Fortunately, every PCI motherboard is equipped with PCI-aware firmware, called the BIOS, NVRAM, or PROM depending on the platform. The firmware offers access to the device configuration address space, even if the processor's instruction set doesn't offer such a capability.

At system boot, the firmware performs configuration transactions with every PCI peripheral in order to allocate a safe place for any address region it offers. By the time a device driver accesses the device, its memory and I/O regions have already been mapped into the processor's address space. The driver can change this default assignment, but it usually doesn't unless there are device-dependent reasons to do so.

---

* You'll find the ID of any device in its own hardware manual.

In Linux, the user can look at the PCI device list by reading */proc/pci*, which is a text file that has an entry for each PCI board in the system. Here is an example of a */proc/pci* entry:

```
Bus  0, device  13, function  0:
  Multimedia video controller: Intel SAA7116 (rev 0).
    Medium devsel.  IRQ 10.  Master Capable.  Latency=32.
    Non-prefetchable 32 bit memory at 0xf1000000.
```

Each entry in */proc/pci* is a summary of the device-independent features of one device as described by its configuration registers. The entry above, for example, tells us that the device has on-board memory that has been mapped to address 0xf1000000. The meaning of some of the more exotic details will become clear later, after I introduce the configuration registers.

Detecting the Device

As mentioned earlier, the layout of the configuration space is device-independent. In this section, we'll look at the configuration registers that are used to identify the peripherals.

PCI devices feature a 256-byte address space. The first 64 bytes are standardized, while the rest is device-dependent. Figure 15-1 shows the layout of the device-independent configuration space.

As the figure shows, some of the PCI configuration registers are required and some are optional. Every PCI device must contain meaningful values in the compulsory registers, while the contents of the optional registers depend on the actual capabilities of the peripheral. The optional fields are not used unless the contents of the compulsory fields indicate that they are valid. Thus, the compulsory fields assert the board's capabilities, including whether the other fields are usable or not.

It's interesting to note that the PCI registers are always little-endian. Although the standard is designed to be architecture-independent, the PCI designers sometimes show a slight bias toward the PC environment. The driver writer should be careful about byte ordering when accessing multi-byte configuration registers; code that works on the PC might not work on other platforms. The Linux developers have taken care of the byte-ordering problem (see the next section, "Accessing the Configuration Space"), but the issue must be kept in mind. Unfortunately, the standard functions *ntohs* and *ntohl* can't be used because the network byte order is the opposite of the PCI order; no standardized functions exist in Linux 2.0 to convert from PCI byte-order to host byte-order, and every driver that builds up multi-byte values from single bytes needs to be careful to deal correctly with endianness. Version 2.1.10 of the kernel introduced a few functions to deal with these byte-order issues; they are introduced in "Conversion Functions," in Chapter 17, *Recent Developments*.

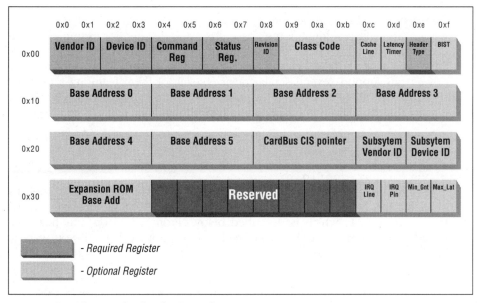

Figure 15-1: The standardized PCI configuration registers

Describing all the configuration items is beyond the scope of this book. Usually, the technical documentation released with each device describes the supported registers. What we're interested in is how a driver can look for its device and how it can access the device's configuration space.

Three PCI registers identify a device: *vendor*, *deviceID*, and *class*. Every PCI peripheral puts its own values in these read-only registers, and the driver can use them to look for the device. Let's look at these registers in more detail:

vendor

> This 16-bit register identifies a hardware manufacturer. For instance, every Intel device is marked with the same *vendor* number, 8086 hex (just a random value?). There is a global registry of such numbers, and manufacturers must apply to have a unique number assigned.

deviceID

> This is another 16-bit register, selected by the manufacturer; no official registration is required for the *deviceID*. This ID is usually paired with the vendor ID to make a unique 32-bit identifier for a hardware device. I'll use the word *signature* to refer to the *vendor/deviceID* pair. A device driver usually relies on the signature to identify its device; the driver writer knows from the hardware docs what value to look for.

class

Every peripheral device belongs to a *class*. The *class* register is a 16-bit value whose top eight bits identify the "base class" (or *group*). For example, "ethernet" and "token ring" are two classes belonging to the "network" group, while the "serial" and "parallel" classes belong to the "communication" group. Some drivers can support several similar devices, each of them featuring a different signature but all belonging to the same class; these drivers can rely on the *class* register to identify their peripherals, as shown later.

The following headers, macros, and functions should be used by a PCI driver to look for its hardware device:

`#include <linux/config.h>`

The driver needs to know if the PCI functions are available in the kernel. By including this header, the driver gains access to the `CONFIG_` macros, including `CONFIG_PCI`, which is described below. From 1.3.73 on, this header is included by `<linux/fs.h>`; you need to include it explicitly if you want to be backward compatible.

`CONFIG_PCI`

This macro is defined if the kernel includes support for PCI BIOS calls. Not every computer includes a PCI bus, so the kernel developers chose to make PCI support a compile-time option to save memory when running Linux on non-PCI computers. If `CONFIG_PCI` is not defined, the rest of the functions in this list are not available, and the driver should use a preprocessor conditional to mask out PCI support and avoid "undefined symbol" errors at load time.

`#include <linux/bios32.h>`

This header declares all the prototypes introduced in this section and should always be included. This header also defines symbolic values for the error codes returned by the functions. The header didn't change between 1.2 and 2.0, so there are no portability issues.

`int pcibios_present(void);`

Since the PCI-related functions don't make sense on non-PCI computers, the *pcibios_present* function tells the driver if the computer supports PCI; it returns a boolean value of true (non-zero) if the BIOS is PCI-aware. Even if `CONFIG_PCI` is defined, the PCI functionality is a run-time option. Therefore, you need to check *pcibios_present* to make sure the computer supports PCI before calling the functions introduced below.

`#include <linux/pci.h>`

This header defines symbolic names for all the numeric values used by the remaining functions. Not every *deviceID* is listed in this file, but you might want to look here before defining your own macros for `id`, `vendor`, and `class`. Note that this header is constantly getting bigger as new symbolic definitions are added for new devices.

```
int pcibios_find_device (unsigned short vendor,
                         unsigned short id,
                         unsigned short index,
                         unsigned char *bus,
                         unsigned char *function);
```

If `CONFIG_PCI` is defined and *pcibios_present* is true, this function is used to request information about the device from the BIOS. The `vendor`/`id` pair identifies the device. `index` is used to support multiple devices with the same `vendor`/`id` identifier and is explained below. The call to *pcibios_find_device* returns the position of the device in the bus and function pointers. The return codes are 0 to indicate success and non-zero for failure.

```
int pcibios_find_class (unsigned int class_code,
                        unsigned short index,
                        unsigned char *bus,
                        unsigned char *function);
```

This function is similar to the previous one, but it looks for devices belonging to a specific class. The `class_code` argument should be passed as the 16-bit *class* register shifted left by 8 bits, because of the way the BIOS interface uses the *class* register. Once again, a return value of 0 means success, while non-zero means there was an error.

```
char *pcibios_strerror(int error);
```

This function can be used to translate a PCI error code, such as the one returned by *pcibios_find_device*, into a string. You might want to print an error message if one of the *find* calls returns neither `PCIBIOS_SUCCESSFUL` (0) nor `PCIBIOS_DEVICE_NOT_FOUND`, which is the expected error code after all the devices have been found.

The code below is typical of the code used by a driver at load time to detect its devices. As outlined above, the lookup can be based on either the signature or the device class. In either case, the driver must store the `bus` and `function` values, which are used later to identify the device. The first five bits if the `function` value identify the device and the next three bits identify the function.

In the code below, every device-specific symbol is prefixed with `jail_` (just another instruction list), lowercase or uppercase depending on the kind of symbol.

If the driver can rely on a unique vendor/id pair, the following loop can be used to initialize the driver:

```
#ifdef CONFIG_PCI
    if (pcibios_present()) {
        unsigned char bus, function;
        int index, result;

        for (index=0; index < JAIL_MAX_DEV; index++) {
            result = pcibios_find_device(JAIL_VENDOR, JAIL_ID, index,
```

```
                                              &bus, &function);
              if (result != PCIBIOS_SUCCESSFUL)
                  break;
              jail_init_dev(bus, function);
         }
         if (result != PCI_BIOS_DEVICE_NOT_FOUND) {
              printk(KERN_WARNING "jail: pci error: %s\n",
                      pcibios_strerror(result));
         }
     }
     if (index == 0)
         return -ENODEV;
#else
    return -ENODEV; /* no PCI bios: no devices */
#endif
```

This code excerpt is correct if the driver deals only with one kind of PCI device, identified by JAIL_VENDOR and JAIL_ID.

However, many drivers are more flexible and can handle both PCI and ISA boards. In that case, the driver probes for the ISA device only if no PCI board is detected or if CONFIG_PCIBIOS is undefined.

It is also common for different vendors to build compatible hardware. The driver should work with all compatible devices even if their signatures are different. To do that, *init_module* should invoke *pcibios_find_class* instead of *pcibios_find_device*.

Using *pcibios_find_class* requires that *jail_init_dev* perform a little more work than in the example. The function returns successfully any time it finds a device belonging to the right class, but the driver still has to verify that the signature is one of the supported ones. This task is performed by a series of conditionals that end up discarding any unexpected device.

Some PCI peripherals contain a general-purpose PCI interface chip and device-specific circuitry. Every peripheral board that uses the same interface chip has the same signature and the driver must perform additional probing to be sure it is dealing with the correct peripheral device. Therefore, sometimes a function like *jail_init_dev* has to be ready to do the device-specific extra checking and to discard a device even though it might have the correct signature.

Accessing the Configuration Space

After the driver has detected the device, it usually needs to read from or write to the three address spaces: memory, port, and configuration. In particular, accessing the configuration space is vital to the driver because it is the only way it can find out where the device is mapped in memory and in the I/O space.

Since the microprocessor has no way to access the configuration space directly, the computer vendor has to provide a way to do it. The exact implementation is therefore vendor-dependent and not relevant to this discussion. Fortunately, the software interface to the transactions described below is standardized, and neither the driver nor the Linux kernel need to be aware of the details.

As far as the driver is concerned, the configuration space can be accessed through 8-bit, 16-bit, or 32-bit data transfers. The relevant functions are prototyped in `<linux/bios32.h>`:

```
int pcibios_read_config_byte (unsigned char bus,
                              unsigned char function,
                              unsigned char where,
                              unsigned char *ptr);
int pcibios_read_config_word (unsigned char bus,
                              unsigned char function,
                              unsigned char where,
                              unsigned short *ptr);
int pcibios_read_config_dword (unsigned char bus,
                               unsigned char function,
                               unsigned char where,
                               unsigned int *ptr);
```

Read 1, 2, or 4 bytes from the configuration space of the device identified by bus and function. The where argument is the byte offset from the beginning of the configuration space. The value fetched from the configuration space is returned through ptr, and the return value of the functions is an error code. The word and dword functions convert the value just read from little-endian to the native byte order of the processor, so you shouldn't need to deal with byte ordering.

```
int pcibios_write_config_byte (unsigned char bus,
                               unsigned char function,
                               unsigned char where,
                               unsigned char val);
int pcibios_write_config_word (unsigned char bus,
                               unsigned char function,
                               unsigned char where,
                               unsigned short val);
int pcibios_write_config_dword (unsigned char bus,
                                unsigned char function,
                                unsigned char where,
                                unsigned int val);
```

Write 1, 2, or 4 bytes to the configuration space. The device is identified by bus and function as usual, and the value being written is passed as val.

The `word` and `dword` functions convert the value to little-endian before writing to the peripheral device.

The best way to access the configuration variables is to use the symbolic names defined in `<linux/pci.h>`. For example, the following two-liner retrieves the revision ID of a device by passing the symbolic name for `where` to *pcibios_read_config_byte*:

```
unsigned char jail_get_revision(unsigned char bus, unsigned char fn)
{
    unsigned char *revision;

    pcibios_read_config_byte(bus, fn, PCI_REVISION_ID, &revision);
    return revision;
}
```

When accessing multi-byte values, the programmer must remember to watch out for byte-order problems.

Looking at a configuration snapshot

If you want to browse the configuration space of the PCI devices on your system, you can compile and load the module *pci/pcidata.c*, in the source files provided on the O'Reilly FTP site.

This module creates a dynamic */proc/pcidata* file containing a binary snapshot of the configuration space for your PCI devices. The snapshot is updated every time the file is read. The size of */proc/pcidata* is limited to `PAGE_SIZE` bytes (this is a limitation on dynamic */proc* files introduced in "Using the /proc Filesystem" in Chapter 4, *Debugging Techniques*). Thus, it lists only the configuration memory for the first `PAGE_SIZE/256` devices, which means 16 or 32 devices (probably plenty for your system). I chose to make */proc/pcidata* a binary file because of this size constraint, instead of making it a text file like other */proc* files.

Another limitation of *pcidata* is that it scans only the first PCI bus on the system. If your computer includes bridges to other PCI buses, *pcidata* ignores them.

Devices appear in */proc/pcidata* in the opposite order than they appear in */proc/pci*. This happens because */proc/pci* reads a linked list that grows from the head, while */proc/pcidata* is a simple look-up loop that dumps everything in the order it is retrieved.

For example, my frame grabber appears second in */proc/pcidata* and (currently) has the following configuration registers:

```
morgana% dd bs=256 skip=1 count=1 if=/proc/pcidata | od -Ax -t x1
1+0 records in
1+0 records out
000000 86 80 23 12 06 00 00 02 00 00 00 04 00 20 00 00
000010 00 00 00 f1 00 00 00 00 00 00 00 00 00 00 00 00
000020 00 00 00 00 00 00 00 00 00 00 00 00 00 00 00 00
```

```
000030 00 00 00 00 00 00 00 00 00 00 00 00 0a 01 00 00
000040 00 00 00 00 00 00 00 00 00 00 00 00 00 00 00 00
*
000100
```

If you juxtapose the dump above and Figure 15-1, you'll be able to make some sense out of the numbers. Alternatively, you can use the *pcidump* program, also found on the FTP site, which formats and labels the output listing.

The *pcidump* code is not worth including here, because the program is simply a long table, plus 10 lines of code that scan the table. Instead, let's look at some selected output lines:

```
morgana% dd bs=256 skip=1 count=1 if=/proc/pcidata | ./pcidump
1+0 records in
1+0 records out
        Compulsory registers:
Vendor id: 8086
Device id: 1223
I/O space enabled: n
Memory enabled: y
Master enabled: y
Revision id (decimal): 0
Programmer Interface: 00
Class of device: 0400
Header type: 00
Multi function device: n
        Optional registers:
Base Address 0: f1000000
Base Address 0 Is I/O: n
Base Address 0 is 64-bits: n
Base Address 0 is below-1M: n
Base Address 0 is prefetchable: n
Does generate interrupts: y
Interrupt line (decimal): 10
Interrupt pin (decimal): 1
```

pcidata and *pcidump*, used with *grep*, can be useful tools for debugging a driver's initialization code. Note, however, that the *pcidata.c* module is subject to the GPL, because I took the PCI scanning loop from the kernel sources. This shouldn't matter to you as a driver writer, because I've included the module in the source files only as a support utility, not as a template to be reused in new drivers.

Accessing the I/O and Memory Spaces

A PCI peripheral implements six address regions. Each region consists of either memory or I/O locations, or it doesn't exist. Most devices substitute a memory region for their I/O ports because some processors (like the Alpha) have no native I/O space and because the I/O space on the PC is quite congested. The structural difference between memory and I/O space has been addressed by implementing a "memory-is-prefetchable" bit;* peripherals that map their control registers to a memory address range declare that range as non-prefetchable, whereas something like video memory on PCI boards is prefetchable. In this section, I'm using the word "region" to refer to a PCI address range whenever the discussion applies to either memory or I/O.

An interface board reports the size and current location of its regions using configuration registers—the six 32-bit registers shown in Figure 15-1 whose symbolic names are `PCI_BASE_ADDRESS_0` through `PCI_BASE_ADDRESS_5`. Since the I/O space defined by PCI is a 32-bit address space, it does make sense to use the same configuration interface for memory and I/O. If the device uses a 64-bit address bus, it can declare regions in the 64-bit memory space by using two consecutive `PCI_BASE_ADDRESS` registers for each region. It is possible for one device to offer both 32-bit regions and 64-bit regions.

I won't go into detail here, because if you're going to write a PCI driver, you will need the hardware manual for the device anyway. In particular, I am not going to use either the prefetchable bit here or the two "type" bits of the registers, and I'll limit the discussion to 32-bit peripherals. It's nonetheless interesting to see how things are implemented in the general case and how Linux drivers deal with PCI memory.

The PCI specs state that each implemented region must be mapped to a configurable address. This means that the device must be equipped with a programmable 32-bit address decoder for each region it implements, and a 64-bit programmable decoder must be present in any board that exploits the 64-bit PCI extension. While 64-bit PCI buses don't exist on PCs yet, some Alpha workstations have them.

The actual implementation and use of a programmable decoder is simplified by the fact that usually the number of bytes in a region is a power of two; for example 32, 64, 4KB, or 2MB. Moreover, it wouldn't make much sense to map a region to an unaligned address; 1MB regions naturally align at an address that is a multiple of 1M, and 32-byte regions at a multiple of 32. The PCI specification exploits this alignment; it states that the address decoder must look only at the high bits of the address bus and that only the high bits are programmable. This convention also means that the size of any region must be a power of two.

Remapping a PCI region is thus performed by setting a suitable value in the high bits of a configuration register. For example, a 1M region, which has 20 bits of address space, is remapped by setting the high 12 bits of the register; writing 0x008*xxxxx* to the register tells the board to respond to the 8MB–9MB address range. In practice, only very high addresses are used to map PCI regions.

---

* The information lives in one of the low-order bits of the base-address PCI registers.

This "partial decoding" technique has the additional advantage that the software can determine the size of a PCI region by checking the number of non-programmable bits in the configuration register. To this end, the PCI standard states that unused bits must always read as 0. By imposing a minimum size of 8 bytes for I/O regions and 16 bytes for memory regions, the standard can fit some extra information into the same PCI register: the "space" bit, which says whether the region is memory or I/O; the two "type" bits; and the prefetchable bit, which is defined only for memory. The type bits select between a 32-bit region, a 64-bit region, and a "32-bit region that must be mapped below one meg." That last value is used for obsolete software that still runs on some PCs.

Detecting the size of a PCI region is simplified by using several bitmasks defined in `<linux/pci.h>`: `PCI_BASE_ADDRESS_SPACE` is set if this is a memory region, `PCI_BASE_ADDRESS_MEM_MASK` masks out the configuration bits for memory regions, and `PCI_BASE_ADDRESS_IO_MASK` masks out the bits for I/O regions. The specification also states that the address regions are allocated in order, from `PCI_BASE_ADDRESS_0` to `PCI_BASE_ADDRESS_5`; as soon as one base address is unused (i.e., set to 0), you know that any subsequent address is also unused.

Typical code for reporting the current location and size of the PCI regions looks like this:

```
static u32 addresses[] = {
    PCI_BASE_ADDRESS_0,
    PCI_BASE_ADDRESS_1,
    PCI_BASE_ADDRESS_2,
    PCI_BASE_ADDRESS_3,
    PCI_BASE_ADDRESS_4,
    PCI_BASE_ADDRESS_5,
    0
};

int pciregions_read_proc(char *buf, char **start, off_t offset,
                int len, int unused)
{
#define PRINTF(fmt, args...) sprintf(buf+len, fmt, ## args)
    len=0;

    /* Loop through the devices (code not printed in the book) */

        /* A device was found: print its regions */
        for (i=0; addresses[i]; i++) {
            u32 curr, mask;
            char *type;

            pcibios_read_config_dword(bus,fun,addresses[i],&curr);
            cli();
            pcibios_write_config_dword(bus,fun,addresses[i],~0);
            pcibios_read_config_dword(bus,fun,addresses[i],&mask);
```

```
                       pcibios_write_config_dword(bus,fun,addresses[i],curr);
                       sti();

                       len += PRINTF("\tregion %i: mask 0x%08lx, now at 0x%08lx\n",
                                       i, (unsigned long)mask, (unsigned long)curr);
                       if (!mask) {
                           len += PRINTF("\tregion %i not existent\n", i);
                           break;
                       }
                       /* extract the type, and the programmable bits */
                       if (mask & PCI_BASE_ADDRESS_SPACE) {
                           type = "I/O"; mask &= PCI_BASE_ADDRESS_IO_MASK;
                       } else {
                           type = "mem"; mask &= PCI_BASE_ADDRESS_MEM_MASK;
                       }
                       len += PRINTF("\tregion %i: type %s, size %i\n", i,
                                       type, ~mask+1);
               },
        return len;
    }
```

This code is part of the *pciregions* module, distributed in the same directory as *pcidata*; the module creates a */proc/pciregions* file, using the code shown above to generate data. Interrupt reporting is disabled while the configuration register is being modified, to prevent a driver from accessing the region while it is mapped to the wrong place. *cli* is used instead of *save_flags* because the function is executed only during the *read* system calls, and interrupts are known to be enabled during system calls.

Here, for example, is what */proc/pciregions* reports for my frame grabber:

```
    Bus 0, device 13, fun  0 (id 8086-1223)
            region 0: mask 0xfffff000, now at 0xf1000000
            region 0: type mem, size 4096
            region 1: mask 0x00000000, now at 0x00000000
            region 1 not existent
```

The computer's firmware uses a loop like the one shown earlier to correctly map the regions at boot time. Since the firmware prevents any collision in address assignment, Linux drivers don't usually change the mappings of the PCI ranges.

It's interesting to note that the memory size reported by the program above can be overstated. For instance, */proc/pciregions* reports that my video board is a 16MB device. This isn't currently true (although I could expand my video RAM). However, since the size information is used only by the firmware to allocate address ranges, region oversizing is not a problem for the driver writer who knows the internals of the device and can correctly deal with the address range assigned by the firmware.

PCI Interrupts

As far as interrupts are concerned, PCI is easy to handle. The computer's firmware has already assigned a unique interrupt number to the device, and the driver just needs to use it. The interrupt number is stored in configuration register 60 (`PCI_INTERRUPT_LINE`), which is one byte wide. This allows for as many as 256 interrupt lines, but the actual limit depends on the CPU being used. The driver doesn't need to bother checking the interrupt number, as the value found in `PCI_INTERRUPT_LINE` is guaranteed to be the right one.

If the device doesn't support interrupts, register 61 (`PCI_INTERRUPT_PIN`) is 0; otherwise, it's non-zero. However, since the driver knows if its device is interrupt-driven or not, it doesn't usually need to read `PCI_INTERRUPT_PIN`.

Thus, PCI-specific code for dealing with interrupts just needs to read the configuration byte to obtain the interrupt number, as shown in the code below. Otherwise, the information in Chapter 9 applies.

```
result = pcibios_read_config_byte(bus, fnct, PCI_INTERRUPT_LINE,
                                  &my_irq);
if (result) { /* deal with error */ }
```

The rest of this section provides additional information for the curious reader, but isn't needed for writing drivers.

A PCI connector has four interrupt pins, and peripheral boards can use any or all of them. Each pin is individually routed to the motherboard's interrupt controller, so interrupts can be shared without any electrical problem. The interrupt controller is then responsible for mapping the interrupt wires (pins) to the processor's hardware; this platform-dependent operation is left to the controller in order to achieve platform independence in the bus itself.

The read-only configuration register located at `PCI_INTERRUPT_PIN` is used to tell the computer which single pin is actually used. It's worth remembering that each device board can host up to 8 devices; each device uses a single interrupt pin and reports it in its own configuration register. Different devices on the same device board can use different interrupt pins or share the same one.

The `PCI_INTERRUPT_LINE` register, on the other hand, is read/write. When the computer is booted, the firmware scans its PCI devices and sets the register for each device according to how the interrupt pin is routed for its PCI slot. The value is assigned by the firmware because only the firmware knows how the motherboard routes the different interrupt pins to the processor. For the device driver, however, the `PCI_INTERRUPT_LINE` register is read-only.

A Look Back: ISA

The ISA bus is quite old in design and is a notoriously poor performer, but it still holds a good part of the market for extension devices. If speed is not important, and you want to support old motherboards, an ISA implementation is preferable to PCI. An additional advantage of this old standard is that if you are an electronic hobbyist, you can easily build your own devices.

On the other hand, a great disadvantage of ISA is that it's tightly bound to the PC architecture; the interface bus has all the limitations of the 80286 processor and is causing endless pain to system programmers. The other great problem with the ISA design (inherited from the original IBM PC) is the lack of geographical addressing, which has led to endless problems and lengthy unplug-rejumper-plug-test cycles to add new devices. It's interesting to note that even the oldest Apple II computers were already exploiting geographical addressing, and they featured jumperless expansion boards.

Hardware Resources

An ISA device can be equipped with I/O ports, memory areas, and interrupt lines.

Even though the x86 processors support 64 kilobytes of I/O port memory (i.e., the processor asserts 16 address lines), some old PC hardware decodes only the lowest ten address lines. This limits the usable address space to 1024 ports, because any address in the range 1KB–64KB will be mistaken for a low address by any device that decodes only the low address lines. Some peripherals circumvent this limitation by mapping only one port into the low kilobyte and using the high address lines to select between different device registers. For example, a device mapped at 0x340 can safely use port 0x740, 0xB40, and so on.

If the availability of I/O ports is limited, memory access is still worse. An ISA device can use only the memory range between 640KB and 1M and between 15MB and 16MB. The 640KB–1MB range is used by the PC BIOS, by VGA-compatible video boards, and by various other devices, leaving little space available for new devices. Memory at 15M, on the other hand, is not directly supported by Linux; this issue is addressed in "Accessing Memory on Device Boards," in Chapter 8.

The third resource available to ISA device boards is interrupt lines. A limited number of interrupt lines are routed to the ISA bus, and they are shared by all the interface boards. As a result, if devices aren't properly configured, they can find themselves using the same interrupt lines.

Although the original ISA specification doesn't allow interrupt sharing across devices, most device boards allow it.* Interrupt sharing at the software level is described in "Interrupt Sharing," in Chapter 9.

ISA Programming

As far as programming is concerned, there's nothing in the kernel or in the BIOS to make using ISA devices easier, except that the Linux kernel offers limited help by maintaining the I/O port and IRQ registries, described in "Using Resources" (Chapter 2) and "Installing an Interrupt Handler" (Chapter 9).

The programming techniques shown throughout the first part of this book apply to ISA devices; the driver can probe for I/O ports, and the interrupt line must be autodetected with one of the techniques shown in "Autodetecting the IRQ Number," in Chapter 9.

The "Plug and Play" Specification

Some new ISA device boards follow peculiar design rules and require a special initialization sequence intended to simplify installation and configuration of add-on interface boards. The specification for the design of these boards is called "Plug and Play" (PnP) and consists of a cumbersome rule-set for building and configuring jumperless ISA devices. PnP devices implement relocatable I/O regions; the PC's BIOS is responsible for the relocation—reminiscent of PCI.

In short, the goal of PnP is to obtain the same flexibility found in PCI devices without changing the underlying electrical interface (the ISA bus). To this end, the specs define a set of device-independent configuration registers and a way to geographically address the interface boards, even though the physical bus doesn't carry per-board (geographical) wiring—every ISA signal line connects to every available slot.

Geographical addressing works by assigning a small integer, called the "Card Select Number" (CSN), to each PnP peripheral in the computer. Each PnP device features a unique serial identifier, 64 bits wide, which is hardwired into the peripheral board. CSN assignment uses the unique serial number to identify the PnP devices. But the CSNs can be assigned safely only at boot time, which requires the BIOS to be PnP-aware. For this reason, old computers can't support PnP without a configuration diskette.

Interface boards following the PnP specs are complicated at the hardware level. They are much more elaborate than PCI boards and require complex software. It's

---

* The problem with interrupt sharing is a matter of electrical engineering; if a device drives the signal line inactive—by applying a low-impedance voltage level—the interrupt can't be shared. If, on the other hand, the device uses a pull-up resistor to the inactive logic level, then sharing is possible. Most ISA interface boards use the pull-up approach.

not unusual to have difficulty installing these devices, and even if the installation goes well, you still face the performance constraints and the limited I/O space of the ISA bus. It's much better in my opinion to install PCI devices whenever possible and enjoy the new technology instead.

If you are interested in the PnP configuration software, you can browse *drivers/net/3c509.c*, whose probing function deals with PnP devices. Linux 2.1.33 added some initial support for PnP as well, in the directory *drivers/pnp*.

Other PC Buses

PCI and ISA are the most commonly used peripheral interfaces in the PC world, but they aren't the only ones. Here's a summary of the features of other buses found in the PC market.

MCA

"Micro Channel Architecture" (MCA) is an IBM standard used in PS/2 computers and some laptops. The main problem with Micro Channel is the lack of documentation, which has resulted in a lack of Linux support for MCA. As of 2.1.15, however, MCA patches that had been floating around have been included in the official kernel; newer kernels can therefore run on PS/2 computers.

At the hardware level, Micro Channel has more features than ISA. It supports multimaster DMA, 32-bit address and data lines, shared interrupt lines, and geographical addressing to access per-board configuration registers. Such registers are called "Programmable Option Select," or POS, but they don't have all the features of the PCI registers. Linux support for Micro Channel includes functions that are exported to modules.

A device driver can read the integer value `MCA_bus` to see if it is running on a Micro Channel computer. `MCA_bus` is non-zero only if the kernel is running in an MCA unit. If the symbol is a preprocessor macro, the macro `MCA_bus__is_a_macro` is defined as well. If `MCA_bus__is_a_macro` is undefined, then `MCA_bus` is an integer variable exported to modularized code. As a matter of fact, `MCA_bus` is still a macro hardwired to 0 for every platform except the PC—the Linux x86 port changed the macro to a variable in 2.1.15. Both `MCA_BUS` and `MCA_bus__is_a_macro` are defined in `<asm/processor.h>`.

EISA

The Extended ISA (EISA) bus is a 32-bit extension to ISA, with a compatible interface connector; ISA device boards can be plugged into an EISA connector. The additional wires are routed under the ISA contacts.

Like PCI and MCA, the EISA bus is designed to host jumperless devices, and it has the same features as MCA: 32-bit address and data lines, multimaster DMA, and shared interrupt lines. EISA devices are configured by software, but they don't need any particular operating system support. EISA drivers already exist in the Linux kernel for Ethernet devices and SCSI controllers.

An EISA driver checks the value `EISA_bus` to determine if the host computer carries an EISA bus. Like `MCA_bus`, `EISA_bus` is either a macro or a variable, depending on whether `EISA_bus__is_a_macro` is defined. Both symbols are defined in `<asm/processor.h>`.

As far as the driver is concerned, there is no special support for EISA in the kernel, and the programmer must deal with ISA extensions by himself. The driver uses standard EISA I/O operations to access the EISA registers. The drivers that are already in the kernel can be used as sample code.

VLB

Another extension to ISA is the "VESA Local Bus" interface bus, which extends the ISA connectors by adding a third lengthwise slot. This extra slot can be used "standalone" by VLB devices; since it duplicates all important signals from the ISA connectors, devices can be built that plug only into the VLB socket without using the ISA sockets. Standalone VLB peripherals are rare, because most devices need to reach the back panel so their external connectors are available.

The VESA bus is much more limited in its capabilities than the EISA, MCA, and PCI buses and is disappearing from the market. No special kernel support exists for VLB. Both the "Lance" Ethernet driver and the IDE disk driver in Linux 2.0 can deal with VLB versions of their devices.

Sbus

While most Alpha computers are equipped with a PCI or ISA interface bus, most Sparc-based workstations use Sbus to connect their peripherals.

Sbus is quite an advanced design, although it has been around for a long time. It is meant to be processor-independent and is optimized for I/O peripheral boards. In other words, you can't plug additional RAM into Sbus slots. This optimization is meant to simplify the design of both hardware devices and system software, at the expense of some additional complexity in the motherboard.

This I/O bias of the bus results in peripherals using *virtual* addresses to transfer data, thus bypassing the need to allocate a contiguous buffer. The motherboard is responsible for decoding the virtual addresses and mapping them to physical addresses. This requires the attachment of some MMU (Memory Management Unit) capability to the Sbus, and the responsible circuitry is called "IOMMU." Another feature of this bus is that device boards are geographically addressed, so there's no need to implement an address decoder in every peripheral or to deal with address conflicts.

Sbus peripherals use the Forth language in their PROMs to initialize themselves. Forth was chosen because the interpreter is lightweight and therefore can be easily implemented in the firmware of any computer system. In addition, the Sbus specification outlines the boot process, so that compliant I/O devices fit easily into the system and are recognized at system boot.

As far as Linux is concerned, there's no special support for Sbus devices exported to modules in kernels up to 2.0. Version 2.1.8 added specific support for Sbus, and the interested reader is encouraged to look in recent kernels.

Quick Reference

This section, as usual, summarizes the symbols introduced in the chapter.

`#include <linux/config.h>`
`CONFIG_PCI`
> This macro should be used to conditionally compile PCI-related code. When a PCI module is loaded to a non-PCI kernel, *insmod* complains about several symbols being unresolved.

`#include <linux/pci.h>`
> This header includes symbolic names for the PCI registers and several *vendor* and *deviceID* values.

`#include <linux/bios32.h>`
> All the `pcibios_` functions listed below are prototyped in this header.

`int pcibios_present(void);`
> This function returns a boolean value that tell whether the computer we're running on has PCI capabilities or not.

```
int pcibios_find_device (unsigned short vendor,
                         unsigned short id,
                         unsigned short index,
                         unsigned char *bus,
                         unsigned char *function);
int pcibios_find_class (unsigned int class_code,
                        unsigned short index,
                        unsigned char *bus,
                        unsigned char *function);
```
> These functions are used to query the PCI firmware about the availability of devices featuring a particular signature or belonging to a particular class. The return value is an error indication, and in case of success, `bus` and `function`

are used to store the position of the device. `index` must be passed as 0 the first time and incremented each time a new device is looked for.

`PCIBIOS_SUCCESSFUL`
`PCIBIOS_DEVICE_NOT_FOUND`
`char *pcibios_strerror(int error);`

These macros and a few more represent the integer return value of `pcibios` functions. `DEVICE_NOT_FOUND` is usually considered a success value, as the query succeeded by finding no device. The *pcibios_strerror* function can be used to convert every integer return value into a string.

```
int pcibios_read_config_byte (unsigned char bus,
                              unsigned char function,
                              unsigned char where,
                              unsigned char *ptr);
int pcibios_read_config_word (unsigned char bus,
                              unsigned char function,
                              unsigned char where,
                              unsigned short *ptr);
int pcibios_read_config_dword (unsigned char bus,
                               unsigned char function,
                               unsigned char where,
                               unsigned int *ptr);
int pcibios_write_config_byte (unsigned char bus,
                               unsigned char function,
                               unsigned char where,
                               unsigned char val);
int pcibios_write_config_word (unsigned char bus,
                               unsigned char function,
                               unsigned char where,
                               unsigned short val);
int pcibios_write_config_dword (unsigned char bus,
                                unsigned char function,
                                unsigned char where,
                                unsigned int val);
```

These functions are used to read or write a PCI configuration register. While the Linux kernel takes care of byte ordering, the programmer must be careful about byte ordering when assembling multi-byte values from individual bytes. The PCI bus is little-endian.

## CHAPTER SIXTEEN

PHYSICAL LAYOUT OF THE KERNEL SOURCE

So far, we've talked about the Linux kernel from the perspective of writing device drivers. Once you begin playing with the kernel, however, you may find that you want to "understand it all." In fact, you may find yourself passing whole days navigating through the source code and grepping your way through the source tree to uncover the relationships among the different parts of the kernel.

This kind of "heavy grepping" is one of the tasks my home computer has been set up to specialize in, and it is an efficient way to retrieve information from the source code. However, acquiring a little knowledge-base before sitting down in front of your preferred shell prompt can be helpful. This chapter presents a quick overview of the Linux kernel source files, based on version 2.0.*x*. The file layout hasn't changed much from version to version, although I can't guarantee that it won't change in the future. So the following information should be useful, even if not authoritative, for browsing other versions of the kernel.

In this chapter, every pathname is given relative to the source root (usually */usr/src/linux*), while filenames with no directory component are assumed to reside in the "current" directory—the one being discussed. Header files (when named with angle brackets—< and >) are given relative to the *include* directory of the source tree. I won't introduce the *Documentation* directory, as its role should be clear.

Booting the Kernel

The usual way to look at a program is to start where execution begins. As far as Linux is concerned, it's hard to tell *where* execution begins—it depends on how you define "beginning."

The architecture-independent starting point is *start_kernel*, in *init/main.c*. This function is invoked from architecture-specific code, to which it never returns. It is in charge of spinning the wheel and can thus be considered the "mother of all functions," the first breath in the computer's life. Before *start_kernel*, there was the chaos.

By the time *start_kernel* is invoked, the processor has been initialized, protected mode (if any) has been activated, the processor is executing at the highest priority (what is sometimes called "supervisor mode"), and interrupts are disabled. The *start_kernel* function is in charge of initializing all the kernel data structures. It does this by calling external functions to perform subtasks, since each setup function is defined in the appropriate kernel subsystem. *start_kernel* also calls *parse_options* (defined in the same *init/main.c* file) to decode the command line passed by the user or program that booted the system.

The command line (along with `memory_start` and `memory_end`) is retrieved from the computer memory by *setup_arch*, which, as the name suggests, is architecture-specific code.

The code in *init/main.c* consists mostly of `#ifdef`s. This happens because initialization takes place in steps, and many of the steps can be run or skipped, depending on the compile-time configuration of the kernel. Command-line parsing also depends heavily on conditionals, as many arguments are meaningful only if a particular driver is present in the kernel being compiled.

Initialization functions called by *start_kernel* come in two flavors. Some of the functions take no arguments and return `void`, while the others take two `unsigned long` arguments and return another `unsigned long` value. The arguments are the current values of `memory_start` and `memory_end`, the bounds of the not-yet-allocated physical memory; the return value is the new `memory_start` (as you already know, the kernel refers to memory addresses as unsigned longs). This technique allows subsystems to allocate a persistent (and contiguous) memory area at the beginning of physical memory, as outlined in "Playing Dirty" in Chapter 7, *Getting Hold of Memory*. The big disadvantage of this allocation technique is that it can only happen at boot time and is thus not available to modules that need a huge memory region suitable for DMA.

After initialization is complete, *start_kernel* prints the banner string, which includes the Linux version number and compile time, and then forks an `init` process by calling *kernel_thread*.

The *start_kernel* function then continues as task 0 (the so-called "idle" task) and calls *cpu_idle*, which in turn is an endless loop that calls *idle*. Things work slightly differently at this point for Symmetric Multi-Processor machines, but I won't describe the differences. The exact behavior of the *idle* function is architecture-dependent, and a few greps in the sources will take you to the location where you can study its functionality.

Before Booting

In the previous section, I treated *start_kernel* as the first kernel function. However, you might be interested in what happens *before* that point.

The code that runs before *start_kernel* is low-level and includes assembly code, so you might not be interested in the details. I'll try nonetheless to introduce what happens in the computer after the firmware (called BIOS in the PC world) gives control to Linux.

If you aren't interested in digging into this low-level code, you can skip to "The Init Process." The following section provides some hints about the Intel, Alpha, and Sparc booting code, as these are the only systems I have access to. (If someone would like to donate the hardware, I'll cover more platforms in the next edition.)

Setting Up the X86 Processors

The personal computer is based on an old design and backward compatibility has always been a high priority. Thus, the PC firmware boots the operating system in an old-fashioned way. Once the boot device has been selected, its first sector is loaded into memory at address 0x7C00 and given control.

The freshly powered-up processor lives in real mode (i.e., it's like an 8086) and can only address the first 640KB of physical RAM, some of which is already occupied by data tables managed by the firmware. Since the kernel is larger than this, the Linux developers had to find a non-trivial way to load the kernel image into memory. The result was the *zImage* file, which is a compressed kernel image that fits (hopefully) into low memory and can unzip itself to high memory after entering protected mode.

So the boot sector finds itself facing five hundred bytes of code and half a megabyte or so of free memory. What exactly the boot code does depends on how the system is being booted. The boot sector can be either the first kernel sector (if you boot the *zImage* file directly from a floppy) or *lilo*. If Linux is booted via *loadlin*, the boot sector is out of the game, because the system has already been booted when *loadlin* runs.

Booting a bare-bones zImage kernel

If the system being booted is the kernel image dumped on floppy, the code that executes as the boot sector is *arch/i386/boot/bootsect.S* (a real-mode assembly source). It moves itself to address 0x90000 and loads a few more sectors from the bootable device, placing them just after its own code (i.e., at 0x90200). The rest of the kernel image is then loaded at address 0x10000 (64KB: after the firmware's data space).

The code at 0x90200 is the so-called "setup" code (*arch/i386/boot/setup.S* and *arch/i386/boot/video.S*), which takes care of various hardware initializations, as well as a preliminary detection of the video board, in order to be able to switch to a different text-mode resolution. These tasks are performed in real mode (or in VM86 mode when using *loadlin*) and therefore can use the BIOS calls and avoid dealing with hardware-specific details.

setup.S then moves the entire kernel from 0x10000 (64KB) to 0x1000 (4KB); this way only one page is wasted before the kernel code—but not even this is really wasted; it has its own role to play in the system. This back-and-forth copying of code is necessary to get rid of the memory layout enforced by the BIOS, while not overwriting important data. Finally, *setup.S* goes into protected mode and jumps to 0x1000.

arch/i386/boot/compressed/head.S (which is written in *gas*, since we are already in protected mode) sets up the stack. It then calls *decompress_kernel*, which places the uncompressed code at address 0x100000 (1meg) and jumps to it.

arch/i386/kernel/head.S is the head of the uncompressed kernel; it establishes the final processor setup (all the register mangling related to hardware paging) and calls *start_kernel*. And that's all that's needed—it's done.

Booting a bare-bones bzImage kernel

As more and more drivers have been developed for the Linux kernel, a full-featured compressed image no longer fits into low memory. This happens, for example, with the installation kernels, which are usually stuffed with drivers in order to be able to work with different configurations. Therefore, an alternative loading mechanism has been devised. The *bzImage* file is a "big" *zImage*, which can be loaded even if it doesn't fit into low memory.

There are several ways to load the *bzImage* depending on the boot loader used. The kernel takes care of each one, and now I'm going to describe how booting works from the raw floppy disk.

The boot sector of a *bzImage* kernel can't simply load all of the compressed data into low memory, so it has to cheat (as most real-mode x86 programs do). If the image being loaded is big, the boot sector loads the "setup" sectors as usual, but a small "helper" routine is called at each iteration of the main loading loop. The helper routine is defined in *setup.S* since the boot sector is too small to host it. Such a routine uses a BIOS call to move data from low to high memory, moving 64KB at a time, and it resets the destination address used by the boot sector for the next data transfer from disk. Thus, the normal loading routine in *bootsect.S* doesn't run out of low memory.

After the kernel has been loaded, *setup.S* is invoked as usual. It does nothing special except change the destination address of the last jump instruction. Since we are loading a big image, the processor jumps to 0x100000 instead of 0x1000, by using a special machine instruction that allows the 386 to use 32-bit offsets in real-mode segments.

Decompression of the kernel works as usual, but the output can't be placed at 0x100000 (1meg), because the compressed image is already there. Uncompressed data is written into low memory until that is exhausted; it's then written past the compressed image. The two uncompressed pieces are then reassembled at 0x100000 by performing other memory moves. But the copying routine also lives in high memory, so it first copies itself to low memory to avoid being overwritten; then it moves the whole image to 0x100000.

At this point, the game is over. *kernel/head.S* doesn't notice the extra work that took place, and everything proceeds as before.

Using lilo

lilo, the Linux Loader, lives in the boot sector—either the master boot sector or the first sector of a disk partition. It uses BIOS calls to load the kernel from a filesystem.

This program faces the same problem as the kernel image: only half a kilobyte of code is loaded into memory when the machine boots, and it's impossible to decode a filesystem structure in a few dozen instructions. *lilo* addresses the problem by building a map of disk blocks at installation time. It uses that map to instruct the BIOS to retrieve each kernel block from the proper place. This technique is efficient, but you have to reinstall *lilo* after you replace or overwrite a kernel image—you have to invoke the *lilo* command in order to reinstall the boot loader with a new table of kernel blocks.

Actually, *lilo* extends the loading mechanism, in that it allows the user to choose at boot time which image to load. The choice is made from an installation-defined list of images. *lilo* can also boot another operating system. It does this by replacing its own boot sector with the boot sector it loads from a different partition.

The biggest benefit of *lilo* over a barebones boot (in addition to being able to boot directly from the hard drive) is that it allows the user to pass a command line to the kernel. The command line can be specified in the *lilo* configuration file or interactively at boot time. *lilo* puts this command line into the second half of the zero-page (the one we kept free before *boot/head.S*). This page is retrieved later by *setup_arch*, which is defined in *arch/i386/kernel/setup.c*.

Recent versions of *lilo* (version 18 and newer) can load a *bzImage*, while older distributions couldn't. The newer versions can load data into high memory using the BIOS call, as *bootsect.S* does.

When *lilo* is done loading, it jumps to *setup.S*, and things proceed as we've seen before.

Using loadlin

loadlin is used to boot Linux off a real-mode operating system. It is similar to *lilo* in that it loads data, passes a command line, and jumps to *setup.S*. But it has the advantage that it can load a kernel from a specific filename in a FAT partition, without needing a block map. This makes it less volatile. If you want to load a *bzImage*, you'll need version 1.6 or newer of *loadlin*.* It's interesting to note that *loadlin* may need to play dirty games to be able to load all of the kernel without trashing the host operating system. Only after all the kernel has been loaded can *loadlin* reassemble it at the proper address and invoke its entry point.

Other booters

There are other programs that can boot a Linux kernel. Two of them are *Etherboot* and *syslinux*, but there are many more. I won't describe them, though, because they are all similar to what I have already described, as far as the kernel is concerned.

Note however that booting a Linux kernel isn't as easy as I've made it seem. Many checks are performed, and version numbers appear in particular places in order to catch any user error and reply in a friendly way. This means that if there is a problem, the system can print a message before it hangs. It's hard to completely avoid hanging on errors within an execution environment as limited as the x86 real mode, and printing a message is better than nothing.

Setting Up Alpha Processors

It's easier to bring an Alpha to the point of being able to run *start_kernel* than it is to boot an Intel processor, because the Alpha has no real-mode or memory limitations to fight. Also, Alpha workstations are usually equipped with better firmware than the PC and can load a whole file from a filesystem. I won't discuss the actual steps involved in loading a file, because the code isn't distributed with Linux and thus you can't examine it—nor can I, to be able to talk about it.

The *milo* (Mini Loader) program is the usual choice for booting. *milo* is smarter than the firmware in that it knows about Linux and its filesystem, but dumber than the kernel because it can't run processes. *milo* is executed by the firmware off a FAT partition and can load the kernel off an ext2 or ISO 9660 block device. Like *lilo* and *loadlin*, *milo* can also pass a command line to the kernel. After Linux has been loaded into memory at the right virtual address, *milo* jumps to the kernel and vanishes.

---

* You'll need 1.6a or newer to load 2.1.22 or newer kernels.

milo relies on the kernel sources for some of its features, because it needs to access the devices and understand the filesystem layout. Being equipped with drivers and filesystem types, it can retrieve the kernel image by pathname from a hard disk or from CD-ROM. The idea behind its design is similar to that of *loadlin*, but *milo* uses code from the Linux kernel instead of being rooted in another operating environment.

milo is not always available for booting Linux on the Alpha. If your system has SRM firmware, you can't install *milo*. Instead, you can use the raw loader from *arch/alpha/boot*. This loader is a simple program that can read a sequential area off the hard disk or floppy drive, the same task performed by the boot sector that heads *zImage* on the PC. Use of the raw loader forces the kernel image to be copied to a contiguous area of the disk, outside of any filesystem.

Regardless of how the system is loaded, control is passed to *arch/alpha/ kernel/head.S*, but "there isn't much left for us to do," Linus says. The source just sets up a few pointers and jumps to *start_kernel*.

Setting Up Sparc Processors

Sparc computers boot Linux using a program called *silo*. It's named after *lilo* and *milo*, but with an "s" for Sparc. Booting a Sparc is easier than booting an Alpha; the firmware can access the devices, and *silo* just needs to access the Linux filesystem and interact with the user. To this end, *silo* is linked to *libext2*, a library that supports file handling over an unmounted partition.

An alternative to using *silo* is to boot the computer from a floppy or from the network. The firmware can load a kernel from an Ethernet using RARP (Reverse ARP) and the `tftp` protocol. In fact, I have never used the floppy to boot my own workstation because the Sparc distribution of Linux allows the system to be installed by booting over the network.

There is really nothing special required for the Sparc. There's no real mode and no memory to be copied. Once the kernel has been loaded into RAM, it begins executing.

The Init Process

The thread created by *start_kernel* forks out `bdflush` (whose code appears in *fs/buffer.c*) and `kswapd` (defined in *mm/vmscan.c*), which are therefore assigned process ids 2 and 3. The *init* thread (pid 1) then performs some further initialization that couldn't be accomplished before; that is, it runs functions related to SMP and, if needed, the `initrd` booting technique, in the form of another kernel thread. After `initrd` is over, the `init` thread activates the "pseudo-root" of the UMSDOS filesystem.

The real role of *init*, after it's done with initialization, is going to user space and executing a program (thus becoming a process). The three `stdio` channels are thus connected to the first virtual console, and the kernel tries to execute *init* from */etc*. If that fails, it looks in */bin* and then */sbin* (where *init* lives in any recent distribution). If *init* fails to run from any of the three directories, the process tries to execute */etc/rc*, and if that also fails, it loops, executing */bin/sh*. In most cases, the function succeeds in running *init*; the other options are there to allow system recovery in case *init* can't be executed.

If the kernel command line specifies a command to execute, using the `init=some_program` directive, process 1 executes the specified command instead of calling `init`.

Whatever the system setup, the *init* process ends up executing in user space, and any further kernel operation is in response to system calls coming from user programs.

The kernel Directory

Most of the critical kernel functions are implemented in this directory. The most important of the source files here is *sched.c*, which deserves special treatment.

sched.c

As the source itself states, this is "the main kernel file." It consists of the scheduler and related operations, such as putting processes to sleep and waking them up, as well as management of the kernel timers (see "Kernel Timers" in Chapter 6, *Flow of Time*), the interval timers (which are related to accounting and profiling), and the predefined task queues (see "Predefined Task Queues" in Chapter 6).

If you are interested in the real-time policies of the Linux scheduler, you'll find the low-level information in the *schedule* function and its relatives. One such relative is *goodness*, which assigns preference values to processes, to help the scheduler choose the next process to run.

The functions (and system calls) related to scheduler control are also defined in this file. This includes the code for setting and retrieving scheduling policies and priorities. The *nice* system call is also found in this source file for every architecture except the Alpha.

In addition, the short system calls to get and set user and group ids are defined in *sched.c* (except on the Alpha), as well as the *alarm* call.*

---

* This call is no longer used by current versions of `libc`, which implement the function by means of timers.

Additional goodies found in *sched.c* include the *show_tasks* and *show_state* functions, which implement two of the "magic" keys described in "System Hangs," in Chapter 4, *Debugging Techniques*.

Process Control

Most of the rest of the directory is in charge of processes. The *fork* and *exit* system calls are implemented in two source files named after the calls, and signal control is implemented in *signal.c*. Most of the signal-handling calls are implemented in a different way for the Alpha, to keep the Alpha port binary-compatible with Digital Unix.

The implementation of *fork* includes the code for the *clone* system call, and *fork.c* shows how the *clone* flags are used. It should be noted that *sys_fork* is not defined in *fork.c*, as the Sparc implementation is slightly different from other versions; most *sys_fork* implementations, however, just call *do_fork*, which *is* defined in *fork.c*. Providing a default implementation (usually called do_*fnct*), while declaring the actual system call (**sys_**_fnct_) within each port, is a technique often used in Linux, and it will probably be extended to other system calls as new ports are made available.

exit.c implements *sys_exit* and the various *wait* functions, as well as the actual sending of signals. (*signal.c* is devoted to signal *handling*, not to *sending*.)

Modularization

The files *module.c* and *ksyms.c* contain the code that implements the mechanisms described in Chapter 2, *Building and Running Modules*. *module.c* holds the system calls used by *insmod* and related programs, while *ksyms.c* declares the public symbols of the kernel that do not belong to a specific subsystem. Other public symbols are declared by the initialization function of specific kernel subsystems, using *register_symtab*. For example, *fs/proc/procfs_syms.c* declares the */proc* interface for registering new files.

Other Operations

The remaining source files in the directory provide the software interface for some low-level operations. *time.c* reads and writes kernel time values from user programs, *resource.c* implements the request and free mechanisms for I/O ports, and *dma.c* does the same for DMA channels. *softirq.c* deals with bottom halves (see "Bottom Halves" in Chapter 9, *Interrupt Handling*) and *itimer.c* defines the system calls to set and get interval timer values.

To see how kernel messaging works, you can look at *printk.c*, which shows the details of several concepts that were introduced in Chapter 4 (i.e., it contains the code for both *printk* and *sys_syslog*).

exec_domain.c includes code needed to achieve binary compatibility with other flavors of Unix and *info.c* defines *sys_info. panic.c* does what its name implies; it also supports automatic reboot of the system when a panic occurs. The reboot takes place after a delay that can be set in */proc/sys/kernel/panic*. The delay is implemented with repeated calls to `udelay(1000)`, because after a panic, the scheduler no longer runs, and *udelay* can be used for delays no longer than one millisecond (see the section "Long Delays" in Chapter 6).

sys.c implements several system-configuration and permission-handling functions, such as *uname, setsid*, and similar calls. *sysctl.c* contains the implementation of the *sysctl* call and the entry points for registering and deregistering `sysctl` tables (lists of entry points for system control). This file also provides the ability to access */proc/sys* files, according to the registered tables.

The mm Directory

The files in the *mm* directory implement the architecture-independent portion of memory management for the Linux kernel. This directory contains the functions for paging, allocation and deallocation of memory, and the various techniques that allow user processes to map memory ranges to their address space.

Paging and Swapping

Surprisingly, *swap.c* doesn't actually implement the swapping algorithm. Instead, it deals with the kernel command-line options `swap=` and `buff=`. These options can also be tuned via the *sysctl* system call or by writing to the */proc/sys/vm* files.

swap_state.c is in charge of maintaining the swap cache and is the most difficult file in this directory; I won't go into detail about it, as it's hard to understand its design, unless a good knowledge of the relevant data structures and policies has been developed in advance.

swapfile.c implements the management of swap files and devices. The *swapon* and *swapoff* system calls are defined here, the latter being very difficult code. For a comparison, several Unix systems don't implement *swapoff*, and can't stop swapping to a device or file without rebooting. *swapfile.c* also declares *get_swap_page*, which retrieves a free page from the swap pool.

vmscan.c is the code that implements paging policies. The *kswapd* daemon is defined in this file, as well as all the functions that scan memory and the running processes looking for pages to swap out.

Finally, *page_io.c* implements the low-level data transfer to and from swap space. The file manages the locking needed to assure system coherence and provides both synchronous and asynchronous I/O. It also deals with problems related to the different block sizes used by different devices. (In the early versions of Linux, it was impossible to swap to a FAT partition, because 512-byte blocks were not supported.)

Allocation and Deallocation

The memory allocation techniques described in Chapter 7 are all implemented in the *mm* directory. Let's start once again with the most frequently used function: *kmalloc*.

kmalloc.c implements the allocation and freeing of memory areas. The memory pool for *kmalloc* is made up of "buckets," where each bucket is a list of memory areas of the same size. The primary function of *kmalloc.c* is to manage the linked lists for each bucket.

When new pages are needed or pages are freed, the file makes use of functions defined in *page_alloc.c*. Pages are retrieved from free memory by _ _get_free_pages, which is a short function that extracts pages from the free-page lists. If there's no memory available on the free lists, *try_to_free_pages* (*vmscan.c*) is called.

vmalloc.c implements the *vmalloc*, *vremap*, and *vfree* functions. *vmalloc* returns contiguous memory in the kernel virtual address space, while *vremap* gives a new virtual address to a specific physical address; it is used mainly to access PCI buffers in high memory. As its name implies, *vfree* frees memory.

Other Interfaces

The most important functions of Linux memory management are part of the *memory.c* file. These functions are generally not accessible through system calls, because they deal with the hardware paging mechanisms.

Module writers, on the other hand, *do* use some of these functions. *verify_area* and *remap_page_range* are defined in *memory.c*. Other interesting functions are *do_wp_page* and *do_no_page*, which implement the kernel's response to minor and major page faults. The remaining functions in the file deal with page tables and are extremely low-level.

Memory mapping is the other big task performed by files in the *mm* directory. *filemap.c* is a complex piece of code. It implements memory mapping of regular files, providing the ability to support shared mappings. Mapped files are supported by means of special `struct vm_operations` structures for the mapped pages, as described in "Virtual Memory Areas" in Chapter 13, *Mmap and DMA*. This source also deals with asynchronous read-ahead; comments explain the meaning of the four read-ahead fields in `struct file`. The only system call that appears in this file is *sys_msync*. The top-level *mmap* interface to memory mapping (i.e., *do_mmap)* appears in *mmap.c*. This file begins by defining the *brk* system call, which is used by a process to request that its highest-allowed virtual address be increased or decreased. The *sys_brk* code is informative, even if you're not a master of memory management. The rest of *mmap.c* is centered on *do_mmap* and *do_munmap*. Memory mapping works, as you might expect, through `filp->f_op`, though `filp` can be NULL for *do_mmap*. This is how *brk* allocates new virtual space. It falls back on memory-mapping the zero-page without needing special code.

mremap.c includes *sys_mremap*. It is an easy file to read if you've figured out *mmap.c*.

The four system calls related to memory locking and unlocking are defined in *mlock.c*, which is a rather simple source. Similarly, *mprotect.c* is in charge of performing *sys_mprotect*. The files are similar in design, because they both modify the system flags associated with the process's pages.

The fs Directory

This directory is, in my opinion, the most interesting in the whole source tree. File handling is a basic activity of any Unix system, and all file-related operations are implemented in this directory. I won't describe the *fs* subdirectories here, as each filesystem type merely maps the VFS layer to a particular information layout. It's important nonetheless to describe the role of most of the files in the *fs* directory because they carry a lot of information.

Exec and Binary Formats

The most important system call in Unix is *exec*. User programs can call one of six different incantations of *exec*, but only one is implemented in the kernel—the rest are library functions that map to the full-featured implementation, *execve*.

The *exec* function uses a table of registered binary formats, to look for the correct loader in order to load and execute a disk file. The first part of the source defines the *register_binfmt* interface. It's interesting to note that the `#!` magic key for script files is handled like a binary format, such as ELF and other formats (although it was a special case of *exec.c* in version 1.2). *kerneld* freaks will also learn how a new binary format is loaded on demand from reading the source.

Each binary format is described by a data structure that defines three operations: loading a binary file, loading a library, and dumping core. The structure is defined in `<linux/binfmts.h>`. Most of the available formats only support the first operation (loading a file), but the interface is nonetheless general enough to be able to support all foreseeable needs for new formats.

devices.c and block_dev.c

We've already used code from *devices.c*, since it is in charge of device registration and unregistration. It is also responsible for the default device *open* method, as well as *release* for block devices. The calls retrieve the correct file operations for the device being opened or closed and dispatch execution to the correct method. Support for the autoloading of modules is implemented in this file. Everything but opening and closing devices appears in the *drivers/** directories, as indicated by each `filp->f_op`.

block_dev.c contains the default methods for reading and writing block devices. As you may remember, a block driver doesn't declare its own I/O methods, but only its request routine. The default read and write implementation in *block_dev.c* is buffer-cache-aware, and does everything for you except the actual data transfer.

The VFS: Superblocks

Execution of programs and devices make up only part of the *fs* directory. Most of the files in *fs*, and all the files in its subdirectories, are concerned with file-related system calls. More specifically, they implement the so-called VFS mechanism: the Virtual File System (or Virtual Filesystem Switch—the interpretation is somewhat controversial).

Conceptually, the VFS is a layer in the Linux file-handling software. This layer offers a unified interface to files by exploiting the features offered by the various filesystem formats. The various techniques for laying out information on a disk are accessed in a uniform way through the VFS interface. In practice, the VFS reduces to a few structures that define "operations." Each filesystem type declares the operations that deal with superblocks, inodes, and files. The `file_operations` structure we have been using throughout the book is part of the VFS interface.

The kernel accesses each filesystem by mounting it. One of *mount*'s tasks is retrieving a so-called "superblock" structure from the disk. The superblock is the main data structure in a filesystem. It gets its name from the fact that, historically, it has been the first physical block of a disk. The file *super.c* includes source code for the interesting operations related to superblocks: reading and syncing them, mounting and unmounting filesystems, and mounting the root filesystem at boot time.

In addition to these interesting (and somewhat complex) operations, *super.c* also returns information about filesystems, including the information provided by */proc/mounts* and by */proc/filesystems*.

register_filesystem and *unregister_filesystem* are the functions used by modularized filesystem types; they are also defined in *super.c*. The file *filesystems.c*, then, is a short table of `#ifdef` statements. Depending on what options were compiled into the kernel, the various init functions for the different filesystems are called. The init function for each filesystem type calls *register_filesystem*, so no other conditional compilation statements are needed.

Inodes and Caching Techniques

The next piece of the VFS interface is the inode. Each inode is identified by a unique key consisting of the device number and inode number. User programs use filenames to access nodes in the filesystem, and the kernel is responsible for mapping the filenames to the unique keys. To achieve better performance, Linux maintains two caches related to inode lookup, the inode cache and the name cache (also known as the directory cache). In addition, the kernel takes care of the more familiar buffer cache.

The inode cache is a hash table used to look up `inode` structures using the device/inode number keys. The implementation of the cache, as well as the routines to read and write inodes, lives in *inode.c*. This file also implements locking techniques for `inode` structures to prevent possible deadlocks.

The name cache is a table that associates inode numbers to filenames. The cache is used to avoid repeated directory lookups when a name is used several times in a row. The source file *dcache.c* includes the software mechanisms that manage the cache. Most system calls and functions that use the name cache are part of *namei.c* (for name-inode), including *sys_mkdir*, *sys_symlink*, *sys_rename*, and similar calls.

The buffer cache is the biggest data cache in the system, and its implementation is laid down in the huge file called *buffer.c*.

As far as files are concerned, *file_table.c* is in charge of allocation and deallocation of `file` structures. This includes *get_empty_filp*, which is called by *open*, *pipe*, and *socket*.

open.c

Most of the other source files in *fs* are responsible for file operations—the same functions that need to be implemented in drivers. The first such file is *open.c*, which includes the code for many system calls. It also includes *sys_open*; its lower-level counterpart, *do_open*; and *sys_close*. These system calls are quite straightforward, mapping onto `filp->f_op`.

open.c includes the system calls that modify the inode: *chown* and *chmod*, as well as their *fchown* and *fchmod* counterparts. If you are interested in looking for security checks and use of the immutable flag, you can browse the source, which can be understood by almost any Unix programmer. Changing the times in the inode is supported as well—*utime* and *utimes* are defined here.

chroot, *chdir*, and *fchdir* are also found in *open.c*, together with the other "change" functions.

The first functions defined in the source are *statfs* and *fstatfs*, which are dispatched to filesystem-specific code using `inode->i_sb->s_op->statfs`.

The *truncate* and *access* calls appear in this file as well. The latter is used to check the permissions on the file using the real uid and gid of the process, temporarily disregarding the fsuid and fsgid.

read_write.c and readdir.c

As its name implies, *read_write.c* contains *read* and *write*, but it also includes both *lseek* and *llseek* (one might guess that the number of leading l's grows by one l every 10 years). *lseek* is the standard call that uses `off_t` (`long`), while *llseek* uses `loff_t` (`long long`). The *llseek* system call maps to the *lseek* file operation, which is implemented as a superset of *lseek* proper. It's interesting to note that version 2.1 of the kernel renamed the method to *llseek*, to be consistent with its implementation.

read and *write* are really simple functions, because the actual data transfer is dispatched through `filp->f_op`; *read_write.c* also contains the code for *readv* and *writev*, which are slightly more elaborate in that multiple chunks of data must be transferred across the kernel/user boundary.

Linux doesn't allow you to directly read a directory file and returns `-EISDIR` if you try. A directory can be read only with the *readdir* system call, which is filesystem-independent, or the newer *getdents*, which "gets directory entries." Reading a directory with *getdents* is faster because one call can return many directory entries, while *readdir* returns only one entry at a time. However, *getdents* is only supported by libc-5.2 and newer libraries.

select.c

The full implementation of *select* lives in *select.c*, with the exception of the *select_wait* inline function. The *select.c* code, though interesting, may be difficult to follow because of the complicated data structures (which were discussed in "The Underlying Data Structure" in Chapter 5, *Enhanced Char Driver Operations*). Nonetheless, *select.c* is a good starting point for looking at kernel code because it is quite self-contained; it doesn't rely on other source files except for some minor details.

Pipes and fifos

The implementation of the pipe and fifo communication channels is quite similar to that of a char driver. Duplication of code is avoided by using the same file operations for the two channels; only the *open* method differs. All the functions except *fifo_open* and *fifo_init* are defined in *pipe.c*. Since fifos appear as filesystem nodes, they need to have a set of `inode_operations` associated with them, in addition to the `file_operations` structure. The right structure is defined in *fifo.c*.

The next interesting thing to note in the implementation of pipes and fifos is that *pipe.c* defines two `file_operation` structures: one for the readable side of the channel and one for the writable side. This permits skipping of the permission check in *read* and *write*.

Control Functions

The "controlling" system calls for files are implemented in two files named after the calls: *fcntl.c* and *ioctl.c*. The former file is almost self-contained, because all the commands defined for *fcntl* are predefined. Since some of them are just wrappers for *dup*, the implementation of *dup* appears in *fcntl.c*. In addition, since the *fcntl* call is responsible for asynchronous notification, *kill_fasync* is also found there.

ioctl.c includes the external interface of the *ioctl* system call. It is a short file that falls back on the file operations for any unrecognized command it receives.

File Locks

Two kinds of locking interfaces are implemented in Linux, the *flock* system call and the *fcntl* commands. The latter is POSIX-compliant.

The file *locks.c* includes code to handle both calls. It also includes optional support for mandatory locks, which is a compile-time option introduced just before 2.0.0 and turned into a mount-time option in 2.1.4.

Minor Files

The *fs* files also support disk quotas. *dquot.c* implements the quota mechanism, while *noquot.c* contains empty functions; it is compiled in place of *dquot.c* if quotas are not included in the kernel configuration.

Finally, *stat.c* implements the *stat*, *lstat*, and *readlink* system calls. Two different implementations of *stat* and *lstat* are defined in 2.0.*x* for backward compatibility with old x86 libraries.

Networking

The *net* directory in the Linux file hierarchy is the repository of the socket abstraction and the network protocols; these features account for a lot of code, as Linux supports several different network protocols. Each protocol (IP, IPX, and so on) lives in its own subdirectory. Unix-domain sockets are treated like another network protocol and their implementation can be found in the *unix* subdirectory. It's interesting to note that version 2.0 of the kernel includes only version 4 of IP, while version 2.1 includes fairly complete support for version 6, the upcoming standard to solve the numbering problems of version 4.

The network implementation in Linux is based on the same file operations that are used to act on device files. This is natural, as network connections (sockets) are described by normal file descriptors. A socket is described in the kernel by a `struct socket (<linux/net.h>)`. The file *socket.c* is the repository of the socket file operations. It dispatches the system calls to one of the network protocols via the `struct proto_ops` structure. This structure is defined by each network protocol to map system calls to the low-level data handling.

Each of the directories under *net* (except *bridge*, *core*, and *ethernet*) is devoted to implementing a network protocol. The *bridge* directory includes an optimized implementation of Ethernet bridging according to the IEEE specifications. Files in *core* implement generic network features like device handling, firewalls, multicasting, and aliases; this includes handling of socket-buffers (*core/skbuff.c*) and socket operations independent of the underlying protocol (*core/sock.c*). Finally, *ethernet* contains generic Ethernet functions.

Almost every directory under *net* hosts a file dealing with system control; information thus exported can be accessed either by means of the */proc/sys* file tree or by using the *sysctl* system call. The kernel interface to *sysctl* allows dynamic addition and removal of system-control entry points and is defined in `<linux/sysctl.h>`.

IPC and lib Functions

Inter-Process Communication and library functions have two small directories dedicated to them.

The *ipc* directory includes a generic file called *util.c* and one source file for each communication facility: *sem.c*, *shm.c*, and *msg.c*. *msg.c* is in charge of message queues and the *kerneld* engine, *kerneld_send*. If IPC is not enabled at compile time, *util.c* exports empty functions that implement IPC-related system calls by returning `-ENOSYS`.

The library functions are like the utilities and variables that you usually use in C programs: *sprintf*, *vsprintf*, the `errno` integer variable, and the `_ctype` array used by the various `<linux/ctype.h>` macros. The file *string.c* contains portable implementations of the string functions, but they are compiled only if the architecture-specific code does not include optimized inline functions. If the inline functions are defined in the header, the implementations in *string.c* are left out of the game by `#ifdef` statements.

The most "interesting" file in *lib* is *inflate.c*, which is the "gunzip" part of *gzip*, extracted from *gzip* itself to allow using a compressed RAM disk at boot time. This technique is used whenever the needed data wouldn't fit on a floppy unless compressed.

Drivers

There is little to say at this point about the Linux *drivers* directory. The source files in this directory have been referenced throughout the book; that's why I left them until last in this walk through the source tree.

Char, Block, and Network Drivers

Although most of the drivers in these directories are specific to a particular hardware device, a few of the files play a more general role in the system's setup.

As far as *drivers/char* is concerned, code that implements the N_TTY line discipline is implemented there. N_TTY is the default line discipline for system ttys, and it is defined in *n_tty.c*. Another device-independent file in *drivers/char* is *misc.c*, which provides support for "misc" devices. A "misc" device is a simplified char driver that has a single minor number.

This directory also includes console support for PCs and some other architecture-dependent drivers; it actually contains a miscellaneous assortment of files that didn't fit elsewhere.

drivers/block is much cleaner. It includes single-file drivers for most block devices and the full-featured IDE driver, which is split into multiple files. Several files in this directory provide general-purpose support; *genhd.c* handles partition tables and *ll_rw_block.c* is in charge of the low-level mechanism for data transfer to and from the physical device. The request structure is the main player in *ll_rw_block.c*.

drivers/net contains a long list of drivers for PC network cards, plus a few for other architectures (e.g., *sunlance.c* for the interface found on most Sparc computers). Some drivers may be more complicated than it appeared when they were introduced in Chapter 14, *Network Drivers*. The driver *ppp.c*, for example, declares its own line discipline.

The general-purpose source files in *drivers/net* are *Space.c* and *net_init.c*. *Space.c* consists primarily of a table of available network devices. This table contains a long list of #ifdef entries that are checked at system boot to detect and initialize the network devices. *net_init.c* contains *ether_setup*, *tr_setup*, and similar general-purpose functions.

SCSI Drivers

As suggested in Chapter 1, *An Introduction to the Linux Kernel*, the SCSI drivers in Linux are not included in the common char and block classes. This happens because the SCSI interface bus has its own standard. Therefore, by distinguishing SCSI devices from other drivers, the developers isolated and shared common code.

Most of the files in *drivers/scsi* are low-level drivers for specific SCSI controllers. The general-purpose SCSI implementation is defined in the *scsi_*.c* files, with the addition of *sd.c* for disk support, *sr.c* for CD-ROM support, *st.c* to support SCSI tapes, and *sg.c* for generic SCSI support. This last source file defines general-purpose support for devices that talk the SCSI protocol. Scanners and other generic devices can be controlled by user-space programs using the */dev/sg** device nodes.

Other Subdirectories

Other hardware drivers have their own subdirectories. *drivers/cdrom* contains drivers for CD-ROM drives that are neither IDE nor SCSI. These are conventional block drivers, which have their own major numbers.

drivers/isdn is (as the name indicates) an ISDN implementation for Linux; *drivers/sound* is a collection of sound drivers for the most common PC sound boards. *drivers/pci* contains a single file, which in turn contains the list of all known PCI devices (vendor/ID pairs). The actual PCI functions are not defined here, but rather within architecture-specific directories.

Finally, *sbus* includes a *char* subdirectory and has the console code for the Sparc architecture. This directory is quickly growing, as 2.1 development continues.

Architecture Dependencies

Versions 2.0 and later of the Linux kernel are fairly portable across platforms, which means that most of the code runs on all the supported architectures without the need to differentiate among them. Everything we have seen in this tour up to now is completely independent of the hardware platform.

The *arch* directory tree is a minor part of the Linux kernel that contains the platform-specific code. Every system-dependent function is replicated in each *arch* subdirectory, so that the structure of all the subdirectories is similar. The most important of these subdirectories is *kernel*, which hosts every system-specific function related to the main *kernel* source directory.

There are two assembly sources that are always found under *kernel*. *head.S* is the startup code executed at system boot; it sometimes includes some of the exception-handling code. The other file is *entry.S*, which includes the entry points to kernel space. In particular, every such file contains the `sys_call_table` for its own architecture; every architecture has a different table to associate system call numbers to functions.

Other commonly found subdirectories are *lib*, which hosts the optimized check-sum routines for network packets and sometimes includes other low-level operations such as string operations; *mm*, which deals with low-level handling of page faults (*fault.c*) and the initialization code called at system boot (*init.c*); and *boot*, which contains the code needed to bring up the system. As you might imagine, *i386/boot* is the most complex of the *boot* subdirectories.

I'm not going to describe the architecture-specific code because it is not very interesting to read and is full of assembly language statements. In order to understand the code, you need to know some of the details of the target architecture. I don't think that there's much fun in reading architecture-specific functions, in any case, because they are the dirty part of the system, dealing with a lot of hardware glitches. It's the rest of the kernel that is interesting.

## CHAPTER SEVENTEEN

RECENT
DEVELOPMENTS

The Linux kernel is subject to relentless development, and the developers feel an urge to improve kernel internals without worrying too much about backward compatibility. This kind of free development shows up in a number of incompatibilities between the device driver interface offered by different versions of the kernel. Nonetheless, no incompatibility is introduced at the application level, with the exception of those few applications whose task requires low-level interaction with kernel features (like *ps*).

The device driver, on the other hand, is directly linked to the kernel image and must therefore comply with any change in the data structures, global variables, and functions exported by the core system. During development, the internals are modified as new features are added or new implementations replace the old ones because they prove faster or cleaner. Although the incompatibilities require programmers to put in some extra work when writing a module, I see continuous development as a winning point of the Linux community: strict backward-compatibility eventually proves harmful.

This chapter describes the differences between 2.0.*x* and 2.1.43, which you can expect to be similar to the upcoming 2.2 release. Linus introduced the most relevant changes in the first few 2.1 versions, so that the kernel could go through several more 2.1 versions, giving driver writers time to stabilize things before the development is frozen to release a stable 2.2 version. The following sections describe how drivers can deal with differences between 2.0 and 2.1.43. I've modified all the sample code introduced throughout the book so that it compiles and runs with both 2.0 and 2.1.43, as well as most versions in between.

The new versions of the drivers are available in the *v2.1* directory in the online examples at the O'Reilly FTP site. Compatibility between 2.0 and 2.1 is achieved by means of the header file *sysdep-2.1.h*, which can be incorporated in your own modules. I chose not to span compatibility back to 1.2 to avoid loading down the

C code with too many conditionals, as 1.2–2.0 differences are already dealt with in the previous chapters. As I'm closing this book, I am aware that other small incompatibilities have been introduced since 2.1.43; I won't comment on them, though, because I can't guarantee complete support for these recent versions.

Note that in this chapter I won't describe all the novelties introduced by the 2.1 development series. What I'm doing here is porting 2.0 modules to work with both 2.0 and 2.1 kernels. Exploiting 2.1 features would require dropping support for release 2.0, which doesn't have such features. Version 2.0 remains the main focus of this book.

In writing *sysdep-2.1.h*, I've tried to accustom you to the new API, and the macros I'm introducing are used to make 2.1 code work with 2.0 instead of the reverse.

This chapter shows incompatibilies in decreasing order of importance; the most relevant differences are described first, while minor details are introduced later.

Modularization

Modularization is becoming more and more important in the Linux community, and the developers decided that a cleaner implementation had to replace the old one. The header file `<linux/module.h>` was completely rewritten in 2.1.18, and a new API was introduced. As you might expect, the new implementation is easier to exploit than the old one.

In order to load your modules, you'll need the package *modutils-2.1.34* or newer (see *Documentation/Changes* for details). The package falls back on a compatibility mode when used with older kernels, so you can replace *modules-2.0.0* with the new package even if you often switch between 2.0 and 2.1.

Exporting Symbols

The new interface to symbol tables is far easier than the previous one and relies on the following macros:

`EXPORT_NO_SYMBOLS;`
> This macro is the equivalent of `register_symtab(NULL);`. It can appear either inside or outside a function, because it instructs the assembler without generating real code. If you want to compile the module under Linux 2.0, the macro should be used from within *init_module*.

`EXPORT_SYMTAB;`
> If you intend to export some symbols, the module must define this macro before including `<linux/module.h>`.

EXPORT_SYMBOL(name);
> This macro states that you want to export the symbol **name**. It must be used outside of any function.

EXPORT_SYMBOL_NOVERS(name);
> Using this macro instead of EXPORT_SYMBOL() forces version information to be dropped, even when compiling code with version support. This is useful for avoiding some unnecessary recompilation. For example, the *memset* function will always work the same way; exporting the symbol without version information allows the developers to change the implementation (and even the data types being used) without *insmod* tagging the incompatibility. It's very unlikely you'll need this macro in modularized code.

If neither of these macros is used in your source, all non-static symbols are exported; this is the same behavior that you get in 2.0. If the module is made up from multiple source files, you can export symbols from any of the sources while still being able to share any symbol within the module's realm.

As you see, the new way to export symbol tables gets rid of a lot of trouble, but the novelty introduces a major incompatibility: a module that exports some symbols and wants to compile and run with both 2.1 and 2.0 must use conditional compilation to include both implementations. This is how the *export* module (*v2.1/misc-modules/export.c*) deals with the problem:

```
#ifdef __USE_OLD_SYMTAB__
    static struct symbol_table export_syms = {
        #include <linux/symtab_begin.h>
        X(export_function),
        #include <linux/symtab_end.h>
    };
#else
    EXPORT_SYMBOL(export_function);
#endif

int init_module(void)
{
    REGISTER_SYMTAB(&export_syms);
    return 0;
}
```

The code above relies on the following lines of *sysdep-2.1.h*:

```
#if LINUX_VERSION_CODE < VERSION_CODE(2,1,18)
#  define __USE_OLD_SYMTAB__
#  define EXPORT_NO_SYMBOLS register_symtab(NULL);
#  define REGISTER_SYMTAB(tab) register_symtab(tab)
#else
#  define REGISTER_SYMTAB(tab) /* nothing */
#endif
```

When using 2.1.18 or newer, `REGISTER_SYMTAB` expands to nothing, as there's nothing to do in *init_module*; using `EXPORT_SYMBOL` outside of any function is all that's needed to export the module's symbols.

Declaring Parameters

The new implementation of kernel modules exploits features of the ELF binary formats to achieve better flexibility. More specifically, when building ELF object files, you can declare sections other than "text," "data," and "bss." A "section" is a contiguous data area, something similar to the concept of "segment."

As of 2.1, kernel modules must be compiled using the the ELF binary formats. As a matter of fact, the 2.1 kernel exploits ELF sections (see "Handling Kernel-Space Faults") and can only be compiled in ELF. So the constraint for modules isn't really a constraint. Using ELF allows informational fields to be stored in the object file. The curious reader can use *objdump —section-headers* to look at section headers and *objdump —section=.modinfo —full-contents* to look at module-specific information. The `.modinfo` section, actually, is the one used to store information about the modules, including which values are considered "parameters" and can be modified at load time.

When compiling with 2.1, a parameter is declared as such by the macro:

```
MODULE_PARM(variable, type-description);
```

When you use the macro in your source file, the compiler is intructed to insert a description string in the object file; such a description states that `variable` is a parameter and that its type corresponds to `type-description`. *insmod* and *modprobe* look in the object file to ensure you are allowed to modify `variable` and to check the actual type of the parameter. Type checking is an important feature for preventing unpleasant errors, such as overwriting an integer value with a string or mistaking long integers for short ones.

In my opinion, the best way to describe the macro is by showing a few lines of sample code. The code below belongs to an imaginary network card:

```
int io[4]  = {0,};   /* io address and irq: at most 4 cards */
int irq[4] = {0,};
short verbose;       /* allow extra messaging to debug problems */
char *options=NULL;  /* textual options */

MODULE_PARM(io, "1-4i");    /* accept 1 to 4 integers */
MODULE_PARM(irq,"1-4i");    /* and the same for irq's */
MODULE_PARM(verbose, "h");  /* a short value */
MODULE_PARM(options, "s");  /* string */
```

The `type-description` string is documented in full detail by the header file `<linux/module.h>` and can be found throughout the kernel sources for your convenience.

One technique worth showing here is how to parameterize the length of an array like `io` above. For instance, suppose the number of peripheral boards supported by the network driver is represented by a `MAX_DEVICES` macro instead of the hard-coded number 4. To this aim, the header `<linux/module.h>` defines a macro (`__MODULE_STRING`) that performs "stringification" of macros using the C preprocessor. The macro can be used in the following way:

```
int io[MAX_DEVICES+1]={0,};
MODULE_PARM(io, "1-" __MODULE_STRING(MAX_DEVICES) "i");
```

In the previous line, the "stringified" value gets concatenated to the other strings to build the informational string in the object file.

The *scull* sample module declares its parameters (`scull_major` and other integer variables) as such using `MODULE_PARM`. This might be a problem when compiling with Linux 2.0, where the macro is undefined. The simple fix I chose is to define `MODULE_PARM` within *sysdep-2.1.h* so that it expands to an empty statement when compiling against 2.0 headers.

Other informational values can be stored in the *.modinfo* section of the module, like `MODULE_AUTHOR()`, but they are currently unused. Refer to `<linux/module.h>` for more information.

/proc/modules

The format of */proc/modules* changed slightly in 2.1.18, when all the modularization code was rewritten. While this change doesn't affect source code, you might be interested in the details, as */proc/modules* is often checked during module development.

The new format is line-oriented like the old one, and each line includes the following fields:

The module's name
    This field is the same as in Linux 2.0.

The module's size
    This is a decimal number reporting the length in bytes (instead of memory pages).

The usage count for this module
    The count is reported as –1 if the module doesn't have a usage count. This is a new feature introduced with the new modularization code; you can write a module whose removal is controlled by a function instead of a usage count. The function asserts whether the module can be unloaded or not. The *ipv6* module, for example, uses this feature.

Optional flags

The flags are text strings, each of which is enclosed in parentheses, and they are separated by spaces.

A list of modules that reference this module

The list as a whole is enclosed in brackets, and the individual names in the list are separated by spaces.

Here is how */proc/modules* might appear in a 2.1.43 system:

```
morgana% cat /proc/modules
ipv6                  75164  -1
netlink                3180   0 [ipv6]
floppy                45960   1 (autoclean)
monitor                 516   0 (unused)
```

In this screenshot, `ipv6` has no usage count and relies on `netlink`; the floppy has been loaded by *kerneld*, as shown by the "autoclean" flag, and `monitor` is a tiny tool of mine that controls some status lights and turns off my computer at system halt. As you can see by its being "unused," I don't care about its usage count.

File Operations

A few of the file operations have different prototypes in 2.1 than they had in 2.0. This is mainly due to the upcoming need to handle files whose size can't fit in 32 bits. The differences are handled by the header *sysdep-2.1.h*, which defines a few pseudo-types according to the kernel version being used. The only serious innovation introduced in the file operations is the *poll* method, which replaces *select* with a completely different implementation.

Prototype Differences

Four file operations feature a new prototype; they are:

```
long long (*llseek) (struct inode *, struct file *, long long, int);
long (*read) (struct inode *, struct file *, char *, unsigned long);
long (*write) (struct inode *, struct file *, const char *,
               unsigned long);
int (*release) (struct inode *, struct file *);
```

The 2.0 counterparts were:

```
int (*lseek) (struct inode *, struct file *, off_t, int);
int (*read) (struct inode *, struct file *, char *, int);
int (*write) (struct inode *, struct file *, const char *, int);
void (*release) (struct inode *, struct file *);
```

The difference, as you see, lies in their return values (which allow for a greater range), and the `count` and `offset` arguments. The header *sysdep-2.1.h* handles the differences by defining the following macros:

`read_write_t`
> This macro expands to the type of the `count` argument and the return value of *read* and *write*.

`lseek_t`
> This macro expands to the return value's type in *llseek*. The change in the method's name (from *lseek* to *llseek*) is not a problem, as you won't usually assign the field by name in your `file_operations`, but will rather declare a static structure.

`lseek_off_t`
> The `offset` argument to *lseek*.

`release_t`
> The return value of the *release* method; either `void` or `int`.

`release_return(int return_value);`
> This macro can be used to return from the *release* method. Its argument is used to return an error code: 0 for success and a negative value for failure. With kernels older than 2.1.31, the macro just expands to `return`, as the method returns `void`.

Using the previous macros, the prototypes of a portable driver are:

```
lseek_t my_lseek(struct inode *, struct file *, lseek_off_t, int);
read_write_t my_read(struct inode *, struct file *, char *, count_t);
read_write_t my_write(struct inode *, struct file *, const char *,
                      count_t);
release_t my_release(struct inode *, struct file *);
```

The poll Method

Version 2.1.23 introduced the *poll* system call, which is the System V counterpart of *select* (which was introduced in BSD Unix). Unfortunately, it is not possible to implement *poll* functionality on top of a *select* device method, so the whole implementation was replaced with a different one, which serves as a back-end to both *select* and *poll*.

With current versions of the kernel, the device method in `file_operations` is called *poll* like the system call, because its internals resemble the system call. The prototype of the method is:

```
unsigned int (*poll) (struct file *, poll_table *);
```

The device-specific implementation in the driver should perform two tasks:

- Queue the current process in any wait queue that may awaken it in the future. Usually, this means queueing the process in both the input and the output queues. The function *poll_wait* is used for this purpose and works exactly like *select_wait* (see "Select" in Chapter 5, *Enhanced Char Driver Operations*, for details).

- Build a bitmask describing the status of the device and return it to the caller. The values of the bits are platform-specific and are defined in `<linux/poll.h>`, which must be included by the driver.

Before describing the individual bits of the bitmask, I'd better show what a typical implementation looks like. The following function is part of *v2.1/scull/pipe.c* and is the implementation of the *poll* method for */dev/scullpipe*, whose internals were described in Chapter 5:

```
unsigned int scull_p_poll (struct file *filp, poll_table *wait)
{
    Scull_Pipe *dev = filp->private_data;
    unsigned int mask = 0;

    /* how many bytes left there to be read? */
    int left = (dev->rp + dev->buffersize - dev->wp) % dev->buffersize;

    poll_wait(&dev->inq, wait);
    poll_wait(&dev->outq, wait);
    if (dev->rp != dev->wp) mask |= POLLIN | POLLRDNORM;  /* readable */
    if (left)               mask |= POLLOUT | POLLWRNORM; /* writable */

    return mask;
}
```

As you see, the code is pretty easy. It's easier than the corresponding *select* method. As far as *select* is concerned, the status bits count as either "readable," "writable," or "exception occurred" (the third condition of *select*).

The full list of *poll* bits is shown below. "Input" bits are listed first, "output" bits follow, and the single "exception" bit comes at the end.

POLLIN
:   This bit must be set if the device can be read without blocking.

POLLRDNORM
:   This bit must be set if "normal" data is available for reading. A readable device returns (`POLLIN | POLLRDNORM`).

POLLRDBAND

This bit is currently unused in the kernel sources. Unix System V uses the bit to report that data of non-zero priority is available for reading. The concept of data priority is related to the "Streams" package.

POLLHUP

When a process reading this device sees end-of-file, the driver must set POLL-HUP (hang-up). A process calling *select* will be told that the device is readable, as dictated by the *select* functionality.

POLLERR

An error condition has occurred on the device. When *poll* is invoked by the *select* system call, the device is reported as both readable and writable, as either *read* or *write* will return an error code without blocking.

POLLOUT

This bit is set in the return value if the device can be written to without blocking.

POLLWRNORM

This bit has the same meaning as POLLOUT, and sometimes it actually is the same number. A writable device returns (POLLOUT | POLLWRNORM).

POLLWRBAND

Like POLLRDBAND, this bit means that data with non-zero priority can be written to the device. Only the "datagram" implementation of *poll* uses this bit, as a datagram can transmit "out of band data." *select* reports that the device is writable.

POLLPRI

High priority data ("out of band") can be read without blocking. This bit causes *select* to report that an exception condition occurred on the file because *select* reports out-of-band data as an exception condition.

The main problem with *poll* is that it has nothing to do with the *select* method used by 2.0 kernels. The best way to deal with the difference, therefore, is to use conditional compilation to compile the proper function, while including both of them in the source file.

The header *sysdep-2.1.h* defines the symbol __USE_OLD_SELECT__ if the current version supports *select* instead of *poll*. This relieves you of the need to refer to LINUX_VERSION_CODE in the source file. The sample drivers in the *v2.1* directory use code similar to the following:

```
#include "sysdep-2.1.h"

#ifdef __USE_OLD_SELECT__
int sample_poll(struct inode *inode, struct file *filp,
                int mode, select_table *table)
{
```

```
/* ... 2.0 (select) implementation ... */
}
#else
unsigned int sample_poll (struct file *filp, poll_table *wait)
{
/* ... 2.1 (poll) implementation ... */
}
#endif
```

The two functions are called with the same name because `sample_poll` is refer-enced in the `sample_fops` structure, where the *poll* file operation replaced the *select* method in place.

Accessing User Space

The first 2.1 versions of the kernel introduced a new (and better) way to access user space from kernel code. The change is meant to fix a long-standing misbe-havior and to enhance system performance.

When you compile code for version 2.1 of the kernel and need to access user space, you need to include `<asm/uaccess.h>` instead of `<asm/segment.h>`. You must also use a different set of functions from those in 2.0. Needless to say, the header *sysdep-2.1.h* takes care of these differences as much as possible and allows you to use the 2.1 semantics when compiling with 2.0.

The most noticeable difference in user access is that *verify_area* is gone, as most of the verification is performed by the CPU instead. See "Handling Kernel-Space Faults" later in this chapter for more details on this subject.

The new set of functions that can be used to access user space is:

`int access_ok (int type, unsigned long addr,`
`                        unsigned long size);`
> This function returns true (1) if the current process is allowed to access mem-ory at address `addr`, false (0) otherwise. This function is a replacement for *verify_area*, although it does less checking. It receives the same arguments as the old *verify_area*, but is much faster. The function should be called to check a user-space address before you dereference it; if you fail to check, the user might be able to access and modify kernel memory. The section "Virtual Mem-ory," later in the chapter, explains the issue in more detail. Fortunately, most of the functions described below take care of such checking for you, so you won't need to actually call *access_ok*, unless you choose to.

`int get_user (lvalue, address);`
> The *get_user* macro used by 2.1 kernels is different from the one we used in 2.0. The return value is 0 in case of success or a negative error code (always `-EFAULT`). The net effect of the function is to assign to `lvalue` data retrieved

using the `address` pointer. The first argument of the macro must be an *lvalue* in the usual C-language meaning.* Similar to the 2.0 version of the function, the actual size of the data item depends on the type of the `address` argument. The function calls *access_ok* internally.

`int __get_user (lvalue, address);`

> This function is exactly like *get_user*, but it doesn't call *access_ok* internally. You should call *__get_user* when you access a user address that has already been checked from within the same kernel function.

`get_user_ret (lvalue, address, retval);`

> This macro is a shortcut that calls *get_user* and returns `retval` if the function fails.

`int put_user (expression, address);`
`int __put_user (expression, address);`
`put_user_ret (expression, address, retval);`

> These functions behave exactly like the *get_* equivalents, but they write to user space instead of reading from it. In case of success, the value `expression` is written to address `address`.

```
unsigned long copy_from_user (unsigned long to,
                              unsigned long from,
                              unsigned long len);
```

> This function copies data bytes from user space to kernel space. It replaces the old *copy_to_user* call. The function calls *access_ok* internally. The return value is always the number of bytes *not* transferred. Thus, if an error occurs, the return value is greater than 0; in that case, the driver usually returns −EFAULT, because the error is caused by a faulty memory access.

```
unsigned long __copy_from_user (unsigned long to,
                                unsigned long from,
                                unsigned long len);
```

> This function is identical to *copy_from_user*, but it doesn't call *access_ok* internally.

`copy_from_user_ret (to, from, len, retval);`

> This macro is a shortcut that calls *copy_from_user* and returns from the current function if it fails.

```
unsigned long copy_to_user (unsigned long to,
                            unsigned long from,
                            unsigned long len);
```

---

* An *lvalue* is an expression that can be the left operand of an assignment. For example, `count`, `v[34+check()]`, and `*((ptr+offset)->field)` are lvalues; `i++`, `32`, and `cli()` are not.

```
unsigned long __copy_to_user (unsigned long to,
                              unsigned long from,
                              unsigned long len);
copy_to_user_ret (to, from, len, retval);
```
These functions are used to copy data to user space, and they behave exactly like their *copy_from* counterparts.

Version 2.1 of the kernel defines other functions for accessing user space: *clear_user, strncpy_from_user,* and *strlen_user.* I won't comment on them because they are not available in Linux 2.0, and because they are rarely needed by driver code. The interested reader is urged to browse `<asm/uaccess.h>`.

Using the New Interface

The new set of functions to access user space may look disappointing at first, but they are meant to ultimately make life easier for the programmer. With Linux 2.1, there's no longer a need to explicitly check user space; *access_ok* won't usually need to be called. The code using the new interface can just go ahead and transfer its data. The *_ret* functions, then, turn out to be very useful when implementing system calls, because a failure in user-space access usually results in a failure in the system call with –**EFAULT**.

The typical *read* implementation, therefore, will look like this:

```
long new_read(struct inode *inode, struct file *filp,
              char *buf, unsigned long count);
{
/* identify your data (device-specific code) */

if (__copy_to_user(buf, new_data, count))
    return -EFAULT;
return count;
}
```

Note that the non-checking *__copy_to_user* function is used because the caller already checked the user address before dispatching data transfer to the file operations. This is just like 2.0, where *read* and *write* didn't need to call *verify_area.*

Similarly, the typical *ioctl* implementation will look like the following:

```
int new_ioctl(struct inode *inode, struct file *filp,
              unsigned int cmd, unsigned long arg);
{
/* device-specific checks, if needed */

switch(cmd) {
    case NEW_GETVALUE:
        put_user_ret(new_value,(int *)arg,-EFAULT);
        break;
```

```
        case NEW_SETVALUE:
            get_user_ret(new_value,(int *)arg,-EFAULT);
            break;
        default
            return -EINVAL;
    }
    return 0;
}
```

Unlike the version 2.0 equivalent, this function doesn't need to check its arguments before the **switch** statement, because each *get_user* or *put_user* does the checking. An alternative implementation is the following one:

```
int another_ioctl(struct inode *inode, struct file *filp,
                unsigned int cmd, unsigned long arg);
{
int retval = -EINVAL, size = _IOC_SIZE(cmd);

if (_IOC_DIR(cmd) & _IOC_READ) {
    if (!access_ok(VERIFY_WRITE, (void *)arg, size))
        retturn -EFAULT;
    }
else if (_IOC_DIR(cmd) & _IOC_WRITE) {
    if (!access_ok(VERIFY_READ, (void *)arg, size))
        return -EFAULT

switch(cmd) {
    case NEW_GETVALUE:
        retval = __put_user(another_value,arg);
        break;
    case NEW_SETVALUE:
        retval = __get_user(another_value,arg);
        break;
    }
    return retval;
}
```

When you want to write code that compiles with both 2.0 and 2.1, on the other hand, things become slightly more complicated, as you can't use the C preprocessor to fake the new behavior with older kernels. You can't just **#define** a *get_user* macro that receives two arguments, because the actual *get_user* implementation in version 2.0 is already a macro.

My own choice for writing code that is both portable and efficient is to set up *sysdep-2.1.h* to provide source code with the following functions. Only the functions that read data are listed; functions that write data behave in exactly the same way.

int access_ok(type, address, size);
    This function is implemented in terms of *verify_area* when compiling against 2.0.

```
int verify_area_20(type, address, size);
```
Usually, when writing code for Linux 2.1, you won't call *access_ok*. On the other hand, *verify_area* is compulsory when compiling for Linux 2.0. This function tries to bridge the gap: it expands to nothing when compiling for Linux 2.1 and is the original *verify_area* when compiling against 2.0. The function can't just be called *verify_area*, because 2.1 still has a macro with the same name as the 2.0 function. The *verify_area* macro as defined in 2.1 implements the old semantics in terms of *access_ok* and exists to ease transition of source code from 2.0 to 2.1. (You could, in theory, leave any *verify_area* in your modules and just rename your functions; the downside of this simple porting technique is that the new version wouldn't compile with 2.0.)

```
int GET_USER(var, add);
int __GET_USER(var, add);
GET_USER_RET(var, add, ret);
```
When compiling with 2.1, these macros expand to the real *get_user* functions, the ones explained above. When they are compiled with 2.0, the 2.0 implementation of *get_user* is used to implement the same functionality as 2.1.

```
int copy_from_user(to, from, size);
int __copy_from_user(to, from, size);
copy_from_user_ret(to, from, size);
```
When compiled with 2.0, these expand to *memcpy_fromfs*; with 2.1, the native functions are used instead. The *_ret* flavor won't ever return with 2.0, because the copying functions can't fail.

This way of implementing compatibility is my personal preference, but it's not the only way to do it. In my sample code, *verify_area_20* must be called before any user-space access (excluding the buffer for *read* and *write*, which is already checked in advance). An alternative would be to be more faithful to 2.1 semantics and automatically generate a *verify_area* at each *get_user* or *copy_from_user* when 2.0 is used. This choice would be cleaner at the source level, but rather inefficient when compiled with version 2.0, both in code size and execution time.

Sample code that compiles with both 2.0 and 2.1 is, for example, the *scull* module, as found in the directory *v2.1/scull*. I don't feel the code is interesting enough to show it here.

Task Queues

Versions of Linux beginning with 2.1.30 don't define the functions *queue_task_irq* and *queue_task_irq_off*, as the actual speed-up over *queue_task* was not worth the effort of maintaining two separate functions. This became evident while new mechanisms were being added to the kernel.

At the source level, this is the only difference between 2.1 and 2.0; the header *sys-dep-2.1.h* defines the missing functions to ease porting drivers from 2.0. The curious reader is urged to look in <asm/spinlock.h> for more details.

Interrupt Management

During 2.1 development, some of the Linux internals were changed. New kernels offer good management of internal locks; race conditions are avoided using several fine-grained locks instead of global ones, thus obtaining better performance—especially with SMP configurations.

One of the outcomes of finer locking is that intr_count no longer exists. Version 2.1.34 got rid of the global variable, and the boolean function *in_interrupt* can be used instead (this function has existed since 2.1.30). Currently, *in_interrupt* is a macro declared in the header <asm/hardirq.h>, which in turn is included by <linux/interrupt.h>. The header *sysdep-2.1.h* conditionally defines *in_interrupt* in terms of intr_count to achieve backward portability to 2.0.

Note that while *in_interrupt* is an integer, intr_count was unsigned long, so if you want to print the value and be portable across 2.0 and 2.1, you should cast the value to an explicit type and specify the suitable format in calling *printk*.

Another difference in interrupt management was introduced in 2.1.37: fast and slow interrupt handlers don't exist any more. The flag SA_INTERRUPT isn't used by the new version of *request_irq*, but it still controls whether interrupts are enabled before the handler is executed. If several handlers share the interrupt line, each can be of a different "type." Interrupts are enabled or not according to the type of the first handler being called. Bottom halves are always executed when the interrupt handler exists.

Bit Operations

Version 2.1.37 slightly modified the role of the bit operations defined in <asm/bitops.h>. The function *set_bit* and its relatives now return void, while new functions like *test_and_set_bit* have been introduced. The new set of functions have the following prototypes:

```
void set_bit(int nr, volatile void * addr);
void clear_bit(int nr, volatile void * addr);
void change_bit(int nr, volatile void * addr);
int test_and_set_bit(int nr, volatile void * addr);
int test_and_clear_bit(int nr, volatile void * addr);
int test_and_change_bit(int nr, volatile void * addr);
int test_bit(nr,addr);
```

If you want to be backward-compatible to 2.0, you can include *sysdep-2.1.h* in your module and stick to the new prototypes.

Conversion Functions

Version 2.1.10 introduced the availability of a few new conversion functions, declared in `<asm/byteorder.h>`. The functions can be used to access multibyte values when the value is known to be stored as either little-endian or bigendian. Since the functions sometimes make a good shortcut in writing driver code, the header *sysdep-2.1.h* takes care of defining them for earlier kernel versions.

The native implementation offered by 2.1 kernel sources is faster than the portable one offered by *sysdep-2.1.h*, because it can exploit architecture-dependent functionalities.

The new functions respond to the following prototypes, where `le` stands for little-endian, and `be` stands for big-endian. Note that strict data typing is not enforced by the compiler, as most of the functions are preprocessor macros anyway; the types shown below are there for your reference.

```
__u16 cpu_to_le16(__u16 cpu_val);
__u32 cpu_to_le32(__u32 cpu_val);
__u16 cpu_to_be16(__u16 cpu_val);
__u32 cpu_to_be16(__u32 cpu_val);
__u16 le16_to_cpu(__u16 le_val);
__u32 le32_to_cpu(__u32 le_val);
__u16 be16_to_cpu(__u16 be_val);
__u32 be32_to_cpu(__u32 be_val);
```

Given the usefulness of such functions when dealing with binary data streams (such as filesystem data or information stored on an interface board), version 2.1.43 added two new sets of conversion functions. These sets allow you to retrieve a value by pointer, or to convert in place the value pointed to by the argument. The functions for 16-bit little-endian respond to the following prototypes; similar functions exist for the other types of integers, leading to a total of 16 new functions.

```
__u16 cpu_to_le16p(__u16 *addr)
__u16 le16_to_cpup(__u16 *addr)

void cpu_to_le16s(__u16 *addr)
void le16_to_cpus(__16 *addr)
```

The "p" functions work like pointer dereferencing, but convert the value if needed; the "s" functions (from the "in situ" clause) can be used to convert the endianness of a value in place (for example, `cpu_to_le16s(addr)` does the same as `*addr = cpu_to_le16(*addr)`).

These functions are defined in *sysdep-2.1.h* as well. The header uses inline functions instead of preprocessor macros as necessary to avoid the side effects of double interpretations.

vremap

The *vremap* function, described in "vmalloc and Friends" in Chapter 7, *Getting Hold of Memory*, got a new name with the advent of version 2.1. Only the name has changed, and the function called *ioremap* takes the same arguments as the old *vremap*. The corresponding free function is *iounmap*, which replaces *vfree* to release remapped addresses.

The change is meant to underline the real role of the function: remapping I/O space to a virtual address in kernel space. The header *sysdep-2.1.h* enforces the new convention, and it #defines *ioremap* and *iounmap* to the 2.0 equivalents when compiled against version 2.0.

Virtual Memory

The Intel port of Linux reached a mature view of virtual memory with version 2.1 of the kernel. Earlier versions stuck to a "segmented" approach to memory management, derived from the beginning of the kernel's lifetime. The change doesn't affect driver code, but is worth outlining anyway.

The new convention matches the behavior of other Linux ports. The virtual address space is built up so that the kernel lives at very high addresses (from 3GB upwards), while user addresses are in the range 0–3GB. When a process is running in "supervisor mode," it can access both spaces. When it runs in user mode, on the other hand, it can't access kernel space because memory pages belonging to the kernel are marked as "supervisor" pages, and the processor inhibits access to them.

This kind of memory layout helped to remove the old *memcpy_to_fs* kind of functions, as there's no longer an FS segment. Kernel space and user space now use the same "segments" and differ only in the priority level the CPU is in.

Handling Kernel-Space Faults

Version 2.1 of the Linux kernel introduced a great enhancement in the handling of segmentation faults from kernel space. In this section, I'm going to give a quick overview of the principle. The way source code is affected by the new mechanism has already been described in "Accessing User Space."

As suggested earlier, recent versions of the kernel fully exploit the ELF binary format, in particular with regard to its capability to define user-defined sections in the compiled files. The compiler and linker guarantee that every code fragment belonging to the same section will be consecutive in the executable file and therefore in memory when the file is loaded.

Exception handling is implemented by defining two new sections in the kernel executable image (*vmlinux*). Each time any source code accesses user space via *copy_to_user*, *put_user*, or their reading counterparts, some code is added to both of these sections. Although this might look like a non-negligible amount of overhead, one of the outcomes of the new implementation is that there's no longer any need to use an expensive *verify_area* mechanism. Moreover, if the user address being used is a correct one, the computational flow will see no jumps at all.

When the user address being accessed is invalid, the hardware issues a page fault. The fault handler (*do_page_fault*, in the architecture-specific source tree) identifies the fault as an "incorrect address" fault (as opposed to "page not present") and takes proper action using the following ELF sections:

__ex_table
> This section is a table of pointer pairs. The first pointer of each pair refers to an instruction that can fail due to a wrong user-space address, and the second value points to an address where the processor will find a few instructions that deal with this error.

.fixup
> This section contains the instructions that deal with each possible error described by the __ex_table section. The second pointer of each pair in the table refers to code that lives in *.fixup*.

The header file <asm/uaccess.h> takes care of building the needed ELF sections. Each function that accesses user space (such as *put_user*) expands to assembly instructions that add pointers to __ex_table and handle the error in *.fixup*.

When the code runs, the actual execution path consists of the following steps: the processor register used for the "return value" of the function is initialized to 0 (i.e., no error), data is transferred, and the return value is passed back to the caller. Normal operation is very fast indeed. If an exception occurs, *do_page_fault* prints a message, looks in __ex_table, and jumps to *.fixup*, where fixing consists in setting the return value to -EFAULT and jumping back just after the instruction that accessed user space.

The new behavior can be checked by using the *faulty* module as it appears in the *v2.1/misc-modules* directory. *faulty* was described in "Debugging System Faults" in Chapter 4, *Debugging Techniques*. *faulty*'s device node transfers data to user space by reading beyond the bounds of a short buffer, thus causing a page fault when reading to an address above the module's page. It's interesting to note that this fault depends on using an incorrect address in kernel space, while in most cases the exception is caused by a faulty user-space address.

When using the *cat* command to read *faulty* on a PC, the following messages are printed on the console:

```
read: inode c1188348, file c16decf0, buf 0804cbd0, count 4096
cat: Exception at [<c28070b7>] (c2807115)
```

The former line is printed by *faulty*'s *read* method, and the latter is printed by the fault handler. The first number is the address of the faulty instruction, while the second is the address of the fixup code (in the *.fixup* section).

Other Changes

There are a few other differences between 2.0 and 2.1.43. They don't deserve special treatment in my opinion, so I'll summarize them quickly.

The *proc_register_dynamic* function disappeared in 2.1.29. Recent kernels use the *proc_register* interface for every */proc* file; if the `low_ino` field in `struct proc_dir_entry` is 0, then a dynamic inode number is assigned. The header *sysdep-2.1.h* defines *proc_register_dynamic* as *proc_register* when compiling for 2.1.29 or newer; this works as long as the `proc_dir_entry` structure being registered features 0 as the inode number.

In the field of network interface drivers, the *rebuild_header* device method has a new prototype from 2.1.15 onwards. You won't be concerned with this difference as long as you develop Ethernet drivers, as Ethernet drivers don't implement their own method; they fall back on the general-purpose Ethernet implementation. The *sysdep-2.1* header defines the macro `__USE_OLD_REBUILD_HEADER__` when the old implementation is needed. The sample module *snull* shows how to use the macro, but it's not worth showing here.

Another change in network code affects `struct enet_statistics`, which doesn't exist any more since 2.1.25. There is a new structure, `struct net_device_stats`, in its place, which is declared in `<linux/netdevice.h>` instead of `<linux/if_ether.h>`. The new structure is just like the old one, with the addition of two fields to store byte counters: `unsigned long rx_bytes, tx_bytes;`. A full-featured network interface driver should increment these counters along with `rx_packets` and `tx_packets`, athough a quick project might disregard the counters. The kernel headers define `enet_statistics` (the name of the old structure) to `net_device_stats` (the name of the new structure) to ease portability of existing drivers.

As a final note, I'd like to point out that the `current` pointer is no longer a global variable; the x86, Alpha, and Sparc kernel ports use smart tricks to store `current` in the processor itself. The kernel developers thus managed to squeeze out a few CPU cycles more. This trick avoids a lot of memory references, and sometimes frees a general-purpose register; the compiler often allocates processor registers to cache a few frequently used memory locations, and `current` is frequently used. Different tricks are used in the different ports to optimize access. The Alpha and Sparc versions use a processor register (one not used by the compiler's optimization) to store `current`. The Intel processor, on the other hand, has a limited number of registers, and the compiler uses all of them; the trick in this case consists in storing `struct task_struct` and the kernel stack page in consecutive virtual-memory pages. This allows the `current` pointer to be "encoded" in the stack pointer. For every platform supported by Linux the header, `<asm/current.h>` shows the actual implementation chosen.

Like any vital piece of software, Linux continues to change. If you want to write drivers for the latest and greatest kernel, you'll need to keep up to date with kernel development. Although dealing with incompatibilities might look like hard work, two observations are due. First, the major programming techniques are in place and are unlikely to change (at least not often). Second, each change makes things better, and usually leaves you less work to do on future development.

INDEX

About the Author

Alessandro Rubini installed Linux 0.99.14 soon after getting his degree as Electronic Engineer. He then received a PhD in Computer Science at the University of Pavia despite his aversion towards modern technology. Alas, he still enjoys digging in technology and discovering the intelligence of people who created it: that's why he now works in his apartment with three PCs, an Alpha, a SPARC, and an Apple—the last without Linux. But you might find him roaming around in the north of Italy on his bike, which doesn't carry an electronic cyclometer.

Colophon

Our look is the result of reader comments, our own experimentation, and feedback from distribution channels. Distinctive covers complement our distinctive approach to technical topics, breathing personality and life into potentially dry subjects.

The image on the cover of *Linux Device Drivers* is of a bucking horse. A vivid description of this phenomenon is given in *Marvels of the New West: A Vivid Portrayal of the Stupendous Marvels in the Vast Wonderland West of the Missouri River*, by William Thayer (The Henry Bill Publishing Co., Norwich, CT, 1888). Thayer quotes a stockman who gives this description of a bucking horse: "When a horse bucks he puts his head down between his legs, arches his back like an angry cat, and springs into the air with all his legs at once, coming down again with a frightful jar, and he sometimes keeps on repeating the performance until he is completely worn out with the excursion. The rider is apt to feel rather worn out too by that time, if he has kept his seat, which is not a very easy matter, especially if the horse is a real scientific bucker, and puts a kind of side action into every jump. The double girth commonly attached to these Mexican saddles is useful for keeping the saddle in its place during one of those bouts, but there is no doubt that they frequently make a horse buck who would not do so with a single girth. With some animals you can never draw up the flank girth without setting them bucking."

The cover layout was produced with Quark XPress 3.32 and Adobe Photoshop 4.0 software, using the ITC Garamond Condensed font.

The interior layouts were designed by Edie Freedman and Jennifer Niederst, with modifications by Nancy Priest and Mary Jane Walsh. Chapter opening graphics are from the Dover Pictorial Archive and *Marvels of the New West*. Interior fonts are Adobe ITC Garamond and Adobe Courier. Text was prepared in SGML using the

DocBook 2.1 DTD. The print version of this book was created by translating the SGML source into a set of gtroff macros using a filter developed at ORA by Norman Walsh. Steve Talbott designed and wrote the underlying macro set on the basis of the GNU *gtroff –gs* macros; Lenny Muellner, with assistance from Chris Maden, adapted them to SGML and implemented the book design. The GNU groff text formatter version 1.09 was used to generate PostScript output.

The illustrations that appear in the book were created in Macromedia Freehand 7.0 by Chris Reilley.

Whenever possible, our books use RepKover™, a durable and flexible lay-flat binding. If the page count exceeds RepKover's limit, perfect binding is used.

 # *More Titles from O'Reilly*

Linux

Linux in a Nutshell, 2nd Edition

By Ellen Siever &
the Staff of O'Reilly & Associates
2nd Edition February 1999
628 pages, ISBN 1-56592-585-8

This complete reference covers the core commands available on common Linux distributions. It contains all user, programming, administration, and networking commands with options, and also documents a wide range of GNU tools. New material in the second edition includes popular LILO and Loadlin programs used for dual-booting, a Perl quick-reference, and RCS/CVS source control commands.

Linux Multimedia Guide

By Jeff Tranter
1st Edition September 1996
386 pages, ISBN 1-56592-219-0

Linux is increasingly popular among computer enthusiasts of all types, and one of the applications where it is flourishing is multimedia. This book tells you how to program such popular devices as sound cards, CD-ROMs, and joysticks. It also describes the best free software packages that support manipulation of graphics, audio, and video and offers guidance on fitting the pieces together.

The Cathedral & the Bazaar

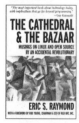

By Eric S. Raymond
1st Edition October 1999
288 pages, ISBN 1-56592-724-9

After Red Hat's stunning IPO, even people outside the computer industry have now heard of Linux and open-source software. This book contains the essays, originally published online, that led to Netscape's decision to release their browser as open source, put Linus Torvalds on the cover of Forbes Magazine and Microsoft on the defensive, and helped Linux to rock the world of commercial software. These essays have been expanded and revised for this edition, and are in print for the first time.

Linux Network Administrator's Guide

By Olaf Kirch
1st Edition January 1995
370 pages, ISBN 1-56592-087-2

One of the most successful books to come from the Linux Documentation Project, *Linux Network Administrator's Guide* touches on all the essential networking software included with Linux, plus some hardware considerations. Topics include serial connections, UUCP, routing and DNS, mail and News, SLIP and PPP, NFS, and NIS.

Running Linux, 3rd Edition

By Matt Welsh, Matthias Kalle Dalheimer &
Lar Kaufman
3rd Edition August 1999
752 pages, ISBN 1-56592-469-X

This book explains everything you need to understand, install, and start using the Linux operating system. It includes an installation tutorial, system maintenance tips, document development and programming tools, and guidelines for network, file, printer, and Web site administration. New topics in the third edition include KDE, Samba, PPP, and revised instructions for installation and configuration (especially for the Red Hat, SuSE and Debian distributions).

Learning the bash Shell, 2nd Edition

By Cameron Newham & Bill Rosenblatt
2nd Edition January 1998
336 pages, ISBN 1-56592-347-2

This second edition covers all of the features of bash Version 2.0, while still applying to bash Version 1.x. It includes one-dimensional arrays, parameter expansion, more pattern-matching operations, new commands, security improvements, additions to ReadLine, improved configuration and installation, and an additional programming aid, the bash shell debugger.

O'REILLY®

TO ORDER: **800-998-9938** • **order@oreilly.com** • **http://www.oreilly.com/**
OUR PRODUCTS ARE AVAILABLE AT A BOOKSTORE OR SOFTWARE STORE NEAR YOU.
FOR INFORMATION: **800-998-9938** • **707-829-0515** • **info@oreilly.com**

Linux

Using Samba

By Peter Kelly, Perry Donham &
David Collier-Brown
1st Edition November 1999
416 pages, Includes CD-ROM
ISBN 1-56592-449-5

Samba turns a UNIX or Linux system into a
file and print server for Microsoft Windows
network clients. This complete guide to
Samba administration covers basic 2.0 configuration, security,
logging, and troubleshooting. Whether you're playing on one note
or a full three-octave range, this book will help you maintain an
efficient and secure server. Includes a CD-ROM of sources and
ready-to-install binaries.

Learning Red Hat Linux

By Bill McCarty
1st Edition September 1999
394 pages, Includes CD-ROM
ISBN 1-56592-627-7

Learning Red Hat Linux will guide any new
Linux user through the installation and use
of the free operating system that is shaking
up the world of commercial software. It
demystifies Linux in terms familiar to Windows users and gives
readers only what they need to start being successful users of this
operating system.

MySQL & mSQL

By Randy Jay Yarger, George Reese & Tim King
1st Edition July 1999
506 pages, ISBN 1-56592-434-7

This book teaches you how to use MySQL
and mSQL, two popular and robust database
products that support key subsets of SQL on
both Linux and UNIX systems. Anyone who
knows basic C, Java, Perl, or Python can
write a program to interact with a database, either as a standalone application or through a Web page. This book takes you
through the whole process, from installation and configuration to
programming interfaces and basic administration. Includes ample
tutorial material.

Programming with Qt

By Matthias Kalle Dalheimer
1st Edition April 1999
384 pages, ISBN 1-56592-588-2

This indispensable guide teaches you how
to take full advantage of Qt, a powerful,
easy-to-use, cross-platform GUI toolkit, and
guides you through the steps of writing your
first Qt application. It describes all of the
GUI elements in Qt, along with advice about when and how to
use them. It also contains material on advanced topics like 2D
transformations, drag-and-drop, and custom image file filters.

Open Sources:
Voices from the Open Source Revolution

Edited by Chris DiBona,
Sam Ockman & Mark Stone
1st Edition January 1999
280 pages, ISBN 1-56592-582-3

In *Open Sources*, leaders of Open Source
come together in print for the first time
to discuss the new vision of the software
industry they have created, through essays
that explain how the movement works, why it succeeds, and
where it is going. A powerful vision from the movement's spiritual
leaders, this book reveals the mysteries of how open development
builds better software and how businesses can leverage freely
available software for a competitive business advantage.

Programming with GNU Software

By Mike Loukides & Andy Oram
1st Edition December 1996
260 pages, Includes CD-ROM
ISBN 1-56592-112-7

This book and CD combination is a complete
package for programmers who are new to
UNIX or who would like to make better use
of the system. The tools come from Cygnus
Support, Inc., and Cyclic Software, companies that provide support
for free software. Contents include GNU Emacs, gcc, C and C++
libraries, gdb, RCS, and make. The book provides an introduction
to all these tools for a C programmer.

UNIX Tools

The UNIX CD Bookshelf

By O'Reilly & Associates, Inc.
1st Edition November 1998
444 pages, Includes CD-ROM
ISBN 1-56592-406-1

The UNIX CD Bookshelf contains six books from O'Reilly plus the software from UNIX Power Tools – all on a convenient CD-ROM. A bonus hard-copy book, UNIX in a Nutshell: System V Edition, is also included. The CD-ROM contains UNIX in a Nutshell: System V Edition; UNIX Power Tools, 2nd Edition (with software); Learning the UNIX Operating System, 4th Edition; Learning the vi Editor, 5th Edition; sed & awk, 2nd Edition; and Learning the Korn Shell.

sed & awk, 2nd Edition

By Dale Dougherty & Arnold Robbins
2nd Edition March 1997
432 pages, ISBN 1-56592-225-5

sed & awk describes two text manipulation programs that are mainstays of the UNIX programmer's toolbox. This edition covers the sed and awk programs as they are mandated by the POSIX standard and includes discussion of the GNU versions of these programs.

lex & yacc, 2nd Edition

By John Levine, Tony Mason & Doug Brown
2nd Edition October 1992
366 pages, ISBN 1-56592-000-7

Shows programmers how to use two UNIX utilities, lex and yacc, in program development. You'll find tutorial sections for novice users, reference sections for advanced users, and a detailed index. Major MS-DOS and UNIX versions of lex and yacc are explored in depth. Also covers Bison and Flex.

Managing Projects with make, 2nd Edition

By Andrew Oram & Steve Talbott
2nd Edition October 1991
152 pages, ISBN 0-937175-90-0

make is one of UNIX's greatest contributions to software development, and this book is the clearest description of make ever written. It describes all the basic features and provides guidelines on meeting the needs of large, modern projects. Also contains a description of free products that contain major enhancements to make.

Writing GNU Emacs Extensions

By Bob Glickstein
1st Edition April 1997
236 pages, ISBN 1-56592-261-1

This book introduces Emacs Lisp and tells you how to make the editor do whatever you want, whether it's altering the way text scrolls or inventing a whole new "major mode." Topics progress from simple to complex, from lists, symbols, and keyboard commands to syntax tables, macro templates, and error recovery.

UNIX Power Tools, 2nd Edition

By Jerry Peek, Tim O'Reilly & Mike Loukides
2nd Edition August 1997
1120 pages, Includes CD-ROM
ISBN 1-56592-260-3

Loaded with practical advice about almost every aspect of UNIX, this second edition of UNIX Power Tools addresses the technology that UNIX users face today. You'll find thorough coverage of POSIX utilities, including GNU versions, detailed bash and tcsh shell coverage, a strong emphasis on Perl, and a CD-ROM that contains the best freeware available.

UNIX Tools

Applying RCS and SCCS

By Don Bolinger & Tan Bronson
1st Edition September 1995
528 pages, ISBN 1-56592-117-8

Applying RCS and SCCS is a thorough introduction to these two systems, viewed as tools for project management. This book takes the reader from basic source control of a single file, through working with multiple releases of a software project, to coordinating multiple developers. It also presents TCCS, a representative "front-end" that addresses problems RCS and SCCS can't handle alone, such as managing groups of files, developing for multiple platforms, and linking public and private development areas.

Practical Internet Groupware

By Jon Udell
1st Edition October 1999
524 pages, ISBN 1-56592-537-8

This revolutionary book tells users, programmers, IS managers, and system administrators how to build Internet groupware applications that organize the casual and chaotic transmission of online information into useful, disciplined, and documented data.

Software Portability with imake, 2nd Edition

By Paul DuBois
2nd Edition September 1996
410 pages, ISBN 1-56592-226-3

This handbook is ideal for X and UNIX programmers who want their software to be portable. The second edition covers version X11R6.1 of the X Window System, using imake for non-UNIX systems such as Windows NT, and some of the quirks about using imake under OpenWindows/Solaris.

O'REILLY®

TO ORDER: **800-998-9938** • *order@oreilly.com* • *http://www.oreilly.com/*

OUR PRODUCTS ARE AVAILABLE AT A BOOKSTORE OR SOFTWARE STORE NEAR YOU.

FOR INFORMATION: **800-998-9938** • **707-829-0515** • *info@oreilly.com*

How to stay in touch with O'Reilly

1. Visit Our Award-Winning Web Site

http://www.oreilly.com/

★ "Top 100 Sites on the Web" —*PC Magazine*
★ "Top 5% Web sites" —*Point Communications*
★ "3-Star site" —*The McKinley Group*

Our web site contains a library of comprehensive product information (including book excerpts and tables of contents), downloadable software, background articles, interviews with technology leaders, links to relevant sites, book cover art, and more. File us in your Bookmarks or Hotlist!

2. Join Our Email Mailing Lists

New Product Releases

To receive automatic email with brief descriptions of all new O'Reilly products as they are released, send email to:
listproc@online.oreilly.com
Put the following information in the first line of your message (*not* in the Subject field):
subscribe oreilly-news

O'Reilly Events

If you'd also like us to send information about trade show events, special promotions, and other O'Reilly events, send email to:
listproc@online.oreilly.com
Put the following information in the first line of your message (*not* in the Subject field):
subscribe oreilly-events

3. Get Examples from Our Books via FTP

There are two ways to access an archive of example files from our books:

Regular FTP

* ftp to:
  ftp.oreilly.com
  (login: anonymous
  password: your email address)
* Point your web browser to:
  ftp://ftp.oreilly.com/

FTPMAIL

* Send an email message to:
  ftpmail@online.oreilly.com
  (Write "help" in the message body)

4. Contact Us via Email

order@oreilly.com
To place a book or software order online. Good for North American and international customers.

subscriptions@oreilly.com
To place an order for any of our newsletters or periodicals.

books@oreilly.com
General questions about any of our books.

software@oreilly.com
For general questions and product information about our software. Check out O'Reilly Software Online at **http://software.oreilly.com/** for software and technical support information. Registered O'Reilly software users send your questions to: **website-support@oreilly.com**

cs@oreilly.com
For answers to problems regarding your order or our products.

booktech@oreilly.com
For book content technical questions or corrections.

proposals@oreilly.com
To submit new book or software proposals to our editors and product managers.

international@oreilly.com
For information about our international distributors or translation queries. For a list of our distributors outside of North America check out:
http://www.oreilly.com/www/order/country.html

O'Reilly & Associates, Inc.
101 Morris Street, Sebastopol, CA 95472 USA
TEL   707-829-0515 or 800-998-9938
       (6am to 5pm PST)
FAX   707-829-0104

International Distributors

UK, EUROPE, MIDDLE EAST AND AFRICA (EXCEPT FRANCE, GERMANY, AUSTRIA, SWITZERLAND, LUXEMBOURG, LIECHTENSTEIN, AND EASTERN EUROPE)

INQUIRIES
O'Reilly UK Limited
4 Castle Street
Farnham
Surrey, GU9 7HS
United Kingdom
Telephone: 44-1252-711776
Fax: 44-1252-734211
Email: josette@oreilly.com

ORDERS
Wiley Distribution Services Ltd.
1 Oldlands Way
Bognor Regis
West Sussex PO22 9SA
United Kingdom
Telephone: 44-1243-779777
Fax: 44-1243-820250
Email: cs-books@wiley.co.uk

FRANCE

ORDERS
GEODIF
61, Bd Saint-Germain
75240 Paris Cedex 05, France
Tel: 33-1-44-41-46-16 (French books)
Tel: 33-1-44-41-11-87 (English books)
Fax: 33-1-44-41-11-44
Email: distribution@eyrolles.com

INQUIRIES
Éditions O'Reilly
18 rue Séguier
75006 Paris, France
Tel: 33-1-40-51-52-30
Fax: 33-1-40-51-52-31
Email: france@editions-oreilly.fr

GERMANY, SWITZERLAND, AUSTRIA, EASTERN EUROPE, LUXEMBOURG, AND LIECHTENSTEIN

INQUIRIES & ORDERS
O'Reilly Verlag
Balthasarstr. 81
D-50670 Köln
Germany
Telephone: 49-221-973160-91
Fax: 49-221-973160-8
Email: anfragen@oreilly.de (inquiries)
Email: order@oreilly.de (orders)

CANADA (FRENCH LANGUAGE BOOKS)
Les Éditions Flammarion ltée
375, Avenue Laurier Ouest
Montréal (Québec) H2V 2K3
Tel: 00-1-514-277-8807
Fax: 00-1-514-278-2085
Email: info@flammarion.qc.ca

HONG KONG
City Discount Subscription Service, Ltd.
Unit D, 3rd Floor, Yan's Tower
27 Wong Chuk Hang Road
Aberdeen, Hong Kong
Tel: 852-2580-3539
Fax: 852-2580-6463
Email: citydis@ppn.com.hk

KOREA
Hanbit Media, Inc.
Sonyoung Bldg. 202
Yeksam-dong 736-36
Kangnam-ku
Seoul, Korea
Tel: 822-554-9610
Fax: 822-556-0363
Email: hant93@chollian.dacom.co.kr

PHILIPPINES
Mutual Books, Inc.
429-D Shaw Boulevard
Mandaluyong City, Metro
Manila, Philippines
Tel: 632-725-7538
Fax: 632-721-3056
Email: mbikikog@mnl.sequel.net

TAIWAN
O'Reilly Taiwan
No. 3, Lane 131
Hang-Chow South Road
Section 1, Taipei, Taiwan
Tel: 886-2-23968990
Fax: 886-2-23968916
Email: taiwan@oreilly.com

CHINA
O'Reilly Beijing
Room 2410
160, FuXingMenNeiDaJie
XiCheng District
Beijing, China PR 100031
Tel: 86-10-66412305
Fax: 86-10-86631007
Email: beijing@oreilly.com

INDIA
Computer Bookshop (India) Pvt. Ltd.
190 Dr. D.N. Road, Fort
Bombay 400 001 India
Tel: 91-22-207-0989
Fax: 91-22-262-3551
Email: cbsbom@giasbm01.vsnl.net.in

JAPAN
O'Reilly Japan, Inc.
Kiyoshige Building 2F
12-Bancho, Sanei-cho
Shinjuku-ku
Tokyo 160-0008 Japan
Tel: 81-3-3356-5227
Fax: 81-3-3356-5261
Email: japan@oreilly.com

ALL OTHER ASIAN COUNTRIES
O'Reilly & Associates, Inc.
101 Morris Street
Sebastopol, CA 95472 USA
Tel: 707-829-0515
Fax: 707-829-0104
Email: order@oreilly.com

AUSTRALIA
WoodsLane Pty., Ltd.
7/5 Vuko Place
Warriewood NSW 2102
Australia
Tel: 61-2-9970-5111
Fax: 61-2-9970-5002
Email: info@woodslane.com.au

NEW ZEALAND
Woodslane New Zealand, Ltd.
21 Cooks Street (P.O. Box 575)
Waganui, New Zealand
Tel: 64-6-347-6543
Fax: 64-6-345-4840
Email: info@woodslane.com.au

LATIN AMERICA
McGraw-Hill Interamericana
Editores, S.A. de C.V.
Cedro No. 512
Col. Atlampa
06450, Mexico, D.F.
Tel: 52-5-547-6777
Fax: 52-5-547-3336
Email: mcgraw-hill@infosel.net.mx

O'REILLY®

TO ORDER: **800-998-9938** • order@oreilly.com • http://www.oreilly.com/
OUR PRODUCTS ARE AVAILABLE AT A BOOKSTORE OR SOFTWARE STORE NEAR YOU.
FOR INFORMATION: **800-998-9938** • **707-829-0515** • info@oreilly.com